Third edition

The airline industry presents an enigma: high growth rates during the last forty years have produced only marginal profitability. This book sets out to explain, in clear and simple terms, why this should be so. It provides a unique insight into the economics and operation of international airlines.

Flying off Course has established itself over the years as the indispensable guide to the inner workings of this exciting industry. This enlarged third edition, completed after September 2001, brings the story fully up to date and includes much new material on key topics such as airline costs, 'open skies' agreements and airline pricing.

Much has happened in the ten years since the second edition of this book first appeared. Airline professionals and transport students will be eager to hear Doganis's views which are given added force by his own experience as Chairman and Chief Executive Officer of Olympic Airways in the mid-1990s.

Rigas Doganis is an airline and airport consultant. He is also Visiting Professor in Air Transport at the College of Aeronautics, Cranfield University and former Chairman and CEO of Olympic Airways in Athens. He is the author of the hugely successful books *The Airport Business* and *The Airline Business in the 21st Century*, also published by Routledge.

Flying off Course

The economics of
international airlines

Third edition

Rigas Doganis

London and New York

First published 1985
by HarperCollins Academic

Second edition 1991
Reprinted 1992, 1993, 1995, 1996, 1998 (twice), 2000, 2001
Third edition 2002
by Routledge
11 New Fetter Lane, London EC4P 4EE

Simultaneously published in the USA and Canada
by Routledge
29 West 35th Street, New York, NY 10001

Routledge is an imprint of the Taylor & Francis Group

© 1985, 1991, 2002 Rigas Doganis

Typeset in Bembo by Graphicraft Limited, Hong Kong
Printed and bound in Malta by
Gutenberg Press Ltd.

British Library Cataloguing in Publication Data
A catalogue record for this book is available from the British Library

Library of Congress Cataloging in Publication Data
A catalog record for this book has been requested

ISBN 0-415-21323-1 (hbk)
ISBN 0-415-21324-X (pbk)

Contents

Tables

Illustrations

Acknowledgements

In February 1995, some time after the previous edition of this book was published, I was lucky enough to be suddenly parachuted into Athens to be Chairman and Chief Executive of Olympic Airways, the Greek national airline. Olympic had been losing money heavily. My task was to implement a restructuring plan and turn the company round. Fourteen months later my Greek colleagues and I were able to announce that Olympic had produced its first profit for eighteen years. Managing a state-owned airline can best be described as 'long periods of crisis management interspersed by short periods of catastrophe management'. My time at Olympic was short, but I learnt a great deal from the experience and from my colleagues. The present edition has been rewritten with the knowledge and confidence gained from having to practise what I had previously been preaching.

The international airline industry is complex, dynamic and subject to rapid change and innovation. What is more, as a result of progressive liberalisation it has become inherently unstable. To understand the industry's economic and operational features one must be close to its pulse beat. In this I have been fortunate. For over twenty-five years, as a researcher, consultant and professor, I have been closely involved in the industry's problems and aspirations. I have taught many in-house air transport seminars or led executive workshops for airlines such as Aer Lingus, Cyprus Airways, Emirates, LOT, Malaysia Airlines, Royal Jordanian, SAS, Singapore Airlines and Thai International. These seminars and workshops provided an open forum for frank discussions of airline trends and problems, where established truths were constantly challenged. In the process I learned much about the airline industry. I am indebted to the numerous participants from these and many other airlines who helped me gain a deeper insight into the workings of their industry. For the same reasons I would like to thank my former students at the University of Westminster and at the Cranfield College of Aeronautics, many of whom now hold key positions in aviation.

In the many years of my involvement with air transport there have been so many who have influenced my thoughts that it is difficult to mention them all. But I would like to single out Dr Fariba Alamdari, Peter Morrell and Ian Stockman of Cranfield University, John Balfour, Paul Clark at Airbus Industrie,

Dr Nigel Dennis from the University of Westminster, Andy Hofton, Andrew Lobbenberg, Stephanos Romeos, formerly of Olympic Airways, Trevor Soames, Stephen Wheatcroft and Dr Conor Whelan. The numerous discussions I have had with them on a variety of air transport topics have contributed significantly to the current edition. I am also indebted to Dr Whelan for helping with several of the figures and to Airbus Industrie, who provided some key diagrams for Chapter 5.

Abbreviations

ACMI	aircraft, crew, maintenance and insurance (type of aircraft operating lease)
AEA	Association of European Airlines
APEX	advance purchase fare
ASK	available seat kilometre
ATB	automated ticket and boarding pass
ATK	available tonne kilometre
BA	British Airways
BAA	British Airports Authority
CAA	Civil Aviation Authority (UK)
CAB	(US) Civil Aeronautics Board
CRM	customer relationship management
DOC	direct operating cost
EASA	European Aviation Safety Agency
EC	European Community
ECAC	European Civil Aviation Conference
EDI	electronic data interchange
EEA	European Economic Area
EU	European Union
FAA	(US) Federal Aviation Administration
FFP	Frequent Flyer Programme
GATS	General Agreement on Trade and Services
GDP	gross domestic product
GDS	global distribution system
GNP	gross national product
GTX	group promotional fare
HHI	Herfindahl–Hirschman index
IATA	International Air Transport Association
ICAO	International Civil Aviation Organisation
IFE	in-flight entertainment
IOC	indirect operating costs
IT	information technology
ITC	inclusive tour charter

ITX	individual inclusive tour fare
JAA	Joint Airworthiness Authority
JAL	Japan Airlines
JAR	Joint Airworthiness Requirement
JIT	just in time
MAS	Malaysian Airline System
MTOW	maximum take-off weight
OPEC	Organisation of Petroleum-exporting Countries
PAL	Philippine Airlines
RPK	revenue passenger kilometre
SAS	Scandinavian Airlines System
SIA	Singapore International Airlines
SITC	Standard International Trade Classification
TCAA	Transatlantic Common Aviation Area
td	time-definite (cargo)
TWA	Trans World Airlines
ULD	unit load device
UPS	United Parcel Service
VFR	visiting friends or relatives

Introduction

In the few weeks that followed the terrorist attacks of 11 September 2001 in the United States, several airlines collapsed or had to be bailed out by their governments. They included Sabena, Swissair and Canada 3000, all of which closed down, while Air New Zealand, the Polish airline LOT and a number of others were saved by capital injections from their governments. By the end of 2001 the airline industry was in turmoil. Other airlines were on the verge of collapse. But the underlying crisis predated 11 September. These airlines were well on the way to collapse before the terrorist attacks. The latter turned crisis into disaster.

The underlying crisis facing many international airlines was already apparent early in 2000. Over-capacity and increased competition were inducing airline managements to reduce fares and tariffs at a time when costs were rising. But it was the airlines themselves which had created the over-capacity in the first place. It looked as if the very profitable years of the late 1990s were to be followed by three or four years of falling, if not vanishing, profits. The airline industry was once again flying off course.

During the last forty-five years the airline industry has undergone an expansion unrivalled by any other form of public transport. Its rate of technological change has been exceptional. This has resulted in falling costs and fares which have stimulated a very rapid growth in demand for its services. A seemingly insatiable demand. In addition, for the first half of this period scheduled airlines enjoyed considerable protection from both internal and external competition. Any other industry faced with such high growth of demand for its products, especially while cushioned from competition, would be heady with the thought of present and future profits. But not the airline industry: it is an exception to the rule. High growth has for the most part spelt low profits. Increased demand has not resulted in long-term financial success. While some airlines have consistently managed to stay well in the black, the industry as a whole has been only marginally profitable.

There is no simple explanation for the apparent contradiction between the industry's rapid growth and its marginal profitability during recent decades. But for the individual airline financial success depends on matching supply and demand in a way which is both efficient and profitable. This is the underlying theme and focus of the book. While airline managements have considerable control over the supply of air services, they have relatively little control over demand. They can influence demand but cannot control it. Hence the matching process is not an easy one. To help in understanding the process this book provides a practical insight into key aspects of airline operations and planning within the conceptual framework of economics.

The book works through the issues logically. Any understanding of the economics of the industry must start with the regulatory framework which circumscribes and constrains airlines' freedom of action. On many international air routes a traditional and highly regulated market environment persists (Chapter 2). Elsewhere the economic regulation of air transport has been progressively relaxed as a result of pressure from the United States, the European Union and several other states (Chapter 3). Thus regulated and so-called 'open skies' markets coexist side by side. In order successfully to match the supply of air services with the demand it is essential to understand both airline costs and the factors that affect them (Chapters 4 and 5) and the nature of the demand. Understanding demand is the first step in the marketing process (Chapter 7). A thorough appreciation of demand must also be used to develop traffic and other forecasts, since every activity within an airline ultimately stems from a forecast (Chapter 8). Supply and demand are brought together in a number of ways, but most crucially through effective product planning (Chapter 9). Price is a key element of the airline product or service. Alternative airline pricing policies and strategies need careful consideration (Chapter 10). While the emphasis throughout is on scheduled operations a large part of international air transport is provided by charter or non-scheduled services. The particular characteristics and advantages of such services require special attention (Chapter 6). While the book focuses primarily on passenger services, the importance and role of air freight should not be forgotten. Freight requires special attention, since many of its economic and operational characteristics are different (Chapter 11). But the book begins with the theme of this introduction. It examines the underlying trends in the airline industry, including its rapid technological change, the high growth rates and the marginal profitability (Chapter 1).

The book is concerned with *international* air transport, which accounts worldwide for about two-thirds of the airline industry's output. Only for the airlines of a few large countries such as the United States, Russia, Brazil and China are domestic operations of greater significance than international, though most of their major domestic airlines also operate internationally. Conversely, in most other countries the larger airlines are primarily concerned with international air services while some of them operate only internationally.

Since the second edition of this book appeared the international airline industry has undergone considerable change. Further liberalisation of international regulations, the privatisation of many government-owned airlines, globalisation and the growing impact of electronic commerce are among the many developments that have led to new operating practices and management concepts. This third edition sets out to reflect the impact of these changes on airline economics and operations. It has been largely rewritten and entirely updated. A separate book entitled *The Airline Business in the 21st Century* takes some of the key issues mentioned here and explores them at much greater depth. They include airline alliances, labour costs, the economics of low-cost no-frills airlines, airline privatisation and survival strategies (Doganis, 2001).

There is no magic wand to ensure success within the international airline industry. This book attempts to flesh out the economic and operational issues which must be understood in order to match supply and demand. Only when this has been done can there be some measure of success in this most dynamic of industries. So come, fly with me.

1 Characteristics and trends in airline operations

At Continental, our biggest focus is not to worry that much about revenue per available seat-mile or cost per available seat-mile; it is to worry about the margin. We target a 10 per cent operating margin.

(Larry Kellner, Chief Financial Officer, Continental Airlines)

1.1 The paradox

The airline industry presents a paradox. For the last fifty years it has been characterised by continued and rapid growth in demand for its services. Yet it has remained only marginally profitable.

Inevitably growth was much faster in the 1950s and 1960s when aviation was a new industry than it is today when it is reaching maturity. But growth rates are still impressive. In the 1950s and 1960s the world's air traffic, measured in terms of tonne kilometres carried, grew on average at around 14–15 per cent each year. In the decade 1970–79 the annual growth was close to 10 per cent. This still meant that air traffic, and the airlines with it, doubled in size every seven years or so. In the following ten years to 1989 growth declined to around 6 per cent annually and in the decade up to 1999 growth was down slightly at 5.2 per cent. In absolute terms, because of the much higher base, a 5 per cent jump in recent years represents a much greater surge in demand than a 10 per cent annual growth thirty years ago. Most long-term forecasts for the first decade of the new millennium are also just above or below the 5 per cent mark.

The airline industry appears to be cyclical and this inevitably impacts on growth rates from year to year. Nevertheless the underlying trend has been one of declining but consistently good growth in demand. Most industries or businesses faced with continued and high growth of demand for their products or services would be basking in substantial profits. Not so the airlines. This is the paradox. The financial performance of the world's airlines taken as a whole has been very marginal, even in the years when the industry was highly regulated and largely protected from internal competition. The traditional measure of profitability, namely the rate of return on assets employed, cannot be applied to the airline industry as a whole. This is because of the difficulty of estimating real

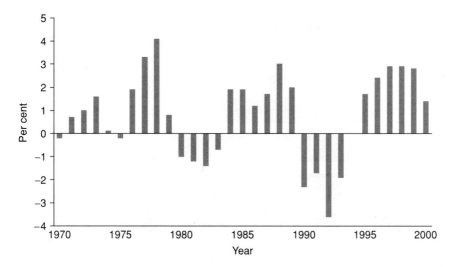

Figure 1.1 Annual net profit or loss as a percentage of total revenue of ICAO member airlines, 1970–2000.

asset values for airlines with varied depreciation policies, using varying proportions of leased equipment and often receiving direct or indirect government subsidy in a variety of forms. Another measure of profitability commonly used among airlines is the operating ratio, which is the annual operating or net profit or loss expressed as a percentage of the total annual revenue. This is calculated annually for the world's airlines by the International Civil Aviation Organisation (ICAO). The net operating ratio is shown diagrammatically in Figure 1.1. This shows the net profit after payment of interest and any other non-operating items.

The cyclical nature of the airline industry is clearly evident. Four to five years of poor or bad performance are generally followed by an upturn and five or six years of improving results. However, even in the good years profit margins are low. The net profits after interest and tax rarely achieve even 2 per cent of revenues. These are of course global figures and mask the fact that some airlines such as Singapore Airlines, Cathay Pacific or British Airways have frequently produced much better profit margins. Nevertheless, such low average profit margins are poor for a new and high-growth industry.

More surprisingly, airlines are the worst performing of any of the individual sectors in the air transport chain. This is clearly evident in Figure 1.2. It is also clear from the diagram that the 6 per cent return on capital earned by the world's airlines in the years 1992–96 was below the cost of capital. For most airlines this would have been at least 8 per cent. The period 1992–96 included some very bad years at the bottom of the cycle and some relatively good years such as 1995 and 1996. The other suppliers of aviation goods and services would also have been affected by the cyclical downturn too. Yet they still outperformed the airlines by a big margin.

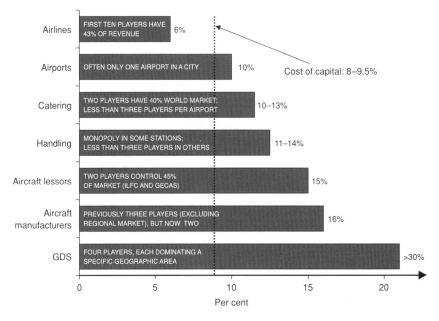

Figure 1.2 The profitability of key players in the air transport chain: estimation of return on capital employed, 1992–96.
Source: Spinetta (2000).

1.2   The essence of airline planning

The paradox of high growth yet poor profitability is amply illustrated by the experience of Europe's major scheduled international airlines which are members of the Association of European Airlines, a trade association based in Brussels. Though some individual airlines did make profits during the cyclical downturn of the early 1990s, as a group these airlines made losses each year from 1990 to 1994. Yet in each of these years, except 1991, their traffic in terms of passenger kilometres grew by over 7 per cent. In fact their worst year in terms of operating results was 1992, yet growth in that year was 14 per cent as demand recovered after a fall in 1991, the year of the Gulf War. Among US airlines during the same period the figures are different but the pattern is the same. The experience of European and US airlines in those years suggests that losses cannot be attributed purely to inadequate growth rates.

There is no simple explanation of the apparent contradiction between the airline industry's rapid growth and its marginal and cyclical profitability. But, for the individual airline, overcoming this contradiction means matching supply and demand for its services in a way which is both efficient and profitable. This is the essence of airline management and planning. It is about matching the supply of air services, which management can largely control, with the demand for such services, over which management has much less influence.

Table 1.1 Operating results, selected airlines, financial year 1999

Airline	Operating cost per ATK (cents) 1	Operating revenue per ATK (cents) 2	Total profit/loss before interest/tax ($ million) 3
Korean	22.2	23.1	+153
Cubana (1998)	25.1	24.9	−1
SIA	25.8	28.6	+467
Malaysian	25.8	23.9	−148
Cathay Pacific	29.3	31.3	+219
Thai Airways	31.2	37.1	+434
Northwest	39.4	42.8	+769
TAROM	40.1	34.4	−28
United	41.9	45.4	+1,358
THY	41.7	34.8	−216
American	42.2	45.0	+1,003
KLM	42.2	42.3	+17
Delta	44.5	48.6	+1,261
Avianca (Colombia)	45.5	43.0	−32
Lufthansa (1998)	46.5	51.7	+1,031
British Airways	49.6	50.3	+156
SilkAir	51.3	48.7	−5
Iberia	53.1	53.6	+35
JAL	53.2	54.7	+260
Middle East Airlines	61.9	50.0	−50
SAS	102.9	103.6	+31
British Midland	132.7	134.6	+15

Source: ICAO *Digest of Statistics*, Series F, *Financial Data*.

To be successful in this an airline can be a low-cost operator or a high-cost operator. What determines profitability is the airline's ability to generate unit revenues which are higher than its unit costs. An airline, within any regulatory constraints, can itself determine the supply of services it offers in the various markets it serves. In turn, the way it organises those services and manages the inputs required to supply them impacts directly on its costs. But cost efficiency and low unit costs are no guarantee of profit if an airline is unable to generate even the low unit revenues necessary to cover such costs.

From a review of a sample of various airlines' costs and revenues in 1999, which was a good year, it is immediately apparent that unit costs vary enormously (Table 1.1, column 1). The high-cost airlines at the bottom of the table, SAS and British Midland, had unit costs that were three or four times as high as the low-cost carriers in the top half. Did that mean they were inefficient high-cost carriers? Far from it. As will become apparent in the course of this book, their high costs were and still are a function of the nature of their operations and the externally determined costs of their inputs rather than a result of poor management. Such factors also explain in part the very low costs of Singapore Airlines (SIA) or Cathay Pacific.

To assess how successful airlines are in matching supply, which they largely control, with demand, which they can influence but do not control, one must examine their unit revenues (column 2). Since revenues per available tonne kilometre are a function of average fares or cargo tariffs and *load factors* achieved they are a good measure of an airline's success in dealing with the demand side. If the unit revenues of the sample airlines are higher than their unit costs then the airlines are profitable. If not they are making losses (column 3). Table 1.1 indicates that low costs are not a guarantee of financial success, though they should make it easier. Thus in its financial year 1998–99 Malaysia Airlines was one of the lowest-cost airlines in the world, helped in part by the devaluation of the Malaysian currency in 1998 as a result of the East Asian financial crisis. Despite its low costs the airline was losing $3 million each week during that year. This was largely due to an over-ambitious fleet and route expansion plan. Fares were cut to capture market share and to fill all the extra capacity. Unit revenues or yields fell to levels which were below unit cost. The airline was in crisis. In fact, control was bought back from private hands by the Malaysian government early in 2001. Other airlines with relatively low costs such as TAROM, the Romanian airline, Northwest and Kuwait Airways also failed to generate revenue levels sufficient to cover their costs and made losses. Surprisingly the two airlines with very high costs, SAS and British Midland, were able, through their product and marketing strategy, to generate very high yields and produce profits. They were successful in the matching process.

Airlines can be low-cost and very unprofitable or high-cost and financially sound. Unit costs or unit revenues are not critical in themselves. For airline executives the key to financial success is to ensure that unit revenues exceed unit costs. This is precisely what Larry Kellner, Executive Vice President and Chief Financial Officer of Continental Airlines, meant in October 2000 when he stated:

> You've got to manage both sides of the equation, the revenue side and the costs side. At Continental, our biggest focus is not to worry that much about revenue per available seat-mile or cost per available seat-mile; it is to worry about the margin.
>
> (Kellner, 2000)

Airlines that fail to focus on the margin end up flying off course. If they do so repeatedly without taking corrective action they are likely to enter a spiral of increasing losses that leads ultimately to collapse – unless they have backers or governments prepared to bail them out.

The difficulties faced by airline executives in trying to match supply and demand have been compounded by the fact that the airline industry is very dynamic and subject to structural instability. Two factors above all have contributed to this: the rapid technological change which is characteristic of air transport, and the liberalisation of economic and market access regulations during the 1980s and 1990s. The latter are discussed in the following chapters. Technology has been a key driver of the airline industry's economic fortunes and merits closer attention.

1.3 Rapid technological change

In the last fifty years technological innovation in air transport has far outstripped that in any other transport mode. The only comparable innovations in other transport sectors have been the emergence of supertankers in shipping and the development of high-speed trains, though the impact of the latter is still limited geographically. Innovation in aviation has centred on the development of the jet engine for civil use, first in a turbo-propeller form and later as a pure jet. Successive developments of the jet engine have consistently improved its efficiency and propulsive power. The emergence of larger and more powerful engines in association with improvements in airframe design and in control systems has resulted over the last thirty years or so in successive and significant improvements in aircraft speed and size. Higher speeds and larger aircraft have in turn produced significant jumps in aircraft hourly productivity. (This is calculated by multiplying the maximum payload an aircraft can carry by its average *block speed*, i.e. the distance it can fly in an hour.)

Even in the era of the piston engine dramatic improvements were made so that the hourly productivity of the Super Constellation was seven times greater than that of the Douglas DC-3 (Table 1.2). The early turbo-prop aircraft also significantly improved productivity. Though the Viscount's productivity was less than that of the Super Constellation, as a DC-3 replacement the Viscount's productivity was four times as great. Likewise, the Britannias were a significant improvement on the Super Constellations they were meant to replace.

The arrival of the turbo-jet engine had a twofold impact. In the 1960s the turbo-jets led to a dramatic increase in speeds, while the size of the aircraft did not increase appreciably. In the later 1960s and early 1970s there was no appreciable increase in speeds, because existing speeds were approaching the sound barrier, but there was a significant increase in the size of aircraft, particularly with the introduction of wide-body fuselages. The earlier increases in speeds combined with these significant jumps in aircraft size together produced major improvements in aircraft productivity so that while the Boeing 720B in 1960 was producing 11,600 tonne-kms per flying hour, only ten years later the hourly productivity of the Boeing 747, the first so-called 'jumbo', was three times as great. The Airbus A300 introduced in 1974 was the first short-haul wide-body aircraft. Its productivity was about twice as high as that of the narrow-body short-haul aircraft then in service.

The next major technological breakthrough was the production of civil aircraft flying faster than the speed of sound. But in economic terms it was a failure. The Anglo-French Concorde, which entered service in 1976, flies more than twice as fast as its predecessors yet is able to do so only through a very

Table 1.2 Impact of technological advance on aircraft productivity

Aircraft type	Year of entry into service	Mean cruise speed (kmph)	Maximum payload (ts)[a]	Passenger payload	Hourly productivity (000 t-kmph)[b]
Piston					
DC-3	1936	282	2.7	21	0.5
Lockheed 1049 Super Constellation	1952	499	1.0	47–94	3.8
Turbo-prop					
Viscount 700	1953	523	5.9	40–53	2.2
Britannia 310	1956	571	15.6	52–133	6.2
Turbo-jet – short haul					
Caravelle VI R	1959	816	8.3	52–94	4.7
Airbus A300	1974	891	31.8	245	19.8
Airbus A320	1988	834	20.4	179	11.9
Turbo-jet – long haul					
Boeing 720B	1960	883	18.7	115–49	11.6
Douglas DC-8-63	1968	935	30.6	259	20.0
Boeing 747-100	1969	908	49.5	430	31.5
Boeing 747-300	1983	908	68.6	420	43.6
Boeing 777-200	1995	869	55.1	305	33.5
Airbus A380	2005	882	85.0	555	52.5
Concorde	1976	2,236	12.7	110	19.3

Source: Compiled by the author.

Notes
a Later versions or developments of these aircraft may have had different maximum or passenger payloads.
b Calculated on the basis of an average block speed assumed to be about 70 per cent of the cruise speed. This is likely to be an underestimate for aircraft on medium- or long-haul sectors.

significant reduction in size. Because of this penalty, supersonic aircraft have lower hourly productivity than their competitors on long-haul routes. This means high costs per seat or seat kilometre and very high fares. It was this factor which made their commercial viability so problematic, even on over-water routes where there were no noise constraints. In practice this aircraft has been operated only by British Airways and Air France, very much as a public relations exercise and only after some of the capital debts arising from its purchase were written off.

From the mid-1970s onwards the rate of technological innovation slackened. Attention switched from the long-haul end of the aircraft market to the develop-ment of more efficient wide-bodied medium-haul aircraft such as the Boeing 767 and the Airbus A310. Developments here were based essentially on existing engine and airframe technology, though there were major developments in avionics, in the use of lighter composite materials in airframe construction and in other areas. At the same time, the trend towards larger aircraft flying at the same speed continued. An example is the Airbus A320 introduced in 1988 which, with up to 180 seats, was significantly larger than the 100–130-seater aircraft it was intended to replace. Thus important gains in hourly productivity have continued to be made as airlines switch to larger, newer aircraft types.

During the 1990s there were two important developments. First was the introduction of extended-range versions of the newer twin-engined jets such as the Boeing 767-200 EQ offering 200 to 250 seats. These allowed more direct non-stop flights on 'thinner' long-haul routes that could not support the large traditional long-haul aircraft such as the Boeing 747 with 400 seats or more. This trend towards medium-size aircraft for long-haul services led to the introduction of the Airbus A340 in 1993 and the Boeing 777 in 1995. The second important development, one which technologically was perhaps more significant, was the development of small, efficient and light jet engines that could be used to power smaller passenger aircraft. Such aircraft had hitherto been dependent on turbo-propeller engines. But they were noisy and aircraft speeds were low. The Canadair fifty-seater Regional Jet which first entered service in November 1992 and the Embraer ERJ 145, also with fifty seats, which launched services in 1997, revolutionised regional air services. They offered faster and more comfortable jet travel on thinner short-haul routes previously the preserve of turbo-prop aircraft.

1.4   Impact of new technology

These developments described so briefly above, which were matched by equally rapid innovations in other areas of aviation technology in the air and on the ground, were due primarily to the increasing efficiency of the jet engine. For a given level of propulsive thrust successive engines were able to carry a larger payload and to carry it faster as well. This, combined with other economies arising from the greater size of aircraft, resulted in ever-decreasing costs per capacity tonne kilometre (see Chapter 5.5 for the impact of size and speed on unit costs). Herein lies the significance of the technological improvements in aviation and of the increase in aircraft productivity which they made possible. They enabled airlines to cut their unit costs rapidly in the 1950s and 1960s when advances in size and speed were most marked and steadily, though less rapidly, in subsequent decades. Between 1960 and 1970 unit costs per available tonne kilometre were halved in constant value terms.

During the 1970s airline unit costs expressed in current values began to rise rapidly as a result of world inflation. They rose particularly sharply following the fuel crises of 1973 and 1978. The airlines tried to counteract the upwards pressure on costs by the accelerated introduction of more modern and usually larger jet aircraft and by more effective cost control. As a result, airline costs did not rise as rapidly as world prices, so that in real or constant value terms airline costs during the 1970s remained stable or moved slowly downwards

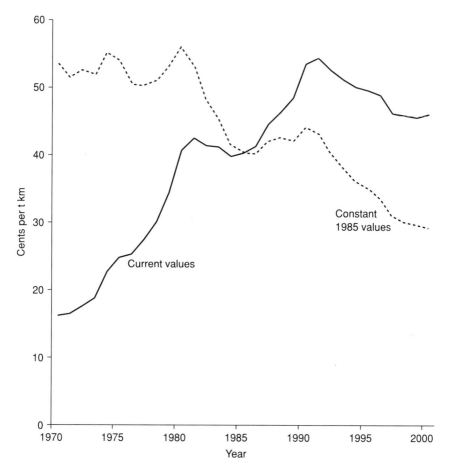

Figure 1.3 Trends in unit operating costs, ICAO scheduled airlines, 1970–2000.
Source: Compiled from IATA data and the US consumer price index.

(Figure 1.3). In the 1980s the price of fuel began to decline in real terms, falling particularly sharply in 1986. It then fluctuated around this low 1986 level. Helped by both the switch to larger aircraft and the fall in the real price of fuel, airline costs again declined in constant value terms during the early 1980s but stabilised in the second half of the decade.

In the 1990s the steady decline in unit costs continued. But during this decade it was driven less by improvements in aircraft technology than by the steady fall in the real price of aviation fuel, at least until 1999, and by the strenuous efforts made by airlines, especially in the early years of the decade, to drive down their costs. Cost reduction was necessary both to climb out of the disastrous downturn in the airline industry's fortunes between 1990 and 1994 and because of the increased price competition as more and more international markets were liberalised. In constant value terms, unit costs fell by about one-third between

1990 and 2000, though the rate of cost reduction slowed appreciably after 1997 (Figure 1.3).

The technological developments in aviation, while they were beneficial in their impact on operating costs and in improving safety, also created problems. The increasing size and capacity of aircraft and the speed with which new, larger aircraft were introduced, often in reaction to competition from other airlines, created a strong downward pressure on load factors. Average load factors of ICAO scheduled airlines dropped from a level of around 60 per cent in the early 1950s to levels below 48 per cent by 1969. There was a significant fall in weight load factors between 1960 and 1963 with the widespread introduction of the first-generation jet aircraft and then again between 1968 and 1971 with the introduction of the early wide-bodied jets. Both these periods of over-capacity were marked by sharply falling profit margins. It was not till the late 1980s that average load factors began to approach the 60 per cent level again. They then steadied at close to 60 per cent. During the last ten years or so they have generally tended to be around 63–5 per cent on international services, though higher in the mid-1990s for some airlines, and lower on purely domestic routes. This means that more than a third of airline capacity each year still remains unsold.

The technical innovations also posed the problem of financing the new capital investment which they made necessary. Whereas up to the mid-1950s short-haul aircraft were costing up to $2 million, by 1974 a 189 seater Boeing 727-200 cost the airlines $8 million to $9 million. (Note: throughout this book all references to dollars are US dollars unless otherwise specified.) Ten years later, in 1984, the same airlines were having to pay around $45 million for a 265-seater Airbus A310 with spares to replace their 727s. By 1990 the price of the same aircraft was up to $60 million. In the early 1970s a fleet of five small short-haul aircraft would have cost about $45 million. A similar fleet ten years later cost over $200 million. In 1981 Singapore Airlines ordered eight Boeing 747-SUDs and six Airbus A300s at a total cost of $1.8 billion. In 1990 the same airline ordered fifty aircraft costing $8.6 billion for delivery between 1994 and 1999. In November 2000 Qantas announced an order for thirty-one aircraft, thirteen Airbus A330-200s, six longer-range Boeing 747-400s and twelve Airbus A380s. These were to cost $4.9 billion. Such figures are indicative of the scale of investment necessary from the end of the 1970s onwards for a large international airline. Not only did aircraft prices rise sharply but interest rates on loans raised to pay for them also escalated from 4 per cent to 6 per cent per annum in the early 1970s to a peak of over 16 per cent, though they decreased subsequently and were around 9–12 per cent for most of the 1980s. They declined further in the 1990s.

Various developments eased the problem of raising capital on this scale. The aircraft manufacturers themselves became increasingly involved with raising capital for their customers, either through the commercial banks in their own country or through special export trade banks, such as the United States Export–Import Bank. Manufacturers vied with each other in trying to get better financing arrangements for their clients and the terms of such purchase loans became an increasingly important factor for airlines in making a choice between aircraft. The banks too helped. With the ability to use aircraft that are very mobile assets as collateral, bankers were very innovative in developing a variety of financial instruments and packages to facilitate airlines in acquiring aircraft (see Morrell, 2002). In the 1970s consortia of banks emerged which purchased aircraft and then leased them to the airlines. The consortia enjoyed tax concessions and also retained ownership of the aircraft, which was a valuable security at a time when the resale value of aircraft was high. During the 1980s these bank consortia were overtaken by the rapid growth of aircraft leasing companies. By 2000 the two largest of these, GECAS and the International Lease Finance Corporation in California, controlled close to 45 per cent of the total aircraft leasing business. It was also estimated that over 25 per cent of the world's commercial airliners were being operated under various leasing arrangements.

Even when the industry as a whole was doing badly or a particular airline's results were poor, the manufacturers' need to sell inevitably ensured that finance would be forthcoming. But for the airlines this was a mixed blessing. It pushed them to invest when they should have been holding back. As a result, during periods of capacity expansion as in the early 1980s, too many international airlines became heavily over-indebted. In other words, the ratio of their debts to their equity capital became much too high. They were under-capitalised. When it is easy to borrow money for aircraft purchase, it is inevitable that growth and expansion will be financed through loans rather than through injections of equity capital. This was especially true of many loss-making government-owned airlines. When traffic failed to reach the forecast levels, airlines were no longer able to service these huge debts. As a consequence, during each downturn in the airline industry's economic cycle, several airlines have collapsed because they could no longer meet their interest and debt charges. In the early 1990s this happened to Air Europe and Dan Air in the United Kingdom and to Pan American, Eastern and others in the United States. It happens with new start-ups all the time. It is easy to acquire aircraft to launch services – much more difficult to keep paying the lease payments or capital charges when traffic levels are less than anticipated.

1.5   Declining yields

The reasons for the relatively rapid overall growth rate which is so characteristic of air transport are not difficult to find. The falling level of operating costs, previously described, enabled airlines to offer tariffs that were lower in real terms. The impact of lower costs on fares was reinforced by the growing liberalisation of international air transport during the 1980s and 1990s. Liberalisation had a double impact. Increased and open competition created further pressures to reduce costs while liberalisation also led to the gradual removal of tariff controls, thereby facilitating price competition.

The yield or average fare charged per passenger kilometre declined rapidly up to 1970 in real terms, that is, in relation to the cost of other goods and services. As with costs, yields in constant value terms were more or less halved between 1960 and 1970. This decline occurred at a time when *per capita* incomes in the developed countries of the world were increasing at a rate of 8 per cent per annum while discretionary incomes were growing at an even faster rate. As a consequence the demand for non-business air travel rose rapidly. At the same time the twenty years to 1970 saw a boom in world trade which generated an increase both in business travel and in the demand for air-freight facilities. The fall in the real cost of freight charges was even more marked than the decline in the real value of passenger fares.

During the 1970s the real cost of air transport in many markets continued to decline but more slowly and with some ups and downs. Disposable incomes also rose, though less rapidly than before. It was not until 1980 and the two or three years that followed that economic recession affecting many developed countries began seriously to undermine demand and annual growth rates declined appreciably. They did so even though real air fares fell rapidly as a result of both over-capacity and the gradual liberalisation of some international markets and the US domestic market (Figure 1.4).

The major downturn in the early 1990s pushed most airlines into several years of losses or sharply lower profits (Figure 1.1). Inevitably attempts were made to stem or even, where possible, to reverse the decline in average yields. Yields did increase for a time in the early 1990s, at least in current values, but not in real terms. After 1995, as the financial fortunes of the industry improved, the downward trend in yield levels was renewed. It was made worse in 1999–2001 by growing over-capacity in long-haul routes and the impact of low-cost carriers on shorter routes in the United States, Europe and Australia. It is difficult to foresee any reversal in this trend in airline yields. This was true even after the September 2001 terrorist attacks. While airlines cut capacity drastically they also had to cut fares to generate demand and restore confidence in flying. Despite short-term fluctuations, airline managements have to live with a stark reality: there will continue to be strong downward pressure on real average yields, especially on international routes. It is clear that falling average yields destabilise the process of matching supply and demand profitably. Falling yields can be offset by further reductions in unit cost levels. When this is not possible airlines must push up their load factors to compensate for the fact that they are receiving less per passenger or per tonne carried. It is when airlines lose control of this dynamic process of matching yields, unit revenues and load factors that they start making losses.

1.6   A cyclical industry

It was pointed out earlier that the airline industry is marginal in terms of its profitability and is also very cyclical. This is evident from Figure 1.1. Each cycle is about eight to ten years in duration. An examination of the last three

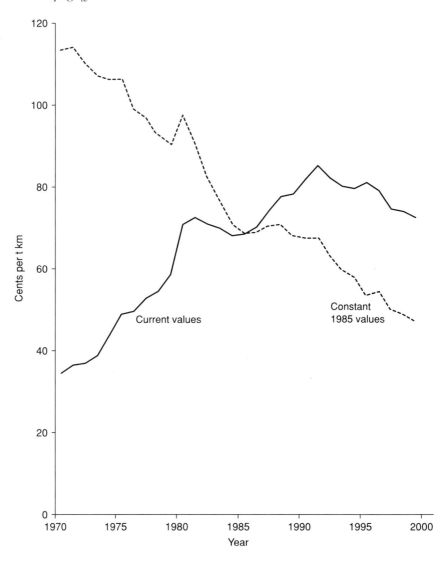

Figure 1.4 Trends in unit revenues, ICAO scheduled airlines, 1970–2000.

complete cycles shows why the industry is inherently unstable. The *early 1970s* started on a low note, with poor financial results, particularly in 1970 and 1971. As a reaction to these poor results the airlines made determined efforts to improve load factors and were partially successful. However, attempts to improve financial results were completely upset by the fuel price crisis which followed the Arab–Israeli war of October 1973. The years 1974 and 1975 were traumatic for the world's airlines. In the first place, the price of fuel escalated at an alarming rate. The average fuel price paid by IATA airlines doubled in the four months between September 1973 and January 1974 and continued to increase thereafter, but at a slower rate. By mid-1975 airlines were paying three times as much for fuel as they had been paying two years earlier. Second, the widespread inflation in most of the world's economies pushed up other areas of operating costs, especially those that were labour-intensive. Finally, the downturn in economic growth, particularly in Europe and the United States, resulted in declining or very low rates of increase in real disposable income which adversely affected the demand for both passenger and freight transport.

The effect of these trends was a large increase in unit costs in 1974 and 1975 (Figure 1.3). Cost escalation, combined with a worldwide recession in traffic development, pushed many airlines into a struggle for financial survival. Airlines operating on the North Atlantic route and in Europe were particularly badly hit.

In *the three years 1975–78* the world's airlines did reasonably well. The price of fuel and other costs declined in real terms, while demand was buoyant and load factors remained at around 55 per cent. This period of well-being was short-lived.

From *1979 to 1983* the international airlines once again entered a period of deep crisis. They were in the anomalous position of enjoying the highest load factors for more than twenty years, while facing increasing losses. The second oil shock, in 1978, resulted in dramatic increases in fuel prices. By 1980 fuel costs represented nearly one-third of total operating costs. High costs, combined with stagnating demand and falling yields generated losses. The high load factors were themselves symptomatic of the crisis, for they resulted from the industry's attempt to compensate for the downward pressure on fares and freight tariffs. They did not compensate enough. In 1980 the world's airlines as a whole made an operating loss before paying interest for the first time since 1961. Further operating losses occurred in 1981 and 1982. Several airlines went bankrupt in this period, including Braniff in the United States and Laker Airways in the United Kingdom, while many others accumulated large debts or had to be financially supported by their national governments. It was not till 1984 that results began to improve.

While all airlines were under pressure during this period, many continued to operate profitably, either by achieving higher than average load factors or by reducing their costs in real terms or both. This was the case with several of the new Third World airlines that were able to benefit from their low labour costs and from the high growth rates in the markets in which they operated. Singapore International Airlines, for example, was very profitable throughout this period.

The *second half of the 1980s* saw a dramatic turn-round in the airline industry's fortunes, though overall profitability remained marginal. While airline chief executives around the world gladly took credit for this turn-round, in reality it was due primarily to two external factors, a significant fall in the real price of aviation fuel and a surge in demand as the world's economies improved.

Airlines that had been making losses for years suddenly found themselves in profit, especially in 1987 and 1988. The underlying financial position, however, was still very weak because the industry as a whole and many individual airlines now found themselves with huge debt burdens. These arose from the need to cover their accumulated losses during the lean years of the early 1980s and to finance the new orders they were placing as traffic growth accelerated. Huge interest payments were needed to finance these debt burdens.

The late 1980s did have one poor year, 1986, when the Chernobyl nuclear disaster, the American bombing of Libya and increased terrorism in Europe and the Middle East led to a sharp fall in US travel to Europe. This adversely affected the financial results of many US and European carriers, especially those with substantial North Atlantic operations.

While the years 1987–89 were highly profitable, the period *1990–93* saw another cyclical downturn. The airline industry faced the worst crisis it had ever known. The crisis started early in 1990 as fuel prices began to rise in real terms while a worsening economic climate in several countries, notably the United States and Britain, began to depress demand in certain markets. The invasion of Kuwait on 2 August 1990 and the short war that followed in January 1991 deepened the crisis for many airlines. Eastern Airlines in the United States and Air Europe in Britain collapsed early in 1991, while Pan American and several smaller airlines such as Midway in the United States and TEA in Belgium had gone by the end of the year. The end of the Gulf War early in 1991 did not lead to any improvement in airline fortunes. In many markets, such as the North Atlantic, liberalisation and insufficient traffic growth were resulting in over-capacity and falling yields as airlines fought for market share. Financial results in 1992 were worse than in 1991, and 1993 was little better. Of the world top twenty airlines, only British Airways, Cathay Pacific, SIA and Swissair made an overall surplus in each of the three years 1991–93. But some of the losses were huge. In 1992 Continental and Northwest each posted net losses after tax of over $1 billion, while in the following year Air France lost on average $4 million every day.

Many airlines required massive injections of capital to survive through the early 1990s. The state-owned airlines within the European Union received over $10 billion in 'state aid' approved by the European Commission plus a further $1.3 billion not categorised as 'state aid' (Doganis, 2001). But many privatised airlines also received capital injections.

The period *1995–98* was one of improving profitability. After 1994, as the cost-cutting measures launched earlier began to have an impact, and as demand growth began to pick up, many airlines returned to profit. While for the industry as a whole 1997 and 1998 were the most profitable years ever, many Asian carriers hit by the meltdown in several East Asian economies posted much reduced profits or even losses. Cathay Pacific, historically one of the industry's most profitable airlines, made its first-ever loss in 1998. In 1999 a few airlines elsewhere, including British Airways and US Air, also posted markedly lower profits. These were the first warning signs.

As 2000 progressed many airline chairmen issued profit warnings. What were the causes of so much concern? Several factors were undermining profits. First, over-capacity in many markets, especially on international routes, as airlines and alliances fought for market share, was pushing average yields down. This trend was exacerbated in Europe and the United States by the pricing strategies of low-cost, no-frills carriers. While yields were going down costs were starting to climb in real terms. During 1999 the OPEC countries had imposed production quotas so as to push up the price of oil. They succeeded. The price of Brent crude oil rose from $10.28 per barrel in February 1999 to $28.14 a year later. It rose to $33–4 by the fourth quarter of 2000. Prices for jet fuel followed the same trend. Aviation fuel prices hit a high of 104c per gallon in September–October 2000. This was more than double the September 1998 price, though they did fall back to around 75c per gallon for much of 2001. Airlines which had not hedged their future fuel purchases were badly hit. The strengthening of the US dollar against many currencies, including the euro, made matters worse, since a significant proportion of airline costs such as fuel, insurance or aircraft lease payments are usually set in US dollars. Finally, many of the collective wage agreements which had been signed in the mid-1990s began to unwind in 2000 and 2001. New agreements coming at the end of several years of profit inevitably resulted in significant wage increases. An example was the trend-setting agreement in September 2000 between United Airlines and its pilots which granted the latter an average 30 per cent wage rise. Similar agreements in the United States and in Europe once again began to push wage costs up after years of restraint.

As a result of all these factors, the top seven US airlines announced marked reductions in net profits for the year 2000 compared with 1999. US Air posted a $269 million loss while TWA filed for bankruptcy protection. All had been hit by rising fuel prices, escalating wage costs, as labour agreements were renegotiated, and increased competition. The only airline to buck the trend was Southwest Airlines. Its net profits actually rose by over $100 million in 2000. Early in 2001 several European carriers also announced falling profits or losses for 2000. These included Swissair ($1.7 billion loss), Sabena ($278 million) and Alitalia ($240 million).

By early 2001 the danger signals were evident. Once more the world's airlines appeared to be flying off course and failing to match supply and demand adequately. Attempts to push up load factors or yields to compensate for rising costs were only partially effective. In fact the economic slowing down in major economies, notably those of Japan and the United States, which began in the second half of 2000, adversely affected both passenger and freight demand. On the passenger side, business travel in key long-haul markets, across the Atlantic and the Pacific, and also between Europe and East Asia, started to fall off during 2001. Far from rising, both traffic levels and average yields were going down in many markets.

By August 2001 it was evident that the airline industry was facing a new crisis. Once again it appeared to be on the verge of a major cyclical downturn.

Table 1.3 Average annual growth of scheduled international passenger tonne-kms by region, 1978–97

Region of airline registration	1978–88 annual % change	1988–97 annual % change
Asia and Pacific	10.4	12.0
North America	8.4	4.5
Middle East	5.8	7.4
Latin America and Caribbean	5.8	7.4
Europe	4.8	3.9
Africa	4.6	4.9
World	7.0	5.9

The terrorist attacks in the United States on 11 September 2001 turned crisis into disaster for many of the world's airlines. This not only because of their immediate impact in terms of a huge drop in demand for travel and increased insurance and security costs, but more especially because 11 September ensured that the economic recession in the United States, Japan and elsewhere would be deeper and longer-lasting. As a result, the industry's cyclical collapse which began in 2000 is likely to be worse than any of the previous downturns. Many airlines with familiar names that were flying at the end of 2000 will have disappeared by the time the airline industry as a whole is in profit again.

In the few weeks preceding 11 September 2001 and in the two months following several airlines went to the wall. In Australia Ansett closed down, while its parent company Air New Zealand had to be rescued by its government. In Europe Swissair and Sabena were declared bankrupt, as were some smaller European airlines which had been part of the Swissair group. In North America Canada's second largest airline, Canada 3000, stopped flying at the beginning of November 2001. These were the first casualties of the cyclical crisis. Others were bound to follow. The key question was whether further closures would facilitate a fundamental restructuring of the international airline industry. Once markets recovered would the industry consolidate around fewer and larger global airlines?

1.7   International focus shifts to East Asia

The high though declining growth rates of air traffic mentioned earlier mark the fact that growth has been very uneven. Wide variations between different parts of the world and between different airlines have been evident. This is particularly true of international air traffic. For the last twenty-five years or so the airlines of Asia and the Pacific have grown much more rapidly than airlines in other parts of the world and at annual rates that are well above the world average (Table 1.3). This is true both of passenger traffic and of cargo.

Much of this growth has been generated by traffic to, from and between the countries of East Asia and Australasia. The explanations are not difficult

Table 1.4 Regional distribution of international scheduled tonne-kms, 1973–99

Region of airline registration	1973 annual % change	1988 annual % change	1997 annual % change	1999 annual % change
Asia and Pacific	14.1	29.0	32.6	30.4
North America	27.5	21.5	19.8	21.0
Middle East	4.0	4.9	4.3	4.5
Latin America and Caribbean	6.3	5.7	5.0	5.0
Europe	44.3	35.5	35.8	35.5
Africa	3.8	3.4	2.5	3.6
World	100.0	100.0	100.0	100.0

to find. For more than twenty years, till the East Asian economic crisis of late 1997 and 1998, Japan and the 'tiger' economies of South East Asia were developing much more rapidly than the traditional economies of Europe and North America. Their export-oriented economies generated considerable business travel while rising *per capita* incomes stimulated leisure and personal travel. At the same time, many of their manufactured exports were high-value goods well suited to carriage by air. Countries such as Thailand, Singapore and Indonesia were also rapidly developing their tourism infrastructure and thereby attracting growing numbers of tourists from both within and without the region. Nor should it be forgotten that most of the countries and many of the major cities of East Asia are separated by large expanses of water. In many cases there is no alternative to air travel. Even when surface travel is possible, as between Kuala Lumpur and Bangkok, the infrastructure is poor and journey times are too slow. The 1970s and 1980s also saw the rapid expansion of new Asian airlines originally state-owned, such as Singapore Airlines (SIA), Malaysia Airlines (MAS), Thai International, Garuda and privately owned Cathay Pacific, Eva Airways and Asiana. Most of these were not IATA members and were able to bypass IATA rules on service standards and traffic. Offering superior in-flight service, and with aggressive marketing, they both stimulated demand and captured a growing share of it.

As a consequence of above-average traffic growth in East Asia and the dynamic expansion of Asian airlines, there has been a dramatic restructuring of the world's international airline industry away from the traditional US and European international airlines and in favour of the East Asian/Pacific airlines (Table 1.4). Whereas in 1973 the Asian and Pacific region airlines carried only 14 per cent of the world's international scheduled traffic, by the late 1990s their share was up to almost one-third, around 30–2 per cent. In terms of tonne kilometres carried on international services four of the world's top ten airlines are now Asian – Singapore Airlines, Japan Airlines, Korean and Cathay Pacific. Conversely, the once dominant US and European airlines have lost market share. In 1973 airlines from these latter two regions carried three-quarters of the world's international traffic. Today their joint share is down to 55 per cent and North American airlines as a group have dropped from second to third place.

Table 1.5 Distribution of traffic and revenue on scheduled services of ICAO airlines, 2000

Traffic	Tonne-kms performed in 2000 (%)			Revenue 1999
	International 1	Domestic 2	All services 3	All services 4
Passenger	61.7	84.7	69.2	86.5
Freight	37.3	12.7	29.3	12.8
Mail	1.0	2.6	1.5	0.7
Total	100.0	100.0	100.0	100.0

Source: Compiled by the author using IATA (2001a, b), ICAO (2000).

However, the data in Tables 1.3 and 1.4 exclude domestic traffic and thus ignore the US domestic market, which is by far the largest single market in the world. If domestic traffic is included, the US airlines are pre-eminent, generating 37 per cent of the world's total traffic (measured in tonne kilometres).

The airlines of the Asia/Pacific region saw their traffic adversely affected by the economic crises in East Asia in 1997 and 1998. As a result, their market share dropped between 1997 and 1999. But by 2000 they were again growing faster than the world average. Long-term forecasts of international air traffic all indicate that growth on routes to/from and within East Asia will continue to outstrip growth elsewhere during the first decade of the current millennium. With a growing market base, these airlines will be well placed to face the challenges of globalisation and consolidation.

In contrast to the airlines of Asia/Pacific the airlines of Africa, the Middle East and Latin America have not increased their market share during the last three decades. With one or two exceptions their international airlines are generally small and financially weak. This means that they are poorly placed to deal with increasing international competition and the challenge of globalisation and consolidation through alliances.

1.8   Passenger and freight business

It is generally assumed that airlines are concerned primarily with carrying passengers and that freight and mail traffic are relatively unimportant in terms of both output and revenue. This is far from being the truth. In 2000 nearly one-third (30.8 per cent) of the world's scheduled airline output was concerned with the carriage of freight and mail, though mail itself is tiny (Table 1.5). Passenger traffic accounted for the rest. On international routes, where distances are greater and air transport becomes more competitive, freight comes into its own. Its share rises to well over one-third of output. Moreover, this share has been slowly increasing. Conversely, freight's share is much less on domestic air services. This is because surface transport, road and rail, is generally more competitive in domestic freight markets.

Table 1.6 Traffic mix on international scheduled services, 2000

Airline	Distribution of tonne-kms carried (%)			
	Passenger	Mail	Freight	Total
Royal Air Maroc	91	a	9	100
Olympic Airways	84	2	14	100
Air Portugal	78	1	21	100
Qantas	73	3	23	100
American	72	2	26	100
Delta	71	1	28	100
United	70	3	27	100
British Airways	69	1	30	100
South African Airways	69	a	31	100
All Nippon Airways	65	1	34	100
Malaysia	63	a	37	100
Varig	63	1	36	100
IATA airlines' average	62	1	37	100
JAL	60	1	39	100
KLM	60	1	39	100
Emirates	59	1	40	100
Air France	59	2	39	100
China Eastern	57	a	43	100
Lufthansa	55	1	44	100
SIA	53	1	47	100
Cathay	52	1	48	100
Lan Chile	35	a	64	100
Korean	33	1	65	100

Source: Compiled by the author from IATA statistics.

Note
a Less than 0.5%.

These global figures hide considerable variations between airlines. A few large international airlines, such as Federal Express or UPS in the United States, are concerned exclusively with the carriage of freight. They are the exception. Most airlines are *combination* carriers, that is, they transport both freight and passengers on their international services (Table 1.6). At one end of the scale are airlines such as Lan Chile, Korean Airlines, Cathay Pacific, Lufthansa or SIA for whom air freight represents close to half or even over half their total production in terms of tonne kilometres. These are clearly quite different airlines from those at the other end of the scale, such as Royal Air Maroc or Olympic Airways, for whom freight and mail together account for less than 15 per cent of their total traffic, despite being based in geographically isolated countries. Interestingly the major US carriers, American, United and Delta, tend to be at the lower end of the scale, generating only around a quarter of their business from freight. This is largely because they have lost much of the US international and, for that matter, most of the domestic freight market to the integrators, that is, the all-cargo door-to-door carriers such as Federal Express, UPS and DHL (see Chapter 11).

It is significant that while freight accounts for over a quarter of total airline production it generates only about one-eighth (12.8 per cent) of total operating revenue. This means that the average revenue per tonne kilometre of freight and, incidentally, of mail, must be very much lower than the average revenue or yield generated by passenger tonne kilometres. Despite this, freight revenue makes an important contribution to many airlines' overall profitability.

Over the airline industry as a whole, the carriage of freight is a significant factor, both in terms of the amount of productive resources it absorbs and in terms of its contribution to overall revenue. For an individual airline the split of its activities between passengers and freight clearly affects both its marketing policy and the structure of its revenues. The importance of mail revenue, however, is very limited and declining. In the early 1960s mail revenue was about 5 per cent of total revenue, whereas now it is below 2 per cent. Inevitably, much of the discussion which follows, except in Chapter 11, concentrates on the passenger aspects of both supply and demand. However, this should not mask the significance of air freight for the international airline industry as a whole.

1.9   The nature of the airline product

As far as passenger services are concerned, there are several contrasting aspects to the airline product. On the one hand, the air journey is seen not as an end in itself but as part of a business trip or of a two-week summer holiday or of a weekend visit to watch a sports fixture. The air journey is a part of a variety of other products or services. A number of important considerations follow. The demand for passenger air services is a derived demand. It is dependent on the demand for these other activities. This means that to forecast the demand for air services one must forecast the demand for all these other types of expenditure. It also means that there has been strong pressure on the airlines to expand vertically into other areas of the travel industry, such as hotels, travel agencies, car hire or tour organisers, in order to gain greater control over the total travel product. There is also a direct effect on airline marketing techniques in the sense that these are frequently oriented to selling and promoting the total product, whether it be a business or holiday trip or a weekend excursion, rather than selling a particular airline. In newspaper and television advertisements many airlines try to interest the reader or viewer in a particular destination or a particular type of trip, and only as an afterthought, almost, do they suggest the airline which might be used.

On the other hand, airlines have to face the realisation that one airline seat is very much like another and that from the passenger's viewpoint there is little difference between one jet aircraft and another. Equally, for the shipper or freight forwarder the major decision will be whether to consign by air or surface: having taken the decision to use air, he may have difficulty in perceiving any difference between one airline and the next serving a particular route. Thus, while air journeys may be only one part of a variety of heterogeneous products or services with different market structures, the air service part of these various products is itself fairly homogeneous. One airline seat is very much like another and one freight hold is no different from the next. Even when airlines wish to differentiate their products, competitive and economic forces and the fact that they are flying similar or identical aircraft mean that they often end up offering very similar products.

The consequences of the homogeneous nature of the airline product are twofold. First, in competitive markets it pushes airlines into making costly efforts to try to differentiate their services and products from those of their competitors. They do this by being first to introduce new aircraft types, by increasing their frequency of service, by spending more on in-flight catering or on ground services and by advertising. Moreover, much of the advertising is aimed at trying to convince the passenger or freight agent that the service they offer is appreciably better than that of their competitors because of the friendliness of the hostesses or the culinary expertise of the chefs, or because of other claims, all of them dubious and difficult to assess. Because of the difficulty of substantiating many claims related to service, quality airlines frequently resort to competing on price, which is tangible, and tariff differences are demonstrable. Second, the homogeneous nature of the airline product makes the emergence of entirely new airlines or the incursion of new airlines on existing routes relatively easy.

This dichotomy between the heterogeneity of the various products, of which the air service is only a part, and the homogeneity of the air services themselves is a constant constraint in airline planning, a constraint which often results in apparently contradictory decisions and actions by airline managements.

2 Traditional bilateralism

A highly regulated industry

> The 1944 [Chicago] Convention was a good thing at the time and has served the airline industry well. But the web of bilateral air service agreements is no longer appropriate.
>
> (Andrew Cahn, Director, Government and Industry Affairs, British Airways, June 2001)

2.1 Two regulatory regimes

Airline managers are not free agents. It has been argued earlier that airline planning and management is the process of matching the supply or provision of air services, which airline managers can largely control, with the demand for such services, which they can influence but not control. It is not as simple as that. Traditionally the airline industry has been one of the most highly regulated of industries. As a result, the actions of airline managers are circumscribed by a host of national, bilateral or international rules and regulations. These are both economic and non-economic in character and may well place severe limits on airlines' freedom of action. An examination of the scope and impact of such regulations is crucial for an understanding of the economics of international air transport.

In the period 1919–49 a framework of international regulation evolved in response to the technological, economic and political developments in air transport. It was uniform and, broadly speaking, worldwide in its application. For the next three decades till the late 1970s this international regulatory framework remained largely unchanged. It was three-sided, based on bilateral air service agreements, on inter-airline pooling agreements and on the tariffs and pricing agreements negotiated through the International Air Transport Association (IATA). Taken together, these three elements created a highly regulated operating environment unlike that of any other international industry – an environment, moreover, that stifled innovation and change. But a review of US international aviation policy in 1979 inaugurated two decades of gradual liberalisation of the economic regulations affecting international air services. This process of liberalisation became more rapid after the mid-1980s when it was adopted by key European countries and eventually by the European Union.

As a result, by the start of the new millennium there were, broadly speaking, two different regulatory regimes in the world. On the one hand, many major routes to and from the United States, those between the member states of the European Union, and some routes between a few European states or the United States and some Asian countries, such as Singapore, were operated under what may be termed 'open skies' regimes. On the other, international air services in many parts of the world were and still are operated within the traditional regulatory structure. In practice it is not a simple twofold division. There are gradations in each of the regulatory regimes. Some traditional bilateral agreements are very restrictive while others are much more open and allow more effective competition. Equally in some liberalised markets, such as that within the European Union, economic deregulation has removed most of the constraints on inter-airline competition, whereas in others some vestiges of traditional regulation survive.

The present chapter examines the traditional regulatory framework and explores the arguments for and against liberalisation. The following chapter deals with the 'open skies' regimes which have emerged progressively in some key markets since the early 1980s.

2.2   Non-economic regulations

The advanced level of aviation technology, the need to ensure passenger safety despite the rapidity of technological innovation, and the international nature of much of the airline industry, have all created pressure for the introduction of more complex and wider-ranging external controls and regulations than are found in most industries. These are broadly of two kinds. First, there are those which are economic in nature and are concerned with regulating the business and commercial aspects of air transport. Second, there is a whole host of technical standards and regulations whose prime objective is to achieve very high levels of safety in airline operations. Such regulations cover every aspect of airline activity and, broadly speaking, they fall into one of the following categories:

1   Regulations which deal with the airworthiness of the aircraft not only in terms of its design and production standards but also in terms of its performance under different operating conditions such as when there is an engine failure during take-off.
2   Regulations covering the timing, nature and supervision of maintenance and overhaul work and the training and qualifications of the engineers who carry out such work.
3   Regulations governing the numbers of flight and cabin crew, their training and licensing, their duties and functions on board and their work loads and schedules.
4   Detailed regulations covering both the way in which aircraft are operated, that is, aspects such as flight preparation and in-flight procedures, and also the operation of the airlines themselves. In all countries, air transport

operators must be licensed by the relevant civil aviation authority and must satisfy certain criteria and operating standards.

5   Finally, there is a complex profusion of regulations and recommended standards dealing with aviation infrastructure, such as airports, meteorological services, en-route navigational facilities, and so on.

Many of the technical and safety requirements are general, that is, not specific to a particular aircraft type, and are promulgated as regulations of the civil aviation directorates or the relevant Transport Ministries of each country. In the United States they are known as Federal Aviation Regulations, while in the United Kingdom such regulations appear in the Air Navigation Order (CAA, 2000c).

In Europe the various national regulations are being progressively superseded by Europe-wide standards, the so-called Joint Airworthiness Requirements (JARs). The latter are agreed through and promulgated by the Joint Airworthiness Authority (JAA), which is made up of thirty-three member states, though by early 2001 only twenty were full members. Working through technical committees composed of experts in each particular field, the JAA promulgates requirements, known as JARs, related to specific areas such as aircraft maintenance or pilot licensing. It is then up to each state to decide whether it wishes to adopt each JAR by incorporating it into its own legislation. In other words, JARs are not as yet mandatory. But the major European states have in fact incorporated the key JARs into their own regulations. The next logical step, which is the establishment of a European Aviation Safety Agency (EASA), with mandatory powers, has been under consideration for a few years. But problems related to the loss of national sovereignty by individual states have bedevilled its creation. Approval by the European Union was expected in late 2001 or early 2002 for the setting up of the first stage of EASA a year later. This stage 1 was likely to regulate aircraft certification and maintenance but not operations. That would come later.

While technical and airworthiness regulations may vary in particular detail from one country to another they are generally based on a whole series of 'International Standards and Recommended Practices' promulgated by the International Civil Aviation Organisation (ICAO) as sixteen annexes to the Convention on International Civil Aviation. This is the so-called Chicago Convention, signed in 1944. For instance, Annex 8 deals with the 'Airworthiness of aircraft' and Annex 1 with 'Personnel licensing'. These are constantly revised and updated. As a result there tends to be considerable uniformity in the technical regulations for air transport in most member states of ICAO. Operational and safety requirements specific to an aircraft type are contained in its flight manual. But the operational constraints and practices recommended in the flight manuals conform to the more general regulations mentioned above and are approved by the relevant national airworthiness authorities. Among other things, the flight manual will impose payload limits on an aircraft at airports with high temperatures or inadequate runway length. In this and numerous other ways airworthiness and other technical regulations have direct economic repercussions on airlines.

While international technical and safety regulations have been adopted by virtually all countries they are not always fully and adequately implemented. This may occur, for instance, if the civil aviation authorities in a country do not have the expertise, the staffing or the financial resources to monitor effectively whether their national airlines are carrying out the required maintenance procedures and checks on their aircraft or whether pilot training is adequate. During the 1990s there was growing concern about the airworthiness and safety standards of aircraft registered in certain countries. As a reaction, in 1996 ICAO began a voluntary programme of audits of individual states' ability to oversee the effective application of safety requirements. This culminated in a mandatory programme of audits of all states (ICAO, 1999a). But, in advance of effective action by ICAO, the US Federal Aviation Administration (FAA) had launched its own 'safety oversight' procedures whereby the FAA itself inspects and monitors the degree to which airworthiness and other safety-related regulations are adequately implemented in certain countries where concern has been raised. The FAA has carried out inspections in close to 100 countries. If the airworthiness standards are deemed inadequate, those states are identified as falling into Category 2. If that happens, aircraft from such countries can no longer fly into the United States. In 1999–2000 a number of states in Central America fell into this category. Their scheduled international airlines had to abandon flights to the United States. Alternatively, their airlines may be prevented from increasing existing frequencies to the United States and have been required to abandon code-sharing agreements with US carriers. In Europe a JAA and ECAC (European Civil Aviation Conference) joint programme 'Safety Assessment of Foreign Aircraft' was launched in 1996. It differs from the FAA approach in that it is based on ramp inspections of aircraft landing at European airports. But the ultimate sanction is the same: to ban a state's aircraft from flying to Europe. The threat of such sanctions imposed by major destination countries is a strong incentive on civil aviation authorities of countries with aspiring international airlines to ensure that airworthiness regulations and standards are met.

These various technical standards and safety procedures undoubtedly constrain airline managers and, at the same time, impose cost penalties on airline operations. But such external controls are inevitable if high safety standards are to be maintained, and significantly all airlines are equally affected by them. No major international airline can enjoy a competitive advantage by operating to airworthiness standards below the generally acceptable level. The implementation of ICAO standards and the safety oversight procedures together ensure that, unlike the shipping sector, there are no 'flags of convenience' in air transport to enable airlines to circumvent national or international safety or manning regulations.

In addition to the various technical regulations and rules, international air transport is circumscribed by a multitude of national, bilateral and multilateral regulations and agreements whose objective is the economic and, sometimes, political regulation and control of the industry. Such economic controls, unlike the technical standards outlined above, do not affect all airlines equally and therein lies their importance.

2.3   The growth of economic regulation

When the Paris Convention, signed in 1919, accepted that states have sovereign rights in the air space above their territory, direct government intervention in air transport became inevitable. A country's air space became one of its valuable natural resources. As a result, the free-trade *laissez-faire* approach to air transport of the early years of aviation was gradually replaced by an incomplete pattern of bilateral agreements between countries having airlines and the countries to or through which those airlines wished to fly. But the restrictive character of 'bilateralism' was soon apparent. Even before the Second World War was over, fifty-two member states met in Chicago in 1944 to consider some form of multinational agreement in three crucial aspects of international transport:

1   the exchange of air traffic rights, or 'freedoms of the air' (see appendix);
2   the control of fares and freight tariffs;
3   the control of flight frequencies and capacity.

From an economist's viewpoint these three aspects together effectively determine the nature of any industry, for they regulate the entry of firms into each market (through traffic rights), the degree of pricing freedom and the nature of controls on production, if any. If there is maximum exchange of traffic rights, which means open market access, combined with little or no control of tariffs or frequencies offered, then a market can be considered to be very competitive. Provided, of course, there are no other barriers to market entry. If, on the other hand, traffic rights, tariffs and frequencies are all tightly regulated, then such markets will be uncompetitive or even monopolistic.

At Chicago there were two conflicting approaches. The United States, whose civil aviation industry was going to emerge from the Second World War largely unscathed and much larger and better equipped than anyone else's, wanted no control of tariffs or capacity and the maximum exchange of traffic rights, including 'fifth-freedom' rights. This 'open skies' policy was supported by states such as the Netherlands or Sweden, whose airlines would have to depend on carrying traffic between other countries because their home base was so small. On the other hand, the United Kingdom and most European countries were more protectionist, understandably so, since their civil airlines had been decimated in the war. They supported tight controls on tariffs and capacity and the limitation of the so-called fifth-freedom traffic rights (see appendix for definition of traffic rights). These two conflicting views could not be reconciled. No multilateral agreement was reached on the three key issues of traffic rights, tariff control and capacity.

The participants at Chicago did manage to agree on the mutual exchange of the first two freedoms – the right to overfly another state while on an agreed service and the right to land in each other's country. This was done through the International Air Services Transit Agreement signed in December 1944 and to which many more states have subsequently adhered. But no agreement was reached on the mutual exchange of commercial traffic rights. These are the third and fourth freedoms, which allow the mutual exchange of traffic rights between two countries, enabling their respective airlines to carry passengers and freight between them. There is also the fifth freedom, which is the right granted by country A to an airline(s) from country B to carry traffic between A and countries other than B (see the appendix).

The most significant result of the Chicago conference was the signing of the Convention on International Civil Aviation, known subsequently as the Chicago Convention. This provided the framework for the orderly and safe development of international air transport. It did this through its various articles and the annexes (mentioned earlier), which deal with every aspect of the operation of aircraft and air services both in the air and on the ground. The convention also set up the International Civil Aviation Organisation, an intergovernmental agency which provided the forum for further discussion of key aviation issues and the basis of the worldwide co-ordination of technical and operational standards and practices. ICAO also provided crucial technical assistance to many countries, especially newly independent states in Africa and Asia, helping them to establish airport and air navigation facilities and to organise other aspects of civil aviation infrastructure.

A further attempt at a multilateral agreement on traffic rights, pricing and capacity was made at the Geneva conference of 1947, but this also failed. In time, government and airlines together found a way of circumventing the failures of Chicago and Geneva. The exchange of traffic rights became a matter for *bilateral air service agreements* between states; the control of capacities and frequencies became a matter for *inter-airline agreements*, and sometimes for bilateral state agreements; tariffs came to be regulated by the International Air Transport Association. As a result, a framework for the international regulation of air transport emerged based on these three separate but interlinked elements.

2.4 Bilateral air service agreements

From the mid-1940s onwards, each country negotiated a series of bilateral air service agreements (known as 'bilaterals') with other states, aimed at regulating the operation of air transport services between them. The prime purpose of such bilaterals has been the control of market access (points to be served and traffic rights) and of market entry, by determining which airlines can be designated to use the traffic rights granted. Some bilaterals also control the flight frequencies or the capacity that can be offered by each airline on the routes between the two countries. Such bilateral agreements – and there are over 1,500 of them still today – became and, in most of the world, remain the fundamental core of the regulatory regime. This is so even when the bilaterals have been renegotiated and have become very liberal or 'open skies' agreements. Air service agreements have three distinct parts.

First, there is *the bilateral itself*. This consists of a number of articles covering a variety of administrative provisions to facilitate the operation of air services. These include articles dealing with exemption from customs duties on imports of aircraft parts, with airport charges, with the setting up of sales offices or the transfer abroad of airline sales revenue, and so on. Of greater significance are the articles dealing with the economic provisions of the agreement. The key articles are those dealing with the regulation of tariffs and those on capacity. Most of the traditional bilaterals specify that passenger fares and cargo tariffs should be agreed by the designated airlines, due regard being paid to all relevant factors, including cost of operation, and a reasonable profit. But in the early years airlines were encouraged to use the tariff-fixing machinery of IATA to reach agreement on fares. Most bilaterals included words such as

> The tariffs . . . shall if possible be agreed by the designated airlines concerned of both Contracting Parties . . . and such agreement shall, wherever possible, be reached by the use of the procedures of the International Air Transport Association for the working out of tariffs.
> (UK–Singapore Air Service Agreement, 1971)

However, both governments were required to approve such fares and tariffs. In other words, ultimate control of tariffs rested with governments, though in practice the vast majority of governments automatically approved the IATA agreed fares. On capacity, some traditional bilaterals require very strict control and sharing of capacity by the airlines of the two countries while others have minimal control.

Another economic issue to be resolved is the number of airlines which will be designated to operate between the two signatory states. In most bilaterals only 'single designation' was envisaged, that is, one airline from each state. Most states, in any case, only had one airline. However, a few bilaterals, especially those with the United States, did allow for 'double' or 'multiple' designation. Irrespective of the number of airlines to be designated, all had to be 'substantially owned and effectively controlled' by nationals of the 'designating state'. This nationality requirement in virtually all bilaterals has proved the biggest obstacle to the normalisation of the international airline industry.

The second part of the bilateral is the annex containing the *Schedule of Routes*. It is here that the traffic rights granted to each of the two states are made explicit. The schedule specifies the routes to be operated by the 'designated' airline(s) of each state. Airlines are never mentioned by name. It is up to each state to designate its airline or airlines subsequently. The points (towns) to be served by each designated airline are listed or, less usually, a general right may be granted such as from 'points in the United Kingdom' without specifying the points. The routes or points granted to the designated airline of one state are not necessarily the reverse image of those granted to the airline of the other state signing the bilateral. If a town or country is not specifically listed in the route schedule a designated airline cannot operate services to it unless the bilateral is amended.

The schedule will also indicate whether the designated airlines have been granted rights to pick up traffic in other countries or from airports lying between or beyond the two signatory states. These are the fifth-freedom rights. But they cannot be used unless the third countries involved also agree. Thus the current US–Singapore bilateral grants the Singapore designated airline fifth-freedom rights between London and New York as an extension of its services between Singapore and London. The London–New York rights cannot be exercised until the UK government agrees in its own air service agreement with Singapore, which hitherto it has been loath to do.

The final part of the bilateral may consist of one or more *Memorandum of Understanding* or 'Exchange of Notes'. These are agreements, often confidential, that amplify or subsequently modify particular aspects of the basic air service agreement. Bilaterals are government-to-government trade agreements. Once negotiated and signed, their validity is indefinite until they are renegotiated. Even then the basic articles and structure tend to remain unchanged and modifications are made through a Memorandum or an Exchange of Notes. If a state wishes to terminate an agreement it must give twelve months' notice. This is sometimes done when the other state is unwilling to open negotiations or refuses to accept any of the modifications being discussed.

Underlying all bilateral agreements from the early days has been the concept of *reciprocity*, of an equal and fair exchange of rights between countries very different in size and with airlines of varied strengths. This has traditionally been enshrined in an article containing the words 'There shall be fair and equal opportunity for the airlines of both Contracting Parties to operate the agreed service on the specified routes between their respective territories.'

Many of the traditional types of bilateral agreement reflect protectionist attitudes. They insist on prior agreement on the capacity to be provided on the route and specify that the agreed capacity shall be shared equally by the designated carriers of the two states, normally only one from each state. In the past some went even further and specified that services must be operated in 'pool' by the airlines concerned. At the same time few if any fifth-freedom rights are granted.

Slightly more liberal but still traditional bilaterals are frequently referred to as Bermuda-type agreements, after the air services agreement signed in 1946 between the United Kingdom and the United States in Bermuda. This was significant because it represented a compromise between the extreme positions taken at the 1944 Chicago conference, and because both the United States and the United Kingdom undertook to try to model all future agreements on the Bermuda pattern. As a result, Bermuda-type agreements became wide-spread. They differ from the protectionist or 'predetermination' type of agreement described above in two respects. First, fifth-freedom rights are more widely available, provided that the total capacity offered by the airline concerned on fifth-freedom sectors is related to the end-to-end traffic potential of the routes. Second, there is no control of frequency or capacity on the routes between the two countries concerned. However, there is one safeguard on capacity: if one airline feels that its interests are being too adversely affected by the frequencies offered by the other, there may be an '*ex post facto*' review of capacity.

The other significant clause of the Bermuda agreement was that on tariffs. While both governments maintained their ultimate right to approve or disapprove the tariffs proposed by the airlines, they agreed that where possible such tariffs should be arrived at using the procedures of the International Air Transport Association. For the United States this was a major compromise. It agreed to approve tariffs fixed by an association of producers, the international airlines, even though such price-fixing was illegal under US domestic anti-trust legislation. In essence, IATA tariff decisions were exempted from the provisions of such legislation. As pointed out earlier, the tariffs article of most bilaterals included wording to the effect that tariff agreements should 'where possible be reached by the use of the procedures of the International Air Transport Association'. Even states such as Singapore or Malaysia, whose national airlines did not become members of IATA until 1990, agreed in their bilaterals to approve where possible tariffs agreed through IATA. Thus approval of the IATA tariff procedures was enshrined in most bilateral agreements. It was this that gave the IATA tariff machinery such force until liberalisation set in after 1978.

Bermuda-type agreements became widespread, but the effect was not as liberal as their terms might suggest. This is because they do not preclude inter-airline pooling agreements which effectively restrict capacity competition. Nor do they preclude subsequent capacity restrictions imposed arbitrarily by governments to prevent foreign designated carriers from introducing a new aircraft type or to limit increases in frequencies.

Today each international airline is faced with a complex web of bilateral air service agreements signed by its home state. If the agreements are of the traditional pre-liberalisation type they will specify which points can be served and what traffic rights have been granted. They will determine whether more than one airline from each state can carry the traffic agreed. Some may impose capacity controls, others will not. A few may even insist that services must be operated in 'pool'. It is the bilateral which tells the airline where it can and cannot fly and how. This is true even where the traditional bilaterals have been renegotiated and liberalised to a greater or lesser extent. The process of liberalisation is discussed in the next chapter. It is the terms of all its own state's air service agreements, and whether these are traditional or more liberal, which will determine what an airline can or cannot do.

2.5 Purchasing traffic rights

Air service agreements are essentially restrictive. They prevent airlines from operating to points or on routes which they may wish to enter, even if it makes economic sense for them to do so, because they do not enjoy particular traffic rights. If their government is unable or unwilling to renegotiate the relevant bilaterals to obtain the additional rights then airlines have only one option left. They can try to purchase such rights by paying royalties or 'revenue compensation' to the airlines whose rights they wish to share.

Royalty payments for traffic rights not granted under existing bilaterals have been most common when airlines have wanted to pick up fifth-freedom rights on medium- or long-haul multi-sector services. For instance, under the terms of the original 1971 Singapore–UK bilateral, Singapore Airlines (SIA) had fifth-freedom rights between Athens and London under the terms of the UK–Singapore bilateral, but could not use those rights unless they were also granted in Singapore's bilateral with Greece. Such was not the case, so when in 1977 SIA operated from Singapore to London via Athens it agreed to pay Olympic Airways a royalty for any local traffic picked up between Athens and London. In other words, SIA bought the Athens–London fifth-freedom rights from the Greek government by paying the Greek airline for them. The royalty in this case was expressed as 20 per cent of the revenue generated from fifth-freedom traffic. Despite the royalty, SIA began to carry so much traffic between Athens and London that Olympic cancelled the royalty agreement a year later in 1978.

Royalty or 'revenue compensation' agreements for fifth-freedom traffic have been fairly common. But in some cases airlines have been forced into making royalty agreements to cover the carriage of the sixth-freedom traffic. The concept of a sixth freedom has rarely appeared in any bilateral agreement, though the expression has been widely used for many years. It involves the carriage of traffic between two points, between which an airline does not have fifth-freedom rights, by the use of two sets of third- and fourth-freedom rights. For instance, Malaysia Airlines can carry traffic between London and Kuala Lumpur using its UK third- and fourth-freedom traffic rights. It can then carry those passengers on to Australia using the third- and fourth-freedom rights, granted under the Australia–Malaysia bilateral. Malaysia Airlines is effectively carrying traffic on a sector, United Kingdom to Australia, for which it does not formally have traffic rights. Up to the mid-1980s attempts were made to limit such sixth-freedom through traffic between London and Australia or on other routes by the imposition of various controls such as the need to make stopovers of several days in Kuala Lumpur or other intermediate points. In fact for many years up to 1985 Malaysia Airlines paid a royalty to British Airways of around $50 for each sixth-freedom passenger it carried on this route. KLM in Europe and SIA, Thai International, and Malaysia Airlines in South East Asia, as well as several Middle East airlines such as Emirates, were so successful in generating sixth-freedom traffic that the various regulatory controls were slowly eroded and eventually abandoned.

Today, the generation of sixth-freedom traffic is common and widespread. The concept of 'hubbing' in international air transport is, after all, about attracting sixth-freedom passengers or cargo. Yet, even as recently as the early 1990s, some airlines were being forced to pay revenue compensation to third- and fourth-freedom carriers for 'stealing' traffic through sixth-freedom operations. For instance, under a 1988 agreement Philippine Airlines continued to pay British Airways substantial compensation for channelling passengers between the United Kingdom and Australia via Manila. Thai International was also paying British Airways for doing the same via Bangkok.

While royalty agreements covering sixth- and more especially fifth-freedom traffic were fairly common from early on, a later phenomenon was the payment of royalties for third- and fourth-freedom traffic. This has occurred when one of the two designated carriers on a route has decided not to operate that particular route. It could then argue that the other country's designated carrier would carry all the traffic, including that which would have been carried by the airline which was not operating. The non-operating airline would want to be compensated for giving up its traffic share and might be able to push the other carrier into a royalty agreement. Under a 1988 agreement between Malev, the Hungarian airline, and Olympic Airways the former paid the latter a royalty for all passengers carried on any scheduled flights between the two countries over and above the four flights weekly originally agreed, because Olympic did not operate any services to Hungary at all. Malev paid $13 for each such passenger on its Budapest–Athens flight and $11 for such additional passengers on Budapest–Salonica. This revenue compensation agreement was terminated in April 1999.

Where royalty payments enable airlines to buy traffic rights they do not have under the terms of existing bilateral agreements, they may improve the viability of certain routes. But if the airlines are forced to pay royalties for third- and fourth-freedom traffic, whose rights they already have under the bilaterals, the result is merely to push costs up. In the past, but much less so today, royalty payments have been an integral part of the bilateral traffic rights system.

2.6   Inter-airline pooling agreements

Prior to liberalisation, the vast majority of international sectors had only two major carriers, the designated airlines of the two countries involved. This is still the case today on most routes. As in many duopolistic situations, there is a strong incentive for formal or informal agreements between the duopolists to share out the market. In the years up to the early 1990s such agreements generally took the form of revenue-sharing pools or, less frequently, revenue- and cost-sharing pools. Where one of the two airlines in a duopolistic market was much weaker or smaller, pooling was a way of guaranteeing its share of capacity and revenue when faced with a much stronger or well-established rival. When the two carriers were of similar strength, pooling helped push load factors up by removing frequency competition. It also helped to reduce costs and rationalise schedules. Without a pooling agreement both competing airlines tended to bunch their departures at peak periods of demand. If all revenue is shared, airlines do not mind operating some flights at less attractive times. Pool partners can plan their schedules so as to offer a good range of departure times throughout the day. This benefits the passengers and stimulates demand.

Pooling agreements were forbidden on routes to or from the United States by that country's anti-trust legislation. But they became very widespread in Europe, where, until the early 1990s, 75–80 per cent of intra-European passenger kilometres were operated on pooled services. They were also common in South East Asia and to a lesser extent in other parts of the world. Agreements can cover a single route or sector or, more normally, all the routes on which the two signatory airlines operate between their two countries. In general, airline pools cover third- and fourth-freedom traffics. But fifth-freedom traffic may be included on long-haul pools, though these are relatively rare. While most pool agreements involve two airlines, three- or four-airline pools are not uncommon, especially in South East Asia. Though it is often known that airlines are operating in pool, the terms of any pooling agreement are a closely guarded commercial secret.

In some instances where the traffic is not considered to be adequate for two-airline operation there may be a *revenue/cost pool*. This means that one airline alone operates the service on behalf of the airlines in the pool, but costs and revenues are shared between them on a prearranged basis. On the Cairns–Tokyo route launched in 1986 there was an operating agreement between JAL and Qantas under which only the latter airline operated the services and revenue and costs were pooled and shared equally.

Some airlines have extended the concept of the revenue/cost pool, which has been seen essentially as a solution to the problem of routes on which traffic is thin, into agreements covering routes which can support two carriers. In such wider cost-sharing pools *both* airlines operate on one or more routes between their countries and all their costs and revenues are shared on the basis of an agreed formula. The flight numbers often carry the code of both airlines. Malaysia Airlines is one airline which has pursued such pools, which it calls 'joint ventures', as a matter of policy. Its agreements include one with Thai International, covering air services between Thailand and Malaysia.

The most widespread pooling agreements have been those involving *revenue sharing*. In these all revenue on a route or sector is shared by the participating airlines in proportion to the capacity they offer on the route. In a two-airline pool, each airline will normally want a half share of the revenue and hence will expect to provide half the capacity. Imbalances in capacity may be permitted by mutual agreement if one carrier cannot or does not wish to increase its own capacity. If an airline does provide 50 per cent of the capacity but obtains only 47 per cent of the revenue generated, compared with its pool partner's 53 per cent, the pool partner will hand over 3 per cent of the revenue. The principle of sharing revenue in proportion to capacity is simple; its application may not be. If several different routes are pooled or if pooled services include multi-stop sectors then estimating each airline's capacity share becomes rather complex.

Another key item is to agree the pool accounting unit. This is the notional fare or revenue which each airline earns from one passenger on each pool sector. The number of revenue passengers carried on each sector by an airline is multiplied by the pool accounting unit for that sector to produce the revenue which that airline has to put into the pool. It is this notional revenue which is pooled, not the actual revenue collected. Such a system is less open to cheating because each airline need not know its pool partner's actual revenue, only the number of passengers carried, which is easy to verify. But it also provides an incentive to keep fares up and a strong disincentive to undercut the market. If an airline sells a ticket for $320 when the pool accounting unit is $300, it can keep $20 and only $300 is credited to the pool. Conversely, if it has sold a ticket for $250, it still has to contribute $300 for that passenger to the pooled revenue. Though a notional figure used purely for accounting purposes, the pool accounting unit is normally related to the average revenue per passenger in the preceding period. There may be a single pool unit irrespective of class or there may be two or three separate unit values applicable to passengers in different classes.

Some revenue-sharing pools allow the unlimited transfer of funds from one airline to the other, provided that the final adjusted revenue of each airline is proportional to its share of the capacity offered. Such agreements remove all competitive incentive. In practice most pools set a limit on the revenue that may be transferred from one airline to the other. This transfer limit may be expressed as a percentage of the total pooled revenue, or as a percentage of the donor's or the recipient's revenue. Alternatively the transfer limit may be an agreed maximum sum of money. Many pool agreements will have fairly low transfer limits, often expressed as 1 per cent or 1.5 per cent of the total revenue. The aim of the transfer limit is to ensure that an airline which is very successful in marketing and selling its services does not end up transferring large sums of money to its inefficient pool partner. Once transfer limits are imposed, particularly if they are very low, competition begins to creep back, for the more passengers a pool carrier can carry the more revenue it can keep. But there is still no competition in terms of frequency or capacity.

Pool agreements may also cover freight. Freight revenue pools are based on the same principles and have the same features as the passenger revenue pools described above. They may relate to all-freighter services or to freight carried on passenger aircraft or both. The effect of all pooling agreements, once entered into, is to reduce the freedom of action of the airlines involved and to reduce or even blunt any competitive tendencies. This is particularly so if there is no transfer limit on pooled revenue or if the limit is relatively high. Then there is little incentive for pool partners to compete, since they are assured of half or close to half of the total revenue, whatever their relative market performance. Another feature of pooling agreements which is anti-competitive is that they require the pool partners to agree jointly on the capacity and frequencies offered. This enables them to push up load factors and tariffs and avoids frequency competition. The joint impact of the bilateral air service agreements with that of inter-airline agreements, where they exist, has been to delimit the routes on which airlines can operate and to determine the capacity shares of the two (or occasionally three) designated carriers in these markets.

It is precisely because they were deemed to be restrictive and anti-competitive collusive agreements between supplies of air services that pooling agreements were never permitted on routes to and from the United States. This was also the reason why in its December 1987 decisions on air transport liberalisation, the so-called 'First Package', the European Council of Ministers deemed that pooling agreements would be illegal unless granted specific exemption by the European Commission. Temporary exemptions were subsequently granted for pooling agreements on intra-EU routes. Nevertheless, during the early 1990s EU airlines gradually unwound their pooling agreements. Today pooling agreements can generally be found only among some Asian, Middle Eastern and African airlines.

A key question arises, however. Pooling agreements have disappeared from most major international routes, especially those involving European airlines. But have they merely been replaced by code sharing, block space or other inter-airline commercial arrangements, whose prime objective is the same – namely, to co-ordinate schedules, avoid capacity or frequency competition and thereby push up load factors and, hopefully, tariffs and yields? After all, most airline alliances involve agreement on some or all of these issues.

2.7   The role of IATA

The International Air Transport Association (IATA) was founded in Havana in 1945 as a successor to the pre-war association, which had been largely European. Its primary purpose was to represent the interests of airlines and to act as a counterweight to ICAO, which was an intergovernmental agency primarily concerned with government interests in aviation. Through its various committees and sub-committees, which bring airline experts together for a few days each year, IATA has been able to co-ordinate and standardise virtually every aspect of international airline operation. Thus the Financial Committee has harmonised methods of rendering, verifying and settling accounts between airlines while the Traffic Committee has standardised aircraft containers and other unit load devices as well as many other aspects of passenger or cargo handling. IATA produces invaluable statistics, surveys and research reports covering many areas of airline activity. IATA also represents the airlines in negotiations with airport authorities, governments or ICAO on matters as diverse as airport charges or anti-hijacking measures. IATA works both as a forum for inter-airline discussion and resolution of key issues and as a pressure group representing the interests of international airlines.

One of IATA's most important functions is to operate the Clearing House for inter-airline debts arising from interline traffic, that is, the carriage by one airline of passengers (or freight) holding tickets issued by other airlines. The sums involved are enormous. In the year 2000 the 217 IATA and forty-two non-IATA airlines using the Clearing House, together with 111 airlines of a US-based clearing house and sixty or so other participants, submitted inter-airline claims amounting to $33.6 billion. The Clearing House settles inter-airline accounts in both dollars and sterling by offsetting members' counter-claims against each other. In 2000, 81 per cent of all claims could be offset without the need for any cash transaction. The Clearing House speeds up and simplifies the process of clearing inter-airline debts and substantially reduces the cost. Airlines that do not use the Clearing House must negotiate individually with each airline whose ticket stubs they may hold. This is slow and laborious. It may involve long delays before debts are cleared as well as additional bank charges.

IATA has made and continues to make a vital contribution in establishing common standards and recommended practices for the selling and distribution of air services. This is crucial, given the vast number of very different airlines involved in international operations and the large number of different countries each of those airlines may be flying to. It is IATA which has made it possible for a passenger to buy a round-the-world ticket from United Airlines in Chicago involving travel on several different airlines and for the passenger to have his ticket accepted for the sector from, say, Port Moresby (in Papua New Guinea) to Hong Kong by an airline he may have never even heard of.

Historically, IATA's most important function has been to set airline fares and cargo rates. Up to 1979 the process for establishing fares was rather rigid (IATA, 1974). It involved the so-called Traffic Conferences, one covering North and South America, the second covering Europe, the Middle East and Africa, and the third the Pacific region and Australasia. Airlines operating in or through these areas belonged to the relevant conference. The conferences, meeting in secret and usually about four to six months in advance, established the tariff structure which would be operative for a specified period, usually of one year. The conferences also agreed on fares between the conference regions. About 200,000 separate passenger fares and over 100,000 cargo rates were negotiated together with complex conditions of in-flight service associated with each fare. The conditions would cover such aspects as seat pitch, the number of meals to be served, whether they were hot or cold, charges for headphones, and so on. Since such detailed service conditions had to be strictly applied by IATA-member airlines there was little scope for competition in service standards or fares. Once each regional conference had agreed on its own tariffs, the three conferences came together in joint session for the tariffs proposed to be voted on. They had to be agreed unanimously. In other words, any airline, no matter how small, could veto the proposed tariffs and force further renegotiation. The tariff process was lengthy and time-consuming. While in the early years unanimity was usually reached fairly quickly, by the early 1970s unanimity became increasingly difficult to achieve.

From the airlines' point of view the Traffic Conference system had clear advantages: it produced a coherent and worldwide structure of interrelated passenger fares and cargo rates, together with tariff-related rules and regulations. The Traffic Conferences were also instrumental in developing standard documents and contracts of air carriage – tickets, waybills, baggage checks, etc.

IATA tariffs were accepted worldwide because in so many bilateral air service agreements governments had explicitly agreed that they would approve fares negotiated through the IATA process. This was the case even with some governments whose airlines were not IATA members. Non-IATA airlines needed to adopt IATA fares in order to get their tickets accepted by IATA carriers. To give added force to its tariff agreements, IATA had compliance inspectors checking that member airlines were not illegally discounting on the IATA tariffs. If caught selling tickets or cargo space at discounted rates, IATA airlines faced heavy financial penalties. Since no IATA airlines were allowed to deviate from the IATA tariffs, no price competition was possible.

There can be little doubt that IATA was effectively a suppliers' cartel, whose object was to maximise its members' profits by mutually fixing the prices at which they sold their services. But it was often argued that three features of the IATA Traffic Conference system safeguarded the interests of the public and the consumers and prevented the airlines' cartel from abusing its power. These were: first, a *de facto* ban on any kind of capacity regulation. This would make it difficult for the airlines to extract monopoly profits by fixing both fares and output at the appropriate levels. In practice, on many routes capacity was controlled either through the bilaterals or through airline agreements such as revenue pools. The second argument was that the unanimity rule favoured those airlines which were pressing for lower fares, since airlines wishing to maintain a higher fare structure would prefer some agreement to none. In fact the unanimity rule appeared to be most effective in preventing an upward movement of fares. It was less effective in ensuring that fares fell to levels proposed by the more efficient airlines. It was claimed that the third safeguard was the requirement under the terms of the bilateral air service agreements for governments to approve any tariff agreements made through IATA. They could, in theory, block any fares they deemed anti-competitive. But, with the exception of the United States, few governments ever did so, since they did not have sufficient expertise in their civil aviation departments to assess tariffs. They were happy to support the fares agreed by their national carriers.

Overall the apparent safeguards against IATA working as a producers' cartel did not seem very effective. But if IATA was a cartel, it was failing to achieve the prime objective of any cartel, namely high profits for its members. Our earlier analysis has shown an industry characterised by poor financial results (Chapter 1.1 and Figure 1.1). Nevertheless, the travelling public and consumer groups remained unconvinced of the benefits of the IATA tariff machinery. During the 1970s pressure began to build up on governments in Europe and North America to allow greater pricing freedom.

At the same time IATA tariff procedures began to prove too rigid and inflexible to deal with two new developments. The first of these, which had started more than a decade earlier, was the growth of non-scheduled or charter air services. Attempts by IATA and many governments to stem their growth had failed. As a result, charter airlines were making serious inroads into scheduled markets in Europe and on the North Atlantic. The second development was the expansion in the 1970s of dynamic new airlines belonging to smaller states in the developing world, especially in South East Asia. Airlines such as Thai International, SIA and Korean began to make an impact on regional and long-haul markets. As non-IATA carriers they captured market share either by offering much higher levels of in-flight service than was permitted under IATA's 'conditions of service' or, less frequently, through greater flexibility in their tariffs. To counter competition both from charters and from new non-IATA carriers the IATA airlines needed much greater pricing freedom than could be obtained within the cumbersome Traffic Conferences.

Faced with these external competitive pressures, IATA airlines found it increasingly difficult to achieve unanimity on the tariff policies to be adopted at the Traffic Conferences. More and more IATA airlines began to offer illegally discounted fares in very competitive markets or to flout the strict controls on in-flight service standards. Several governments, particularly that of the United States, began to push for a system which allowed consumers to benefit from greater pricing freedom. Openly disregarded by some of its own members, and under pressure from a number of governments, IATA's tariff machinery began to disintegrate.

IATA was forced to change. The aim of new rules introduced in 1979 was to allow greater flexibility in tariff setting and offer greater freedom to airlines to opt out of the agreed tariffs. The unanimity rule was abandoned and greater weight was given to the interests of the third- and fourth-freedom carriers on a route when agreeing fares. The various regulations on conditions of in-flight service, such as those relating to meals, gifts, in-flight entertainment, etc., which related to different fares, were also abandoned. But passenger fares still relate to different classes of travel and may have booking or travel restrictions. Finally the secretive and confidential Traffic Conferences of earlier days have been replaced by the much more open and public Tariff Co-ordinating Conferences. Observers from governments and international organisations may attend and third parties may make written or oral presentations to the conferences.

Perhaps the most radical change was that after 1978 airlines could join IATA as a trade association without participating in the Passenger or Cargo Tariff Co-ordinating Conferences. By mid-2001, of IATA's 246 active member airlines, about half did not take part in Tariff Co-ordination. Nor are trade association members obliged to implement IATA tariffs. IATA's more open structure and its role in pursuing airline interests on many issues, such as airport charges or infrastructure, made it increasingly attractive to airlines that had previously stayed aloof. A major breakthrough occurred in July 1990 when four Asian airlines, SIA, Cathay Pacific, Malaysia Airlines and Royal Brunei joined as trade association members for the first time. The last real objection to their joining was removed earlier when IATA had agreed to modify its strict rules on IATA-accredited travel agents so as to allow carriers to deal with virtually any agent. Previously only IATA-accredited agents could be used. This represented a further relaxation in IATA's hitherto rigid membership rules.

The restructuring of IATA and the introduction of more flexible and open tariff-setting procedures have enabled IATA to survive despite the considerable pressures towards deregulation during the 1980s and 1990s. By the mid-1990s IATA's mammoth annual Tariff Conferences, where airlines from all regions were represented, had been replaced by a series of smaller, separate, regional and sub-regional meetings conducted throughout the year. IATA tariffs remain the government-approved tariffs for the majority of international air routes. Such IATA-agreed tariffs are widely accepted as providing the basic tariff structure and level of fares, even in markets or on routes where tariff discounting is widespread by both non-IATA and IATA airlines. More important, IATA tariffs, by establishing a structure for airlines to share revenues, also provide a basis for the issue and pricing of interline tickets, enabling passengers to use a single issued ticket to fly on several sectors using different airlines (see Table 10.9).

2.8   Limited regulation of non-scheduled air services

Unlike scheduled rights, non-scheduled traffic rights were traditionally not regulated by bilateral air service agreements. At the time of the 1944 Chicago Convention non-scheduled air services were not expected to be of any significance, and a more liberal attitude was therefore adopted. Whereas, under Article 6 of the Convention, scheduled air services specifically required 'special permission or other authorisation' from the destination countries, Article 5 left the authorisation of non-scheduled services to the discretion of individual states (ICAO, 1980).

In practice most countries have insisted on giving prior authorisation to incoming non-scheduled flights, but attitudes towards authorisation have varied significantly. Some countries, such as India, have been restrictionist in their approach and have refused to authorise charter flights unless they are operated by their own national carrier or unless it can be shown that no scheduled traffic will be diverted. Others may insist, before authorising an incoming charter, that one of their own airlines should be allowed to tender for the charter contract. In contrast, many other countries, particularly tourist destinations such as Spain, Morocco or Tunisia, have followed a more liberal 'open skies' policy and have readily authorised non-scheduled services.

In 1956 the member states of the European Civil Aviation Conference (ECAC) agreed to mutually waive the requirement for any prior authorisation from the destination country for a wide range of non-scheduled flights (HMG, 1956). This agreement greatly facilitated the development of charter services, particularly inclusive tour charters, within Europe. It was subsequently superseded by the various liberalisation measures agreed within the European Union during the 1990s, though these did not cover as many states as the 1956 ECAC agreement.

While access to many non-scheduled markets was relatively open even from the early days, most countries, especially those with new airlines emerging, brought non-scheduled operations within some form of national regulatory control. Such regulation was aimed at clearly delineating the area and scope of non-scheduled operations so as to protect scheduled airlines, while giving non-scheduled operators considerable freedom of action within their defined area. For example, British airlines have had to obtain an 'air transport licence' from the Civil Aviation Authority for all operations, as well as different licences for specific types of charter flights.

In the United States the Civil Aeronautics Act 1938 had allowed non-scheduled operations under a general exemption from regulations which affected scheduled carriers. But in 1962 Public Law 87-528 confined the role of supplemental carriers, as US charter airlines were then called, exclusively to non-scheduled operations and authorised the Civil Aeronautics Board (CAB) to certify supplemental carriers to operate in designated geographical areas. In time, thirteen supplemental carriers were certified. The final breakthrough came in 1968 with the Inclusive Tour Charter Bill which empowered the CAB to authorise the operation of inclusive tour charters (ITCs). An inclusive tour is a holiday package where a single charge includes travel, hotel accommodation and possibly local ground transport, visits, etc. Inclusive tour charters were developed in parallel with 'affinity' group charters operated by both supplemental carriers and scheduled airlines. Such affinity charters arose when societies or clubs, whose total membership was normally limited to 20,000 members and whose prime purpose was other than travel, chartered aircraft for their members, who shared the cost equally. Rapidly developing new holiday markets with affinity group charters and ITCs, and bolstered by the operation of substantial military charters in support of the Vietnam War, US non-scheduled operations grew at a phenomenal rate during the 1960s. High growth continued until about 1971 when military charters began to decline.

The European airlines meanwhile had based their own non-scheduled operations on developing inclusive tour charters, and were less dependent than their American counterparts on affinity group or military charters, though several were operating affinity charters to the United States or Canada.

Initially IATA tried to regulate the non-scheduled activities of its own members by trying to fix minimum charter rates as a function of the scheduled fare and by other rules governing who could have access to charter flights. In the 1960s many governments, under pressure from IATA, and to protect their own scheduled airlines, imposed arbitrary and often restrictive regulations on charter services. But as the tide of public opinion in many European countries and in North America swung strongly in favour of cheap charter flights, governments were forced to gradually dismantle the various domestic controls on charters. This process was given added impetus by the moves in the United States after 1978 to deregulate both domestic and international air transport. In particular, the United States set out to remove all price and other controls on charters while at the same time making the granting of non-scheduled traffic rights explicit within bilateral air service agreements.

The gradual liberalisation of non-scheduled services and the dismantling of often arbitrary regulations led to a rapid growth in charter traffic. By 1977, 29 per cent of passengers flying across the Atlantic were on inclusive tour or affinity group charters. That was the peak year. Then in 1978 the long-haul charter market collapsed. This was a direct result of deregulation of fares and entry on many North Atlantic scheduled routes. Several new entrant and lower-cost airlines, such as Laker Airways, began operating scheduled services. Competitive pressure pushed both new and existing scheduled carriers to offer fares which were charter-competitive. With little price advantage to offer, charter airlines found their traffic shrinking rapidly. Today charters account for well below 10 per cent of North Atlantic passenger traffic. However, in other areas, especially in European holiday markets, charter operations have continued to grow rapidly, normally outstripping the growth rates of scheduled carriers. Today, around 14 per cent of the world's international passenger kilometres are generated by charter services (see Table 6.2).

Generally speaking, non-scheduled operations have been subject to two different regulatory regimes. While in many parts of the world, such as the European–Mediterranean market or that of the North Atlantic, they have traditionally been subject to less regulatory controls than scheduled carriers, at least until the 1990s, in some states there has been a virtual ban on allowing incoming or even outgoing charter flights, except in exceptional circumstances. But here too the need to encourage tourism arrivals is leading to a gradual relaxation of the regulatory constraints.

2.9 Operational constraints imposed by the regulatory framework

The traditional three-pronged structure of international regulation based on the bilaterals, the inter-airline agreements and IATA has constrained the freedom of action of individual scheduled airlines in a number of ways.

First, their markets have often been restricted. Airlines could not enter any market at will, but have been dependent on government action and support – first in making bilateral agreements to open up air routes and obtain the necessary traffic rights and, second, in negotiating the points which should be served on these routes. This is not always straightforward, particularly if an existing bilateral has to be renegotiated. The other country may refuse to negotiate or may want to exact a high price for accepting changes in routes or traffic rights granted under the existing bilateral. Singapore Airlines had long wanted to operate from Singapore to Kota Kinabalu in eastern Malaysia (Sabah) but the Malaysia–Singapore bilateral granted traffic rights only to the

Malaysian designated carrier. The Malaysians had not been prepared to renegotiate on this, so SIA was excluded from a potentially lucrative route until the mid-1990s. To obtain fifth-freedom rights some airlines have had to pay royalties to other carriers. Some have even had to pay royalties to exercise third- and fourth-freedom rights granted to them under air service agreements.

Second, the level of output of each airline has not been entirely at its own discretion. Its production may be limited through bilateral agreements on capacity control or on equal sharing of capacity, or through any inter-airline agreements on revenue sharing and capacity. An airline wishing to increase its capacity and output on routes where there is some form of bilateral or inter-airline capacity control has often found that the other airline in the duopoly may be unable or unwilling to increase its own capacity, and therefore may veto the expansion plans. Thus competing in terms of frequencies offered became virtually impossible. Singapore Airlines had long wanted to increase its flights from Singapore to Hong Kong from fourteen to twenty-one weekly as permitted under the air service agreement with the United Kingdom. But it could not do so unless Cathay Pacific matched any frequency increase, which it was not prepared to do. SIA waited several years before getting Cathay's agreement to an increase of frequencies in 1989. Capacity limitations are widespread but have not existed in all markets. For instance, on many routes to or from the United States there was little effective capacity control even before deregulation, though the cities served at both ends of the route were limited.

Finally, airlines' pricing freedom has also been limited. This is partly because, until liberalisation in the 1980s, most tariffs have traditionally been set by the IATA Tariff Conferences in which the influence of any individual airline was limited and partly because governments must ultimately approve all tariffs. Even non-IATA airlines have frequently been required by governments to apply IATA tariffs on most of their international routes. Prior to international liberalisation, pricing freedom existed only in markets where either there was widespread discounting of IATA tariffs or where, with the connivance of governments, the IATA tariff process had been abandoned. Under traditional bilateralism, airline managers have not been free to choose and set their own tariffs at will. Tariffs have had to be approved by IATA or by the two governments concerned. In practice, such government approval has usually depended on the agreement of the other airline(s) on the route in question. Pricing freedom was further restricted if airlines were in revenue pools with other carriers.

From 1978 onwards many international air transport markets have been progressively liberalised. This is the topic of the next chapter. Where it has happened, many of the constraints imposed on airlines which have been summarised here have been relaxed or removed altogether. However, there are many point-to-point markets which are still operated under more traditional bilateral regulatory regimes. This means that market access or points to be served, as well as capacity and frequencies offered, are tightly controlled in many markets. But on pricing there is more variability, since attempts to prevent price competition in many bilateral markets have failed.

In practice most airlines have to operate under two different regulatory regimes. On many of their routes they will be constrained by having to operate within the limitations of traditional bilaterals while on some other routes they may be operating in an 'open skies' regime. Singapore Airlines is a case in point. It has 'open skies' bilateral agreements with the United States, Brunei and New Zealand and fairly open agreements with some European states such as Germany. But SIA operates the majority of its services to other Asian countries, to points in the Middle East, Africa or Eastern Europe, with the constraints arising from the traditional bilateral regime. Even the United States, which has pursued 'open skies' bilaterals so vigorously, still had a very large number of bilaterals in 2002 that had not been liberalised. But, as one can see in the following chapter, even 'open skies' regimes do not allow airline managers unlimited freedom of action. Whatever the regulatory regime, restrictive or 'open', airlines are still constrained in what they can do to a greater or lesser extent. Airline planning and economics can be understood only in the context of this mixed regulatory environment.

3 Liberalisation

Open markets and open skies

> The development of international air transportation as a commercial market driven industry has outpaced progress in the regulatory environment.
> (Andrew Lobbenberg, J. P. Morgan, November 2001)

3.1 The case for and against regulation

In the period up to the late 1970s economists had justified the tight regulation of both international and domestic air services on several grounds. In the United States the Civil Aeronautics Act of 1938 had been introduced to regulate and control competition between US domestic carriers because the unregulated competition which had prevailed up to then had led to chaotic economic conditions, little security for investors and low safety margins. For many years the US view was that, while air transport is not a natural monopoly, regulation was required because 'unregulated competitive market forces may have adverse consequences for the public at large' (Richmond, 1971). The same philosophy had been widely adopted to justify the regulation of international air transport as well. It was argued that, whereas there were strong oligopolistic tendencies in air transport, the absence of any regulation of market entry would inevitably lead to wasteful competition. This is because the industry has a non-differentiated product and relative ease of entry. At the same time economies of scale are not very marked, so small new entrant airlines would not be disadvantaged when operating against much larger incumbents. The latter would not have lower costs merely because of their size. On the other hand, new entrants in a particular market would try to establish themselves by undercutting existing fares, and a price war would result, with adverse consequences for all participants.

The second economic argument favouring regulation was based on the concept that air transport is a public utility, or at least a quasi-public utility. It was argued that the external benefits arising from civil aviation were such that the industry needed to be regulated in order to ensure that any benefits were not jeopardised. These benefits were assumed to be not only economic but also strategic, social and political. The public utility nature of air transport has, rightly or wrongly, been considered so important that most countries, except the United States, concentrated on developing one major scheduled operator, usually with direct government participation. The same carrier often operated domestic services and acted as the designated foreign carrier. It was a natural extension of this point of view to believe that free and unregulated competition on international air routes would endanger national interests because it might adversely affect that national state-owned airline.

A third argument supporting regulation of international air transport was linked with the rapid development of non-scheduled air traffic. In 1969 a committee of inquiry which examined British air transport came out strongly in favour of protecting scheduled services on most routes because they had 'public service' features which imposed certain costly obligations upon them and which made them particularly vulnerable to price competition (CICAT, 1969). Once an airline is committed to operate a series of scheduled services the marginal cost of any empty seats is virtually nil, since services cannot be withdrawn at short notice. If fares were not regulated, a fare war would result in disastrously low fares and marked financial instability among scheduled airlines.

The UK committee also argued that in the long run scheduled operations could not compete with charter operations because the former satisfied a 'collective' demand which necessitated the ready availability of spare seats on particular routes at short notice. In order to satisfy that demand scheduled operators must inevitably operate at lower load factors than charter airlines. Ready availability is after all one aspect of 'public service'. Lower load factors in turn mean higher passenger-kilometre costs than those achieved by non-scheduled operations. Where states wish to have scheduled services providing regular and readily available capacity with the minimum of special conditions for the public at large, some form of protection against the encroachment of lower-cost charter operators is required. This is particularly so where the scheduled traffic is relatively thin, for even a small loss of traffic may jeopardise the continuation of scheduled operations.

During the 1960s economists in the United States and elsewhere began to question the benefits of regulation and argued the advantages of freer competition in air transport. The then existing international regulations, described in the previous chapter, limited pricing freedom and product differentiation, restricted capacity growth and excluded new entrants. If these regulations were relaxed, a more competitive environment would provide considerable benefits to the consumer in lower fares, innovatory pricing and greater product differentiation. Lower tariffs would push airlines to re-examine their costs and would force them to improve their efficiency and productivity. Lower costs would facilitate further reductions in tariffs. Some inefficient airlines might be forced out of particular markets. But it was argued that the economics of the airline industry did not justify the fear that freer competition would lead to economic instability. The capacity of most large international airlines to fight tariff wars on a limited number of routes at a time, combined with a strong sense of self-preservation, would prevent the established carriers from going too far in a price war because of the dangers of getting 'locked in'. In other words, they would avoid successive fare reductions which would ultimately leave each airline with much the same share of the market but with very low and possibly unprofitable fare levels. Fear of new entrants would almost certainly push fares down to a level where only normal profits were being secured. Excess profits would attract new entrants. By the same token cross-subsidisation of unprofitable routes from the more profitable ones, which was prevalent up to then, would be largely eliminated, since it implied excess profits on particular routes. But in deregulated markets excess profits would draw in new entrants, until profits dropped to normal levels. Where airlines did enter new markets or routes they were likely to be innovative in their pricing and in their products. Existing carriers, hitherto protected by the regulatory environment, would be shaken out of their complacency. This could only be good for consumers. They would be offered more air-service providers to choose from and a wider choice of fares and service standards. The number of point-to-point services was also likely to increase, obviating the need for connecting flights and the concomitant delays.

At a more general level, many economists argued, there was little reason to believe that the airline industry was so different from other industrial and service sectors that both suppliers, that is, the airlines, and consumers needed special protection. Surely the normal anti-monopoly regulations would be enough to safeguard consumer interests? Since entry by new airlines was assumed to be easy, there was no need to protect incumbent carriers. If through bad management they collapsed, others would step in.

3.2   Mounting pressure for liberalisation

Whatever the economic arguments, political and consumer pressures for liberalisation of the tight regulatory regimes were building up. Consumers in the United States and Europe could not understand why various rules were needed to prevent them from having free access to much cheaper charter flights or cheaper and unrestricted fares on scheduled services. Despite the numerous restrictions they faced, charter or non-scheduled airlines were capturing a significant and growing share of the transatlantic and intra-European leisure market (see Chapter 2.8). In East Asia the newly established airlines of former colonies such as Singapore Airlines, Malaysian Airline System or Garuda Indonesia were operating outside the confines of the IATA tariff system. By offering service standards well above those specified by IATA they were capturing a growing share of the scheduled traffic on trans-Pacific routes and on services from East Asia to Europe. Under this pressure, agreements on tariffs within IATA became increasingly difficult to achieve.

In the United States pressures for domestic deregulation became very vocal in late 1974 during the hearings of the Senate Judiciary Subcommittee on Administrative Practice and Procedures. These so-called Kennedy hearings focused attention on the need for reform of the Civil Aeronautics Board's procedures and controls. A few months later, the 'Report of the CAB Special Staff on Regulatory Reform' came out strongly in favour of the deregulation of US domestic air services. It argued that the undesirable effects of the existing system included: (1) *de facto* exclusion of new airlines from long-haul trunk line markets; (2) protection of the relatively inefficient carriers; (3) unduly high labour costs and unduly high-cost types of service; and (4) lack of emphasis on price competition and on variations in the price/quality mix in response to consumer preference (CAB, 1975). In 1977 the newly elected President Jimmy Carter made airline deregulation one of his key objectives and on 24 October 1978 the Airline Deregulation Act was signed into law.

The Act provided for the complete elimination of the Civil Aeronautics Board by 1985, bringing an end to all controls over *domestic* routes and fares. Other aspects of the Board's responsibilities would be taken over by other branches of the federal government. The law instituted gradual decontrol between 1978 and 1985 primarily by making new domestic routes easier to obtain and unprofitable routes easier to give up. The Board retained authority over maximum and minimum fares until 1982, when tariffs were to become completely deregulated. Charter rules were relaxed, as were limits on the right of scheduled carriers to operate charters. In practice, the Board reduced its own regulatory controls even more quickly than was envisaged by the Act. The significance of US domestic deregulation, which was so rapid and total, was that the pressure for change inevitably spilled over to international air transport.

In Europe there were similar winds of change. In the United Kingdom the Civil Aviation Authority became increasingly liberal in its licensing decisions from 1975 onwards. One example of this was the virtual deregulation of international freight charters in 1976. The European Parliament in Strasbourg and the European Commission in Brussels all began to discuss various aspects of deregulation within Europe. The European Commission went one step further and actually produced a series of proposals or draft directives on the liberalisation of air transport that were sent by the Commission to the Council of Ministers, though none was actually approved. It was not until 1983 that the first directive, on the deregulation of regional air services between member states of the European Community, was approved (CEC, 1983). This directive, a watered-down version of earlier proposals, had little impact, but it did mark the first step towards liberalisation on an EU-wide basis. It should be borne in mind that whereas domestic deregulation in the United States was implemented very quickly and almost overnight, in Europe the process was more gradual. It moved slowly from limited liberalisation in the mid-1980s to a more fully deregulated intra-EU market ten years later. This meant that European airlines responded much more slowly to the opportunities created by deregulation than did their American counterparts.

3.3 Reversal of US aviation policy

In the international arena, the three-pronged structure of economic regulation which emerged following the 1944 Chicago conference had resulted in an industry characterised by a high degree of regulation and a very limited scope for competition. Most markets were duopolies or oligopolies. The only real competition was in certain non-scheduled markets. The United States had acquiesced in this pattern of regulation for more than thirty years. Then late in 1977 US international aviation policy began to change dramatically. Far from accepting the existing regulatory framework, the United States suddenly appeared to be hell-bent on deregulation, on reducing existing regulatory controls to a minimum. It was supported in this by several other governments, especially those of the Netherlands and Singapore, but it was the United States that was the prime generator of change.

The change in US policy was linked with the Carter administration which took over at the White House in January 1977. Three key factors explain the moves towards a new policy. First, 'consumerism' had been a key element in Carter's election campaign. In international air transport this meant reducing fares, facilitating access to air services and opening new direct links from US cities not previously served by international services. There was considerable public and congressional pressure for international deregulation and the Carter administration was eager to harness such pressure in its own support. A second factor was that the Carter administration had a fundamental belief in the benefits of greater competition. The early stages of domestic deregulation in the United States appeared to be producing lower fares for consumers and higher airline profits without any marked instability for the industry. The protected position of Pan American, TWA and other US international airlines could not be justified. If greater competition was proving beneficial domestically it would also do so internationally. The third factor was a need to increase US airlines' share of international air transport. The once dominant US position had been eroded. The regulatory system together with the lack of drive of the established American international airlines had resulted in a declining market share for these airlines. By 1977 US airlines had only about 40 per cent of the market between the United States and Europe and on some routes, such as those to the Netherlands or Scandinavia, their market share was below 20 per cent. More liberal bilateral air service agreements and the entry of the new US carriers would enable the US industry to increase its market share. Here one can discern an element of self-interest behind the pressure for deregulation.

Following public hearings a statement on 'International Air Transport Negotiations' was signed by President Carter on 21 August 1978 (Presidential Documents, 1978). This stated that the United States' aim was 'to provide greatest possible benefit to travellers and shippers' and that 'maximum consumer benefits can best be achieved through the preservation and extension of competition between airlines in a fair market place'. This broad aim was to be achieved through the negotiation or renegotiation of bilateral agreements. In such negotiations, the United States would henceforth have the following objectives:

1　The 'creation of new and greater opportunities for innovative and competitive pricing that will encourage and permit the use of new price and service options to meet the needs of different travellers and shippers'.

2   The 'liberalisation of charter rules and the elimination of restrictions on charter operations'.
3   The 'expansion of scheduled services through the elimination of restrictions on capacity, frequency and route operating rights'.
4   The 'elimination of discrimination and unfair competitive practices faced by US airlines in international transportation'.
5   The 'flexibility to designate multiple US airlines in international air markets'.
6   The encouragement of maximum traveller and shipper access to international markets by authorising more US cities for non-stop or direct service.
7   The 'flexibility to permit the development and facilitation of competitive air cargo services'.

The United States set out to achieve these objectives in a series of crucial bilateral negotiations which took place in the period 1977–85. The major objective of US policy was general liberalisation. This made sense given the free-enterprise and competitive aviation environment in the United States. But in most of the countries with which the United States was negotiating there was only one airline or only one large scheduled airline which was usually state-owned and was the 'chosen instrument' of each country's aviation policy. As a result most countries negotiating with the United States did not favour multiple designation and several, such as Japan or Italy, still wanted capacity controls. Others, including the United Kingdom and France, actually wanted to reduce existing US fifth-freedom rights rather than expand them. On the decontrol of tariffs, the liberalisation of charters and air cargo the position of several countries was more flexible and closer to that of the United States.

The reversal of US international aviation policy in 1978 inaugurated the first steps towards liberalisation. The period 1978–91 is best described as the 'open market' phase, when international markets were opened up to increased competition but many constraints on airline operating freedom still remained.

3.4   Open market phase of liberalisation, 1978–91

3.4.1   *Renegotiation of US bilaterals*

Picking off a country at a time, the United States began renegotiating its bilateral air service agreements. Because of the importance and size of the US international market, most countries wanted to serve more gateway cities in the United States. Increased access to the US market was the carrot used by American negotiators to obtain most of the policy objectives outlined above. The key bilaterals that were renegotiated were those across the Pacific with states in East Asia and those with certain European states. On these long-haul routes from the United States a more liberal regulatory regime was progressively introduced. By the mid-1980s similar concepts were being introduced in markets outside the United States through the renegotiation and revision of bilateral air service agreements. The years 1978–91 are best characterised as the period during which markets were liberalised and opened up. Several regulatory restrictions remained which were not to be removed until after 1991, when the 'open skies' phase began.

It was the revised US–Netherlands air services agreement, signed in March 1978, which was to set the trend for subsequent US 'open market' bilaterals. The Dutch wanted to maximise opportunities for their own airline, KLM, which suffered from having a relatively small home market. Since the Dutch were starting from a viewpoint very similar to that of the United States it was inevitable that the US–Netherlands bilateral agreement would be a particularly liberal one. Both sides set out to reduce the role of the government in matters of capacity, frequency, tariffs and in the setting of market conditions. The key terms of the agreement can be summarised as follows:

1   Multiple designation accepted (i.e. more than one airline from each state).
2   US airlines given unlimited authority from any points in the United States via intermediate points to Amsterdam and points beyond, with full traffic rights (i.e. fifth-freedom rights).
3   Dutch airlines given only five points in the United States (New York, Chicago, Houston, Los Angeles and one additional US point) (i.e. the Dutch were given only a limited number of US gateways).
4   No capacity or frequency restrictions.
5   No restrictions on sixth-freedom traffic (see appendix).
6   Unlimited charter rights between any points in either territory (i.e. charter rights included in a bilateral for the first time).
7   Country-of-origin rules for scheduled tariffs (i.e. each government to set its own rules for tariffs originating in its own country). Subsequent bilaterals introduced double disapproval of tariffs (i.e. only disapproval by both governments can block a filed fare).

Not wishing to see their traffic diverted to Amsterdam, Belgium and Germany concluded bilaterals with the United States at the end of 1978 which were very similar to the US–Netherlands agreement. There were variations but the pattern was set. Other countries in the European area were under pressure to follow suit in their own negotiations with the United States. One or two of the larger European aviation powers, notably the French and the Italians, held out against the trend towards deregulation, though they too had to compromise on some issues.

Liberalisation through bilateral renegotiation was also being pursued by the United States in other international markets. The most important after the North Atlantic for American airlines was perhaps the north and mid-Pacific market. Here the United States negotiated several key bilaterals between 1978 and 1980 with Singapore, Thailand, Korea and the Philippines. These bilaterals followed the same pattern as those in Europe. As with the Netherlands agreement, the United States offered these countries a handful of gateway points in the United States, usually less than five, in exchange for most if not all of the US objectives previously outlined. One of the first renegotiated bilaterals was that between the United States and Singapore. The main features of the US–Singapore air services agreement of March 1978 as amended by a Memorandum of Understanding agreed in June 1979 broadly mirrored those in the US–Netherlands agreement, though the cities granted to the Singapore designated carrier were different.

The other bilaterals between South East Asian countries and the United States renegotiated in the early 1980s generally incorporated the above features, though with some variations. The only countries of significance to try and slow down the rush to total liberalisation on the trans-Pacific routes were Japan and Australia. They took a tougher negotiating stance during the 1980s and did not give way on all the issues requested by the US negotiators.

United States' moves towards deregulation had an impact on other countries, such as Canada and the United Kingdom, and induced them to be more liberal in their own aviation policies. For example, under the 1987 UK–Canada air services agreement all capacity controls were removed and route access was opened up. This meant that there was no limit on the number of airlines designated on each route or on the routes or points that could be served. Increased fifth-freedom rights were also granted to both countries' airlines. Such agreements were, however, relatively few, since there was little attempt by other countries to follow the US example and systematically renegotiate all their key bilaterals.

3.4.2   Focus switches to Europe

In Europe consumer pressures for liberalisation of air transport built up throughout the 1980s. They were reinforced by the mounting pressure both from within the European Parliament and from the Commission of the European Communities for major changes in the structure of regulations affecting air services between the member states of the Common Market. But it was not till the mid-1980s that the first significant breakthroughs were achieved. Changes in the regulatory environment were introduced in two ways. First, bilaterally through the renegotiation of air service agreements between pairs of countries. Second, multilaterally, through actions initiated by the European Commission in Brussels or the European Court of Justice.

The more liberal and free-market attitudes towards air transport prevailing in the United Kingdom pushed it to renegotiate most of its key European bilaterals in the period from 1984 onwards. The first major breakthrough was in June 1984 when a new air services agreement was negotiated with the Netherlands, another country set on liberalisation. This agreement, together with further modification in 1985, effectively deregulated air services between the two countries. Free entry of new carriers, access by designated airlines to any point in either country, no capacity controls and a 'double disapproval' regime for fares were the key features introduced. These features, some of which were first introduced in the revised US bilaterals discussed earlier, represented a clear break with the traditional European bilaterals which had prevailed till then.

The UK–Netherlands agreement set the pattern for the renegotiation of European bilaterals. Later in 1984 the United Kingdom signed a new air services agreement with Germany and in the following year agreements were concluded with Luxembourg, France, Belgium, Switzerland and the Irish Republic, though not all these agreements went as far as the UK–Netherlands agreement had done in removing constraints on competition.

While the United Kingdom set the pace, other European states also began to renegotiate their bilaterals in this period. Though they did not usually adopt all the features of the UK–Netherlands agreement in one go, the aim of such negotiations was usually to introduce gradual liberalisation. The impact of this bilateral liberalisation was greatest in countries where domestic liberalisation had encouraged the emergence of several airlines with the potential for international operations. Where the domestic air transport regime was highly regulated and controlled the impact of liberalisation was more muted.

The European Commission's Directorate General of Transport espoused liberalisation early on and had been trying to push various proposals through the Council of Ministers since 1975. Initially its only limited success was the July 1983 Council Directive on Inter-regional Air Services (CEC, 1983). This allowed airlines flying aircraft with seventy seats or less to develop air routes freely between regional airports within the European Community. But by excluding air routes from regional centres to capitals or major hubs, this directive had relatively little effect. However, it set the precedent for action on air transport at EC level. More significant was the so-called 'December 1987 Package' of measures, agreed at that time by the European Council of Ministers. This was the first step towards liberalisation of air transport within the Community as a whole. It introduced a more liberal fares regime, including the concept of fare zones. These allowed airlines some pricing flexibility within agreed upper and lower limits, the so-called fare zones. It abandoned the previous practice of equal sharing of capacity by airlines of each state and facilitated the entry of new airlines by opening up market access (CEC, 1987a).

The 1987 'package' was important because it explicitly acknowledged that the competition articles of the Treaty of Rome applied to air transport (CEC, 1987b). In turn this meant that many of the inter-airline agreements then in existence, such as those dealing with capacity planning, revenue pooling or pricing, would be illegal unless specific exemptions were granted. Block exemptions were published by the European Commission in August 1988. But these block exemptions were granted at that time and subsequently only if certain demanding conditions were met (CEC, 1988), the aim of such conditions being to avoid the abuse of oligopolistic power or discrimination against new entrants or airlines not wishing to join such agreements. One consequence was that revenue-pooling agreements between European airlines (see Chapter 2.6) were progressively abandoned.

In June 1990 the Council of Ministers agreed the details of a second liberalisation package. This made only marginal improvements to the 1987 package. The more significant liberalisation in Europe in the 1980s came about through the renegotiation of bilateral air service agreements rather than through action at EC level.

3.4.3   Liberalisation spreading

Outside Europe and North America a number of other countries began to move cautiously towards reducing controls on their air transport industries. In Japan, JAL's effective monopoly of international air services was broken when from 1986 onwards a domestic carrier, All Nippon Airways or Japan Air Systems, was designated as the second Japanese carrier on a number of key international routes. In several South East Asian countries new airlines were allowed to emerge to operate both domestic and international air services, often in direct competition with the established national carrier. In South Korea, for instance, Asiana Airlines was formed in February 1988, launching domestic services at the end of that year and regional services to Tokyo, Bangkok and Hong Kong in 1990. The emergence of Eva Air in Taiwan and Dragonair in Hong Kong were other examples. In Australia in 1987 a new government aviation policy reaffirmed Qantas's continued role as the country's sole designated international carrier but announced the complete deregulation of domestic air services from October 1990. This meant that the government would withdraw from regulating domestic fares or capacity. The previous policy of limiting domestic trunk operations to only two carriers, Ansett and Australian, was also abandoned, though Qantas would still be precluded from operating purely domestic services.

In the East Asian–Pacific region such attempts at liberalisation were often localised, haphazard and unco-ordinated as between neighbouring countries. Their impact was fairly limited. On most routes, single designation continued to prevail (except on routes to Japan), third- and fourth-freedom capacities and frequencies were still regulated and many services were covered by revenue-pooling agreements. On tariffs there was more flexibility. In many countries governments, aviation authorities and airlines turned a blind eye to illegal discounting of government-approved IATA fares. In this way *de facto* liberalisation of tariffs was introduced on many international routes.

3.4.4   The new rules of the game

In the process of renegotiating many of its key bilaterals between 1977 and 1985 the United States introduced some new concepts into international regulation which significantly changed the rules of the game as far as airlines were concerned, offering them greater freedom of action. In the second half of the 1980s these were incorporated into the revised bilaterals negotiated by some European states which in some respects went even further than the US

Table 3.1 Key features of traditional and post-1978 'open market' bilaterals

Feature	Traditional bilaterals	New 'open market' bilaterals
Market access	Only to points specified	Open access – airlines can fly between any two points[a]
	Limited fifth freedoms granted – more in US bilaterals	Extensive fifth-freedom rights granted in US bilaterals but still very limited in intra-European bilaterals
	Charter rights not included	Unlimited charter rights granted (in Europe granted earlier under 1956 ECAC agreement)
Designation	Single – some multiple in US bilaterals	Multiple
	Airlines must be 'substantially owned and effectively controlled' by nationals of designating state	
Capacity	Capacity agreed or shared 50:50	No frequency or capacity controls
	No capacity/frequency controls in liberal bilaterals, but subject to review	
Tariffs	Double approval by both governments required	Double disapproval (i.e. only *both* governments can block)
	To be agreed using IATA procedures	Country-of-origin rules (in some US bilaterals)

Note
a While US 'open market' bilaterals gave US airlines rights from any point in the United States, foreign airlines were restricted to a handful of named points in the United States.

bilaterals. These are summarised in Table 3.1. (For more details see Doganis, 2001.)

A significant change was the opening up of market access. Whereas under the traditional bilaterals the number of points to be served in each country was strictly limited, under the 'open market' bilaterals, *access was opened up to several new points*. The US bilaterals were somewhat unbalanced in this respect. While US airlines were granted the right to fly from any point in the United States to specified points in the other country, the other country's airlines could fly only to/from a larger but still limited number of points in the United States. Revised bilaterals between European states and states outside Europe also limited the points to be served. The intra-European bilaterals, however, were generally more liberal in allowing flights *between any points* by carriers from either state. On the other hand, the US bilaterals granted more *extensive fifth-freedom rights* than did the European ones. All the new bilaterals also tended to allow *unlimited charter rights*, though some permitted governments to establish their own regulations for charters originating in their own state, so-called 'country-of-origin' rules.

On traffic rights the other significant development was the adoption of *unlimited or multiple designation*. This is the right of each party to a bilateral to designate as many airlines as it wishes to operate its own agreed routes. Some earlier bilaterals, such as the 1946 UK–US agreement, had accepted double or multiple designation but they were the minority. In addition, many of the new US bilaterals include *break-of-gauge* rights. This is the right to change from a larger to a smaller aircraft in the other country's territory on a through service that is going beyond the other country, usually, but not necessarily, with fifth-freedom rights. In order to use its break-of-gauge rights an airline would need to station smaller aircraft at the airport where the change of 'gauge' took place.

The major change introduced in terms of capacity was to *remove limits on the frequencies or seat capacity* offered by airlines on the routes they operated. Most earlier bilaterals had imposed some attempts to balance or control capacity and the European bilaterals had mostly required a fifty–fifty sharing of capacity by the airlines of each state.

On pricing, the new concept introduced in the 'open market' bilaterals was that of *double disapproval*. Under traditional air service agreements tariffs could not become operative unless approved by both governments. In other words, either government on its own could block any tariff filed by an airline or proposed by IATA. However, under a double disapproval regime a tariff can be blocked only if *both* governments reject it. One government may not like a particular fare or cargo tariff but cannot prevent an airline from implementing it if the other government is prepared to approve it. In other words, in agreeing to double disapproval governments gave up their veto powers on tariffs. This was a major step in freeing airline pricing.

These new rules of the game, wherever applied, represented a significant shift towards a more liberal and competitive environment for international airlines. But the spread of 'open market' bilaterals was somewhat haphazard and geographically rather patchy. By the early 1990s the most liberalised markets for scheduled air transport were those to and from the United States and Canada. On the North Atlantic routes, for instance, capacity or frequency constraints had largely disappeared and the entry of new carriers was in theory easy because of multiple designation. The number of US gateway points had more or less doubled and on many routes US carriers could add new gateway points almost at will, though European carriers did not have the same freedom. The tightly regulated tariffs agreed through the IATA mechanism had been replaced by a more flexible system of fare zones, with airlines free to pitch their fares anywhere within the relevant agreed zones for each fare type. Attempts to control and standardise in-flight service had been abandoned. On the trans-Pacific routes the situation was similar in many respects but not so liberal. Route access was fairly open for US airlines, less so for Asian carriers. But while capacity or frequency controls were imposed only on certain routes, there was probably greater pricing freedom than on the North Atlantic, since the agreed fares were widely discounted.

Within Europe the situation was very mixed. The most liberalised markets were those between the United Kingdom and the Netherlands and the United Kingdom to Ireland. At the other extreme the Austria–Greece scheduled market or air services to Eastern Europe were still categorised by capacity controls, revenue-pooling agreements and the enforcement of IATA tariffs.

Elsewhere in the world real liberalisation had not proceeded very far by 1991. On long-haul routes from Europe to Central and South East Asia and Australasia there was some pricing freedom through widespread discounting of IATA- and government-approved fares to which many governments turned a blind eye. The same was true of air services within South East Asia and the Pacific region. On the other hand, traffic rights and capacities were strictly regulated and revenue-pooling agreements were widespread. In Africa, South America, the Middle East and Western Asia deregulation had had even less impact and the traditional regulatory framework remained largely intact.

3.5   The United States pushes for 'open skies', 1992 onwards

By 1991 the regulatory environment appeared patchy and mixed, but the trend to further liberalisation and eventually to deregulation could not be reversed or even stemmed. On the contrary, the need for further liberalisation became increasingly apparent as a result of several developments.

First, there was a growing body of expert opinion that the airline industry should be normalised, that is, it should be allowed to operate as any other major international industry. It is true that most governments had willingly accepted the traditional bilateral system (as described in Chapter 2) and a smaller number grudgingly acquiesced to it while wishing to modify it more or less radically. Wide acceptance of the system, despite apparent shortcomings, suggests that most countries considered the perceived benefits to their own airlines and consumers to be greater than any disbenefits. But there was a strong counter-argument, namely that the airline industry was no longer different from other industries and should not be treated any differently. This view gained ground during the 1980s both among aviation specialists and among government officials in several key countries.

A second and perhaps stronger argument against bilateralism was that the system, though worldwide, was and is inherently restrictive. This is because even when countries signed the more liberal open-market bilaterals, the market opportunities opened up tended to be those considered acceptable by the less liberal of the two countries. The frequent occurrence of disputes between countries over the application and interpretation of their bilateral agreements suggests that, too often, one of the two countries has felt disadvantaged in some way.

Disputes in 1991–92 between Thailand and the United States, Canada and Singapore or between the United States and both France and Germany showed that this happened with the new liberal 'open market' bilaterals as much as, if not more so than, with the more traditional and restrictive agreements.

The third factor pushing towards further liberalisation was that the airline industry had matured during the previous decade. As a result of the liberalisation that had already taken place after 1978 the industry had undergone structural changes which made it progressively more difficult for airlines to operate within the confines of the bilateral system. Such structural changes included:

1   Growing concentration within the US airline industry as the smaller post-1978 new entrant carriers collapsed or were taken over by the more successful majors. At the same time one saw the emergence of the US domestic majors, such as American or United Airlines, as big players in international markets
2   The search by many international airlines outside the United States for the marketing benefits of very large-scale operations was being achieved through mergers with other airlines in their own country and minority share purchases or strong marketing alliances with airlines in other countries (Doganis, 2001). Here too there was growing market concentration and the need to search for new markets.
3   Airline ownership outside the United States was changing. In many parts of the world there was a growing view that governments should not be running commercial businesses. This view, combined with fiscal pressures to reduce government exposure, was pushing many governments to privatise their airlines, in part or fully. The UK government set the trend here with the successful privatisation of British Airways in 1987. Privatised airlines would be expected to stand on their own without regulatory protection.

These structural changes created a critical need for successful airlines, whether private or state-owned, to be able to operate more easily outside the narrow confines of their own national markets, while freed from the remaining constraints imposed by bilateralism.

Again the initial motor of change was the United States. At first in the early 1980s the US carriers had lost market shares on the North Atlantic and the trans-Pacific as more dynamic European and new Asian carriers entered new routes and competed against the rather slow and unresponsive traditional US airlines such as Pan Am and TWA. But as the latter were progressively replaced by the powerful and very large domestic majors such as American, Delta and United, the market share of US airlines began to rise. These carriers benefited from having huge domestic networks to feed their international services and enjoyed great marketing power from their sheer size. In some markets they reinforced their marketing strength by setting up hubs in foreign destination countries such as Delta's hub in Frankfurt and Northwest's in Tokyo. They could outsell the competition on selected routes by high frequencies and innovative pricing made possible by lower unit costs. But many of the existing bilaterals, even if of the 'open market' type, still limited their scope and freedom of action. American, United, Delta among others pushed for further liberalisation for two basic reasons. As major domestic carriers relatively new to large-scale international operations, they saw that the long-term opportunities for expansion were much greater in international markets than within their more mature US domestic market. At the same time they felt that in a fully liberalised open skies environment they would do better than their foreign competitors because of the traffic feed that they would obtain from their huge domestic US networks and from their sheer size. In addition, they had lower unit operating costs than most of their foreign competitors, especially in Europe, and they were also more commercially oriented. The US State Department and the Department of Transportation also felt that open skies would benefit both American consumers and their airlines. At the same time, developments within the European Community, later to become the European Union, were also pushing inexorably towards open skies.

In the case of the US bilaterals, the first key breakthrough came in 1992 in negotiations with the Netherlands, whose government and airline, KLM, were also keen to adopt open skies. KLM had done well under the earlier 1978 'open market' agreement with the United States and by the mid-1980s its market share on the US–Amsterdam routes was over 80 per cent. Much of this traffic was travelling to other points in Europe through KLM's well-operated hub at Amsterdam Schiphol airport. KLM was anxious to reinforce its position, while its government felt that as a small country the Netherlands had much to gain from further liberalisation of international air services, especially if it was the first in Europe to do so.

In September 1992 the Dutch and US governments signed what was effectively the first 'open skies' agreement and inaugurated a new phase of international deregulation. In brief the new features of this bilateral, which had not been included in the earlier open-market bilateral, were as follows:

1   open route access – airlines from either country can fly to any point in the other with full traffic rights;
2   unlimited fifth-freedom rights;
3   no tariff controls (unless tariffs too high or too low);
4   airlines free to code share or make other commercial agreements;
5   break of gauge permitted.

At the same time the new 1992 agreement reiterated some of the newer articles of the old 1978 'open market' agreement, namely:

1   multiple designation of airlines;
2   no frequency or capacity control;
3   open charter access.

The new features represented a further and significant easing of the regulatory environment. Open and free-market access, together with no pricing controls, when added to the absence of capacity restrictions and multiple designation, already granted in the earlier bilateral, meant that one had moved from a liberalised regime to one that appeared to be deregulated. But not quite. As discussed later the open skies agreements still left some regulatory issues unresolved. Nevertheless, they represented a major step forward.

But after the US–Netherlands agreement there was a lull. The fortunes of the airline industry deteriorated dramatically in the period 1990–93. After three years of record losses, numerous bankruptcies and the demise of well-known airlines such as Pan American and Eastern, the US Congress in May 1993 established the National Commission to ensure a Strong Competitive Airline Industry. Three months later the commission, among its many recommendations, suggested that the US government should renegotiate its bilateral air service agreements to achieve an open and liberal market environment in which US airlines could operate without restriction or discrimination.

Spurred on by the findings of the National Commission, the Clinton administration shortly afterwards undertook its own review of aviation policy and in April 1995 Secretary of Transportation Federico Pena issued the first formal statement of international air transport policy in seventeen years. According to Secretary Pena the Clinton administration was taking steps to 'ensure that global marketing and services will lead to improved services for travellers and shippers' while it was also seeking to 'find ways to help strengthen the US airline industry so that it may continue its leadership role in international air services' (Pena, 1995).

To achieve these twin objectives, the US government clearly saw the urgent need to create open aviation markets with unrestricted access for the airlines of the countries concerned and with freedom for airlines to develop types of services required by the market place. This could involve commercial agreements such as code sharing, which hitherto had been doubtful on anti-trust grounds. These objectives were to be achieved primarily by entering into 'open skies' aviation agreements initially with like-minded states and later with less liberal states. (For more details of the development of US aviation policy see Doganis, 2001.) But for those countries not willing to advance market liberalisation the threat of US counter-measures was explicit in the 1995 policy statement. The United States could limit their airlines' access to the US market and restrict commercial relations with US carriers. In particular, foreign airlines should not expect code-sharing arrangements with US airlines to be approved and be given anti-trust immunity if their states did not agree to 'open skies' bilaterals.

As mentioned, prior to the 1995 policy statement, the United States had already negotiated 'open skies' agreements with the Netherlands. Shortly after the 'open skies' agreement with the United States, KLM applied for and obtained anti-trust immunity from the US authorities to enable it to exploit more fully the potential benefits from its partnership with Northwest, an airline in which it had bought an almost 20 per cent share three years earlier. Both airlines wanted to code share on many of their flights, not just those between the United States and Amsterdam but also on services beyond each other's gateways. For instance, Northwest wished to put its code on KLM flights beyond Amsterdam to points in Germany so as to capture and carry German traffic across the Atlantic without actually flying there. Immunity provided KLM-Northwest with considerable freedom jointly to plan their code shares, schedules and pricing policy.

European airlines negotiating commercial alliances with US carriers appreciated the potential benefits which anti-trust immunity could provide. The US government grabbed the opportunity. In the 1980s it had offered access to more US gateway points in order to persuade countries to sign up to 'open market' bilaterals. Now it offered an even more enticing exchange – anti-trust immunity for alliance partners in return for agreement on new 'open skies' bilaterals.

In 1995 the United States signed such bilaterals with a group of nine of the smaller West European countries. But the big prizes – the United Kingdom, Germany and France, together representing over 60 per cent of the transatlantic passenger market – eluded it. There had been a transitional agreement with Germany in 1994 but the breakthrough came in 1996 when pressure from Lufthansa and United Airlines pushed the German government to bring forward the implementation of a full 'open skies' agreement. Interestingly it refused to sign the bilateral until *after* anti-trust immunity had been granted.

By mid-2001 over fifty new 'open skies' agreements had been signed by the United States. These were with most of its major aviation partners except the United Kingdom and Japan, which are the two largest markets for US carriers. But in January 1998 the United States and Japan did sign a new bilateral which went some of the way towards open skies, especially for incumbent carriers. All these agreements, such as the one with Singapore signed in 1997, were very similar to the US–Netherlands agreement detailed above. Some countries, reluctant to jump to a full 'open skies' agreement in one step – often to protect their own airlines – signed phased bilaterals. In these the full 'open skies' features were introduced gradually over a two-year period. The US–Italy agreement signed in November 1998 was such a phased agreement, whose aim was to allow anti-trust immunity to be granted for the imminent link-up between Alitalia and Northwest (which in the end did not materialise). The US–France agreement signed earlier that year also had anti-trust immunity as an objective.

Open skies policies have also been adopted and actively pursued by a few other states. New Zealand, which signed an open skies bilateral with the United States, had secured similar deals with Singapore, Malaysia, Brunei, the UAE and Chile by the end of 1999. This was in addition to the Single Aviation Market pact concluded earlier with Australia. The latter country plans to pursue its own open skies agreements and signed the first one with the UAE. This represented a major policy shift. Australia was prepared to offer not only all the key features of US-style open skies agreements but was also willing to

Table 3.2 US 'open market' and post-1991 'open skies' air service agreements

Feature	1978–91 'open market' bilaterals	Post-1991 'open skies' bilaterals
Market access	Named number of points in each state – more limited for non-US carriers	Unlimited
	Generally unlimited fifth freedom	Unlimited fifth freedom
	Domestic cabotage not allowed	
	Seventh freedom not granted	
	Open charter access	
Designation	Multiple	
	Substantial ownership and effective control by nationals of designating state	
Capacity	No frequency or capacity control	
Tariffs	Double disapproval or country-of-origin rules	Free pricing
Code sharing	Not part of bilateral	Code sharing permitted[a]

Note
a Co-operative arrangements, e.g. code sharing, blocked space or leasing allowed between airlines
   of signatory states or within airline(s) of third states if they permit reciprocal arrangements.

consider granting seventh-freedom rights for stand-alone air services between the bilateral partner and a third country on a case-by-case basis. Domestic cabotage, however, was not negotiable. On the other hand, in a new aviation policy, Australia relaxed its ownership rules to allow foreign interests or airlines to own up to 100 per cent of Australian domestic airlines. This made it possible for Ansett Australia to become majority-owned by Air New Zealand.

The 'open skies' agreements, generally very similar to the US–Netherlands agreement described earlier, were a significant improvement on the 'open market' agreements they replaced in several respects, most notably in relation to market access and tariff regulation (Table 3.2). They opened route access to any point in either country whereas the earlier bilaterals had tended to limit the number of points that could be served by foreign carriers in the United States. Also mutual fifth-freedom rights were granted without restraint compared with the more limited fifth freedom in earlier bilaterals. On tariffs, double disapproval or the 'country-of-origin' rule were replaced by a clear decision that governments should not meddle in tariffs except *in extremis* to prevent discriminatory practices, to protect consumers from unreasonably high or restrictive prices or to protect airlines from artificially low fares due to government subsidies or support.

A further innovation was the inclusion of an article dealing specifically with inter-airline commercial agreements such as code sharing (this is when airlines add their partner's code to their own flight number) and block space or leasing agreements. This was critically important. Close-knit commercial agreements, which went further than simple code sharing on routes between the two countries, risked falling foul of US anti-trust legislation. As mentioned earlier, this new article in the 1992 'open skies' bilateral effectively granted KLM and Northwest immunity from prosecution for a commercial agreement which might otherwise be considered anti-competitive.

3.6   'Open skies' within the European Union

In parallel to the United States, Europe was also moving towards open skies but the approach was structurally quite different. The US strategy was essentially bilateral. The implementation of open skies was being promoted by one country through a series of bilateral air service agreements. In contrast to this the development of a single open aviation market in Europe was to be achieved through a comprehensive multilateral agreement by the member states of the European Union. This multilateral approach to opening up the skies enabled the Europeans to go further in pursuit of deregulation than was possible under US bilateralism.

Within the European Union (until 1993 known as the European Community) the push towards multilateral liberalisation of air transport among the member states was driven by two complementary lines of approach. The Directorate General of Transport espoused airline liberalisation early and had been trying since about 1975 to push various proposals through the Council of Ministers. The second driver for change was the Directorate General of Competition, which was trying to ensure that competition between producers and service providers within the Union was not distorted by uncompetitive practices imposed by governments or introduced by the industries themselves. The twin objectives of air transport liberalisation and fair and open competition were achieved only in stages. In the late 1980s the first two packages of liberalisation measures, described earlier, did not go very far but they did set the trend and identify the direction of Community aviation policy. The major breakthrough was achieved through the so-called 'Third Package' of aviation measures, which came into force on 1 January 1993 (CEC, 1992a, b, c).

The Third Package consists of three interlinked regulations which have effectively created an 'open skies' regime for air services within the European Union. There is open market access. Airlines from member states can operate with full traffic rights on any route within the Union and without capacity restrictions even on routes outside their own country (CEC, 1992b). Governments may impose restrictions only on environmental, infrastructure capacity, regional development or public service grounds, but any restrictions would have to be justified. There are no price controls. Airlines have complete freedom to determine their fares and cargo tariffs but there are some limited safeguards to prevent predatory or excessive pricing (CEC, 1992c). The third regulation harmonises the criteria for granting operating licences and air operators' certificates by EU member states (CEC, 1992a). Apart from technical and financial criteria which have to be met, the airline must be majority-owned and controlled by any of the member states or their nationals, or companies, but not necessarily by nationals or companies of the state in which the airline is registered. Henceforward all regulations apply equally to scheduled and charter services, with no distinction being drawn between them.

The Third Package went further than the US-style open skies bilaterals in two important respects. First, it was a multilateral agreement to open up the skies covering not just pairs of states but a whole region, the fifteen eventual member states of the European Union plus Norway and Iceland, which adopted the package of measures without joining the Union. Second, whereas the open skies bilaterals did not change the nationality rule at all, the Third Package for the first time explicitly allowed cross-border majority ownership. It gave EU nationals or companies from any member state the right to set up and operate an airline in any other EU member state or to buy such an airline. This has enabled British Airways to own and manage Deutsche BA in Germany or KLM to buy and operate a British airline, KLM UK, previously known as Air UK. However, this so-called right of establishment is restrictive in one important sense. While KLM UK can operate freely within the area of the European Union it cannot, as a Dutch-owned airline, operate international services from London to, say, Moscow, because the UK–Russia air services agreement contains the traditional article regarding substantial ownership and effective control by nationals of the designating state.

In parallel with the liberalisation of air transport regulations, the European Commission felt that greater freedom for airlines had to be accompanied by the effective implementation and application to air transport of the European Union's so-called 'competition rules'. These were designed to prevent monopolistic practices or behaviour which was anti-competitive or which distorted competition to the detriment of consumers. The competition rules cover three broad areas, namely cartels and restrictive agreements, monopolies and mergers and state aid or subsidies to producers. The basic principles on competition were originally laid down in Articles 81–90 of the Treaty of Rome and the separate Council Regulation on Mergers of 1989 (Regulation No. 4056/89).

The European Commission has used Articles 84 and 85 which relate to transitional measures to take action on air transport between the Union and third countries and in particular on the alliances between European airlines and major US carriers. In its decisions in the late 1990s on both the proposed American Airlines–British Airways alliance, which has not progressed, and the Lufthansa–SAS–United alliance the Commission required the partners to give up substantial numbers of runway slots at their European hubs to competitors so as to ensure effective competition.

The subsidisation of airlines by central or local government clearly distorts competition. Articles 88 and 89 of the Treaty of Rome specifically prohibit 'state aid' of any kind. Yet during the 1980s and early 1990s most of Europe's numerous state-owned airlines were being heavily subsidised by their governments. To overcome this contradiction, the European Commission in a series of decisions between 1991 and 1997 approved major injections of state aid to a number of airlines but with strict conditions the purpose of which was to ensure their transformation into profitable enterprises. The state aid had to be used for financial and operational restructuring of the airline through debt repayment, early retirement of staff, and so on. Moreover, the state aid was approved on the basis of a 'one time, last time' principle. In other words, no further requests for approval of additional state aid would be considered. But when in 2001 several of the state-owned airlines in Europe started reporting huge losses, a question arose whether government aid might have to be allowed for a second time to prevent the total collapse of airlines such as Sabena, Air Portugal or Olympic Airways. With the exception of the authorised state aid schemes no direct or indirect subsidisation of any kind by governments or their airlines is permitted within the European Union. For example, governments can no longer guarantee airline borrowings or offer reduced airport charges to their owned airlines. But governments can offer support for the operation of air services to meet social service needs but in a manner which is transparent.

Following the closure of US airports for four days after the 11 September terrorist attacks, the European Commission in October 2001 agreed that EU governments could grant aid to their airlines to cover losses arising directly from these airport closures. The Commission also approved government support for increased insurance costs and government funding for increased security measures. All this because of the 'exceptional circumstances' created by the terrorist attacks. The Commission also allowed the Belgian government to extend a major loan to Sabena (subsequently transferred to its subsidiary regional airline DAT) to enable the airline to keep flying long enough to find a buyer. It appears that the rules on state aid can be flexible to deal with unexpected crises! In such crises it is deemed to be 'rescue' aid.

The final element of the competition rules is the EU's Regulation on Mergers, first agreed in 1989 and subsequently modified in 1997 (Regulation 1310/97). Any mergers or acquisitions which exceed the stated threshold in terms of turnover must be first notified to the Commission. It will give its approval only if the transaction does not lead to the strengthening or creation of a dominant position. To ensure that this does not happen the Commission may impose demanding conditions. Thus when Air France took over the French independent long-haul airline UTA in 1990 and thereby also obtained a majority share in the domestic airline Air Inter, the Commission forced Air France to divest itself of its shareholding in TAT, the second largest domestic carrier in France.

The merger regulations even enable the Commission to examine mergers between non-EU companies which are deemed to have the potential to restrict or distort competition within the Union. It was on this basis that in June 2001 the Commission blocked the proposed $42 billion merger between

General Electric and Honeywell unless the two companies agreed to $4 billion worth of asset disposals. Yet this merger had been approved by the US authorities. Thus even here there is an extraterritorial dimension to the EU competition rules. This was again evident in October 1999 when the Commission launched an investigation into the proposed merger of Air Canada and Canadian Airlines on the grounds that it would reduce competition on services between London and Canada.

In addition to its decisions arising directly out of the application of the competition rules, the European Commission, acting through the Council of Ministers, has passed various directives, regulations or codes of conduct both to ensure greater competition in areas where competition was previously limited and to ensure that competition is not distorted through unfair practices. The code of conduct on slot allocation at airports (Council Regulation 95/93) and the directive on ground handling services (Council Directive 96/97) were both aimed at ensuring greater competition. On the other hand, the code of conduct on computer reservation systems aimed at avoiding unfair practices (Council Regulations 3089/93 and 323/99). Such directives and regulations were in addition to the numerous measures introduced to protect consumers directly or to ensure the safety of aircraft, and so on.

If the aim of transport deregulation and open skies is to encourage much greater competition, competition rules appear to be necessary to ensure that the increased competition is effective and is not undermined by anti-competitive practices or the abuse of dominant market positions. Hence the parallel development in the European Union of an 'open skies' regime and a raft of competition rules.

3.7 The missing pieces

By the start of the new millennium the pursuit of 'open skies' bilaterals by the United States and the creation of 'open skies' within the European Common Aviation Area had gone much of the way towards normalising the economic and regulatory framework for international and domestic air transport in certain major markets. But the process of normalisation was not complete in two respects. First, while air transport was largely deregulated for services within and between the countries of the European Union, most of the bilaterals between EU states and countries outside the Union, except those with the United States and Canada and possibly Singapore, were of the traditional type. Equally while the United States had over fifty 'open skies' bilaterals, virtually all the bilaterals between non-European states, with only a few exceptions, were again of the traditional kind. Many were and still are very restrictive. Thus open skies coexist side by side with skies that are relatively closed and protected.

Second, even within those markets that claim to be operating under 'open skies' regimes many clouds are still visible. This is especially so outside the European Common Aviation Area. While, outside Europe, the fifty or so

US-style 'open skies' agreements, together with the few similar agreements between pairs of other like-minded states, represent a significant leap forward, they have not in fact resulted in the total economic deregulation of international air services. Nor have they 'normalised' the air transport industry. While much more liberal and open than anything that preceded them, they still contain certain restrictive features. To start with, not all traffic rights are freely exchanged. Two types of services in particular are still excluded in virtually all cases (Table 3.2). The first is the right of an airline to carry domestic traffic between two airports within the territory of the other signatory country to the bilateral agreement. This would normally be on an extension of international flights within that country. This is referred to as cabotage. In the case of the United States it is claimed that a change in legislation is required to grant such rights and that it is unlikely that Congress would agree. Another right which has not been yet given away is the so-called 'seventh freedom'. This is the right to carry passengers between points in two foreign countries by an airline operating entirely outside its home country, though the United Kingdom did get some seventh-freedom rights from Belgium, Germany and the Netherlands in the 1991 round of negotiations with the United States. Perhaps the most glaring anomaly is the continued restriction on foreign ownership of airlines. Airlines still have to be 'substantially owned and effectively controlled' by their own nationals even though minority ownership by foreign individuals or companies may be permitted. In the United States the position is still that only up to 25 per cent foreign ownership of its airlines may be allowed, despite the recommendation of the 1993 National Commission to go to 49 per cent. Clearly, even the most free-enterprise economy, the United States, feels that the national ownership of its airlines needs to be protected.

In other respects, too, the new 'open skies' bilaterals were not as open as one might imagine. In fact they continued to be blatantly protective of US carriers in several respects. Under the so-called 'Fly America' policy, officials or others travelling on behalf of the US government were and still are required to fly on US airlines or flights operated by foreign airlines but with a US carrier code share. International airmail contracts by the US Post Office are also effectively limited to US carriers even though the latter can bid for UK or other mail contracts. Also, while US airlines cannot lease in foreign aircraft and crews, they can offer their own aircraft on wet leases to foreign carriers. For instance, most of Atlas Air's forty or so Boeing 747 freighters are wet-leased to European and Asian carriers (see Chapter 11.2). Finally, cargo generated as a result of US government contracts also has to 'Fly America'.

In terms of both traffic rights and ownership the 1993 European so-called 'Third Package' of liberalisation measures went further than the US-style 'open skies' bilaterals, but only in respect of intra-European air services. As we have seen, airlines of the member states were granted unlimited traffic rights on routes to, from and within any of the other member states. This included 'seventh-freedom' rights and domestic cabotage. At the same time ownership and nationality constraints on airlines registered in any member state were also removed, provided the owners or purchasers were from another EU member state. Ownership by nationals or companies of non-member states is still limited in theory to 49 per cent. However, this totally 'open skies' regime is in respect only of intra-EU air services. Any services or routes to points outside the European Union are still governed by the air service agreements that each individual EU state has with third countries.

Despite all the progress achieved so far in moving from a restrictive bilateral regulatory regime to a more open competitive environment for international air transport, much remains to be done. In order to normalise the airline industry the missing pieces of the jigsaw need to be filled in.

First, it is essential that more markets operate under 'open skies' regimes. Clearly, it would be faster and more effective to do this through multilateral agreement(s) between like-minded states than through the slow and laborious process of renegotiating hundreds of bilateral air service agreements. The member states of the European Union have shown that this is possible, though the 1993 so-called 'Third Package' of liberalisation measures was underpinned by the political will among those states to create a single European market. However, three intergovernmental conferences organised by the International Civil Aviation Organisation in Montreal in 1992, 1994 and 1997 also underlined how difficult it is to reconcile the conflicting views of governments on the future of international regulation. The ICAO was planning a further conference in 2004, but worldwide intergovernment agreement on the abandonment of the bilateral system in favour of a more open multilateral system seems unlikely because of the divergent interests of so many governments.

A possible alternative approach might be to use the new round of negotiations which started in 2000 on the extension of the General Agreement on Trade and Services, the so-called GATS/2000, to introduce much greater liberalisation of air services. But there are two difficulties in using GATS for further liberalisation of air transport. The first is that there are some very specific issues relating to air transport, particularly in relation to the commercial traffic rights – that is, the third, fourth and fifth freedoms – that cannot be dealt with satisfactorily as part of a comprehensive agreement covering all sectors. It is best if they continue to be considered within a specific sectoral basis. The second problem is that because of divergent government views a global agreement through GATS on these so-called hard rights would appear unlikely.

Rather than a multilateral solution, perhaps the easier way forward would be through regional agreements between like-minded states. The US government has raised the possibility of interlocking 'open skies' bilateral agreements. The first step was taken in 2000 in negotiating a multilateral Pacific region 'open skies' agreement between the United States, Chile, New Zealand, Brunei and Singapore. It is hoped that other states will join. The European Union had earlier started to negotiate an agreement with ten Central European states (as well as with Switzerland and Cyprus) for those countries to adopt the European

Union's air transport measures and the related competition rules even before joining the European Union as full members. By mid-2001 the agreements were awaiting ratification by the relevant governments. The final entry of up to twelve additional European states into the European Common Aviation Area was expected to be completed during 2003 or 2004 and would create a single 'open skies' market covering most of Europe.

Other parts of the world have also been moving towards liberalisation on a regional basis. In South America there have been moves among the Andean states and the members of ECOSUR to jointly liberalise their air transport markets. The African states, meeting in November 1999 in Côte d'Ivoire, adopted a new policy framework, the so-called Yammoussoukro II agreement, for the liberalisation of the continent's air transport industry. Though still awaiting ratification by the Assembly of the Organisation of African Unity and individual states, the agreement aims to liberalise market access by the year 2002 in order to create a single African aviation market. The target date seems unlikely to be met. But the agreement is far-reaching. Signatory states would grant each other unlimited third-, fourth- and fifth-freedom rights. There would be no control or capacity or frequencies operated or of tariffs, though the number of designated airlines might be limited. The agreement proposes to abandon the traditional nationality rule in favour of allowing states to designate airlines having their headquarters, central administration and princi- pal place of business in the designating state, and being 'effectively controlled' from within that state. A state would also be able to designate an airline from another state to operate on its behalf (*African Aviation*, December 1999). If ratified and implemented, even by a limited number of states, Yammoussoukro II would show one way towards achieving clear skies.

Apart from widening the geographical scope of 'open skies' markets, the second requirement must be to find a way of removing the clouds which exist even in 'open skies' markets. Previously these were identified as being the nationality clauses in bilaterals which require airlines to be substantially owned and effectively controlled by nationals of the designating state, the failure to grant domestic cabotage and seventh-freedom rights and the pre- ference given by some governments to their airlines for the carriage of government-related business. Of these the most critical issue to resolve is that of nationality. Once strict nationality and ownership rules are relaxed, the case for not granting cabotage or seventh-freedom rights is seriously weakened. As is the case for maintaining preference for 'national' airlines. The whole issue of the nationality rule and how to move away from it has been explored at length elsewhere (Doganis, 2001). Suffice it to say that the simplest way to move forward is to change the criterion for designating airlines. Instead of focusing on ownership and nationality, airlines should be designated if their 'principal place of business' is in the designating state and subject to its laws, irrespective of who the beneficial owner is. This principle has been used by the Hong Kong government in the past to permit the designation of Cathay Pacific, an airline effectively controlled by UK interests. The principal place of business has also been adopted as the nationality criterion in the multilateral open skies agreement between the United States, Chile, New Zealand, Brunei and Singapore.

Abandoning national ownership in favour of principal place of business would seem to be a simple and logical step. It appears to go a long way to fully normalising international air services. But not quite! If the United States or other states do not allow ownership of their own airlines by foreign nationals or companies, this liberalisation will be fairly one-sided. Thus the move towards 'principal place of business' to identify an airline's nationality must be accompanied by removing restrictions on foreign ownership of a country's airline companies.

One way of both enlarging the geographical scope of 'open skies' and taking steps to remove the remaining clouds in those 'open skies' would be through the creation of a Transatlantic Common Aviation Area (TCAA) linking Europe with the United States and Canada. In December 1999 the US Transportation Secretary Rodney Slater hosted an inter-ministerial meeting in Chicago on the theme 'Beyond Open Skies'. For the US government this was an opportunity to open up discussion on the final push towards free trade in the air – in other words, on how to go beyond 'open skies' bilaterals. The Europeans surprised everyone by stating they were ready to open negotiations with the United States aimed at creating a TCAA. This would involve a long and laborious process in order to achieve convergence between the Union and the United States on several contentious issues. However, the establishment of a TCAA need not wait until all issues have been resolved and all details have been agreed. One could initially establish the TCAA by agreeing to those issues on which there is already common ground or on which agreement is not far off. During the lengthy preparatory and negotiating phases existing bilateral air service agreements would need to remain in force and could be amended further.

A TCAA or any other similar regional agreement on clear skies would need to address four key issues. The first would be that of open market access within the common aviation area itself. Airlines of the signatory states should be free to operate between any two points, including domestic sectors, without capacity or price controls. In effect the so-called seventh freedom would also be available. So a British airline would be able to operate services between, say, Copenhagen and New York without such services originating or stopping in the United Kingdom.

The second issue is that of the nationality or ownership rules and the right of establishment. A fundamental change is required here in view of the economic pressures towards industrial concentration within the airline industry, which is currently being distorted by restrictions on ownership. The simplest and first step would be to allow ownership of TCAA airlines by nationals or companies from any of the states within the TCAA. This would be similar to the current regime within the European Union. Once this was agreed it would be possible for a US airline to buy Eurowings in Germany or for Lufthansa to buy a majority share in America West, since these are airlines operating wholly within the TCAA. In other words, some cross-border mergers and acquisitions would become possible. But air services to countries outside the TCAA would still be governed by the conventional bilateral agreements with the traditional nationality requirement. To open up and normalise the industry, the next logical step would be for the TCAA member states when renegotiating their own bilaterals with third countries to insist that designated airlines should have their principal place of business in the designating states and that the traditional ownership rule should be abandoned.

A key requirement within any regional aviation area is to ensure that competition is open, fair and safeguarded. Therefore a third issue to resolve in creating a TCAA would be to try and harmonise competition policy. The EU competition rules (section 3.6 above) and US anti-trust legislation both have the same basic principles and objectives. But in applying them the Union and the United States often reach different conclusions. The aim should be, however, to try and ensure that in their application of these competition rules the relevant authorities converge as much as possible. This would minimise the possibility of conflicting decisions and would remove the current uncertainty and delay that distort airline decisions on alliances and co-operative agreements.

Finally, linked with the issue of competition policy, one would need to establish a common approach and convergence on a range of regulatory issues on which there are still a few remaining differences on either side of the Atlantic. The most critical of these are slot allocation rules at congested airports, bankruptcy protection regulations and the leasing in of foreign-registered aircraft. Issues on which convergence would be easier include government subsidies or state aid, cargo and mail preference rules and codes of conduct for computer reservation systems.

The large number of issues that need to be covered in moving towards a Transatlantic Common Aviation Area highlights the difficulties involved. It is clear that progress will be slow. The United States in 2001, under the new Bush administration initially, appeared hesitant to move forward on the TCAA concept. Nevertheless a TCAA appears such a logical next step in creating a truly 'open skies' market covering around 40 per cent of the world's international and domestic traffic. The creation of the TCAA would be phased and in steps once agreement was reached on policy and convergence in different areas. Transitional arrangements might also be necessary on particular issues or for specific markets. The real question is whether and when there will be the political will on both sides of the Atlantic to move in this direction.

4 The structure of airline costs

4.1 The need for costing

The costs of supplying airline services are an essential input to many decisions taken by airline managers. The way that an airline's costs are broken down and categorised will depend on the purpose for which they are being used. In airline planning, cost information is generally needed to meet four key requirements. First, airlines need an overall breakdown of their total expenditure into different cost categories as a general management and accounting tool. They require a general breakdown of costs to show cost trends over time, to measure the cost efficiency of particular functional areas such as flight operations or maintenance, and ultimately to enable them to produce their annual accounts and their operating and non-operating profit or loss. Second, airlines require very detailed cost information by flight and route in order to make operating decisions such as whether to add more frequencies on a sector or reduce them, or whether to operate that route at all. Third, cost identification is crucial in the development of pricing policies and pricing decisions, for both passengers and cargo. Finally, an assessment of costs is essential in any evaluation of investments, whether in new aircraft or in new routes or services.

No single cost categorisation is capable of satisfying all these management requirements simultaneously. A cost breakdown developed for general management and accounting purposes may be useless as a guide to pricing strategy and may be of little help in making operating decisions. As a result, most airlines break their costs down in two or more different ways, depending on the purpose for which the cost breakdown is required.

While the approach to cost categorisation used by each airline is strongly influenced by accounting practices in its home country, it is also influenced by the cost classification adopted by the International Civil Aviation Organisation (ICAO). The governments of the member states of ICAO are required to provide ICAO each year with financial data about their airlines on a standard form. These data provide the basis for ICAO's annual *Digest of Statistics*, Series F, *Financial Data*, which contains the balance sheets and profit and loss statements of all the ICAO member airlines, though in practice each year data for several airlines are missing. The need to provide ICAO with a particular breakdown of costs and the ability once this is done to compare one's costs on a fairly straightforward basis with other airlines have over time induced many airlines to adopt a cost classification similar to that of ICAO. The ICAO cost classification was in any case based fairly closely on prevailing cost practices in the United States and among several European airlines. Thus worldwide, throughout the airline industry, there tends to be a fairly standard and traditional approach to the categorisation of costs for general management use.

4.2   The traditional approach to airline costs

It is normal practice to divide airline accounts into operating and non-operating categories. The aim is to identify and separate out as non-operating items all those costs and revenues not directly associated with the operation of an airline's own air services. Following ICAO and US practice, most airlines have adopted this approach, which identifies as *non-operating* the following five items:

1   The gains or losses arising from the retirement of property or equipment, both aeronautical and non-aeronautical. Such gains or losses arise when there is a difference between the depreciated book value of a particular item and the value that is realised when that item is retired or sold off.

2   Interest paid on loans, as well as any interest received from bank or other deposits. It is considered that bank interest paid or received has little to do with the business of flying. For some costing purposes, however, such as aircraft evaluation, some airlines would include interest paid on aircraft-related loans as an operating cost.

3   All profits or losses arising from an airline's affiliated companies, some of which may themselves be directly involved in air transport. In some cases this item may be of some importance in the overall financial performance of an airline. Early in 2000 British Airways, for example, had over eighteen majority-owned subsidiaries and shareholdings of 50 per cent or less in another sixteen aviation companies.

4   An assortment of other items which do not fall into the previous three categories, such as losses or gains arising from foreign exchange transactions or from sales of shares or securities. In recent years airlines have from time to time made large losses or profits as a result of sudden marked fluctuations in exchange rates. These are clearly a non-operating item.

5   The final item includes any direct or indirect government subsidies or taxes on profit or other corporate taxes. In the case of some airlines, subsidies have at times been very substantial. Thus in the mid-1990s Air France, like several other state-owned airlines in Europe, received massive injections of state funds to enable it to reduce its debts and restructure its operations (see Doganis, 2001). Subsidies have also been paid periodically to most government-owned airlines outside Europe. Such subsidies would appear as non-operating items. Similarly, profit taxes or other corporate taxes would also be categorised as non-operating.

Table 4.1 Sources of Singapore Airlines' profits, financial year 1999–2000

Source	US $ (million)	% share of profits
1 Non-operating:		
Surplus on sale of aircraft	51	5
Dividends from subsidiaries	118	12
Income from deposits/investments	79	8
Exceptional items:		
(a) Special dividend from SATS and SIA Engineering Co.	221	23
(b) Disposal of shares in Delta, Swissair and Equant	101	10
Total non-operating	570	58
2 Airline operations	407	42
3 Total profit before tax	977	100

Source: Compiled by the author from SIA (2000).

For some airlines non-operating items may have a major impact on their financial results. Thus in the financial year 1999–2000 Singapore Airlines (SIA) produced an overall net profit before tax of $977 million. Of this, only $407 million or 42 per cent was from airline operations (Table 4.1). The remainder came from non-operating items. As much as $118 million was dividends from subsidiary companies; there was a surplus on the sale of aircraft of $51 million, which was much lower than in previous years. The airline earned a further net income of $79 million from investments and deposits. There were also two exceptional items in that year. A special gross dividend of $221 million was received from SIA's ground handling subsidiary, SATS, and from Singapore Engineering Company as a result of restructuring prior to these two companies' flotation. In addition, a total profit of $101 million came from the disposal of shares in Delta Airlines, Swissair and Equant (SIA, 2000). The SIA case amply illustrates why it is essential to separate out non-operating items.

Non-operating items are not necessarily profits or surpluses as in SIA's case. They may well be losses or costs. Most airlines normally pay out a great deal more in interest charges on their loans than they receive from their own cash deposits at the bank. This is particularly so of state-owned airlines whose development has been financed by a succession of loans rather than through injections of equity capital. But even many privatised airlines face large interest payments on their debts. Thus in the financial year 1999–2000 British Airways had a net interest charge for the year of £679 million sterling. In other words, it was paying almost £2 million in net interest each day. In 1998 Air Canada turned an operating surplus of $71 million into a deficit of about $18 million before tax by the inclusion of two large non-operating costs – $107 million of interest and a further $17 million of other non-operating losses. These were only partially offset by a surplus of $36 million from affiliated companies, and from the retirement of assets (ICAO, 1999b).

The nature of each airline's non-operating costs and revenues is probably unique, in that many non-operating items are influenced by circumstances which are very particular to each airline. As a result inter-airline comparisons of net profits or total costs including non-operating costs are of little value.

In fact, in years when their profits decline, many airlines 'massage' their non-operating costs or revenues to improve their bottom line results. For instance, it is common for hard-pressed airlines to sell some of their aircraft and then lease them back. This generates a substantial cash inflow which appears as a positive non-operating item which may offset any operating losses. Because of such anomalies and complexities it is better when assessing an airline's costs or revenues to leave non-operating items aside and to focus on its operating costs or revenues. These are the best descriptors of its performance as an airline.

On the operating side, airline accounts are divided into *operating revenue* and *operating costs*. The latter can be further subdivided into direct operating and indirect operating costs. But direct and indirect have a different meaning in the airline industry from that in normal accounting usage.

In theory, the distinction between these two cost categories is fairly clear. *Direct operating costs* should include all those costs which are associated with and dependent on the type of aircraft being operated and which would change if the aircraft type were changed. Broadly speaking, such costs should include all flying expenses (such as flight crew salaries, fuel and oil), all maintenance and overhaul costs and all aircraft depreciation costs. *Indirect operating costs* are all those costs which will remain unaffected by a change of aircraft type because they are not directly dependent on aircraft operations. They include areas of expenditure which are passenger-related rather than aircraft-related (such as passenger service costs, costs of ticketing and sales, and station and ground costs) as well as general administrative costs. In practice, however, the distinction between direct and indirect operating costs is not always clear-cut. Certain cost items, such as maintenance administration or costs of cabin staff, are categorised as direct costs by some airlines and as indirect costs by others. The main categories of airline operating costs are shown in Table 4.2. The cost categories shown are those currently accepted and used, with some modification, by most international airlines around the world. They are broadly based on the cost categorisation traditionally used by ICAO.

4.3 Direct operating costs

4.3.1 Cost of flight operations

This is undoubtedly the largest single element of operating costs which is aircraft-dependent. It includes, in the first place, all costs associated with *flight crew*. Such costs cover not only direct salaries and travelling and stopover expenses but also allowances, pensions, insurance and any other social welfare

Table 4.2 Traditional categorisation of airline operating costs

---

DIRECT OPERATING COSTS *(DOC)*

1 Flight operations:

- Flight crew salaries and expenses
- Fuel and oil
- Airport and en-route charges[a]
- Aircraft insurance
- Rental/lease of flight equipment/crews[b]

2 Maintenance and overhaul:

- Engineering staff costs
- Spare parts consumed
- Maintenance administration (could be IOC)

3 Depreciation and amortisation:

- Flight equipment
- Ground equipment and property (could be IOC)
- Extra depreciation (in excess of historic cost depreciation)
- Amortisation of development costs and crew training

INDIRECT OPERATING COSTS *(IOC)*

4 Station and ground expenses:

- Ground staff
- Buildings, equipment, transport
- Handling fees paid to others

5 Passenger services:

- Cabin crew salaries and expenses (could be DOC)
- Other passenger service costs
- Passenger insurance

6 Ticketing, sales and promotion

7 General and administration

8 Other operating costs

Notes
a ICAO classifies airport and en-route charges as an indirect operating cost under 'Station and ground expenses'.
b The US practice is to classify rentals under 'Depreciation'.

payments. While most jet aircraft now have two-man cockpit crews, their salaries normally depend on the type of aircraft being flown. For safety reasons, pilots and co-pilots are licensed to fly only one aircraft type during any period of time. As a general rule the larger the aircraft the higher the salaries paid. So pilot costs are aircraft-specific. However, cockpit commonality in some aircraft types such as the Airbus 319 and Airbus 320 are allowing some airlines to use pilots who are common-rated to fly two aircraft types. Flight crew costs can be directly calculated on a route-by-route basis or, more usually, they are expressed as an hourly cost per aircraft type. In the latter case the total flight crew costs for a particular route or service can be calculated by multiplying the hourly flight crew costs of the aircraft being operated on that route by the block time for the route. (See the glossary for definition of block time.)

The second major cost element of flight operations is *fuel*. Again, it is very aircraft-specific. Fuel consumption varies by aircraft type, depending on the number and the size or thrust of the engines and the type and age of those engines. During operations, actual fuel consumption varies considerably from route to route in relation to the sector lengths, the aircraft weight, wind conditions, the cruise altitude, and so on. Thus an hourly fuel cost tends to be even more of an approximation than an hourly flight crew cost, and it is normal to consider fuel consumption on a route-by-route basis. In addition to aviation fuel, aircraft also use up *oil*. But the oil consumption is negligible and, rather than try to calculate it directly for each route, the normal practice is to have an hourly figure for oil consumption for each type of engine. The oil consumption on a particular route is then calculated from the number of engines on the aircraft flying the route multiplied by the hourly oil consumption for that engine and by the block time. Fuel and oil costs include any fuel throughput charges levied by some airport authorities on the volume of fuel uplifted, the fuel handling charges paid to fuel suppliers for the loading of fuel and any relevant fuel taxes or duties levied by governments, though these are not usual.

Another significant element of flight operation costs is made up of *airport and en-route charges*. Airlines have to pay airport authorities for the use of the runway and terminal facilities. Airport charges normally have two elements: a landing fee related to the weight of the aircraft, usually its maximum take-off weight, and a passenger charge levied on the number of passengers boarded at that airport. (Occasionally it is calculated on the number of disembarked passengers.) Many Third World airports do not charge the airlines for the number of passengers embarked but collect a fee directly from each passenger on departure. This slows down passenger check-in. It is contrary to the recommendations of ICAO, which wants passenger-related charges to be paid by the airlines and included in the price of the ticket. (For details of airport charging practice see Doganis, 1992.) When passengers pay an airport charge directly to the airport authority on departure, this cost does not appear as an airline cost. At most airports a free parking period of two to six hours is covered by the basic aircraft landing fee. If an aircraft stays at an airport beyond this free time period, it will have to pay additional aircraft parking or hangarage fees. These are relatively small compared with the basic landing and passenger charges.

Airlines must also pay en-route navigation charges to cover the cost of en-route navigation aids that their aircraft use while flying. The actual level of the navigation charge is related to the weight of the aircraft and the distance flown over a country's air space. As a result, airport charges, where they are not passenger-related, and navigation service charges will both vary with the type of aircraft used and are therefore considered as a direct operating cost. On the other hand, passenger-related charges do not vary with aircraft type. This may partly explain why ICAO insists on treating landing and en-route charges as an indirect cost, though few airlines follow its lead. Since landing and en-route charges vary by individual airport and country, they must be calculated separately for each flight or route.

A relatively small cost in flight operations is that of the *insurance of the flight equipment*. The insurance premium paid by an airline for each aircraft is calculated as a percentage of the full purchase price. The annual premium may be between 1.5 per cent and 3 per cent, depending on the airline, the number of aircraft it has insured and the geographical areas in which its aircraft operate. If the airline wants full war risk cover, if it wants to be covered against terrorist action, or if it is operating in or through an area where there is armed conflict, an additional premium of up to 2 per cent may have to be paid. In the aftermath of the terrorist attacks in the United States in September 2001 war risk and third-party premiums shot up so sharply that governments agreed to provide the cost of additional cover themselves in order to help their airlines. The annual premium, which is fixed, can be converted into an hourly insurance cost by dividing it by the projected aircraft utilisation, that is, by the total number of block hours that each aircraft is expected to fly during the year.

Many airlines may, in addition, have to meet *rental* or *lease charges* for the hiring or leasing of aircraft from other airlines or leasing companies. Lease charges are usually considered as part of flight operation costs. Several of the small national airlines were originally launched on the basis of leased aircraft, though over the last twenty years leases have become widespread even among larger airlines. They are broadly of two kinds: operating leases, which are generally for five years or less, with ownership resting with the lessor, and financial leases under which after ten or more years aircraft ownership is transferred to the airline. (For details of leasing arrangements see Morrell, 2002.) In such cases, rental or lease charges are high, pushing up the airline's total flight operation costs to abnormally high levels. This is because the rental charges for leased aircraft effectively cover both the depreciation and the interest charges paid by the owners of the aircraft. Conversely, airlines heavily dependent on leased equipment tend to have very low depreciation charges, since they pay for depreciation indirectly through the rental charge. It is because rentals include a large element of depreciation that the American practice is to categorise rental charges under the heading of depreciation rather than to treat them as a cost of flight operations. Lease costs and depreciation taken together can be considered as aircraft ownership costs.

Lastly, there may be some costs related to flight operations which do not fall into any of the above categories. Such additional costs may include costs of *flight crew training* or of *route development*. However, if training costs are amortised over two or three years they are grouped together with depreciation.

4.3.2 Maintenance and overhaul costs

Total maintenance costs cover a whole series of separate costs, related to different aspects of maintenance and overhaul, which ideally ought to be treated separately. In practice there are so many joint costs in the separate maintenance areas that it is difficult, if not impossible, for many airlines to break total maintenance costs down into separate cost categories. While ICAO groups all maintenance and overhaul expenditure into a single undivided cost item, the UK Civil Aviation Authority in its own airline statistics splits maintenance into two categories, fixed and variable. The latter are those costs which are dependent on the amount of flying done. Maintenance costs cover not only routine maintenance and maintenance checks carried out between flights or overnight but also the more extensive periodic overhauls and major checks. They encompass two major cost areas. First, the very extensive use of labour and the expenses related to all grades of staff involved directly or indirectly in maintenance work. Where possible, costs of maintenance staff at out-stations should be separated out from station costs and included under maintenance. Second, there is a major cost associated with the consumption of spare parts. Most parts of each engine and airframe have a usable life which is measured in terms of block hours or numbers of flight cycles, that is, landings and take-offs. Once its certified life has expired, each part must be removed and checked or replaced. Hence the consumption of spare parts is high and costly. The costs of workshops, maintenance hangars and offices are also included. Finally, if an airline is subcontracting out any of the maintenance done on its own aircraft, the charges it pays for any such work should be allocated to the maintenance and overhaul category.

In the United States, the Department of Transportation requires airlines to split their flight equipment maintenance costs into three categories: direct maintenance on the airframe; direct maintenance on the engines; and a maintenance burden. The maintenance burden is essentially the administrative and overhead costs associated with the maintenance function which cannot be attributed directly to a particular airframe or engine but are allocated on a fairly arbitrary basis. United States' airlines are obliged to furnish the federal government with these three categories of maintenance costs separately for each aircraft type that they operate. The data are published and provide an excellent basis for the comparison of maintenance costs between airlines and also between different aircraft types and engines.

Outside the United States, airlines also try to apportion their maintenance costs between different aircraft types, but there is no standard way of doing this, so inter-airline comparisons would not be valid even if such data were publicly available. Individual airlines, having estimated the total maintenance costs of one particular aircraft type, may then convert those costs into an hourly maintenance cost by dividing them by the total number of block hours flown by all the aircraft of that particular type operated by the airline.

4.3.3 *Depreciation and amortisation*

Depreciation of flight equipment is the third component of direct operating cost, since it is very much aircraft-dependent. Airlines tend to use straight-line depreciation over a given number of years with a residual value of 0–15 per cent. The residual value is the predicated or assumed resale value of the aircraft at the end of the depreciation period. Up to the mid-1970s depreciation periods were generally twelve years or less. The introduction of wide-bodied jets led to a lengthening of the depreciation period, first, because the capital cost of such aircraft was very much higher than that of the previous generation of aircraft; second, because air transport technology appeared to have reached a plateau. It became much more difficult than it had been previously to predict that further developments in technology might adversely affect and shorten the economic life of the wide-bodied jets. Their economic life was dependent on the strength and technical life of their various components and was unlikely to be affected by any new leaps forward in aircraft technology which might make them obsolescent. In response to these two factors, airlines throughout the world have tended to lengthen the depreciation period of their large, wide-bodied jets to fourteen to sixteen years with a residual value of around 10 per cent. For smaller short-haul aircraft, especially if they are turbo-props, depreciation periods are shorter, generally eight to ten years.

The purpose of depreciation is twofold. First, it aims to spread the cost of an aircraft over the useful life of that aircraft. If the full cost of a new aircraft was all debited in the year in which the aircraft was bought it would seriously inflate costs and undermine profits in that year, especially if a fleet of aircraft was bought. Instead, only a proportion of an aircraft's full cost is charged against revenues each year. The depreciation policy chosen determines how much that proportion should be. Second, depreciation allows money out of each year's revenues, equivalent to the depreciation charge, to be put into a general reserve fund. These monies, together with any retained profits, can be used to pay back the loans with which the aircraft were bought together with any accrued interest. If the aircraft have been bought fully or in part with the airline's own cash, the accumulated depreciation reserve can be used to fund the new aircraft when the current aircraft are replaced.

The annual depreciation charge or cost of a particular aircraft in an airline's fleet depends on the depreciation period adopted and the residual value assumed. An airline buying several Boeing 747-400 aircraft in mid-2000 might have paid $170 million for each aircraft and, say, another $30 million per aircraft for a spares holding, making a total of $200 million. Assuming it depreciated each aircraft over sixteen years to a 10 per cent residual value, the annual depreciation charge would be $11.25 million:

Annual depreciation

$$= \frac{\text{Price of aircraft and spares (\$200 million)} - \text{residual value (10\%)}}{\text{Depreciation period (16 years)}}$$

$$= \frac{\$200 \text{ million} - \$20 \text{ million}}{16} = \frac{\$180}{16} = \$11.25 \text{ million}$$

If an airline chooses a shorter depreciation period, the annual depreciation cost will rise. Thus until 2001 Singapore Airlines had been depreciating its aircraft over ten years with a 20 per cent residual value. On this basis, the annual depreciation cost of the Boeing 747-400 aircraft purchased in 2000 would rise from $11.25 million to $16.0 million. The immediate effect would be to increase annual operating costs by pushing depreciation costs up.

So why would SIA or any other airline choose a faster depreciation policy if the effect is to push up operating costs? If an airline wants a young fleet and renews its fleet every three to five years the faster depreciation is compensated for by higher non-operating profits when its young aircraft are sold. For instance, using a traditional depreciation period of sixteen years for a new Boeing 747-400 as described above, this aircraft at the end of four years would have a book value in the airline's asset registry of $155 million ($200 − 4 × $11.25 million). For the airline depreciating faster at $16.0 million per year, the book value of its aircraft at the end of the fourth year is $136 million ($200 million − 4 × $16.0 million). All other things being equal, a four-year-old aircraft will have a market price which reflects the more widely used depreciation policy, namely the longer one. So such an aircraft, plus its bank of spares, will be valued at around $150 million to $160 million. If the airline wishing to renew its fleet sells its aircraft, which it values in its own books at $136 million, in the market where prevailing second-hand prices are much higher, it will make a profit. If it sells, say at $160 million, it will have made a profit on the sale of assets of $24.0 million ($160.0 million − $136.0 million). Higher depreciation costs in the short term are counterbalanced by high profits on aircraft sales four or five years later. This strategy is reinforced if there are significant tax allowances which reduce an airline's tax liability when it undertakes new investments. This is the case in Singapore. While SIA's unit depreciation charges were relatively high it was consistently making substantial non-operating profits from selling relatively new aircraft (top row in Table 4.1).

Once the depreciation policy has been determined, the annual depreciation cost of each aircraft becomes a fixed cost. But the hourly cost is dependent on the hours of flying that an aircraft undertakes each year. The hourly depreciation cost of each aircraft in any one year can be established by dividing its fixed annual depreciation cost by the aircraft's annual utilisation, that is, the number of block hours flown in that year. Thus, if the Boeing 747-400 aircraft above flew 3,260 block hours in a year, as Saudi Arabian Airlines flew its 747-400s in 1999, its hourly depreciation cost would be $3,450 ($11.25 million divided by 3,260). If the annual utilisation could be pushed up to 5,000 hours, which is what Thai Airways managed in 1999, the hourly cost would be cut to $2,250 ($11.25 million divided by 5,000). This is why pushing up the annual utilisation is so crucial. The more an aircraft flies each day and year the lower is the depreciation cost per block hour. It is evident that any changes in the depreciation period, in the residual value or in the annual utilisation will all affect the hourly depreciation cost.

A major issue for airline accountants in recent years has been whether to use the historical purchase price of the aircraft as the basis for calculating its annual depreciation cost or the current cost of replacing that asset, which may be substantially higher, especially for aircraft that are more than five or six years old. Current or replacement cost depreciation would result in substantially higher annual depreciation charges, and few airlines have adopted it. Some airlines, however, have adopted a policy of charging extra depreciation in good years when profits are high. This enables them to put more money aside for fleet replacement.

It is ICAO practice to include depreciation of ground property and equipment as a further item of direct operating costs. This practice is questionable in that such depreciation charges are not directly related to the operation of aircraft and, except where they relate to ground equipment which is specific and unique to a particular aircraft type, they will remain unaffected if an airline changes its fleet.

Many airlines amortise the costs of flight crew training as well as any developmental and pre-operating costs related to the development of new routes or the introduction of new aircraft. In essence this means that such costs, instead of being charged in total to the year in which they occur, are spread out over a number of years. Such amortisation costs are grouped together with depreciation.

4.4 Indirect operating costs

4.4.1 Station and ground expenses

Station and ground costs are all those costs incurred in providing an airline's services at an airport other than the cost of landing fees and other airport charges. Such costs include the salaries and expenses of all airline staff located at the airport and engaged in the handling and servicing of aircraft, passengers or freight. These should include all costs associated with an airline's lounges for business or first-class passengers. In addition there will be the costs of ground handling equipment, of ground transport, of buildings and offices and associated facilities such as telex machines, telephones, and so on. There will also be a cost arising from the maintenance and insurance of each station's buildings and equipment. Rents may have to be paid for some of the properties used. Clearly, by far the largest expenditure on station and ground staff and facilities inevitably occurs at an airline's home base.

At some airports, especially the smaller ones it serves, an airline may decide to contract out some or all of its check-in and handling needs. Handling fees charged by third parties should appear as a station expense. An airline may contract out of all of its handling, including passenger check-in, baggage and freight handling and loading, aircraft cleaning and so on, or only some of these activities. It may pay a global fee irrespective of the aircraft type actually used. However, if the fees paid for handling to be provided by a handling agent or another airline vary with the size or type of aircraft being used then such handling charges may legitimately be considered a direct operating cost.

Some aircraft maintenance may be done at an airline's out-stations and the costs arising from such maintenance work should ideally be included as a direct operating cost under the 'maintenance and overhaul' category. But maintenance expenditures are frequently difficult to disentangle from other station costs and are in many cases left as part of station and ground costs.

4.4.2   Costs of passenger services

The largest single element of costs arising from passenger services is the pay, allowances and other expenses directly related to aircraft cabin staff and other passenger service personnel. Such expenses would include hotel and other costs associated with overnight stops as well as the training costs of cabin staff, where these are not amortised. Unlike pilots, cabin crew are licensed to work on any aircraft type in an airline's fleet. They are not restricted to one or two types only. Hence cabin crew costs are assumed to be independent of the type of aircraft being used. On the other hand, as the number and grading of cabin staff may vary by aircraft type, some airlines consider cabin staff costs as an element of flight operation costs, that is, as a direct operating cost.

A second group of passenger service costs are those directly related to the passengers. They include the cost of in-flight catering, the cost of accommodation provided for transit passengers, the cost of meals and other facilities provided on the ground for the comfort of passengers, and expenses incurred as a result of delayed or cancelled flights.

Lastly, premiums paid by the airline for passenger liability insurance and passenger accident insurance should also be included. These are a fixed annual charge based on an airline's total passenger kilometres produced in the previous year. The premium will depend on each airline's safety record but is likely to be within the range of 35–55c per 1,000 revenue passenger kilometres.

4.4.3   Ticketing, sales and promotion costs

Such costs include all expenditure, pay, allowances, etc., related to staff engaged in reservation ticketing, sales and promotion activities as well as all office and accommodation costs arising through these activities. The costs of retail ticket offices or shops, whether at home or abroad, would be included, as well as the costs of telephone call centres, of the computerised reservation systems and the operation of the airline's internet web site. Problems of cost allocation arise. It is frequently difficult, especially at foreign stations, to decide whether particular expenses should be categorised as station and ground expenses or as ticketing, sales and promotion. For instance, where should an airline allocate the costs of ticketing staff manning a ticket desk at a foreign airport who may also get involved in assisting with the ground handling of passengers? The same difficulty arises with the costs of an airline's 'country manager' in a foreign country who may have overall responsibility for sales as well as the handling of passengers at the airport.

A significant cost item within this area is that of commission or fees paid to travel agencies for ticket sales. Commission is also paid to credit card companies for sales paid for by card as well as to the global distribution systems for all reservations made on their worldwide computer systems. Finally, all promotional expenditure, including the costs of all advertising and of any other form of promotion, such as familiarisation visits by journalists or travel agents, also fall under this heading.

4.4.4 General and administrative costs

General and administrative costs are normally a relatively small element of an airline's total operating costs. This is because, where overhead costs can be related directly to a particular function or activity within an airline (such as maintenance or sales), they should be allocated to that activity. Thus, strictly speaking, general and administrative costs should include only those cost elements which are truly general to the airline or which cannot readily be allocated to a particular activity. Inter-airline comparison of these general costs is of little value, since airlines follow different accounting practices. While some airlines try to allocate their central costs to different cost centres as much as possible, other airlines do not do so either as a matter of policy or because their accounting procedures are not sophisticated enough to enable them to do so.

Where airlines cannot legitimately include a particular expense under one of the cost categories discussed above, they may include it as a separate item under 'Other operating expenses'. If the sums shown under this heading for a particular airline are large, it is usually an indication of poor cost control and/or inadequate accounting procedures.

4.5 Trends in airline costs

The distribution of total operating costs between the various cost elements discussed above can be seen in Table 4.3. It is apparent that for the world's scheduled airlines as a whole just over half of total operating costs now arise from direct costs, though at the start of the 1980s the figure was generally around 60 per cent. The rest are indirect costs. While this is a useful generalisation, it hides the fact that there may be differences between airlines in their cost structures. A number of factors may cause variations in airline cost composition, but for most airlines direct operating costs are generally between 45 per cent and 60 per cent of total operating costs. Direct operating costs tend to be well above 50 per cent for long-haul carriers such as Singapore Airlines or Virgin Atlantic and below 50 per cent for short-haul carriers. It is only in non-scheduled operations that direct costs generally surpass 60 per cent of total operating costs and may reach as high as 75 per cent or 80 per cent. This is also the case with low-cost no-frills carriers such as Southwest in the United States and Ryanair or easyJet in Europe. This is because both charter

Table 4.3 Operating costs: scheduled airlines, ICAO member states, 1980–99

	1980 %	1990 %	1999 %
DIRECT OPERATING COSTS *(DOC)*			
1 Flight operations:	44	32	35
• Flight crew	(8)	(7)	(8)
• Fuel and oil	(28)	(15)	(11)
• Airport and en-route charges	(5)	(4)	(7)
• Aircraft rental, insurance, etc.	(3)	(6)	(9)
2 Maintenance	11	11	11
3 Depreciation: aircraft and ground facilities	6	7	7
Total DOC	60	50	53
INDIRECT OPERATING COSTS *(IOC)*			
4 Station/ground expenses	11	12	11
5 Passenger services	9	10	11
6 Ticketing, sales, promotion	14	16	14
7 Admin. and other costs	6	11	12
Total IOC	40	50	47
Total operating costs (TOC)	100	100	100

Source: ICAO *Digest of Statistics*, Series F, *Financial Data*.

and low-cost operators achieve most of their cost savings in the area of indirect costs.

The most significant factor affecting the overall level and distribution of unit costs during the last two decades has been the variation in the price of aviation fuel. In the early 1970s general inflation, particularly wage inflation, had begun to push up airline costs. But it was the rapid and unprecedented rise in fuel prices following the Arab–Israeli war in the autumn of 1973 that had the most dramatic impact on unit costs (Figure 4.1). International aviation fuel prices stabilised between 1974 and 1978 but at a level which in real terms was about three times that of early 1973. Towards the end of 1978 and early in 1979 political instability in Iran and the ensuing war with Iraq created a sudden shortage of crude oil. This, together with the pricing policies of OPEC, led to a new escalation of fuel prices even more dramatic than that of 1974 (Figure 4.1). By the end of 1979 the price of aviation fuel had doubled, compared with its level at the start of 1978. Fuel prices stabilised in 1981/82 and then began to decline slowly in dollar terms in the latter part of 1982. This steady decline continued till 1986, when a more dramatic price fall occurred. This brought the real price of fuel to a level below that of 1974. This large drop in the fuel price was a major factor in the improved financial performance of many airlines in the period 1987–89 (Figure 1.1).

The two price hikes of 1974 and 1978–79 had a major impact on airline cost structures. By the early 1980s fuel had shot up from around 11 per cent ten years earlier to almost 30 per cent of total operating costs (Table 4.3). In

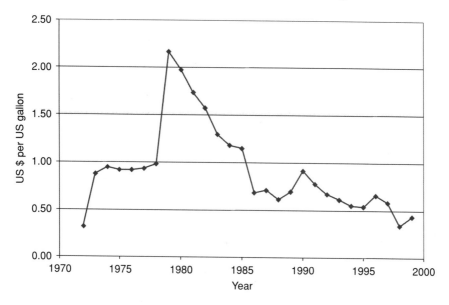

Figure 4.1 The trend of fuel prices, 1972–99 (Rotterdam spot prices at constant 1992 values).

the process direct operating costs were on average around 60 per cent of total operating costs and for some airlines such as the all-cargo operators they reached over 70 per cent.

As the real price of fuel declined after 1982 so did its share of total costs, so that by 1990 this was down to 15 per cent. After 1986 fuel prices fluctuated but around a fairly steady base level. Thus there were short-term upward shifts in 1990–91 as a result of the Kuwait crisis and Gulf War and again in 1996. By 1998 the fuel price had in real terms fallen to the same levels as those of the early 1970s (Figure 4.1). This helped the airlines achieve record profits in 1997 and 1998. The good news could not last. In 1999 and 2000 fuel prices rose steadily to a peak in October 2000. This was a result of OPEC decisions to limit oil production. In real terms, aviation fuel prices in mid-2000 were still well below the high prices of the early 1980s, though they were significantly higher than the exceptionally low levels of 1998. During 2001 fuel prices declined as economic slowdown in many economies meant a slackening of demand for petroleum products.

One cost element of flight operations which has shown a marked tendency to increase in relative terms is that of airport and en-route charges. As airports have become more independent of governments, especially when they have been privatised, they have come under growing pressure to be financially self-supporting. The same is also true of air traffic services. So their charges have remained high or have increased in real terms.

The two other elements of direct operating costs – maintenance costs and depreciation – were not as adversely affected by the general inflation of costs

as were flight operations. Both these cost elements, but particularly depreciation, were helped by the more widespread use of wide-bodied jets during
the 1980s and 1990s, which were technically more proficient and had lower
maintenance requirements. At the same time, their annual productivity was
such that, despite their high purchase price, their unit cost of depreciation
was actually lower in real terms than that of the aircraft they were replacing.
As a result, the share of both maintenance and depreciation in total costs has
been fairly stable.

However, the depreciation figure in Table 4.3 does not cover the full cost
of aircraft ownership because during the last twenty years a growing proportion of aircraft are leased in rather than purchased. This explains why, in
Table 4.3, rental and insurance of flight equipment (together with other similar
items) went up from 3 per cent to 9 per cent of total costs between 1980 and
1999. In 1999 aircraft rentals, or lease costs, were 7.4 per cent of total costs,
aircraft insurance was 0.2 per cent and aircraft depreciation was 5.4 per cent.
Thus ownership costs total on average around 13 per cent of total costs.

Changes in the relative importance of different indirect costs have been less
marked over the last twenty years. Ticketing, sales and promotion remain by
far the most significant indirect cost element, accounting for around 14 per
cent of total costs (Table 4.3). A worrying trend is the increase in the proportion of expenses attributed to general and administrative functions. This
would suggest some airlines are having difficulty categorising their costs.

The ICAO data discussed above are very much a global average since they
include both domestic and international services. A better guide to the latter
is provided by IATA statistics, which are also much more reliable (Table 4.4).
When one assesses the cost structure of international scheduled services, in
1999 the overall split between direct and indirect costs was similar to that of
airlines in general. However, certain characteristics related to international
operations stand out:

1   Fuel costs represent around 12–13 per cent of total operating costs. But
    this was in a year when fuel prices were relatively low. A figure of around
    15 per cent is more typical of recent years. Certainly with the increase in
    fuel prices seen in 2000 the relative importance of fuel costs was certain
    to increase.
2   Taken together, the cost of flight and cabin salaries and expenses account
    for around 14 per cent of total costs. They are a very expensive labour
    input. This is why airlines aiming to reduce or contain their labour costs
    place so much emphasis on these two staff categories (see Chapter 5.4).
3   Surprisingly, airport and en-route charges together total around 9 per
    cent of total costs. Twenty years earlier they were closer to 5 per cent.
    Airlines have some control over most of the other input costs and have
    been able to reduce them, in some cases not only in relative but also in
    absolute terms. But airport and en-route charges are non-negotiable and
    they have tended to increase in real terms as airport authorities and
    providers of air traffic control services have become more commercially

Table 4.4 Distribution of costs, IATA international scheduled services, 1999

	%	%
DIRECT OPERATING COSTS *(DOC)*		
Flight operations:		28.0
• Flight crew	(7.1)	
• Fuel and oil	(12.1)	
• Landing fees and en-route charges	(8.8)	
Maintenance		10.4
Depreciation/Rentals/Insurance		13.2
Total DOC		51.6
INDIRECT OPERATING COSTS *(IOC)*		
Station and ground		11.7
Passenger services:		13.9
• Cabin attendants	(7.2)	
• Other pax services	(6.7)	
Ticketing, sales and promotion		16.6
General and admin.		6.1
Total IOC		48.4
Total costs		100.0

Source: IATA (2000).

oriented and have been forced by governments to become more self-sufficient financially.

4 Aircraft ownership costs, that is, depreciation, lease rentals and aircraft insurance, account for around 13 per cent of total costs. For international airlines that own all their aircraft, depreciation alone will normally account for between 8 per cent and 12 per cent of their costs. The exact share will depend on the depreciation policy adopted and the age of the fleet; the younger the fleet the higher the relative impact of depreciation. When depreciation represents such a high proportion of total costs, changing the depreciation policy can reduce or increase *total costs* by 1–2 per cent.

5 Ticketing, sales and promotion costs are the major item of indirect operating costs, at around 16–17 per cent of total costs. In response to the growing liberalisation of international air services, competition in many markets has become more acute. As a result sales and promotion costs have tended to increase in importance. For instance, British Airways, which operates in many liberalised markets, found in the financial year 1999–2000 that ticketing, sales and promotion accounted for 19 per cent of its total costs.

6 Increased international competition has also tended to push up the relative significance of passenger service costs. While globally for all services they represent around 11 per cent of total costs (Table 4.3) for IATA airlines' international services the figure rises to 14 per cent. Growing efforts to

brand their product mean that many airlines are trying to differentiate their in-flight services by improved catering, more cabin attendants, better in-flight entertainment, and so on. Costs in this area are inevitably increasing.

4.6 The concept of escapability

4.6.1 An alternative approach to costing

The traditional classification of costs described above is essentially a functional one. Costs are allocated to particular functional areas within the airline, such as flight operations or maintenance, and are then grouped together in one of two categories, as either direct or indirect operating costs. This cost breakdown is of considerable value for accounting and general management purposes. It is particularly so where the organisational structure of an airline corresponds fairly closely to the same functional areas as may be used for costing purposes – in other words, where an airline has a flight operations division, an engineering (maintenance) division, a sales division, and so on. A functional classification of costs is useful for monitoring an airline's performance over time and also for inter-airline comparisons. Costs can be broken down relatively easily to produce disaggregate costs within a particular functional area. For instance, one could analyse separately labour costs in the maintenance area as opposed to the labour costs in station and ground operations.

In addition, the broad division into direct and indirect costs is especially useful when dealing with aircraft evaluation. The indirect costs of a particular network or operation can be assumed to remain constant, since they are unaffected by the type of aircraft used. An evaluation of a new aircraft type or a comparison between several aircraft for a particular network can then be based purely on an assessment of the direct operating costs. This simplifies the process of evaluation.

The great advantage of the traditional approach to cost classification is its simplicity and the fact that in allocating costs by functional area it avoids many of the problems associated with trying to allocate joint or common costs. For instance, station and ground costs common to a number of different services are grouped together and are not allocated to particular flights or services. However, the simplicity of this cost classification is also its major drawback. It is of only limited use for an economic evaluation of particular services or routes; or for pricing decisions; or for showing how costs may vary with changes in the pattern of operations on a particular route.

To aid decision making in these and other related areas the concept of *escapability* of costs needs to be introduced. The degree of escapability is determined by the time period required before a particular cost can be avoided. Some costs may be immediately escapable, as a result of a particular management decision, while others may not be avoided except in the very long run. The concept of escapability involves a temporal dimension. Different costs will require different periods before they can be avoided, but ultimately all costs are escapable. There is also a technical dimension to the concept, in that the degree of escapability also varies with the size and nature of the airline service or activity being considered. Thus, if all services on a particular route were to be cut, the nature of the escapable costs would be different from what it would be if only the flight on a particular day of the week was cancelled on the same route. The first course of action might involve not only a saving of flight operation costs but also the closure of a complete station or a reduction in the number of crews or even the number of aircraft in the fleet. Cancellation of only one flight a week might involve a reduction in some flight operation costs but little else. This is because many costs are joint or common costs which will go on being incurred to support the remaining flights even if one flight a week is cancelled. The interaction of the temporal and technical aspects of escapability must be constantly borne in mind by airline managers.

Airlines vary in the way they introduce the concept of escapability into their costing procedures. The most usual way is by adopting the traditional accounting distinction of fixed and variable costs. Airlines do this by taking those elements of cost generally accepted as being direct operating costs, together with some of the indirect costs, and further subdividing them into 'fixed' and 'variable' costs. There are several ways in which it can be done because of the temporal and technical considerations outlined above. The larger and more sophisticated airlines may use one breakdown of costs for, say, pricing decisions and a different one for evaluating the profitability of particular services or routes. One possible approach is discussed below.

4.6.2   Variable and fixed direct operating costs

Variable or *flying costs* are costs which are directly escapable in the short run. They are costs which would be avoided if a flight or a series of flights was cancelled. They are immediately escapable costs, such as fuel, flight crew overtime and other crew expenses arising in flying particular services, landing charges, the costs of passenger meals, and so on. These are fairly self-evident. Less self-evident are the engineering or maintenance costs which should be classified as variable. Certain maintenance checks of different parts of the aircraft, involving both labour costs and the replacement of spare parts, are scheduled to take place after so many hours of flying or after a prescribed number of flight cycles. (A flight cycle is one take-off and landing.) Undercarriage maintenance, for example, is related to the number of flight cycles. Since a large part of direct maintenance is related to the amount of flying or the flight cycles, cancelling a service will immediately reduce both the hours flown and the flight cycles and will save some engineering expenditure, notably on the consumption of spare parts, and some labour costs.

Fixed or *standing costs* are those direct operating costs which in the short run do not vary with particular flights or even a series of flights. They are costs which in the short or medium term are not escapable. They are certainly not escapable within one scheduling period. That is to say, having planned its schedules for a particular programme period and adjusted its fleet, staff and maintenance requirements to meet that particular schedules programme, an airline cannot easily cut back its schedules and services, because of public reaction and its own obligations to the public, until the next schedules programme is introduced. New schedules would normally be introduced twice a year. If the airline decided to cut back its frequencies when the next schedules programme was introduced, it could reduce its fleet by selling some aircraft and it could reduce its staff numbers and cut its maintenance and other overheads. Fixed or standing direct operating costs may be escapable but only after a year or two, depending on how quickly the airline could actually change its schedules and cut back on aircraft, staff, and so on. Thus most staff costs for pilots, cabin crew or maintenance engineers are fixed in the short term but staff travel expenses or pilots' bonuses related to flying activity would be a variable cost.

While most *indirect operating costs* are fixed costs in that they do not depend in the short term on the amount of flying undertaken, others are more directly dependent on the operation of particular flights. This is particularly true of some passenger service costs such as in-flight catering and hotel expenses and some elements of cabin crew costs. Fees paid to handling agents or other airlines for ground handling of aircraft, passengers or freight can be avoided if a flight is not operated. Some advertising and promotional costs may also be escapable in the short run. Airlines breaking their costs down according to their escapability take some or all of the above expenses previously categorised as indirect costs and redefine them as fixed or variable direct operating costs. This leaves within the indirect cost category costs which are not dependent on the operation of particular services or routes. They are fixed in the short term.

One possible division of costs based on the concept of escapability is shown in Table 4.5. All direct operating costs have been divided into fixed or variable. In addition, all cabin crew costs, handling fees paid to others and the costs of in-flight catering and passenger hotels, all previously categorised as indirect operating costs (in Table 4.2), are here shown as direct costs. Handling and passenger service costs are now deemed to be variable costs, as are some cabin crew costs. But most cabin crew costs are fixed direct costs.

The concept of cost escapability has been applied to British Airways, whose cost structure is fairly typical for a major international airline with a well-developed short-, medium- and long-haul network. Using published operating cost data for the financial year April 1999 to March 2000, it proved possible to break down British Airways' costs in the way suggested earlier. The breakdown is shown in greater detail in Figure 4.2. It is clear that in 1999–2000 more than a third of BA's total operating costs, or 40 per cent, were immediately escapable. Just over a quarter of costs, 27 per cent, were fixed direct operating costs and a further third or so, 33 per cent, were indirect operating costs. Clearly, variable costs are significant. By cancelling a scheduled flight one may save up to 40 per cent of total costs but in the short run not

Table 4.5 Cost structure based on fixed and variable direct operating costs

Variable direct operating costs	Fixed/standing direct operating costs	Indirect operating costs
1 Fuel costs:[a] • Fuel • Oil consumed • Water methanol (if any)	7 Aircraft standing charges: • Depreciation or lease rentals • Aircraft insurance	11 Station and ground expenses
2 Variable flight crew costs:[a] • Flight crew subsistence and bonuses	8 Annual flight crew costs:[a] • Fixed salaries and other expenses unrelated to amount of flying done • Flight crew administration	12 Passenger services: • Passenger service staff • Passenger insurance
3 Variable cabin crew costs: • Cabin crew subsistence and bonuses	9 Annual cabin crew costs: • Fixed salaries and other expenses unrelated to amount of flying done • Cabin crew administration	13 Ticketing, sales and promotion
4 Direct engineering costs: • Related to number of flight cycles • Aircraft utilisation	10 Engineering overheads: • Fixed engineering staff costs unrelated to number of flying hours • Maintenance administration and other overheads	14 General and administrative
5 Airport and en-route charges: • Landing fees and other airport charges • En-route navigation charges		
6 Passenger service costs:[a] • Passenger meals/hotel expenses • Handling fees paid to others		

Note
a These items were previously categorised as 'indirect' (Table 4.2).

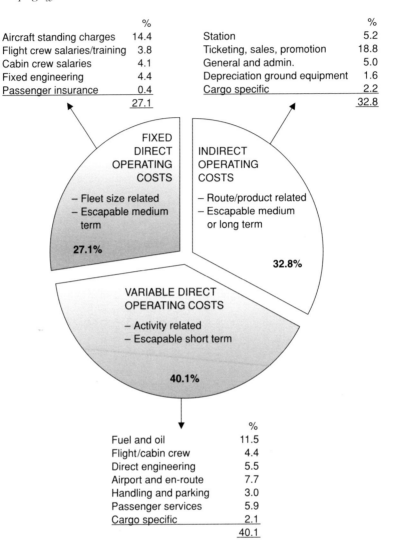

	%		%
Aircraft standing charges	14.4	Station	5.2
Flight crew salaries/training	3.8	Ticketing, sales, promotion	18.8
Cabin crew salaries	4.1	General and admin.	5.0
Fixed engineering	4.4	Depreciation ground equipment	1.6
Passenger insurance	0.4	Cargo specific	2.2
	27.1		32.8

FIXED
DIRECT
OPERATING
COSTS

– Fleet size related
– Escapable medium
  term

27.1%

INDIRECT
OPERATING
COSTS

– Route/product related
– Escapable medium
  or long term

32.8%

VARIABLE DIRECT
OPERATING COSTS

– Activity related
– Escapable short term

40.1%

	%
Fuel and oil	11.5
Flight/cabin crew	4.4
Direct engineering	5.5
Airport and en-route	7.7
Handling and parking	3.0
Passenger services	5.9
Cargo specific	2.1
	40.1

Figure 4.2 British Airways' costs in terms of escapability, 1999–2000.

much more. Thus in the months after September 2001 when most airlines were cutting routes or reducing frequencies in order to cut capacity by 15–20 per cent, the short-term impact on cost reduction was much less. A 20 per cent cut in capacity flown might produce only an 8 per cent or so cut in costs (i.e. only the variable costs would be cut in the short term). It would take much longer to cut staff numbers, reduce aircraft standing charges or other fixed costs. This is why the crisis was so deep. There is always a lag between cutting capacity or output and achieving a similar reduction in operating costs.

Variable costs are related to an airline's activity level, that is, the amount of flying it actually does. The high proportion of variable costs indicated in the British Airways example has important implications for operations planning and for pricing. It shows that significant savings can be achieved in the short term by cancelling a flight or a series of flights. The potential savings are greatest when the price of fuel is high, since that increases the relative proportion of variable costs. For example, because fuel prices in much of 1998 were very low, the share of fuel costs in BA's overall cost structure in the financial year 1998–99 was unusually low at 8 per cent, compared with 11.5 per cent in the following year.

Variable costs are those that are immediately escapable. In the medium term – that is, within a period of a year or so – many fixed direct operating costs previously considered fixed start to become variable. Such costs are essentially related to the size of the fleet. If the fleet size is reduced, many fixed costs can be reduced too. Aircraft can be sold, cutting depreciation costs, flight and cabin crew numbers can be run down or staff redeployed, and engineering staff facilities can be reduced in size.

Indirect operating costs tend to be related primarily to the number of routes being operated, the quality of service offered and the nature of the sales and distribution systems built up to support the network. Advertising and promotion costs are also influenced by the route structure. The number of routes operated can be cut back in the medium term and over a longer period the whole network can be modified. Thus even some indirect operating costs are escapable in the medium term and most are escapable in the longer term. In short, elements of both fixed direct costs and indirect costs are escapable in the medium term. Ultimately all costs are escapable. What is perhaps more significant and often forgotten is that as much as 90 per cent of total costs can be varied in the medium term, that is, after a year or so, either by discontinuing all operations or by a partial withdrawal of certain operations. Airlines can disinvest or drastically cut their operations more easily than most forms of public transport because they do not have fixed investments in navigational aids, runways or terminals, though there may be some exceptions, as in North America, where airlines may own and operate their own terminals.

4.7   Allocation of costs for operating decisions

In order to be able to use the concept of cost escapability in making operating decisions – such as whether to reduce or increase frequencies on a route or whether to open an entirely new route – the various fixed and variable costs need to be allocated to individual flights or routes. Broadly speaking, the approach adopted by various airlines is similar, though there may be differences in the details.

Allocating *variable direct operating costs* is fairly straightforward, since nearly all of them are specific to individual flights. Fuel costs, variable flight and cabin crew costs, airport and en-route charges and passenger service costs (as defined in Table 4.5) depend directly on the type and size of the aircraft used and the route over which it is being flown. They are clearly very specific and can easily be measured. The exceptions are the variable engineering or maintenance costs. Here some averaging out is required.

Some direct maintenance work and checks are related to the amount of flying that an aircraft undertakes, while other checks depend on the number of flight cycles. Maintenance on those parts of the aircraft which are most under pressure on landing or departure, such as the undercarriage or the flaps, is clearly related to the flight cycles undertaken. For each aircraft type an airline will normally work out an average cost of maintenance per block hour and a separate average cost per flight cycle. The variable maintenance cost of an individual flight can then be calculated on the basis of the number of block hours and flight cycles required for that flight.

An airline's *fixed direct operating costs* are normally converted into a cost per block hour for each aircraft type in its fleet. They can then be allocated to each flight or route on the basis of the aircraft type(s) being used and the block times for the sector or route. The first element of fixed direct operating costs is aircraft standing costs, that is, depreciation and any rentals for leased aircraft plus aircraft insurance. Such costs are aircraft type-specific, since they depend on the purchase price or lease rate of the aircraft. They are a fixed annual cost, based on the number of aircraft of a particular type, which when divided by the annual utilisation of the aircraft produces a depreciation and insurance cost per block hour (see section 4.3 above). If aircraft are leased there is normally an annual leasing cost made up of twelve equal monthly payments. These are fixed annual costs independent of how much flying is undertaken. Therefore the hourly lease cost, as with depreciation, depends on the number of hours flown each year. In addition airlines may have to pay a separate hourly charge per block hour into a 'maintenance reserve'. This is a fixed hourly charge. The total annual amount paid is dependent on the amount of flying undertaken. Its purpose is to build up a cash reserve for costly major overhauls known as D checks. Though needed for maintenance, the hourly maintenance reserve charge is often included under rentals.

It is relatively easy to identify and allocate the fixed annual flight crew costs, since each aircraft type has its own dedicated complement of pilots, co-pilots and, for older types, flight engineers. In many cases, if there are several aircraft of a particular type, that fleet will have its own administrative managers as well. Some flight crew overheads, however, will not be aircraft type-specific and will need to be allocated on some basis between the different aircraft types, usually the number of aircraft or annual utilisation. The total annual fixed flight crew cost for a fleet of aircraft of a particular type can then be divided by the total annual utilisation (that is, block hours flown) of all the aircraft in that fleet to arrive at a flight crew cost per block hour for that aircraft type.

A similar approach is adopted with other fixed elements of direct operating costs. In the case of cabin crew, problems of allocating fixed annual costs between aircraft types arise because, unlike flight crew, cabin crew can work on different aircraft types at any time. Nevertheless, the annual cabin crew costs can be apportioned to different aircraft types on the basis of the number and seniority of the cabin crew they use and the sectors they fly on. Some fixed maintenance costs will be aircraft type-specific, others will be common costs that need to be allocated between aircraft types, usually on the basis of maintenance man hours required for different aircraft. Thus, for each aircraft type, airlines can estimate an hourly flight crew and cabin crew cost and an hourly maintenance cost to cover the fixed element of such costs. Some airlines take this process a step further and calculate different hourly crew and maintenance costs for different types of routes. For instance, some carriers use a higher hourly flight crew cost for a given aircraft type when it is flying on short sectors than when it is used on longer sectors.

Since all the fixed direct costs discussed above are allocated to specific aircraft types, some airlines refer to them as 'fleet' costs, associated with operating a fleet of aircraft of a particular type.

When one turns to *indirect operating costs* difficult problems of allocation arise, since by definition such costs are independent of the type of aircraft being operated. Some indirect costs may be route-specific and may be escapable in the medium term if a whole route operation is closed down. If an airline operates a single route to another country, the sales and advertising costs in that country as well as the station and ground costs at the airport served can be readily identified as a cost specific to that route. But most indirect costs are fixed joint and common costs that cannot be easily allocated to individual flights or routes except on some arbitrary basis. Most station costs, passenger insurance expenses and the costs of ticketing, sales and promotion as well as overhead administrative costs will normally be allocated to particular services or routes on the basis of some output measure such as the revenue tonne kilometres or revenue generated. Each approach has its advantages and drawbacks. Using a traffic measure, such as the revenue tonne kilometres generated on each route, may penalise long-haul routes where tonne kilometres generated are high but revenues per kilometre are low because fares, like costs, taper with distance. Allocating indirect costs on the basis of the revenue earned on each route or flight may appear more equitable, but would entail bias against shorter routes where fares per kilometre are high. More than one allocative method may be used. Sales, ticketing and passenger service costs may be divided between flights on the basis of passenger kilometres produced, while cargo-specific costs may be apportioned using freight tonne kilometres carried.

Using an allocative method such as that outlined above, but adapted to its own particular requirements and accounting procedures, an airline can allocate costs to individual flights or routes. Such costs would be made up of four elements:

1   All *variable direct operating costs*. These can be calculated per flight or aggregated to arrive at the variable direct operating costs for a particular

route. (Such costs are likely to be in the range of 30–45 per cent of total operating costs.)

2   Those *indirect operating costs which are route-specific* such as advertising in the destination country or region or station costs. Such costs can, if necessary, be broken down further and allocated to individual flights on the route (generally 5–10 per cent of total operating costs).

3   *The fixed direct operating costs* which are joint costs and are normally allocated to each flight or route on the basis of the block hours flown, as shown earlier (ranging between 25 per cent and 30 per cent of total costs).

4   Those *indirect operating costs which are not route-specific* and which have been allocated to each flight or route on the basis of some output or revenue measure (25–35 per cent of total costs).

By comparing these costs with the revenues generated, airline planners are in a position to make decisions as to the number of frequencies that should operate on a route or whether the route should be operated at all. Some airlines and analysts assess flights or routes in terms of their contribution to overhead or fixed costs. In other words, a particular flight or route is expected at least to cover its flight or route-specific costs (items 1 and 2 above) out of the revenues it generates. If it does not do so at present and is unlikely to do so in the near future then its continued operation must be in doubt. Revenues in excess of the route- or flight-specific costs are deemed to make a *contribution* to fixed direct costs and to non-specific indirect costs. Ideally, revenues should cover all these allocated costs too. Even if they do not, the key issue is the level of the contribution that revenue generated by a particular route makes to such costs. Discontinuing flights will not save any of the fixed direct and indirect costs in the short term. Thus some contribution to meeting these costs is better than none. In the medium and longer term fixed direct operating costs can be cut by reducing fleet size, while indirect costs can be reduced by abandoning routes or downsizing the network and level of operations.

If there are many routes which cover their variable and specific costs but make only a marginal contribution to overheads, that is, fixed direct and indirect costs, an airline is haemorrhaging. It would be wise in the medium term to cut out those routes which make only a minimal contribution and have little prospect of improving and to downsize both the fleet and the operations. Unfortunately airline managers are generally reluctant to take such corrective action, even when the need becomes obvious, except at times of real crisis. This occurred after September 2001 when US airlines cut up to 30 per cent of their services and European airlines 10–20 per cent. But many routes and frequencies cut then, especially in international markets, should have been cut well before September. But few airline executives have the nerve to cut services quickly when market conditions begin to worsen.

5 Determinants of airline costs

It is vital that if we are to survive in the current climate we continue to examine and drive down costs.

(Austin Reid, CEO, British Midland, November 2001)

5.1 Management control of costs

It was suggested in the previous chapter that variable operating costs, which may represent up to 40 per cent or so of total operating costs, can be escaped in the short term by the cancellation or withdrawal of services. In the medium term a very much higher proportion of costs is escapable. Perhaps as much as 90 per cent of costs can be saved by the disposal of aircraft, reduction of staff, closing of offices and so on within two years or so. Through the ability to increase or reduce the scale and pattern of operations airline managements can directly affect their total costs. In this sense management control over costs may be absolute and constrained only by the desires of shareholders, whether governments or private individuals or firms. Clearly, overall costs are broadly determined by the level of supply, that is, the volume of output, decided upon by the management. But once a level of output has been decided and is being planned for, what factors then determine the precise level of unit costs, that is, costs per tonne kilometre or seat kilometre, that will be incurred?

The theme of this book is that airline planning and management are about the process of profitably matching supply, which within certain constraints an airline can very largely control, with demand, which it can influence but cannot control. Low unit costs in themselves do not ensure efficiency or guarantee profitability if an airline fails to generate sufficiently high revenues. Nevertheless, controlling and, if possible, reducing costs is a key management objective. As both domestic and international markets have become liberalised, competition and especially price competition has intensified. In virtually all markets average yields per passenger kilometre have tended over time to drift downward in real terms. This has reinforced pressure to reduce unit costs. But can airline managements influence and reduce unit costs? Or are such costs very largely determined externally by factors and developments beyond management control?

Table 5.1 Unit operating costs of major international airlines, financial year 1999 (cents per available tonne kilometre)

Rank	North American		European		East Asian	
1			Lufthansa	58.6		
2			Alitalia	57.0		
3					All Nippon (1998)	56.2
4					JAL	53.2
5			Iberia	53.1		
6	Continental	50.5				
7			British Airways	49.6		
8	Delta	44.5				
9	Air Canada	42.4				
10			KLM	42.2		
11	American	41.9				
12	United	41.7				
13			Air France	41.5		
14	Northwest	39.4				
15					Thai Airways	31.2
16					Cathay	29.3
17					SIA	25.8
18					Korean	22.2

Source: Compiled using ICAO (1999b) data.

It is evident that among international airlines unit costs vary widely. Table 5.1 shows the unit costs of the six largest international passenger carriers in each of three regions of the world. Together these eighteen airlines carried over half (around 55 per cent) of the world's international tonne kilometres in 2000. The unit costs are for their total operations. (Subsequent tables also refer to these eighteen airlines except where data are unavailable.) The table amply illustrates both the wide range in cost levels between airlines and the existence of marked regional variations. High-cost airlines such as Lufthansa, Alitalia or Japan Airlines have unit costs around twice as high as Singapore Airlines or Cathay Pacific at the bottom of the table. East Asia is the region which clearly stands out as having the lowest cost airlines, though it also encompasses one or two high-cost operators, notably the Japanese airlines Japan Airlines and All Nippon Airways. The North American majors are moderately low-cost operators and it is noticeable that, if one excludes Continental, there is relatively little variation in unit cost levels between them. In contrast, five of the European carriers tend to be grouped at the top of the list, indicating relatively high costs.

To gain an insight into the causes of such a wide diversity of unit costs between airlines one needs to assess the determinants of operating costs, paying particular attention to the degree to which they can be influenced by management.

The numerous factors which affect airline operating costs can be grouped into three broad categories according to the degree to which they are under

Table 5.2 Factors affecting airline operating costs

Factor	Degree of management control		
External economic factors	Little		
Cost of labour		Some	
Type/Characteristics of aircraft used		Some	
Route structure/Network characteristics		Some	
Airline marketing and product policy			High
Airline financial policy			High
Corporate strategy			High
Quality of management			High

management control (Table 5.2). First, one can identify a number of external economic factors over which airlines have little control. Such factors include the prevailing fuel prices, airport and en-route navigation charges and certain distribution costs. An airline has to accept these as more or less given and can only marginally mitigate their impact through negotiations with service providers or fuel suppliers. The levels and patterns of demand that an international airline is trying to satisfy are also largely externally determined by economic and geographical factors beyond its control.

Second, there are three major determinants of costs over which airlines have somewhat greater but still limited control. These are staff costs, the type of aircraft used and the pattern of operations for which the aircraft are used. While the latter two of these may seem to be entirely at the discretion of airline management, in practice managements' hands are tied to some extent by factors beyond their control. The geographical location of an airline's home base, the bilateral air service agreements signed by its government, the traffic density on its routes and other such factors will strongly influence the type of aircraft required and the network operated. Management does not have an entirely free hand to do as it wishes. This is particularly true of national airlines in countries with only one flag carrier, especially if it is majority-owned by the government.

The third category of cost determinants is that over which management has a high level of control or even total control. Marketing, product planning and financial policy fall into this category, as does corporate strategy. In the final analysis one must also consider the quality of management and its efficiency as a cost determinant. It is crucial because management determines the degree to which the impact of the other factors mentioned above, whether favourable or unfavourable, can be modified to the benefit of the airline concerned.

The analysis in this chapter of the effect of different variables on costs is qualitative rather than quantitative. Some earlier studies have used various forms of multivariate analysis to establish the influence of a range of independent variables (for instance, airline size, pilot wage levels or stage length) on a dependent variable such as unit costs or labour productivity. For instance, Pearson (1977) used a multivariate approach in a comparative assessment of

European airlines in the mid-1970s. In theory multivariate analysis should be able to establish the relative impact of the various independent variables on the unit costs of the airlines concerned. Certainly Pearson in his work was able to produce high coefficients of determination, suggesting that a high proportion of the variations in the dependent variable could be explained by variations in the independent variables. Subsequent work by the UK Civil Aviation Authority (1977, appendix B) questioned the value of multivariate analysis. The CAA carried out its own multivariate analysis of European airline performance. For instance, it examined labour productivity as a dependent variable. Using different independent variables from Pearson but comparable ones, it was able to produce equally high coefficients of determination. But one or two airlines that were labour-efficient when analysed by Pearson were inefficient in their use of labour when assessed by the CAA model. Such discrepancies occurred in other areas too. Two models using the same technique and broadly comparable sets of explanatory variables should have produced consistent results. The fact that they did not raises serious doubts about the validity of multivariate analysis for comparative studies of international airlines.

It has subsequently been argued by some economists that studies such as those mentioned above are essentially inductive. They can correlate events rather than establish cause and effect between them. This is an added shortcoming of such an approach. The alternative might be to develop a deductive approach which by using selected measures of total factor productivity allows comparisons between airlines in different countries by adjusting for differences in factor prices, network characteristics, aircraft size, and so on (see, for example, Tae Hoon Oum and Chunyan Yu, 1995). This is an interesting and potentially valuable approach, but it is mathematically complex. While a good descriptor of an airline's overall productivity, total factor productivity is of more limited value as a management tool that can pinpoint where corrective action is needed. In order to provide a better conceptual understanding of the determinants of airline costs a more qualitative approach would appear to be preferable to both the above techniques and has been adopted in the analysis which follows.

5.2   The influence of demand on costs

Before assessing the factors which directly impact on the costs of supplying airline services it is important to appreciate that demand too impacts on unit costs. It is generally understood and accepted that airline costs have a direct impact on the demand for air services, since they influence the prices at which those services are sold. Costs also reflect service quality and other product features. What is frequently forgotten, however, is that costs are not entirely independent of demand. They are themselves influenced by demand. There is a two-way relationship between supply (costs) and demand. Each affects the other. There are two aspects of demand, in particular, which impact on costs, namely *route traffic density* and *sector length*.

The traffic density on a route and the sector length(s) on that route will influence the size and type of aircraft chosen for that route. Aircraft type, and more especially the size of the aircraft, is a key determinant of unit costs. Route traffic density also influences the frequencies which are needed and will thereby affect the annual utilisation, that is, the number of hours flown by each aircraft. The higher the utilisation the lower the costs. Traffic density also affects the level of station costs per passenger or per tonne of cargo. Since station costs do not go up in proportion to the traffic handled, more traffic going through a station means lower costs per unit of traffic. These relationships will become clearer in the following sections. There is one other aspect of demand which impacts on costs and that is the variations in demand over time. Marked seasonal peaks create a need for extra capacity in terms of aircraft, crew, ticketing and sales staff, catering facilities and so on which may be grossly underutilised in off-peak periods. Carrying that extra capacity during the off-peak is costly. From a cost point of view airlines are better off if they are trying to satisfy a pattern of demand that is more or less constant throughout the year (Chapter 7.6).

In a truly open and competitive environment airlines would be free to choose their own markets in terms of the length of routes and traffic densities that they wished to serve. This may be the case among US domestic airlines and to a more limited extent among European charter airlines and airlines operating entirely within the European Union. But the vast majority of international airlines do not have a free hand with regard to the demand that they set out to satisfy. The routes they serve and the density of demand on those routes are determined largely by the interplay of geographical, political, economic and social factors outside the airlines' control. The starting point for any international airline is its home base. The geographical location of the home base, together with the level of business and tourist interaction between the home country and other countries, will influence the potential sector lengths and traffic densities that can be fruitfully operated. Australia and Malta represent the two extremes. A major international airline based in Australia must operate a long-haul network with some very long sectors because of Australia's geographical isolation and the long distances to key markets. Conversely the national airline of Malta, as a result of the island's location on the southern periphery of Europe and its small size, is predestined to be a short- to medium-haul airline with only a small number of relatively thin routes.

Where an airline is a country's only international airline, as is frequently the case, it may also be under political pressure to operate some routes which it would otherwise ignore. Conversely, where there are several international carriers, as in the United Kingdom or the United States, these may have much more choice as to the routes they can serve.

Though constrained by some of the above factors airlines do have some ability to influence the patterns of demand on the routes they serve or wish to serve. First, they can as a matter of policy concentrate on the denser traffic sectors. Second, they can try to increase the total traffic on their routes through their marketing policy and their promotional activity. Third, they can try to improve their own traffic density by increasing their market share when they have competitors on the route. Many airlines put considerable marketing effort into increasing their market share on their major routes. Greater market share is seen as a key objective, not merely because it increases their revenues but also because it can help them to reduce costs.

5.3   Externally determined input costs

The costs of a number of key airline inputs or factors of production are determined by external economic variables and are largely outside the control of individual airline managements. Since the external variables vary between countries and regions the factor input costs of different airlines may also vary significantly. While airlines can try to reduce the prices of their inputs, in the case of some key inputs they can do so to only a limited extent. They have to accept the general level of these input prices as given and they have only limited scope to negotiate downwards from that given level. Another feature of these input prices is that they are subject to sudden and often marked fluctuations. Adjusting to sudden changes in the price of fuel or in the level of charges at a particular airport is a common headache among airline managers.

5.3.1   *Price of aviation fuel*

The price of aviation fuel at any airport depends partly on the companies supplying the fuel and partly on the government of the country concerned. As far as the fuel companies are concerned, the price of crude oil and of refinery costs are broadly similar worldwide. But distribution and handling costs vary considerably. While oil refineries are widely scattered around the world, only a relatively small number refine jet fuel. The supply of fuel to some airports may involve lengthy and costly transportation especially if the airport is well away from a seaport. Transport costs also rise if the total volume of fuel supplied to an airport is small. Handling costs at airports vary in relation to the facilities used and the volume of fuel uplifted. Governments may influence the price of jet fuel in two ways. They may impose import duties or some other kind of tax, though most governments do neither of these things to fuel supplied for international flights. Some governments may also try to control or fix the price of fuel as a matter of policy. During the 1970s both the US and Australian governments maintained domestic crude oil prices and the prices of refined products at well below world levels but subsequently abandoned the policy. As a result, in both countries the price of jet fuel is now closer to prices in other countries. But some states still continue to impose price controls on aviation fuel.

Because of the above factors there are quite marked regional variations in jet fuel prices. African airlines seem particularly disadvantaged by the very high fuel prices at most African airports, especially those south of the Sahara. Inland locations, long distances from oil refineries producing aviation fuel and

Table 5.3 Average fuel prices paid by international scheduled airlines, September 1999

Region	Average fuel/oil price paid (cents per US gallon)	Index (North America = 100)
Africa	88.3	134
Middle East	85.8	130
Eastern Europe	77.1	117
Mediterranean	74.3	113
Latin America	72.5	110
Far East/Pacific	72.3	110
Western Europe	67.1	102
North America	66.0	100
World average	70.4	

Source: IATA.

relatively small volumes of fuel uplift seem to be the root cause of fuel prices which are on average a third higher than those in North America or Europe (Table 5.3). Surprisingly, Middle East airports also have expensive fuel, largely because the nearby refineries do not produce sufficient jet fuel. The lowest fuel prices are in the United States and Canada, closely followed by prices in West European airports.

The interplay of crude oil prices, oil company costs and pricing strategies and individual government policies on taxation and on fuel price control determines the posted fuel prices at airports around the world. The posted price is the price that an airline without regular scheduled services may have to pay. In practice few airlines pay the posted price. Regular users of an airport will negotiate their own contract price with the fuel suppliers. This will be at a discount on the posted price, the level of the discount depending on the total tonnage of fuel that an airline expects to uplift during the contract period. This in turn will depend on the number of daily departures an airline operates from that particular airport, the size of the aircraft being used and the sector distances over which they will be flying. Clearly an airline is likely to pay the lowest price at its own home base airport, as it will be by far the biggest user of fuel.

The discount will also be influenced by the number of fuel suppliers. If there is only one oil company providing fuel, the scope for pushing the price down is clearly limited. At most airports around the world there are generally only a few available fuel companies. In the United States, on the other hand, the existence of a large number of small refineries and of common carrier pipelines open to use by any company has resulted in a very large number of companies competing for fuel supply contracts. This creates a strong downward pressure on jet fuel prices. In a few countries such as India fuel prices may be fixed by the government and may be non-negotiable.

While the prices negotiated in individual fuel contracts are confidential there are prevailing discount levels at each airport depending on an airline's

Table 5.4 Average fuel prices paid by international airlines at twenty-five selected airports, October 2001 (cents per US gallon)

Rank	Africa		Middle East		Asia/Pacific		Europe/USA	
1							Budapest	113.4
2	Lagos	110.9						
3					Delhi	107.0		
4			Jeddah	101.2				
5	Dakar	100.2						
6					Karachi	98.9		
7							Zurich	98.5
8							Vienna	97.0
9			Dubai	96.1				
10			Bahrain	95.6				
11	Nairobi	95.4						
12					Tokyo	89.5		
13							Madrid	88.5
14			Cairo	87.6				
15							Athens	87.4
16							Paris CDG	87.2
17							Rome	86.4
18							Frankfurt	85.8
19							London LHR	83.7
20							Amsterdam	83.4
21					K. Lumpur	82.4		
22					Singapore	80.8		
23					Bangkok	79.7		
24							Chicago	75.9
25							New York	72.3

Source: Compiled by the author using IATA data.

total fuel uplift. Each airline has a fairly good idea what other airlines are paying. Thus airlines each operating twice-daily long-haul departures from London Heathrow airport with Boeing 747 aircraft will all end up paying very similar prices. The exact price will depend on the negotiating skill of each airline's fuel buyer. The latter may try to get a better price by negotiating with one fuel company for the supply of fuel at several airports.

But ultimately it is the prevailing market price at each airport and the accepted discount levels that will determine the fuel prices at any airport. The airline fuel buyer who is a good negotiator may shave one or two or even more tenths of a US cent off the price per gallon, but he can do little more. Fuel prices are largely externally determined by prevailing market conditions at each airport.

The level of fuel prices paid by airlines varies markedly between airports – even between airports in the same region. This is evident from Table 5.4, which shows the average fuel prices paid by international airlines at twenty-five selected airports around the world in October 2001. This was after the sharp increases in fuel prices that occurred during 2000 owing to external factors, namely OPEC cutbacks in production. While fuel prices dropped back during 2001, the October 2001 prices were generally 15–20 per cent higher than they had been in October 1999. Fuel prices were highest at African and Middle East airports and, as expected, fuel at New York and other US airports was the cheapest. In Europe and Asia there is great diversity in price levels. Clearly, Malev, the Hungarian airline based in Budapest, and Air India flying out of Delhi face the problem that fuel at their main base, where their fuel uplift is greatest, is relatively expensive. Even though as the largest buyers they will be paying less than the average price shown (Table 5.4), high fuel prices at their home base will inevitably push up their operating costs. On the other hand Singapore Airlines or Malaysia Airlines benefit from very low fuel prices at their home airport, as do US carriers.

Airlines can try to mitigate the impact of high fuel prices at certain airports by reducing their fuel uplift at those airports to the minimum necessary. Instead, captains may be instructed to tanker as much fuel as possible at airports where fuel prices are low. Such a policy, however, needs careful monitoring, since extra fuel will be burnt during the flight to carry the additional fuel loaded. This is because fuel consumption increases as the total weight of the aircraft increases.

An added problem for airlines is that oil companies insist on escalation clauses in fuel supply contracts. These allow the fuel price to move up or down in response to changes in the price of crude oil. Airlines can no longer use fixed-price contracts to isolate themselves from external economic factors leading to a sudden jump in the price of aviation fuel. However, they can hedge against future increases in fuel prices by buying fuel forward for future delivery at fixed prices. Some did this in early 1999 as prices began to rise. As a result they were temporarily shielded from the more hefty price rises in late 1999 and 2000.

Delta Air Lines provides an interesting example of how airlines were hedging against increases in fuel costs during 1999 and 2000 when prices were rising sharply. Delta hedged by taking out so-called *call options* on heating oil because its prices closely track those of jet fuel. Call options give the airline the right but not the obligation to buy heating oil at set prices on given future dates. The airline paid a premium for this right. If actual prices on the date set were below the agreed set prices, the airline could walk away but lose the premium. If market prices were above the set price plus the premium, the airline could buy heating oil at the previously agreed set price and resell at the market price, making a profit. Such profits could then be used to offset any higher prices for aviation fuel. In the fifteen months to September 2000 Delta had paid around $100 million in premiums on call options but had netted a surplus of $600 million from hedging (*International Herald Tribune*, 23 October 2000). But, to reduce the risks of hedging, Delta would normally take out call options to cover only around half its fuel needs. Delta had been hedging in this way against fuel price increases since about 1996.

The differential impact of fluctuating exchange rates may also adversely affect some airlines, since fuel prices in most parts of the world are quoted in US dollars. If the dollar exchange rate of a particular currency drops rapidly the cost of fuel in that country in terms of its own currency will rise equally rapidly. This will hit hardest the country's own national airline, most of whose earnings will be in local currency. This happened in several countries such as Thailand and Indonesia in 1997–98 as a result of the economic crisis which hit East Asia. The deep devaluation of their currencies pushed up their airlines' fuel costs significantly.

Fuel prices are largely externally determined, yet for most airlines they represent between 10 per cent and 15 per cent of total operating costs. While able to influence the basic price of fuel only marginally, airlines can lower their fuel costs by trying to reduce their fuel consumption. A number of options are open to them. They can try and reduce the weight of their various aircraft by using lighter equipment in the cabin, and less paint on the fuselage. They can also reduce weight by avoiding unnecessary 'tankering', that is, carrying more fuel than is required to meet safety minima on a particular sector. Then they can save fuel by reducing the aircraft cruising speed. A 3–4 per cent reduction in the cruising speed of a jet aircraft on a sector of one hour or more may reduce fuel consumption by 6–7 per cent at the cost of a few minutes' extra flying. Computerised flight planning can also help. By choosing slower rates of climb or descent and higher cruise altitudes, where available, airlines may be able further to reduce the fuel consumed. But ultimately the biggest savings come from switching to newer more fuel-efficient aircraft, especially where one can replace three or four-engined jets by aircraft having fewer and more advanced engines.

5.3.2 User charges

For the world's airlines as a whole user charges, that is, airport charges and en-route facility charges, account for just over 7 per cent of their total costs. For international airlines the figure rises to 9 per cent (Tables 4.3 and 4.4). But these are global figures. For those international airlines operating relatively short sectors, where landings occur more frequently, the impact of user charges is much greater. Thus in 1999 Finnair and British Midland, both primarily short-haul airlines, found that airport and en-route navigation charges together represented well over 10 per cent of their total costs. For Finnair it was 16.6 per cent and for British Midland 14.5 per cent. For KLM UK, an operator with even shorter sectors, such charges represented 23.5 per cent of its total costs in 1999. Yet for some airlines such as Iberia or SIA the proportion dropped to below 6 per cent, while for US carriers it was generally 2–4 per cent.

User charges, like fuel prices, are largely externally determined. But, unlike fuel, user charges allow little room for manoeuvre. While the airlines as a whole, acting through IATA, may try to hold increases in landing fees or

Table 5.5 Representative airport charges for a Boeing 747-400 aircraft,[a] October 2000 ($ per turn-round)

	Airport charge related to:		Airport charges Total	Government taxes
	Aircraft 1	Passenger 2	3	4
New York JFK	10,681	5,614	16,295	8,308
Tokyo NRT	9,779	6,265	16,044	0
Nairobi	1,969	13,400	15,369	0
Buenos Aires EZE	4,372	6,868	11,240	3,350
Atlanta	340	10,272	10,612	8,308
Vienna	4,176	4,502	8,678	0
Frankfurt	3,366	4,909	8,276	0
Miami	1,298	6,973	8,271	8,308
Amsterdam	3,523	4,166	7,689	0
Manchester	2,891	4,549	7,439	9,683
Paris CDG	3,591	2,404	5,995	678
Delhi	1,954	3,618	5,572	0
Hong Kong	3,714	1,676	5,390	2,149
London LHR[b]	1,797	3,583	5,380	9,683
Bangkok	1,541	3,836	5,376	0
Singapore	2,220	2,864	5,085	0
Cairo	2,399	2,651	5,051	0
Rome FCO	2,250	2,763	5,013	0
Johannesburg	1,740	3,121	4,862	4,425
Madrid	2,644	1,929	4,574	0
London LGW[b]	1,410	3,050	4,461	9,683

Source: Aeronautical Charges Unit, Air Transport Group, Cranfield University.

Notes
a With 395 t MTOW, 335 passengers and parking for three hours.
b London-Heathrow (LHR) and Gatwick (LGW) are a weighted average of peak and off-peak charges.

en-route charges down in a particular country, an individual airline has no scope for negotiating better rates for itself. All are in the same boat. This is because under Article 15 of the 1944 Chicago Convention all airlines are to be treated equally. There should be no discrimination. In practice, some airports may offer reduced charges for two or three years to airlines opening new routes. But such reductions are in theory open to all operators of new services.

The level of *airport charges* will depend partly on the costs at the airports and partly on whether the airport authority or the government is trying to recover those costs fully or even make a profit. As a result, landing and passenger-related charges vary enormously between different airports. It is evident from Table 5.5 that JAL, operating a Boeing 747 flight from Tokyo, has to pay around $5,400 when landing at London Heathrow. But on returning to Tokyo the airport charges are three times as high. Clearly airlines based in high-cost airports such as Tokyo or Nairobi face a significant cost disadvantage, since a high proportion of their landings will be at their high-cost base airport.

Airport charges consist of two major elements: a landing fee based on the weight of the aircraft and a passenger charge levied on a per passenger basis. In the United States a passenger-related charge, known as the Passenger Facility Fee, was not introduced until 1991. In addition to the two basic charges, there may be further charges for the use of air bridges, for aircraft parking beyond a short free period, for the use of terminal air navigation services, or for security, and so on. At many airports the balance of charging in recent years has moved towards generating more revenue from the passenger fee than from the aircraft-related charges (Doganis, 1992).

ICAO recommends that the passenger charges should be levied on the airlines and their cost recouped through the ticket. Most European and some Third World airports do this. Elsewhere the fee is collected directly from passengers on departure and therefore does not appear as an airline cost. Airlines based in or operating through airports where passenger charges are levied directly on passengers enjoy a cost advantage. This is reinforced if the aircraft landing fee is also low.

The position in the United States is unique. Landing fees and passenger charges are generally very low. On the other hand, at most airports major airlines run and may even build their own terminals, which clearly increases their costs. Elsewhere in the world it is very unusual for airlines to operate their own passenger terminals, though they may have their own cargo complexes.

Unlike most other countries, the US government has for many years levied a variety of taxes on passengers at its airports. These include an international passenger tax, plus separate charges for agricultural inspection and for immigration and customs facilities. The latter three are not included under passenger-related charges in Table 5.5, but are shown for US airports in column 4. In the 1990s a number of governments elsewhere also began to introduce fiscal taxes on passengers purely to raise government tax revenues, since the funds raised are not to be used for airport investments. This happened in the United Kingdom, Norway and Denmark. These were in addition to the normal charges levied by the airport authorities (final column of Table 5.5). Strictly speaking such government taxes should not be considered as an airline cost, but rather as a transfer of funds collected by the airlines on behalf of governments. They are increasingly shown as a separate item on the tickets over and above the fare.

En-route charges are imposed by civil aviation authorities on aircraft flying through their air space to cover the cost of air traffic control and navigational and other aids provided. The charges are generally levied on the basis of the weight of the aircraft and the distance flown within each country's air space. But there are variations. Some countries, Egypt, India and Thailand among them, base the charge on distance alone and aircraft weight is ignored. A few, such as Japan and Korea, have a fixed charge irrespective of aircraft size or distance travelled. As a result, while there is some uniformity in the method of

Table 5.6 Comparative en-route charges in selected countries for Airbus A321, 2001 ($ per 700 km overflight)

	$	*Distance-related*
Japan	717	No
Germany	560	
Italy	465	
France	431	
Spain	405	
India	362	No
Argentina	330	
Australia	167	
Indonesia	142	
USA	141	
Egypt	125	No
South Africa	125	
Korea	92	No
Brazil	28	

Source: Aeronautical Charges Unit, Air Transport Group, Cranfield University.

charging, the level of charges varies enormously, as can be seen in Table 5.6. By far the highest charges are those in Japan and in Europe.

A few state-owned airlines have been able to persuade their governments or airport authorities to give them preferential treatment on airport or en-route navigation charges. They are either exempted from payment altogether or they may get a substantial discount. The Greek airline Olympic, for instance, was until 1995 not paying landing fees at Athens on its international flights. Elsewhere, one finds some national airlines that are billed but do not pay their bills to the civil aviation authorities. Such cases are relatively few, however, because such preferential treatment runs counter to Article 15 of the Chicago Convention and to the principle of equal treatment of each other's airlines which is enshrined in bilateral air service agreements.

5.3.3   *Commission payments for sales and distribution*

According to IATA, distribution costs, that is, the cost of sales, ticketing and promotional activities, represent around one-sixth, that is, 16–17 per cent, of the total operating costs of international scheduled airlines (Table 4.4). The costs of distribution are the second highest functional cost area after flight operations. A major element of distribution costs is the payment of commission to third parties who assist the airlines in selling and reservations. The level of such payments or commission is largely externally determined.

The highest commission payments are those made to travel agents or other airlines. According to an IATA 1996 study commission paid, net of commission received, represented almost 43 per cent of airlines' distribution costs. This was equivalent to 7–8 per cent of *total operating costs* (IATA, 1996). The rate of commission paid, expressed as a percentage of the ticket price, varies between markets and between countries. The rates for international ticket sales tend to be between 5 per cent and 6 per cent, but they are usually lower for domestic tickets. All airlines will pay agents identical or very similar rates in any particular market.

It is very difficult for an individual airline to negotiate a separate and lower commission rate than the prevailing rate in a market unless it is very dominant in that market. It may be possible in some smaller domestic markets where the one national carrier may be in a very powerful and possibly monopolistic situation. Elsewhere, if an airline tries to pay lower commission than competing airlines, it may well lose the loyalty or support of travel agents. Unilateral action on commission rates by one airline is generally avoided because it may prove counterproductive. Commission rates can be cut effectively only if there is concerted action by all airlines in a market. Thus when in October 1999 United Airlines announced that it would cut the commission paid to US agents from 8 per cent to 5 per cent and cap it at $50 for a domestic round trip and $100 for international tickets, other major US carriers followed suit, as did many of the smaller airlines. The lower commission rate stuck. But once that had happened, all airlines paid the new commission rate. It was not individually negotiable. Commission rates are determined by market conditions.

Surprisingly, while airlines may have little discretion to pay lower commission rates, they are able to offer higher rates to generate or buy agents' loyalty. This is done by offering commission 'overrides'. That is, higher commission rates to larger agents when sales volumes in monetary terms surpass certain benchmark levels. However, in more competitive markets the override rates offered by different carriers may end up being fairly similar.

Airlines also pay a fixed charge per booking made on the worldwide computer reservation systems, even though most of the bookings will be made by travel agents. The airlines even have to pay if they themselves book passengers on their own flights using one of these global systems. Galileo, Sabre and Amadeus are the three major global distribution systems (GDSs) and they all charge airlines the same booking fee. They match each other on price and for obvious reasons they cannot discriminate between airlines. The sum paid appears relatively small; in 2000 it was $3 per sector booked. But it represents around 7–8 per cent of airline distribution costs, equivalent to about 1.5 per cent of total operating costs. Once again the unit charge is not negotiable. It is determined by the GDS providers.

Finally, airlines need to pay commission to credit card companies for any tickets bought directly from the airlines' sales offices, telephone sales or internet sites and paid for by credit card. Again the commission rates are largely non-negotiable. Commission on credit card sales makes up around 4 per cent of distribution costs, equivalent to just under 1 per cent of total operating costs.

Taken together, these three types of commission payment, namely those paid to travel agents and others, those exacted by computer reservation systems and payments to credit card companies, may make up to 10 per cent of total operating costs.

In summary, the three input costs which are largely externally determined, namely the costs of fuel, airport and air navigation charges and sales commission paid to others, together represent between 30 per cent and 35 per cent of most airlines' total expenditure. Therefore the prices or commission rates that any airline pays for these inputs have a significant effect on its cost levels. Differences in these input prices may explain some of the variation in costs between airlines. Yet airlines can influence the level of these input prices only marginally.

5.4 The cost of labour

For most airlines wage costs and associated social security and pension payments for staff represent the largest single cost element. Among major North American carriers such costs including social charges generally account for 30–40 per cent of total operating costs. Among European airlines the figure is somewhat lower at 25–35 per cent. It is lowest for Asian carriers. Among airlines of East Asia labour costs frequently represent only 15–20 per cent of total costs. In countries such as Indonesia or Korea where the currency was heavily devalued in 1997–98 labour costs have become an even smaller proportion of total airline costs. Since staff costs represent such a high proportion of overall costs, variations in the average level of wages paid have a direct effect on an airline's total costs and may also lead to appreciable cost differences between airlines.

Until the early 1990s the salaries and wages paid by an airline seemed to be much more dependent on prevailing salary levels and the labour market in its home country than on management action or the negotiating skills of its personnel department. Wage costs seemed to be largely beyond management's control. Earlier editions of the present book treated labour costs together with fuel and user charges as costs which were externally determined. However, the major economic crisis faced by the airline industry in the period 1990–94 forced airline managers to take a more direct and active role in reducing staff costs. They were successful in showing that it could be done in many but not all cases. Thus today one should consider labour as a factor input whose costs are largely determined by prevailing economic and social factors in an airline's home country but in many countries they can also be influenced by management action.

In a country with free wage bargaining it is the interplay of supply and demand for the categories of labour required by the airline(s) together with the strength of particular unions which will broadly determine the level of wages that an airline has to pay for its various categories of staff. In other countries wage levels may be set by national agreements between governments or employers' associations and the trade unions. In some cases governments themselves virtually determine the levels to be paid and impose them on employers and employees alike. In all cases the prevailing wage levels are related to the standard and cost of living in the country concerned.

In addition to the basic cost of salaries and wages, airlines will normally also have to pay a variety of social charges such as social security or pension contributions or medical expenses. They are frequently enshrined in the social legislation of the country concerned and are mandatory and non-negotiable. Their impact on staff costs can be very substantial. For example, in 1999 the average cost to Air France of social charges was $15,300 for each of its employees. These social charges increased Air France's wage bill by 37 per cent. British Airways, on the other hand, paid only $6,000 per employee, which increased its overall staff costs by 14 per cent (Doganis, 2001).

For most airlines the three most expensive groups of employees tend to be the flight crews, the cabin attendants and the maintenance engineers. The pilots and cabin attendants alone represent on average around 14 per cent of total operating costs (Table 4.4). The significant variations which exist in wage levels for similar categories of staff between regions and between airlines in the same region are illustrated in Table 5.7. This shows the average annual remuneration or wage of the three key groups of airline employees in a selection of airlines, including most of those airlines whose costs were given in Table 5.1. Some variation in pilot salaries may be due to differences in flight equipment, since pilot salaries vary with the type of aircraft flown, or with the age and seniority of the pilots. Nevertheless, allowing for this and other minor discrepancies, some interesting conclusions emerge.

As one would expect, the wage levels of the larger US airlines tend to be very similar, as they have the same home base and are competing in the same labour market. In 1998 pilots at the US majors shown were being paid between $121,000 and $155,000 per year, while among cabin crew salaries varied within a narrow band of $30,700 to $37,400. With the exception of those at Delta Air Lines maintenance engineers were all getting around $48,000 to $50,000. For smaller US airlines, such as TWA, or low-fare carriers such as Southwest, remuneration levels were lower.

But it is significant that by 1998 several European and East Asian airlines were paying higher salaries to key categories of staff than their US competitors. Salary differentials were widest among East Asian airlines. Because of heavy dependence on expatriate crews, Cathay Pacific was paying its pilots $215,000, which was over 50 per cent more than many US airlines. This differential is slightly misleading because Cathay, unlike US carriers, does not operate smaller short-haul aircraft whose pilots are on lower salaries. Nevertheless the high cost of its pilots was a major cause of concern for Cathay management. Unit costs of Japan Airlines and All Nippon Airways are very high compared with other Asian carriers (Table 5.1) in part because of their high wage costs, made worse by the steady appreciation of the yen over the last two decades. Among major European airlines, salary levels at Alitalia and Iberia were especially high, which is one explanation for their high unit costs (Table 5.1), while British Airways' were the lowest.

Table 5.7 Average annual remuneration of key staff of selected major airlines in 1998 ($)

Airline	Pilots/co-pilots	Cabin attendants	Maintenance/overhaul staff
North America			
Continental	154,400	34,600	n.a.[b]
American	143,300	37,400	48,200
Northwest	142,600	30,700	49,900
United	140,500	33,300	47,100
USAir	138,600	36,400	50,300
Delta	121,900	35,100	38,800
Air Canada	83,200	20,500	27,800
Europe			
Alitalia	201,600	58,500	n.a.
Iberia	190,900[a]	61,800	38,500
SAS	163,700	72,600	60,400
Lufthansa	155,100	51,900	n.a.
British Airways	125,200	29,600	45,200
East Asia/Pacific			
JAL	229,900[a]	62,900	n.a.
Cathay Pacific	215,800	39,400	33,000
All Nippon	167,400	32,600	60,000
SIA	120,700	36,200	n.a.
Qantas	114,600	42,000	44,100
Thai Airways	83,800	13,200	14,300
Malaysia Airline	50,800	19,200	15,000
Korean	35,500	n.a.	22,600
Philippine Airlines	18,700	4,000	· 6,200

Source: *Digest of Statistics*, Series F-P, Fleet and Personnel 1998. ICAO, Montreal, 1999.

Notes
a Includes flight engineers.
b n.a. = Not available.

Marked currency fluctuations can have a significant impact on salary levels when expressed in US dollars. Following currency devaluations in 1997, all Thai, Korean and Malaysia Airlines staff were paid less in US dollar terms, though their salaries did not change. Their pilots received less than $85,000 per year, while their flight attendants too were by far the lowest paid (Table 5.7). The most dramatic impact of currency devaluation on staff costs can be seen in the case of Philippine Airlines, where pilots in 1998 were paid less than $19,000 per year and engineers received only $6,200. Yet these wage levels were reasonably good by Philippine standards. During 2000 the steady devaluation of the euro against the US dollar (by October 2000 it was down 30 per cent on its January 1999 value) significantly reduced the dollar value of many European airlines' wage levels.

The traditional view long held within the airline industry was that management could do little about the unit cost of labour because salaries and social

charges were largely externally determined. As a consequence, airline executives focused their attention on improving labour productivity through the
introduction of large aircraft, computerisation, and so on, while holding back,
as much as possible, any increases in staff numbers as output increased. But
during the 1980s management attitudes to labour began to change drastically
as a result of deregulation and the successive cyclical economic crises that
affected the airline industry. Growing domestic and international competition, accompanied by falling fares and yields, made it increasingly clear that
trying to improve labour productivity in itself was not enough to contain
labour costs. This was especially so as the latter became a growing proportion
of total operating costs following the decline in the real price of fuel. Airlines
were forced to try and reduce the unit cost of labour.

The US airlines were the first to tackle the issue of labour costs head-on in
the early 1980s. In Europe action came later during the crisis years of the
early 1990s when so many European airlines faced very large and mounting
losses. Experience in Europe has shown that the unit cost of labour can be
reduced in a number of ways while acting within any legal constraints such
as national labour regulations. The most common strategy adopted has been
to renegotiate terms and conditions of employment with the twin aims of
cutting the unit cost of labour while also improving the productivity of
labour. This means attempting to freeze wages for one or two years, or even
to cut them, while at the same time reducing staff numbers or agreeing
higher work loads with existing staff. Thus Olympic Airways as part of its
restructuring programme froze all salaries for two years in 1994 and 1995. At
about the same time Swissair negotiated new labour contracts which enabled
it to cut the cost of flight crew per block hour by 23 per cent (Bruggisser,
1997). Airlines in dire financial straits have been able to negotiate wage cuts,
as Sabena did in 1993 when its staff agreed to wage reductions of 2.5–17 per
cent. In the second half of the 1990s privatisation of state-owned airlines
enabled the latter to offer employees shares in exchange for concessions on
wages or work practices. Air France, for instance, reached such an agreement
late in 1998 with its pilots, who ended up owning 7 per cent of the company.
The Europeans were in this respect doing what US airlines had done a few
years earlier through so-called employee stock option plans (Doganis, 2001).

A different approach has been to transfer employment to countries where
wage rates are much lower. This effectively means relocating certain activities
away from an airline's home base. Swissair was the first to do this by moving
some of its revenue accounting services to Mumbai in India. It was followed
by others, including Austrian Airlines. Meanwhile both British Airways and
Singapore Airlines have transferred much of the software development for
their management information systems to India. Another way of achieving
lower wage costs is by employing flight or cabin crews who have as their base
and point of employment countries with lower wage rates. Swissair has done
this by employing Asian flight attendants. Cathay Pacific has been trying to
reduce its high pilot costs (Table 5.7) by taking on pilots based in London at

UK pilot wage rates rather than having them based in Hong Kong, where salary levels are very high. In the mid-1990s Japan Airlines set up a subsidiary company, Japan Air Charter, which hired most of its pilots and cabin crew abroad, mainly in Thailand. The salaries of Thai pilots and stewardesses employed and based in Bangkok are about one-fifth of those of Japanese pilots and stewardesses. JAL leases in Japan Air Charter to operate scheduled services on holiday routes and JAL gets the benefit of much lower unit labour costs. This trend to relocate airline jobs to lower-wage economies is bound to increase.

Some airlines have tried to overcome the adverse impact of their own high salary levels by setting up or acquiring low-wage airlines which are then used to operate services on their behalf. It may also be the case that the smaller carrier has lower costs in other areas as well as cheaper labour costs. Lufthansa, for instance, has set up a separate subsidiary called Lufthansa CityLine which operates regional jet services on its behalf with staff employed on terms different from those of the parent company. Until its own virtual collapse in October 2001 Swissair used Crossair, which was then 69 per cent owned by Swissair, to operate a network of routes radiating from Zurich, Geneva and Basle. Crossair staff had more flexible and more demanding terms and conditions of employment and were paid less, sometimes much less, than comparable Swissair staff. Some airlines franchise smaller airlines to operate on their behalf, again to take advantage of their lower wage rates. In 1999 British Airways had ten franchisees flying services on its behalf while using BA aircraft livery and uniforms. The effect of all the above measures is not to reduce the major airlines' own unit labour costs but to mitigate their impact by utilising other airlines with lower wage rates to operate certain services.

The ultimate cost of labour depends not only on the average wage rates paid for different categories of staff but also on the productivity of that labour. This partly depends on institutional factors such as working days in the week, length of annual holidays, basic hours worked per week and so on, and partly on the ability of management to get more output per employee. This in turn is a function of the collective agreements between each airline and its staff which determine work practices, such as number of rest days for pilots or cabin crew after long-haul flights. It is also a function of the number of staff actually employed. In the early and mid-1990s most European airlines found that they were grossly over-staffed, especially in areas other than flight operations. Many of them set out to make significant cuts in staff numbers by offering staff financial inducements to encourage voluntary redundancy and/or early retirement. Several restructuring programmes were financed by government financial aid to airlines following approval of such schemes by the European Commission. Thus during the mid-1990s Iberia, Air Portugal and Olympic all reduced staff numbers by 13–18 per cent. The airlines' response to the worsening crisis facing the industry after September 2001 again included massive cuts in staff numbers. Where staff cuts were proportionally greater than the reduction in routes and frequencies labour productivity would inevitably rise.

In summary, airlines do have some flexibility in reducing the unit cost of labour, that is, the average wage cost plus social charges per employee. But they can also reduce the overall cost of labour by employing fewer people to produce a given level of output. In other words they can strive to increase labour productivity. However, labour productivity is not only a function of the collective agreements and work practices or of the number of staff employed. It is also very much influenced by the type of aircraft being flown by the airline as well as the characteristics of the network which is being served.

5.5   Aircraft type and its characteristics

Many technological aspects of each aircraft type have a direct effect on that aircraft's operating costs. The most important from an economic viewpoint are likely to be the size of the aircraft, its cruising speed and the range or distance which the aircraft can fly with a full payload. The significance of size, speed and range is reinforced in that, taken together, they determine an aircraft's hourly productivity, which in turn also affects costs.

5.5.1   Aircraft size

As a general rule, though there are exceptions, the larger an aircraft the lower will be its direct operating costs per unit of output, that is, per tonne kilometre available or per seat kilometre. In other words, other things being equal, the direct operating costs of aircraft do not increase in proportion to their size or their payload capacity. The cost per hour of the larger aircraft will be higher than that of a smaller aircraft but when converted into a cost per seat kilometre or per tonne kilometre it is lower. For example, in 1998, in the United States, Boeing 737-500 aircraft flown by US carriers with on average 110 seats incurred on average direct operating costs of about $1,783 per block hour (*Airline Monitor*, 1999). A larger Boeing 737-400 aircraft with 142 seats cost about $1,933 per block hour to fly. The larger aircraft's hourly costs were 8.4 per cent higher than those of the Boeing 737-500 but its capacity in terms of seats was about 29 per cent more. The greater capacity of the Boeing 737-400 more than compensated for its higher hourly cost. As a result its unit cost was 3.94c per available seat kilometre. This was significantly less than the smaller and newer Boeing 737-500, whose seat-kms cost was on average 4.68c or 19 per cent higher.

Aircraft size influences costs in two ways. In the first instance, there are certain aerodynamic benefits from increased size. Larger aircraft have proportionally lower drag and more payload per unit of weight. At the same time larger and more efficient engines can be used. Thus the 215-seater Boeing 767-300 has a maximum take-off weight which is nearly three times as great as that of the Boeing 737-400, yet its hourly fuel consumption is only slightly more than twice as high (*Airline Monitor*, 1999). It is relatively easier and

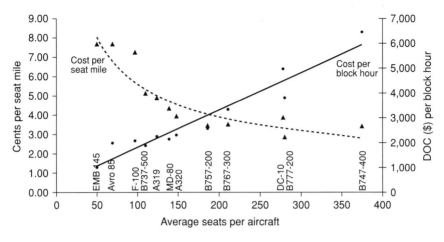

Figure 5.1 The impact of aircraft size on direct operating costs, US airlines, 1999.

cheaper per unit of weight to push a large mass through the air than a smaller one. The same applies to mass in water. Hence the development of supertankers. Second, there are other economies of size related to the use of labour. Maintenance costs, a large part of which are the costs of labour, do not increase in proportion to increases in aircraft size. One can see this clearly when comparing two aircraft from the same manufacturer, the Boeing 737-300 and the Boeing 757-200. The hourly maintenance costs among US airlines in 1998 of the larger Boeing 757-200 was 14 per cent higher, yet the 757 could carry up to 40 per cent more passengers. In addition large economies also arise in flight crew costs, since larger aircraft do not require more flight crew, though the pilot and co-pilot may be paid slightly more for flying a larger aircraft.

The close relation between aircraft size and unit costs for the major aircraft types operated by US trunk airlines can be seen in Figure 5.1. It shows, on the right-hand axis, how hourly costs increase in a linear progression as aircraft size, measured in seats, rises. However, since hourly costs increase less than proportionately to size when they are converted to costs per seat kilometre, there is a strongly downward sloping curve (left-hand axis). The relation between increasing size or seating capacity and declining unit costs is clear, though there are deviations and outlyers. Such deviations relate either to new and improved versions of existing aircraft types or to the launch of a newer generation of twin-engine aircraft. An example of the latter is the Boeing 777, with hourly and unit costs about 25 per cent lower than those of the similar but older generation DC-10. It should always be borne in mind that the aircraft illustrated are in practice flown on different average sector lengths and this, as is discussed later, influences the unit costs shown in the diagram. The diagram also highlights the very high unit operating costs of the new generation of small regional jets such as the Embraer 145 and the Avro 85.

This cost disadvantage is largely a function of their small size. On the other hand their hourly costs are low, so they may be suitable for thin routes provided fares are high enough to cover the very high seat-mile costs.

Finally, it is important to emphasise that while larger aircraft generally produce lower seat-kms or tonne-kms costs than smaller aircraft when flown on the same sectors, their total round-trip costs are in most cases higher. This creates the basic conundrum of airline planning. Does an airline choose the aircraft with the lower seat-kms costs or the one with the lower trip costs?

5.5.2   Aircraft speed

Apart from size, aircraft speed also affects unit costs. It does this through its effect on an aircraft's hourly productivity. Since hourly productivity is the product of the payload and the speed, the greater an aircraft's cruising speed the greater will be its output per hour. If an aircraft flies at an average speed of 800 kmph and has a 20 tonne payload, its hourly output is 16,000 tonne-kms. An aircraft with a similar payload flying at 900 kmph would generate 18,000 tonne-kmph, or about 12.5 per cent more than the slower aircraft. Some elements of cost might be higher for a faster aircraft. Fuel consumption might be slightly higher unless the faster speed was due to improved aerodynamic design. But many costs, particularly those that are normally estimated on a per block hour basis, would be similar. Flight and cabin crew costs, maintenance costs, insurance, landing fees and depreciation would certainly be fairly similar. These similar hourly costs would be spread over 12.5 per cent more tonne kilometres. Therefore, assuming other things are equal, the cost per tonne kilometre for the faster aircraft would be lower. Since in practice the faster aircraft are frequently larger as well, the cost advantages of size and speed reinforce each other, producing the lowest seat-kms or tonne-kms costs.

5.5.3   Take-off performance and range

The lower unit costs of larger and faster aircraft do not mean that airlines should always choose to operate such aircraft in preference to smaller, slower aircraft. Airlines must resolve the conundrum previously mentioned. The larger aircraft with the lower unit costs per tonne kilometre will have higher trip costs than smaller aircraft. In making a choice between aircraft types other factors must also be considered, such as the level and pattern of demand on the routes for which aircraft are needed and the design characteristics of the aircraft in relation to those routes. Aircraft are designed to cater for particular traffic densities and stage lengths. As a result each aircraft type has different take-off and range characteristics and these in turn influence unit costs. An aircraft requiring particularly long runways or with engines adversely affected by high ambient temperatures at airports suffers cost penalties. In either case it can overcome its design handicap by reducing its payload so as

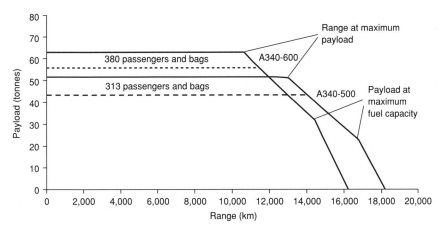

Figure 5.2 Payload–range diagrams for two versions of the Airbus A340. The 500 series has an extended-range version but achieves it by sacrificing payload. Both aircraft have a three-class layout. Passenger weight is 95 kg. Capacity above the dotted line is freight.

to reduce its take-off weight. This would enable it to take off despite a runway or temperature limitation. But the reduced payload immediately results in higher costs per tonne kilometre, since the same costs need to be spread over fewer units of output.

An aircraft's range performance is illustrated in payload–range diagrams such as the one in Figure 5.2. Each aircraft is authorised to take off at a maximum take-off weight (MTOW). This weight cannot be exceeded for safety reasons. The MTOW is made up of the 'operating weight empty' of the aircraft plus some combination of fuel and payload. With maximum payload the aircraft taking off at its MTOW will be able to fly up to a certain distance for which it has been designed. This is known as the 'range at maximum payload'. To fly beyond this distance the aircraft must substitute fuel for payload, always ensuring that it does not exceed its MTOW. Initially the reduction in payload may be in terms of belly-hold freight rather than passengers.

The aircraft's range can be progressively increased by further uplift of fuel and a continuing reduction in payload. This process continues until the fuel tanks are full and no extra fuel can be uplifted. The range at this point is known as 'payload at maximum range'. This is the effective maximum range of the aircraft. In practice, an aircraft could fly further without more fuel by reducing its payload, since a lighter aircraft consumes less fuel per hour. This is why the payload line beyond maximum payload in Figure 5.2 is not exactly vertical but steeply sloping. The shape of each aircraft's payload range line is different, since aircraft are designed to satisfy particular market needs.

Aircraft size, speed and range together determine an aircraft's productivity curve and hence its unit costs. The relationships are illustrated in Figure 5.3.

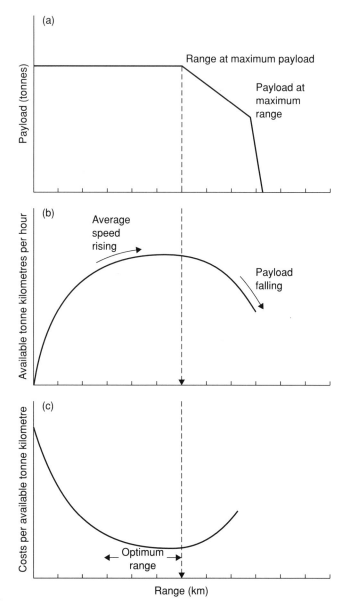

Figure 5.3 Payload–range, productivity and cost relationship: (a) payload–range, (b) hourly productivity, (c) unit cost.

Hourly productivity is the product of aircraft size and speed. As sector length increases average aircraft speed rises. This is because aircraft speed is calculated on the basis of the block time for a journey. Block time is from engines on to engines off. It therefore includes an amount of dead time on the ground.

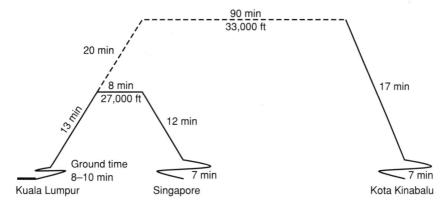

Figure 5.4 The impact of sector distance on block time and block fuel. Case study: Boeing 737-500, Kuala Lumpur–Singapore 0:48 min. block time, Kuala Lumpur–Kota Kinabalu 2:24 min. block time.

Ground time will vary with runway, taxiway and apron layout at each airport and with the number of aircraft movements during a given period. On departure from a very busy international airport such as London Heathrow or Frankfurt, aircraft may spend up to twenty minutes from engine start-up to lift-off. This time may be spent on being pulled out from the stand, disconnecting from the ground tractor unit, waiting further clearance from Ground Traffic Control, taxiing to the end of the take-off runway, which may be some minutes from the stand, perhaps waiting in a queue of aircraft for clearance to taxi on to the runway and take off. On landing the ground time is usually less, though at peak periods an aircraft may have to wait for a taxiway to be clear or even for a departing aircraft to vacate a stand. The total ground manoeuvre time at both ends of a flight may amount to twenty or thirty minutes at large and busy airports and will rarely be less than fifteen minutes on any international air services. When airborne, the aircraft may have to circle the airport of departure and it will then climb to its cruise altitude. The climb and descent speeds are relatively slow, especially if based on the horizontal distance travelled. On short sectors an aircraft may spend most of its airborne time either in climb or in descent, that is, at slow speeds, and may fly at its higher cruising speed and altitude for only a few minutes. As the stage distance increases more and more time is spent at the cruising speed and the ground manoeuvre, climb and descent phases become a smaller proportion of block time. Average block speed therefore increases.

The flights operated by Malaysia Airlines in 2000 from Kuala Lumpur to Singapore and Kota Kinabalu (on the island of Borneo) provide a vivid illustration of the impact of sector distance on average aircraft speed (Figure 5.4). On the very short sector Kuala Lumpur to Singapore the total block time with a Boeing 737-400 aircraft is on average forty-eight minutes. But of this fifteen to seventeen minutes are spent on the ground at either end of the route, with engines running. Around half the total block time, twenty-five minutes, is spent in the ascent (thirteen minutes) or descent (twelve minutes) phases when speeds are relatively low. Only eight minutes are spent at a cruise altitude and at close to a cruising speed. On the much longer sector from Kuala Lumpur to Kota Kinabalu the time on the ground is still the same, fifteen to seventeen minutes. Because the cruise altitude is higher it takes a few minutes longer to climb and also to descend than it does on the Singapore flight. But once the cruise altitude is reached, the aircraft spends ninety minutes or 60 per cent of the block time flying at a relatively high cruising speed. The impact on average block speed is dramatic. The average block speed on Kuala Lumpur–Singapore is 400 kmph while on the longer Kota Kinabalu sector it is 680 kmph.

Initially, increasing sector distance has no impact on an aircraft's payload capacity. It remains at its maximum and constant. But, as sector distance increases, the rising average speed ensures that hourly productivity rises (Figure 5.3b). It continues to rise until the range at maximum payload is reached. For distances beyond this, payload falls and though average speed may still be rising marginally the net effect is that hourly output falls.

Hourly productivity directly affects unit costs because all the costs which are constant in hourly terms, such as flight crew costs or depreciation, are spread over more units of output. Thus a unit cost curve can be derived from the productivity–range curve showing how unit costs decline as range and hourly productivity increase (Figure 5.3c). Unit costs continue to decline until payload has to be sacrificed to fly further and hourly productivity begins to drop. The unit cost curve will vary for each aircraft type, depending on its size, speed and range characteristics. For each aircraft type it is possible to identify a range of distance over which its unit costs are uniformly low. This may be considered the optimum cost range of that aircraft. The preceding discussion has assumed that total costs per hour are constant irrespective of sector length. The next section on the effect of stage length on costs will indicate that costs decrease relatively with distance. This reinforces the effect of increasing hourly productivity. More of this later.

5.5.4   Engine performance

A key characteristic of any aircraft type is the engine it uses. Increasingly, the same engines or engines with similar thrust made by different manufacturers are being used by broadly similar types of aircraft. This is because there are only three major manufacturers of civil jet engines in the Western world and competition to get their engines into the same aircraft drives them to produce similar products. This should not obscure the fact that even similar engines may have different fuel consumption. In particular newer engines are likely to be more fuel-efficient. Thus in the early 1980s when Qantas was introducing newer 747s into its own fleet but with Rolls Royce RB-211 engines, it found that the Rolls Royce engines were saving 5–7 per cent on fuel compared with the older Pratt & Whitney engines and were cheaper to maintain.

But there was a weight penalty because the new engines were heavier. Early in 2000 BAE Systems launched the RJX, a new version of its successful Avro 100–20-seater regional jet powered by new Honeywell AS-977 engines. It was claimed that these new engines would reduce fuel burn per sector by 10–15 per cent and cut maintenance costs by up to 20 per cent. It is clear from these two examples that the type of engines in an airline's fleet and in particular whether they are new or old versions of the engine type may influence operating costs. In assessing the costs of different airlines one needs to consider the impact not only of the aircraft type being used but also the version of engine which powers it.

In conclusion, there can be little doubt that the type of aircraft operated has a significant effect on cost levels. With this in mind the key question is how far an airline has the freedom to choose any aircraft type it wishes or how far the choice is constrained by the sector lengths and the traffic densities on the routes concerned, or other factors. The choice of aircraft occurs in two stages and management influence is critical only in the second. The first stage is shortlisting the possible aircraft types for a given operation. As previously emphasised, an international airline's route structure and demand pattern are dependent on its geographical location and on economic and political factors largely beyond its control. The route structure, the airports used, in particular the runway lengths available, and the traffic density on those routes will broadly delimit the type of aircraft that is needed or can be used. For particular parts of its network, the sector lengths and traffic densities taken together will reduce the options open to the airline to perhaps only two or three aircraft types. In some cases only one type may fit the requirements. In the year 2000, airlines operating relatively long-haul routes of say over 4,000 km but with traffic flows that were too thin to support a 400 seater Boeing 747 with a commercially acceptable frequency would have been looking for a 250–300 seater. Given these market constraints the choice would probably have been between an Airbus A340 or a Boeing 777. At another level, an airline planning to operate international charters from northern Europe into the smaller Aegean islands of Greece, such as Myconos or Skiathos, can use only Boeing 737 or Airbus A320 series aircraft because of runway limitations even if the traffic flows could support larger aircraft. In both the above examples it is a combination of external factors that produce the shortlist of possible aircraft.

It is only when one moves to the second stage, that of choosing between the shortlisted aircraft, that the role of management becomes critical. Management has to make several key and related decisions. It must not only choose the aircraft which best meets its airline's needs and objectives, but it must also choose the number of aircraft and optimise the mix of aircraft in the fleet. Fleet planning is pulled in opposite directions. On the one hand an airline needs to choose the optimum aircraft in terms of size and range characteristics for each route, but at the same time it must minimise the number of different types of aircraft in its fleet so as to reduce maintenance and crewing costs (Clark, 2001). Thus a compromise must be found between having a different aircraft type for each route and having only one aircraft type to serve all routes. Management must also decide on the engines which will power its aircraft, if more than one engine type is available. All these decisions will eventually affect the airline's cost levels.

Once an airline has made its choice and invested in particular aircraft types for various parts of its network then those aircraft types have to be considered as given. They cannot be changed from year to year. Because of investment in flight crew training, maintenance and ground facilities, aircraft types are unlikely to be changed except after several years. Once aircraft have been introduced into an airline's operation the most significant factor which will then affect their costs of operation, other than the level of input costs, is the route structure on which they will be operated.

5.6   Route structure and network characteristics

5.6.1   Stage length

Several aspects of an airline's operating pattern may influence its costs but the most critical are the stage or sector lengths over which it is operating its aircraft. The average stage lengths will vary within an airline by aircraft type, since it is likely that different aircraft will have been chosen for different types of routes within the total network. For each aircraft type, nevertheless, the longer the stage length which can be flown the lower will be the direct operating costs per unit of output. This is so until sectors get so long that payload has to be sacrificed.

The rapid decline of unit costs as stage distance increases is a fundamental characteristic of airline economics. A number of factors help to explain this relationship. One of them, the effect of stage length on block speed, has already been discussed in the previous section. It was pointed out that ground manoeuvre time and the relatively slow climb and descent phases of a flight become a decreasing proportion of the total block time as stage length increases. Consequently, the average block speed increases. In turn, the hourly productivity in terms of tonne kilometres or seat kilometres also rises. Fixed costs, both direct and indirect, are spread over more units of output and therefore the total operating cost per available tonne kilometre or seat kilometre goes down.

The same considerations which affect block speed also influence block fuel. During ground manoeuvre time on departure or arrival aircraft are burning fuel. In twenty to thirty minutes on the ground they can burn a considerable amount of it (Figure 5.4). During climb, and to a lesser extent during the descent phase, fuel consumption is relatively high in relation to the horizontal distance travelled. Conversely, fuel consumption is least in the cruise mode and is reduced at higher altitudes. The earlier example of the two flights out of Kuala Lumpur to Singapore and Kota Kinabalu (Figure 5.4) highlights the

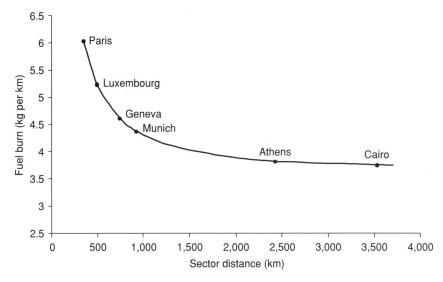

Figure 5.5 The impact of sector distance on fuel burn, Airbus A321-200 on routes
from London. Fuel burn is the average of outward and return trips, based
on 75 per cent passenger and 50 per cent cargo load factor.

impact of sector distance on fuel burn. On the longer sector, time on the
ground and time spent in ascent and descent are a much smaller proportion
of the total block time. Conversely, not only is more than half the block time
spent in cruise, when fuel consumption is lowest, but it is also spent at a
much higher altitude than on the shorter sector, thereby further reducing fuel
burn. In short, ground manoeuvre and climb and descent fuel becomes a
decreasing proportion of total fuel burn as stage distance increases. The net
result is that fuel consumption does not increase in proportion to distance.
Thus if an Airbus A310 or a Boeing 767 doubles its stage distance from, say,
500 km to 1,000 km the fuel burnt will not double. Depending on the
particular circumstances of the route, the fuel consumed will increase by only
about 60 per cent to 70 per cent. Looking at an actual example, the Airbus
A320-200 on London to Paris with a full passenger load and no cargo
consumes about 1,700 kg of fuel. Flying to Geneva, where the distance from
London is 118 per cent greater, the Airbus burns about 2,800 kg, an increase
of only 65 per cent. As a result the fuel burned per kilometre and the fuel
cost per kilometre drops by up to 25 per cent. This is a major saving, given
that fuel may be a significant proportion of total costs. On longer sectors
beyond 2,500 km the fuel savings from additional sector distance become
marginal. The fuel burn of the larger Airbus A321 on sectors out of London
is shown in Figure 5.5.

Stage length not only affects fuel consumption but also influences aircraft
and crew utilisation and this too impacts on costs. An aircraft is a very

expensive piece of capital equipment. It is earning revenue and paying back its high initial cost only when it is flying. The more flying it does the lower become its hourly costs. This is because the standing annual charges, notably depreciation and insurance, can be spread over a greater number of productive hours. It is much easier to keep aircraft in the air if stage lengths are longer. On short sectors such as New York–Boston, London–Paris or Singapore–Kuala Lumpur, where aircraft have to land after every forty or fifty minutes of flight and then spend up to an hour on the ground, achieving more than five or six block hours per day with an aircraft becomes very difficult. Higher utilisation requires either a reduction in the aircraft turn-round time so as to carry out more flights within the operating day, or an extension of the operating day by scheduling very early morning or late evening departures. Charter airlines in Europe achieve very high utilisation on relatively short sectors by extending the operating day. Low-cost no-frills airlines achieve the same result by reducing turn-rounds to thirty minutes or less.

Conversely, when one looks at longer sectors involving, say, five block hours, an aircraft can fly out and back and with just two flight sectors achieve a daily utilisation of ten block hours while spending only a couple of hours or so on the ground. The close relation between stage length and aircraft utilisation can be seen by examining British Airways' Boeing 737-400 aircraft in 1999. Out of London Heathrow airport these aircraft were being flown on relatively short sectors, averaging around 560 km, and achieved a daily utilisation of 6.1 hours. But out of London Gatwick BA operated the same aircraft on longer sectors averaging 978 km. On Gatwick operations daily utilisation jumped to 8.3 hours, a third more than on the Heathrow routes (CAA, 2000a).

Flight and cabin crew, like aircraft, are a valuable and costly resource. A high proportion of crew costs are fixed and do not vary in the short term. The more flying that crews can actually do the lower will be the crew costs per block hour. On short sectors crews spend relatively more of their time on the ground. On one to one-and-a-half-hour sectors, crews may actually be flying only for four to six hours during a twelve- to fourteen-hour duty period. As stage lengths increase they should be able to spend more of their duty period actually flying.

A more obvious implication of short stages is that airport charges, station costs and any handling fees paid to others are incurred more frequently than on longer stages. Their impact on total costs is therefore greater. One can see this when examining the cost structure of short-haul airlines, whether international or domestic. In 1999 British Midland had an average stage length of only 589 km. Its landing and other airport charges and station costs, together with handling fees, came to a staggering 30.8 per cent of its total costs. For KLM UK, a small British-based airline whose average sector distance was shorter, only 472 km, this figure came to 28.9 per cent. Yet in the same year British Airways, operating with an average sector distance of 1,980 km, found that airport charges, station costs and handling fees accounted for only 14.6 per

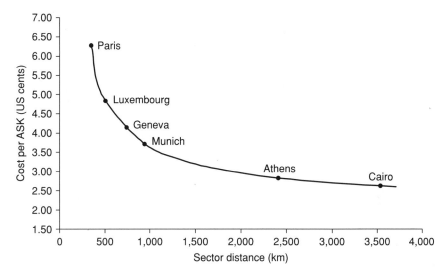

Figure 5.6 The impact of sector distance on unit costs for the Airbus A321 on routes from London.

cent of its total operating costs. For Virgin Atlantic, an exclusively long-haul airline, with an average sector distance of over 6,000 km, these costs drop to only 13.5 per cent of their total costs (CAA, 2000c, 2001).

Some elements of maintenance expenditure are also related to stage length. This is because certain maintenance checks and spare parts replacement schedules are related to the number of flight cycles, that is, take-offs and landings. These occur less frequently as stage length increases. The part of the aircraft where maintenance is most obviously related to the number of flight cycles is the undercarriage, though there are others too.

All the above factors reinforce the cost–range relationship, based on aircraft productivity, discussed in the preceding section. Together they result in a typically U-shaped cost curve for every aircraft type. Unit costs fall rapidly at first as stage length increases, then gradually flatten out until they rise sharply as payload restrictions begin to push up costs. A cost curve based on a route costing study of the Airbus A321 is shown in Figure 5.6. The A321 study and other similar analyses indicate that the most significant economies with respect to distance occur by increasing stage lengths at the short to medium range. The implication for airlines is clear. They must avoid short sectors, because they impose much higher costs, and should try and operate each aircraft at or near the stage distances where costs are at their lowest. This means the distances for which each aircraft has been designed.

The relationship between sector distance and unit costs is one of the fundamental rules of airline economics. Short sectors are inherently more costly to operate, in terms of cost per seat kilometre or available tonne kilometre, than longer sectors. Other things being equal, short-haul airlines will tend to

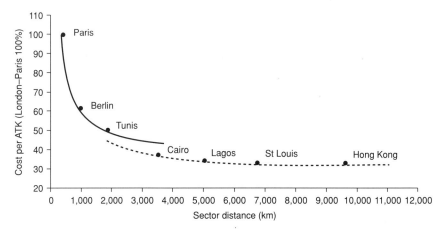

Figure 5.7 The impact of sector distance and aircraft size on unit costs, Airbus A320-200 and Airbus A340-600 on routes from London. The A320 is a 150-seater twin jet; the A340 has four engines and is here operated with around 300 seats.

have higher unit costs than airlines with longer average sector distances. This should be borne in mind when comparing airline costs. Several airlines' unit costs were compared in Table 5.1. Of these airlines, two, Singapore Airlines and Cathay Pacific, have average sector lengths which are very much higher than those of any other carrier. In 1999 they were 3,970 km and 3,480 km respectively. The next longest average sector length was Japan Airlines' 2,430 km and KLM's 2,030 km. All the others were below 2,000 km. Given that Singapore Airlines and Cathay Pacific are way ahead in terms of sector distance, it is hardly surprising to find that their unit costs are so low when compared with other airlines' in Table 5.1. Though, of course, other factors also impact on costs.

In so far as larger aircraft tend to be used on longer stages the twin effects of aircraft size and stage length frequently reinforce each other. The result is that operating costs per tonne kilometre on long sectors flown by large wide-body aircraft may be as low as 20–25 per cent of the costs on short-haul sectors flown by smaller aircraft. This is vividly illustrated by comparing two newer Airbus aircraft on routes out of London, the 150-seat short to medium range A320 and the much larger 300-seater long-haul A340 (Figure 5.7). The larger aircraft's direct operating costs on long sectors are less than 40 per cent of those of the smaller aircraft on London–Paris. The unit cost discrepancy would be even greater if an older generation of aircraft was being used on the shorter sectors.

Airlines operating primarily large aircraft over long sectors will always appear to have lower unit operating costs than airlines flying smaller aircraft on domestic and short-haul international services. But their lower costs will be primarily a function of aircraft size and sector distance rather than of better managerial efficiency! It is no coincidence that two of the three airlines with the lowest unit costs in Table 5.1 above, namely Singapore Airlines and Cathay Pacific, operate very large aircraft over average sector distances which are well above the average for all the eighteen airlines in the group. The only other airline which is in any way comparable to these two in having above-average aircraft size and sector distances is Japan Airlines, but as mentioned earlier it is penalised by high wage rates (Table 5.7).

If sector distances flown have such a critical impact on unit costs, to what extent can they be influenced by management decisions? As previously pointed out, an airline's route structure and therefore its sector distances are a function of the location of its home base(s), the geographical location of the markets it is serving and the degree to which the regulatory regimes within which it operates allow free access to those markets. But there is some scope for action. Management must constantly assess and reassess the viability of short sectors to establish whether revenues generated exceed the high costs or at least make a sufficient contribution to fixed costs. Short sectors which have little prospect of achieving long-term profitability and do not generate significant transfer traffic for other routes may be discontinued. Multi-sector services, usually on domestic routes, can be re-examined to see whether certain en-route stops can be cut out or replaced by non-stop services. Short hops at the end of long-haul routes are especially costly because the distances are usually very short and the aircraft used are large wide-bodied ones. For instance, in 2000 Singapore Airlines was operating a Singapore–Zurich service with a Boeing 747-400 which continued on to Brussels, a one-hour hop. Very costly!

5.6.2 Frequency of services

High frequencies provide airlines with greater flexibility in schedule planning, thereby enabling them to increase aircraft and crew utilisation. The availability of further schedules to be operated whenever an aircraft and crew return to base makes it much easier to keep them flying throughout the operating day. Airlines operating low frequencies on short to medium sectors face the problem of what to do with their aircraft when they have completed their first round trip of the day. This problem is especially acute if for commercial reasons most departures even for low-frequency destinations need to be early in the morning. It follows that by early afternoon most aircraft will be back at their home base with insufficient further flights to absorb all of them. To avoid under-utilisation of aircraft and crews certain flights will be rescheduled to later in the day to utilise aircraft that have returned from early morning departures. But later departures may be at commercially less attractive times. On long-haul routes high frequencies also enable airlines to reduce the length and cost of crew stopovers. Conversely, low frequencies prove costly.

Olympic Airways' route from Athens to Melbourne and Sydney in Australia in 1999 amply illustrates the cost problems created by low frequencies on long-haul services. Olympic operated the service with a Boeing 747 but only twice a week and with a stop in Bangkok. On the way out, after a nine-hour sector to Bangkok, a complete set of crew, twenty in all (two pilots, a flight engineer and sixteen or seventeen cabin crew), would disembark. They would wait three or four days to take over the next outward flight on to Melbourne and Sydney. At Sydney they would spend a further three or four days before flying the return sector to Bangkok. Then another three- or four-day stopover in Bangkok waiting to take over the next returning flight back to Athens. Each set of crew was away for thirteen or fourteen days. The pilots were originally entitled to eleven rest days on their return! Thus during a twenty-five-day period each pilot crew on this route would have undertaken only four duty periods. Not only was crew utilisation and productivity inevitably very low but crew expenses were extremely high. At all times there were two complete sets of crew, forty or so people, staying in Bangkok, one set in Sydney and one on the aircraft. This meant very substantial hotel costs plus associated daily out-of-base allowances and expenses for all sixty crew members. To make matters worse the Boeing 747 operated a very short and expensive one- and-a-quarter-hour sector between Melbourne and Sydney. With very low yields and high costs this route inevitably lost money and should have been discontinued. In 2000 Olympic switched from the Boeing 747 to a smaller A340. This enabled frequencies to be increased to three per week and rest days at the end of the rotation to be reduced. So crew utilisation improved. But this was unlikely to be enough to ensure profitability.

The aircraft which an airline has available, the demand patterns in the markets concerned, together with constraints imposed by bilateral air service agreements or inter-airline agreements influence or even determine the frequencies to be operated. But an airline has some scope to try to increase its frequencies by changes in the type of aircraft used or in the operating pattern or route structure. Higher frequencies also have marketing benefits.

5.6.3 *Length of passenger haul*

Many costs associated with sales, ticketing and the handling of passengers are related to the number of passengers rather than to the distance that each passenger travels with the airline on a particular journey. This is true with the costs of reservation, of ticketing and of the handling of both passengers and their baggage. It is also frequently true of airport passenger charges when paid by airlines. In other words, a passenger who buys a single ticket and travels 3,000 km on an airline network will cost the airline less than three separate passengers each travelling 1,000 km. In the latter case each of the three will impose his own ticketing and handling costs and the airline may have to pay a separate airport charge for each. From the cost point of view an airline is better off carrying fewer passengers travelling long distances rather than many more passengers on short journeys. However, the shorter-haul passengers may produce higher yields and generate more income because of the way fares are structured (see Chapter 10). Long-haul passengers pay much less per kilometre travelled because unit fares decline as distance increases, to mirror the drop in unit costs. But purely in cost terms the long-haul passenger is to be preferred. The average length of passenger haul, that is, distance travelled, on each airline's services depends primarily on two factors: first, the airline's average sector or stage distance, which is a function of its network; second, on the airline's success in attracting passengers who travel on two or more sectors, usually by transferring flights at the airline's hub.

Most of the major airlines whose costs were compared earlier (Table 5.1) have an average passenger haul of between 2,000 km and 2,500 km. Four stand out for carrying their passengers on average for much longer distances. These are two Asian carriers, Singapore Airlines and Cathay Pacific, whose passenger haul in 2000 was 4,760 km and 3,980 km respectively, and the two European airlines KLM (3,710 km) and British Airways (3,110 km). The first two achieve this because they have the initial advantage of having very long sectors. The two European carriers, however, are much more successful in generating on-line transfer passengers. In fact early in 2000 British Airways' then chief executive claimed that the airline had been very successful in attracting transfer passengers but that this undermined the airline's profitability because average yields for such business were so low! The cost advantages of selling to passengers travelling long distances on the BA network were apparently not sufficient to offset the lower yields. As a result the airline changed its strategy. It reduced capacity on many long-haul routes by switching from large Boeing 747 to smaller Boeing 777 aircraft and refocused its marketing away from economy-class passengers transferring from short- to long-haul flights. These were the passengers who had been paying very low fares to travel thousands of kilometres but had been needed to fill the large Boeing 747s.

5.6.4   Airline and fleet size

Early studies of airline economics, particularly in relation to US airlines, had suggested that there might be significant economies of scale, particularly at the lower end of the size scale. Such economies were expected to arise through the ability of larger carriers to gain the benefits of bulk buying and of spreading contingency provision over more units of output. Large carriers would also benefit from their ability to themselves undertake discrete activities such as major maintenance checks or computerised reservation systems, for which a minimum scale of operations was necessary. Increasingly during the 1960s and 1970s the view that there are cost economies of scale in airline operations began to be questioned. Studies both in the United States (Reid and Mohrfield, 1973) and elsewhere failed to establish any economies of scale in airline operations. These findings were confirmed in practice following US domestic deregulation and liberalisation elsewhere. During the last twenty years or so many small new entrant carriers have emerged in the United States and in other deregulated markets. Many of these were able to be price-competitive against very much larger and well-established airlines. Their unit costs were in many cases actually lower because of leaner management and fewer administrative and other overheads.

The airline industry appears to be characterised by constant returns to scale. In other words, there are no marked cost economies of scale. Such a conclusion has important implications on regulatory policy. It means that in the absence of entry or capacity controls new small carriers should be in a position to enter existing markets and be cost-competitive with established carriers. On the cost side, the economics of the airline industry indicate a natural tendency towards competition rather than monopoly. In practice in international air transport that tendency is distorted by bilateral agreements, by the lack of airport capacity at major airports and by other constraints discussed in earlier chapters on regulation. Moreover, post-deregulation experience in the United States and the emergence of so-called mega-carriers and global alliances suggest that while there may be no cost advantages of larger size, the larger airlines with a wide network spread enjoy distinct scale benefits in terms of marketing. Thus new smaller entrants into an established market may be competitive in terms of costs but may not be competitive in their marketing because of the small scale of their operations. As a result many new entrant airlines have not survived long. This reinforces a tendency towards oligopolistic rather than perfect competition.

If there are no cost economies of scale related to airline size, what about the related question of fleet size? Varied stage lengths and differing traffic densities impose the need on many airlines to have quite mixed fleets. This in turn means that some airlines, especially smaller Third World airlines, may operate only two or three aircraft of one type. When the number of aircraft of one type in a fleet is so small there are likely to be higher costs. The cost of holding spares will be higher, since the spares holding expressed as a proportion of the purchase price of the aircraft goes up as the number of aircraft purchased drops below a certain level. For instance, one spare engine may be enough whether an airline has three or fifteen aircraft of a particular type. Flight crew training and engineering training costs have to be spread over fewer aircraft and are therefore higher. Maintenance costs will be particularly high for small fleets if engines or aircraft have to be sent elsewhere for major overhauls. The small numbers may preclude the installation of more advanced or very specific maintenance facilities. Conversely, if maintenance or ground handling equipment which is very specific to one aircraft type is installed to service only two or three aircraft it will push up the costs of maintenance or handling. Sets of flight crews per aircraft may be higher for very small mixed fleets because of the inability in emergencies to switch crews between aircraft if they are of different types. Pilots are certificated for only one aircraft type at a time.

All the above considerations mean that it is relatively expensive to operate small fleets of aircraft. Hourly direct operating costs go down by 5–10 per cent as the fleet size of aircraft of a particular type increases from two or three to fifteen aircraft. Fleets larger than this do not appear to achieve further significant cost economies. This means that airlines with small mixed fleets have a cost disadvantage. In 1999 Air Madagascar operated eighteen aircraft of six different types. No fleet contained more than four aircraft of the same type. In contrast Aloha, the Hawaiian airline, had nineteen aircraft, but they were all Boeing 737-200s. For Aloha the degree of commonality of spare parts, maintenance procedures and flight crews must have produced marked cost economies. The low-cost or budget airlines have learned this lesson. Despite having large fleets they tend to fly only one or at most two aircraft types.

5.7 Airline marketing and product policy

Product and service quality is both an integral part of an airline's marketing strategy and a significant cost determinant. It is also an area of cost over which an airline has much greater control. However, airlines do not have complete control over such marketing costs except in those few cases where an airline operates on its own, as a monopolist, on all or most of its network. This is most likely to occur in domestic operations. On their international operations, where they face direct or indirect competition, airlines do not have an entirely free hand. Several factors will influence how much they spend on product features and quality. The sector distances, or rather the travel times, of the different routes that they operate are important. Clearly service standards must be different on a six-hour sector compared with a one-hour sector. They will also differ according to the time of day or night that a flight is operated. Above all, service quality must be responsive to competitive pressures from other carriers operating in the same or in parallel markets. Such pressures will even impact on routes where an airline may be the only operator, since it must offer the same consistent product throughout its network. It cannot afford to alienate customers by providing a poorer service on routes where it enjoys a monopoly.

Within the constraints imposed by sector times and by what competitors are doing, an airline has considerable freedom to decide its marketing strategy. This means not only deciding which markets to service, it also includes pricing policy as well as decisions on the types of product and the quality of services that the airline wishes to offer in those markets. The whole issue of marketing is discussed in Chapter 7. But it is important to appreciate that several aspects of marketing policy impact directly on cost levels. They can be grouped under two headings: costs associated with product and service features and those costs more directly related to sales, distribution and related promotional activities.

5.7.1 Product and service features

Airlines have to decide on the nature and quality of the product they are going to offer in the various freight and passenger markets that they serve.

This must be done within certain constraints. For commercial and competitive reasons airlines may have to conform to certain minimum standards of product quality. They must also conform to a variety of international or national safety and technical regulations. These affect many aspects of the cabin layout such as the seat pitch next to emergency exits, or the minimum number of cabin staff, and so on. Within these constraints airlines enjoy considerable freedom to decide on the quality of the product they are going to offer, both in the air and on the ground, and on the costs they are prepared to incur.

In the air, three aspects of cabin service standards are particularly important for passenger services. *Cabin layout and seating density* are frequently the most significant in terms of their impact on unit costs. Each aircraft type has a maximum design seating capacity based on an all-economy layout at a given minimum seat pitch. The actual number of seats that an airline has in its own aircraft of a particular type depends on a number of key decisions which the airline itself takes. It must decide whether it is going to offer a one-, two- or three-class product in each part of its network. A large number of airlines, such as Continental, Delta, SAS, Garuda or KLM, have abandoned first class on their long-haul routes and offer only business and economy cabins. Some offer fully reclining seats in first class that turn into flat beds but take up a great deal of space. In 2000 British Airways launched fully reclining seats in their long-haul business cabins and other airlines began to follow suit. In November 2000 KLM announced it was spending $38 million to improve its in-flight product. Much of this was to be spent on new flat-bed business-class seats. In the mid-1990s many European airlines began to upgrade their short-haul business product – first class had long been abandoned in Europe – by installing convertible seating in the front section of their narrow-bodied aircraft. This convertible seating is more expensive but it enables them to convert six-abreast economy seats (three plus three) into five-abreast (two plus three) more spacious business seating. As a result they can expand the business section further back into the aircraft by converting the seats in response to daily demand.

The distribution of space between fare classes, if there is more than one, the type of seating and the seat pitch adopted for each class and the number of seats abreast are the more crucial determinants of seating capacity. The distribution of cabin space between seating areas, galleys, toilets and storage is another factor. In certain wide-body aircraft extra space for seating can be provided by positioning one or more of the galleys in the freight hold, though only at the expense of freight capacity. The fewer the number of seats on offer, the higher will be the cost per seat kilometre, since the aircraft's trip costs need to be divided among the fewer seat kilometres generated.

The range of seating densities used by international airlines in two aircraft types is illustrated in Table 5.8. Some scheduled airlines, as part of a superior product strategy, choose cabin and seating configurations which may result in a reduction in the number of seats by 20 per cent or more when compared

Table 5.8 Impact of different airline seating density on costs per seat, 1997

Airline	Airbus A320		Airline	Boeing 767-300/ER	
	No. of seats	Cost per seat[a]		No. of seats	Cost per seat[a]
Scheduled airlines					
All Nippon	166	100	Delta	254	100
Air Portugal	156	106	KLM	224	113
British Airways	149	111	LOT Polish Airlines	221	115
Iberia	147	113	British Airways	219	116
Royal Jordanian	140	119	Aero Mexico	209	122
Kuwait Airways	135	123	United	206	123
Charter airlines					
Monarch	180	92	Britannia	325	78
Airtours	180	92	Airtours	325	78
Aero Lloyd	174	95	Condor	269	94

Source: Compiled by the author using ICAO *Digest of Statistics*, Series F-P, *Fleet and Personnel* (1998).

Note

a Scheduled airline having most seats indexed at 100 and assumes airlines have similar operating costs for each aircraft type.

with the seating capacity offered by other scheduled carriers in the same type of aircraft. The airline's product may be improved but the cost implications are serious. For example, in 1997 the seat-kms costs of United Airlines with only 206 seats in its Boeing 767–300 aircraft were 23 per cent higher than they would have been if it had adopted Delta's much higher seating density. The impact of different scheduled seating densities on costs is normally not so marked and involves unit cost variations of up to 15 per cent. The charter airlines shown in Table 5.8 push their seating densities way above those found acceptable for scheduled services with a concomitant reduction of seat-kms costs. Very high seating densities are a key feature of the economics of non-scheduled operations and of low-cost airlines.

A second aspect of cabin service standards which has important cost implications is the *number of cabin crew* used. Safety regulations impose a minimum number for each aircraft type. It is up to each airline to decide how many more than the minimum it wishes to use. This is partly a function of the number of cabin classes it decided to offer and partly a function of the sector distance. On short- to medium-haul sectors, where there is less time for meals and other in-flight services, cabin crew numbers may be close to the minimum. On long-haul sectors airlines have more scope to try and differentiate their product through their in-flight services, and one aspect of this may be more cabin staff. In 1999 Singapore Airlines were flying their Boeing 747–400 aircraft with nineteen cabin crew when the minimum required was eleven.

Other South East Asian airlines had fewer cabin crew on their own 747s. Cathay Pacific had eighteen while Thai International and Malaysian had seventeen. Philippine Airlines had fewer, at only fifteen. When cabin crew wages are low by international standards, the cost of improving the in-flight product by having more cabin staff is not high. This is the case with these Asian carriers (Table 5.1 above). Conversely, it is more costly for high-wage airlines to compete in terms of cabin staff numbers.

The third key element of cabin service standards is that of *in-flight catering and related cabin product features*. As a result of international liberalisation the need and the scope for management initiative in this area increased. Many airlines place great emphasis on trying to persuade potential customers that they offer the best meals, cooked by well-known master chefs, together with the most expensive and sought-after wines, the best spirits and the finest coffee. This is done despite the fact that passenger surveys repeatedly show that in-flight catering is way down the list of factors that influence choice of airline. Moreover competitive pressures push most carriers to more or less match what their competitors are doing. For this reason, while in-flight catering costs may vary between airlines, they are unlikely to be important in explaining difference in total unit costs between those airlines. The same is also true of the minor elements of cabin service such as the range of newspapers and magazines on offer, free give-aways, toiletry bags on long-haul flights, and so on. There may be greater cost differentiation in the provision of in-flight entertainment because the options available to airlines are much greater. For instance, some long-haul carriers, such as Emirates in Dubai, have for some years offered seat-back screens for all economy class passengers with a multiple choice of channels. This is clearly an expensive marketing decision, since it means refurbishing all aircraft with complex and more expensive seats, as well as installing more expensive equipment. Moreover the video and audio programmes are also expensive to buy and must be changed frequently.

There is also scope for product differentiation on the ground. Airlines can rent and operate more check-in desks to reduce passenger waiting times and they may also decide to provide more ground staff for passenger handling and assistance in general. Some international airlines go further and provide sometimes quite luxurious and costly first- or even business-class lounges at airports, while their competitors may provide neither. An example is Singapore Airlines, which has decided, as a matter of product policy, to provide its own exclusive first/business-class lounges at all the airports it serves irrespective of the frequency of its services or the number of first- or business-class passengers handled. In this way it imprints its own brand and product style on the lounges. On the other hand, some other carriers share executive lounges with one or more different airlines in order to save costs.

It is difficult to assess the impact of the product quality decisions of different airlines on their comparative costs because of the paucity of reliable data. One way of doing it, however, is to establish the expenditure on passenger

Table 5.9 Passenger services expenditure on intra-European services, 1999

Airline	cents per 100 scheduled pass-kms
SAS	386
KLM[b]	347
Swissair	274
Austrian	247
British Airways	234
Lufthansa	226
Iberia	209
Air France	209
Alitalia	200
Sabena	177
Malev	91

Source: Compiled by the author using Association of European Airlines data.

Notes
a Annual expenditure: includes cabin crews and passenger-related costs.
b Figures for 1998.

services per 100 passenger-kms of traffic carried. Passenger service expenditure, essentially, covers the costs of cabin crews and passenger service personnel as well as passenger-related costs such as in-flight catering and hotel accommodation. By expressing such expenditure per 100 passenger-kms rather than per passenger one can partially adjust for the fact that there will be quite different average passenger hauls on the airlines selected.

The relative passenger service expenditure levels on their intra-European services for a group of selected European carriers are shown in Table 5.9. The carriers selected all had broadly similar sector lengths on their intra-European routes, namely between 776 km and 1,148 km, though only three had average sectors of over 1,000 km. The range of expenditure on passenger services is high, as illustrated by a comparison of SAS and Sabena from either end of the table. SAS spent more than twice as much as Sabena per 100 passenger-kms. As a result of this high expenditure, resulting from SAS's focus on the high-yield business market, 34 per cent of SAS intra-European passengers in 1999 were travelling in business class. Sabena's performance, not surprisingly, was abysmal in this respect. Only 11 per cent of its European passengers were in business class. This was not only poor in relation to SAS but was half the average for all European airlines, which was 20 per cent. Sabena's management had clearly made a decision not to target the business market, and therefore its expenditure on passenger services in Europe was low. But poorer service standards also impacted adversely on traffic and yields in its economy class too. In 1999 Sabena lost $125 million on its European services. SAS also lost money but proportionally much less. Within two years Sabena had collapsed but SAS was still flying.

5.7.2   *Sales distribution and promotion policies*

Scheduled airlines enjoy considerable discretion in the way they organise and run their sales and distribution activities. They decide on the extent to which they should sell their services through their own sales offices, telephone call centres and Web sites rather than through other airlines or travel agents. Such decisions have cost implications. While setting up and operating its own sales outlets costs money, the airline saves the commission it would otherwise have to pay to travel agents. (The impact of commission payments on costs was discussed in section 5.3.) A key issue in recent years has been the switch to selling on the internet through an airline's own web site. The low-cost no-frills airlines such as Southwest in the United States and easyJet in Europe were the first to grasp fully the value of the Internet in reducing distribution by cutting out commission to agents, which can represent between 6 per cent and 10 per cent of total costs. By the end of 2001 easyJet was selling close to 90 per cent of its tickets through its web site. Conventional scheduled carriers have been slow to follow, especially some of the smaller ones. Few were achieving even 5 per cent of sales through their web sites by the end of 2000.

Several other important decisions have to be made in relation to sales and distribution. An important issue is whether an international airline should set up off-line sales outlets, that is, outlets in cities or countries to which it does not fly. Equally crucial may be the decision on whether it should itself staff and operate sales offices at some of its less important overseas destinations or whether to appoint a general sales agent, who may or may not be another airline. When airlines enter into cross-border alliances they may cut the costs of distribution by merging their sales offices and sales staff in each other's country or in third countries to which two or more of the alliance partners operate. This has been done by SAS and Lufthansa. Following their alliance in 1996, Lufthansa pulled out all its sales staff and closed its sales offices in Scandinavia. SAS did likewise in Germany. Each now sells and distributes for the other in its own home market.

Having taken these decisions on whether to provide its own sales outlets, an airline has to decide on their location and size within each city. If opening a sales outlet in London, does it insist on its being with many of the other airlines in a small area bordered by Bond Street, Piccadilly and Regent Street, one of the most expensive shop locations in the world, or does it, like Philippine Airlines, choose a less expensive location in central London but somewhat away from the other airlines? Or could it follow Cyprus Airways' example and set up its sales outlet in much cheaper facilities well away from central London on the grounds that most sales are done through agents or its call centre?

Decisions on advertising and promotional activity are very much at management's discretion. It is open to airlines themselves to decide how much to spend on advertising and promoting their services and how to spend it.

Table 5.10 Advertising spend in UK by selected Asian airlines, 1995

Airline	Annual spend (£000)	Flights per week	Annual advertising spend per flight (£000)
Qantas	1,729	14	124
Singapore Airlines	1,989	17	117
Korean Air Lines	440	4	110
Garuda Indonesia	283	3	94
Cathay Pacific	1,412	17	83
Thai Airways	521	7	74
Emirates	1,100	19	58
All Nippon	185	9	21
Japan Airlines	193	15	13
Malaysia Airlines	173	14	12

Note: Includes advertising spend on television, radio and the press.

Numerous promotion channels are open to them from television, radio or national press advertising aimed at large numbers of potential customers at one end of the scale to promotional activities or trade press advertising involving relatively small numbers of freight and travel agents or travel journalists at the other. Many airlines target an advertising and promotional budget equivalent to about 2 per cent of their revenue. They may spend much more than this in particular markets, especially when they are launching a new service, or in foreign countries where they are less well known than the home-based carriers. Advertising spend is also likely to be higher in markets where competition is more intense.

Different management attitudes to advertising can be seen in Table 5.10, which shows advertising expenditure in the UK press, radio and television of all the East Asian airlines in 1995. Some interesting differences emerge in airline policies. The key issue is not the total annual spend, since that should vary with the number of services operated, but the annual expenditure per weekly frequency (column 3 in Table 5.10). Of the established carriers Qantas, SIA and Korean spent much more, in that year, per weekly flight than any of the other carriers. Because of their high advertising spend and excellent in-flight service Qantas and SIA were getting particularly high loads in first and business class. Some airlines were spending remarkably little on advertising, notably Malaysian, Japan Airlines and All Nippon Airways. The latter two did this because they clearly focus their marketing at the Japanese end of the route. Malaysia Airlines claimed it did not need to spend more as its load factors were already very high on the London–Kuala Lumpur route. These examples show that advertising spend is purely a management decision.

Ticketing, sales and promotion represent around 14 per cent of the total operating costs of scheduled airlines of ICAO member states but rise to

Table 5.11 Expenditure on ticketing, sales and promotion, selected airlines, financial year 1999 ($ per 100 revenue tonne kilometre)

Rank	North American Airline	Expend.	European Airline	Expend.	East Asian Airline	Expend.
1					All Nippon[a]	18.70
2			British Airways	14.67		
3					Japan Airlines	13.05
4			Iberia	12.92		
5	Continental	12.00				
6	Delta	11.90				
7	American	11.81				
8			Alitalia	11.75		
9	United	11.00				
10			Lufthansa	10.99		
11	Northwest	10.68				
12			Air France	10.16		
13	Air Canada	9.86				
14					Korean Airlines	6.27
15			KLM[a]	5.90		
16					SIA	5.44
17					Thai Airways	5.12
18					Cathay Pacific	3.50

Source: Compiled using ICAO (2000) data.

Note
a Figures for 1998.

16.6 per cent on the international scheduled services of IATA airlines (Tables 4.3 and 4.4). As such, it is clearly a major item of expenditure, yet one which is very much influenced by the policies adopted by individual airlines.

As a result the expenditure on ticketing, sales and promotion per unit of traffic generated varies considerably between airlines, as can be seen in Table 5.11. This shows for the financial year 1999 the spend per 100 revenue tonne-kms (passengers and freight) for the world's major international airlines. While Japanese and one or two Asian or European carriers are high spenders, as a group the US airlines have the highest spend. It is also noticeable that the sales and promotion expenditures of these US carriers per unit of output sold are all fairly similar. But they are also significantly higher than those of their East Asian counterparts. The sales and promotion costs of some Asian carriers were low in 1998 in part because of the devaluation of their currencies that year. In the case of SIA and Cathay Pacific they were also low because of the very long-haul nature of their operations. Among European airlines, British Airways, in particular, appears to spend relatively more than others on ticketing, sales and promotion.

5.8   Financial policies

5.8.1   *Depreciation policy*

The hourly depreciation cost of an aircraft (as discussed in Chapter 4.3) depends on the length of the depreciation period, the residual value of the aircraft at the end of that period and the annual utilisation of the aircraft. The annual utilisation, that is, the block hours flown during the year, is dependent on the pattern of operations, on the stage lengths flown and on the scheduling efficiency of an airline's management. The depreciation period adopted and the residual value assumed are determined by an airline's financial policy. In many countries legislation or accounting convention may require the adoption of a particular depreciation policy or may impose certain minimum requirements. Most international airlines, however, have some flexibility in deciding on the effective commercial life of their aircraft and their residual value at the end of that life. This flexibility is important. If an airline can adopt the practice of depreciating its wide-body aircraft over sixteen years to a 10 per cent residual value, its hourly depreciation costs (assuming the same annual utilisation) will be 30 per cent less than they would have been had it used a ten-year life for the aircraft with a 20 per cent residual value.

Both these depreciation policies are currently in use by different airlines and they show the significant variations in depreciation costs that can result from the adoption of different policies. Since, on average, depreciation charges represent around 8–10 per cent of airlines' total operating costs, the depreciation policy adopted can influence total costs by as much as 3 per cent.

Many airlines change their depreciation policy in order to increase or reduce their costs. Depreciation periods are frequently lengthened or residual values increased in periods of falling profitability in order to reduce costs and improve financial results. It is less usual for depreciation periods to be shortened when times are good. In the 1970s Singapore Airlines adopted a policy of using depreciation periods which were exceptionally short by international airline standards. The airline estimated the life of its aircraft to be between five and six years with zero residual value. The purpose appears to have been to build up reserves from the depreciation charges to finance the rapid renewal of the fleet and also to mask the large operating profits that were being made. When in 1979 the fortunes of the airline industry were hit by the rise in the price of fuel, Singapore Airlines promptly lengthened the life of its aircraft to eight years to reduce its costs. It thereby still managed to show a profit. During the 1980s Singapore Airlines continued to use an eight-year life for its aircraft with appropriate residual values. This was still very short compared with most international airlines. It explains why Singapore Airlines' depreciation costs per tonne kilometre available were among the highest when compared with international airlines with roughly similar average stage lengths. Then in April 1989 SIA again lengthened its depreciation period, to ten years, with 20 per cent residual value, so as to be more in line with industry practice.

SIA's rapid depreciation is also linked with its policy of rapid fleet renewal and the investment allowances available in Singapore which can be used to offset taxation. As the crisis of 2001 began to bite into airline profits, SIA announced that it would once again change its depreciation to bring it in line with industry practice. For the financial year 2001–02 it would stretch its depreciation period from ten to fifteen years and halve the residual value from 20 per cent to 10 per cent. These changes would reduce its depreciation cost for the year by $151 million!

5.8.2   Current or historical cost accounting

The theoretical justification for depreciation is not only to spread the cost of the asset over its useful commercial life. It is also to set aside money each year as a depreciation charge in order to build up a reserve fund, from which new aircraft or equipment can be bought to replace existing aircraft when the latter are retired or sold off. Failure to cover depreciation charges out of revenue means that an airline is not generating enough revenue to renew its assets. Inevitably, however, new aircraft cost more than the aircraft being replaced, so there is normally a shortfall between the funds set aside through depreciation based on the historical cost of the aircraft and the capital required to finance the new purchases. At times of relatively low inflation this shortfall is of manageable proportions and can be covered by raising loans. But when the annual rates of inflation begin to reach abnormally high levels, as in the second half of the 1970s, the difference between the historical cost of aircraft and their replacement cost becomes excessively large. A number of airlines at that time began to consider whether they should depreciate their aircraft and other assets on the basis of their current replacement cost rather than on the basis of their historical cost.

Different methods can be used to calculate the current replacement cost of an asset or aircraft purchased some years ago, but they all involve inflating the historical cost through some price index such as the index of manufacturing costs or aircraft prices. By inflating the cost of assets to be used for depreciation purposes, one of the effects of current or replacement cost accounting is to increase depreciation charges and thereby an airline's operating costs. In the early 1980s a few airlines embraced current cost accounting, but the practice was then largely abandoned as inflation rates declined. The adoption or otherwise of current cost accounting is another aspect of financial policy which influences airline costs.

Some airlines have adopted a compromise position of charging extra depreciation in addition to historical cost depreciation without formally adopting current cost accounting. This is done on an *ad hoc* and arbitrary basis. For instance, in the past Swissair charged increased depreciation in years when profits were high. It could also be argued that using relatively short asset lives, as Singapore Airlines did up to 2001, has the same result as current cost accounting. It accelerates the accumulation of reserves needed to finance new aircraft purchases.

An additional problem when considering depreciation costs is how to treat aircraft which have been leased rather than purchased, since legally the airline is not the owner. One approach is to differentiate between *finance lease agreements* that give the airline rights approximating to ownership, often involving the transfer of ownership at the end of the lease period, and so-called *operating leases* which do not give such rights and are usually of shorter duration. In the case of finance leases the aircraft can be depreciated in the normal way so that its depreciation cost appears under the airline's direct operating costs in the profit and loss account. However, while the interest element which is included in the lease payment is added to the other interest payments in the airline's accounts, the capital repayment element is not charged to the profit and loss account but is shown only as a liability. This is to avoid double counting, since the capital cost of the asset is already covered by a depreciation charge. Conversely, annual lease payments on operating leases would appear as a flight operating cost and there would be no separate depreciation charge. This is the approach adopted by Singapore Airlines. It follows that the type of aircraft leases that an airline negotiates will affect the absolute and relative level of its depreciation costs.

5.8.3 Methods of finance

Interest charges on loans are considered within the airline industry as a non-operating item. As such they do not affect operating costs or the operating results. However, they do affect each airline's overall profit or loss after the inclusion of interest and other non-operating items. The bulk of interest charges relate to loans raised to finance aircraft acquisitions, though some airlines may also be paying interest on bank overdrafts arising from cash flow problems or from the need to finance losses incurred in previous years. An airline can reduce or avoid interest charges by financing part or all of its aircraft purchases internally from self-generated funds.

Self-financing is clearly cheaper than borrowing, especially at a time when interest charges are high. To do this airlines must first build up their cash reserves from accumulated profits and possibly depreciation charges. But even highly profitable airlines may be able to self-finance only part of their capital expenditure. Singapore Airlines, through a policy of rapid depreciation previously referred to, and as a result of its high profits, has been able to build up substantial reserves during the last fifteen years or so. Yet even SIA has been no more than 70 per cent self-financing in most years. There are few airlines in as favourable a position as SIA. Most are still heavily dependent on external sources of finance.

Airlines would prefer to be self-financing but may be unable to generate sufficient reserves from their depreciation charges and retained profits to do so except to a limited extent. Their remaining capital requirements can be met in one of two ways. First, there may be an injection of equity capital into the airline. The advantage of equity finance is that airlines pay interest on it in the form of dividends only if they make a profit. Many of the larger international airlines outside the United States are partly or totally government-owned, but governments have been loath to put in more capital to finance aircraft purchases, especially as the sums involved are very large. This is one of the reasons which have been pushing governments to partially or fully privatise their airlines. By injecting some of the funds raised through the privatisation back into the airlines concerned, the latter's debts and finance charges could be reduced.

If equity finance is unavailable, airlines must borrow in one form or another from commercial or government banks. Several different forms of loan finance are available, but either directly or indirectly they all involve interest charges. This is true even of finance or operating leases. In the past, the traditional reliance of state-owned airlines on external loan finance rather than self-financing or equity capital pushed them into having very high debt:equity ratios. In other words, too many of their investment requirements were financed by loan capital and too few by equity. Many airlines have been under-capitalised and have needed an injection of capital if the interest burden was to be kept within manageable proportions, and if they were to be in a position to order new aircraft without bankrupting themselves. It is generally believed that a debt:equity ratio of 25:75 is desirable and that a ratio of up to 50:50 is acceptable. Given the very high cost of new aircraft, airlines can stay within acceptable limits only by injections of new capital. Most governments have been loath to put more equity capital into their airlines. Their airlines' debt:equity ratios have consequently deteriorated, especially during each of the cyclical downturns.

As previously mentioned, an alternative solution for airlines with inadequate financial resources is to lease aircraft from specialist aircraft leasing companies, such as GECAS Capital, ILFC or smaller companies, such as Oryx, or from finance houses that provide the same facility. This solution is particularly attractive for airlines that are too small to obtain the best prices from the manufacturers or airlines that are not themselves in a position to get any tax advantages from direct purchase. The leasing companies by doing both can provide aircraft which may be cheaper in real terms.

5.9   Corporate strategy

An airline's corporate strategy and objectives are likely to have a major impact on its cost structure and cost levels. It is self-evident that an international airline that sees its mission as being to operate primarily charter or non-scheduled services will have lower costs than a conventional scheduled network carrier. The same is also true of an airline that sees its prime mission to be a scheduled low-cost no-frills operator.

A key strategic decision is the degree to which an airline focuses on the carriage of freight as well as on the passenger business. On average, the world's scheduled airlines generate around 29 per cent of their total traffic, domestic plus international, from the carriage of freight (Table 1.5). Yet several airlines as part of their corporate strategy are much more heavily involved in freight. In 2000, 63 per cent of Korean Airlines' revenue tonne kilometres was generated from freight. The comparable figures for other airlines whose corporate strategy was to place particular emphasis on the development of air freight were as follows: Lan Chile 59 per cent, Cathay Pacific 48 per cent, Singapore Airlines 47 per cent and Lufthansa 43 per cent. On the other hand US carriers have more or less given up the carriage of freight as anything other than fill-up on their passenger services, especially on domestic flights, and even here they have been outsold by the integrators such as FedEx and UPS. As a result freight is of little importance. For United in 2000 it represented only 16 per cent of traffic carried, for American Airlines 14 per cent and for Delta only 11 per cent, though purely on their international services freight was more significant (Table 1.5). Since the costs of carrying freight are significantly lower than those of carrying an equivalent volume of passengers, airlines which focus on freight will have lower overall costs than those that focus primarily on carrying passengers. This is one further reason why Cathay Pacific, SIA and Korean Airlines have the lowest costs of all the airlines shown in Table 5.1.

Another strategic issue is whether an airline sets out to be a major network operator or whether it sees its role as being that of a more restricted 'niche' carrier. The 'niche' may be geographical in scope or it may be a particular type of operation such as providing feeder services into a network carrier's hub. The niche carrier may be able to reduce its costs through greater specialisation. For instance, it may operate only one type of aircraft and it may also be able to increase flight crew and staff productivity through the simple pattern of its operations. Airlines that try to be all things to all men and serve every possible market end up with very mixed fleets of aircraft and pilots, complex maintenance arrangements and large over-staffed head and regional offices. Inevitably their costs are pushed up.

Airlines with domestic networks in countries where there is only one major national carrier often find that their corporate mission is heavily influenced by government policies. This is particularly so if they are government-owned. Such airlines may be required to provide domestic air links whose primary objective may be the social and economic cohesion of the country or the stimulation of domestic tourism rather than the provision of commercially justified and financially self-supporting air services. Services provided with social objectives in mind are usually on thin routes, with small aircraft and often at frequencies that are too high in relation to the demand. Olympic Airways, Malaysia Airlines, Air Algérie and Philippine Airlines are among the many airlines whose corporate objectives have traditionally included the provision of services to isolated and small domestic communities. By their very nature such services are inherently high-cost. Since in many cases the governments that expected this of their airlines also held back increases in domestic air fares, such social services became a constant financial haemorrhage on the airlines concerned.

Airlines, like most business enterprises, will normally have several, sometimes mutually conflicting, corporate objectives. Invariably operating profitably is one of the objectives. But the key question is the degree to which profitability is pursued as the prime and key corporate objective. If it is, then airline managers will be under pressure to do all they can to reduce costs. This is the case with most privatised airlines or airlines which, though not fully privatised, such as Singapore Airlines, are nevertheless operated as fully commercial enterprises. Many government-owned airlines are expected to operate profitably. But this objective is often lost and blunted among a whole series of other corporate objectives which are often imposed by the government as the major or only shareholder. When profit is not clearly the prime corporate objective, costs are likely to creep up as other objectives are pursued.

5.10   The quality of management

The analysis so far indicates that the most important variables affecting airline costs are the level of input prices, including the cost of labour, the type and size of aircraft used and the stage lengths over which the aircraft are operated. In so far as the last two of these variables are themselves influenced by the pattern and levels of demand that an airline is trying to satisfy, demand may also be considered an important variable. Other, though less important, variables have also been discussed. Many of the latter are particularly prone to management decision and choice. But there is a further dimension of management whose importance may be absolutely crucial in establishing an airline's unit cost levels, but may be difficult to define or measure. One might broadly define it as the quality of management, and it permeates through to most areas of an airline's activities

The quality of management affects the efficiency with which the management of an airline brings together the various factors of production at its disposal in order to meet different levels and types of demand in different markets. In theory it is management ability or the lack of it which should explain cost differences between airlines which cannot be attributed to variations in input costs, aircraft types operated, stage lengths or any of the other cost variables.

In practice no airline management is likely to be equally efficient or inefficient in all areas of the business. It may well be efficient in one area, such as flight crew scheduling, but relatively inefficient in the organisation of maintenance procedures. Thus the total unit cost of an airline may mask wide variations of performance in discrete areas of activity such as flight operations or maintenance management. Ideally, inter-airline comparisons should be on a disaggregate basis, looking at such discrete areas separately.

6 The economics of passenger charters

Charter airlines are the original low-cost airline . . . they must not be ignored.
(Robert Parker-Eaton, Deputy Managing Director,
Britannia Airways, November 2000)

6.1 The charter enigma

Charter airlines present an enigma. They fly passenger aircraft similar to those of their scheduled counterparts, often on the same routes. Most of their input costs, such as those for fuel or maintenance, are similar too. Yet, when they compete head-on with scheduled airlines they can sell their seats at one-third of the latter's average fares and still make a profit. How do they do it? This is the enigma.

There are three distinct business models for passenger services. The traditional and most widespread model is that of the conventional scheduled airline. Much of the present book is concerned with this model. Conventional airlines are network-oriented. They aim to maximise the travel link offered by their networks by operating point-to-point services, but also by offering convenient transfer connections at one or more hub airports. They target both business and leisure markets and, where possible, combine the carriage of passengers and freight on the same aircraft. The nature of their operations makes them inherently costly and their passenger fares are relatively high. This is in marked contrast to the other two business models, where the prime focus is to offer low fares. The older of the two models is that of the *charter* or *non-scheduled* airline. Such airlines expanded rapidly in the 1960s and 1970s, especially on European holiday routes and on the North Atlantic, in part because they were less strictly regulated than scheduled services (Chapter 2.8).

The second and more recent low-cost model is that of the *low-cost no-frills* airlines, also referred to as budget airlines. These have a different product and market strategy from the charter carriers. But their focus is the same, namely to offer low-price services. This business model was successfully developed for domestic services in the United States in the two decades after 1978, most notably by Southwest Airlines. The model was transferred to Europe and to international services in the mid-1990s by airlines such as Ryanair, easyJet

Table 6.1 Conventional scheduled and charter fares, London–Athens, summer (July–September) 2000

Type of fare	Return fare (£)	Fare index (excursion = 100)
Scheduled[a] – *publicly available*		
Unrestricted:		
Club/business class	848	236
Eurobudget	758	211
Restricted:[b]		
Excursion	359	100
Advanced purchase fares:		
Weekend (K class)	287	80
Weekday (K)	267	74
Weekend (M class)	246	69
Weekday (M)	222	62
Scheduled – *available to agents*		
For inclusive tours or consolidation (average)	150	42
Charter – *cost per passenger*[c]		
Friday day flight	133	37
Tuesday day flight	130	36
Tuesday night flight	110	31

Source: Compiled by the author from various sources.

Notes
a Olympic and British Airways. Low-cost carrier easyJet offered return fares ranging from around £100 to £300.
b Restrictions vary but include requirement to stay Saturday night plus no booking change, full payment on reservation, etc.
c Charter cost assumes 90% seat occupancy.

and Go. The economics of the low-cost no-frills model have been explored elsewhere (Doganis, 2001).

Today, around 13 per cent of international passenger traffic, in terms of passenger kilometres, is generated by charter flights, though a proportion of these are flown by conventional scheduled carriers. The success of charter operations is due in no small measure to the very low fares they offer. The fare advantage offered by charters in Europe, where they are most developed, can be gauged by examining the London–Athens route during the peak summer months of 2000 (Table 6.1). The cost of a charter round trip per passenger was only one-third of the scheduled excursion fare and around half the cheapest advance purchase fares offered by British Airways or Olympic. The charter fare advantage was much less when compared with the scheduled consolidation or inclusive tour fares of around £150 which could be bought by travel agents. However, the number of seats on any scheduled flight available for consolidation or group fares is limited, especially during periods of peak summer demand when scheduled carriers have little difficulty in filling seats at the higher rates. Also agents normally combine these low fares with holiday packages, so they are not publicly available. At the other extreme, the unrestricted business class fare was six times as high as the most expensive charter seat. From 1996 onwards one or two low-cost no-frills carriers, notably easyJet, entered the London–Athens market. In theory their prices ranged from around £100 return to £300 or so. In practice they too exercised yield management, so that it would have been difficult to fly at their lowest fares in the peak months unless passengers had booked several months earlier (Chapter 8).

It is the charter airlines' ability to offer such low seat costs which has enabled them to capture between a third and half of all international passenger traffic within the European Union. On most holiday routes between northern Europe and the Mediterranean, charters are dominant. On very many such routes, for instance those from Germany or the United Kingdom to Crete and other Greek islands, or to Turkish holiday resorts, charter airlines are the only operators.

In Canada too the charter industry is well developed, focusing on winter flights to Florida and the Caribbean. From the United States there are holiday charter flights to Europe, and to a lesser extent across the Pacific. However, the US charter airlines, the so-called 'supplemental carriers', which grew successfully on the back of military charters and expanded into leisure markets, such as the North Atlantic in the 1960s and 1970s, were adversely affected by domestic and international deregulation after 1978. They used the opportunities offered to launch scheduled services and all of them collapsed in the years that followed, except World Airways, which eventually abandoned its own scheduled services. As a result charters are much less significant in US markets than in Europe. Another market of particular importance is the very large number of charters from countries with large Moslem populations, which carry pilgrims to Saudi Arabia during the Haj season. Elsewhere the passenger charter market is less significant. Also, unlike Europe and Canada, a higher proportion of the charter flights in other markets are operated by the conventional scheduled airlines.

6.2   The nature of non-scheduled passenger services

In 1944 the Chicago Convention asserted that non-scheduled flights were those 'not engaged in scheduled international air services'. But no attempt was made to define 'scheduled' until 1962, when the Council of the International Civil Aviation Organisation agreed that a scheduled international air service is one 'operated so as to serve traffic between the same two or more points, either: (i) in accordance with a published timetable, or (ii) with flights so regular or frequent that they constitute a recognisable systematic series'. Within a few years of this definition being drafted it was meaningless as the basis of any real distinction between scheduled and non-scheduled services. Since the 1970s many inclusive tour and affinity group charters have been operated as a 'recognisable systematic series' of flights and though the time-tables may not be published by the charter airlines themselves they are to all intents and purposes published by the tour operators and travel agents who sell seats on them. The formal distinction between the two types of service has become increasingly blurred. In fact the 'Third Package' of air transport liberalisation measures which came into force within the European Union in January 1993 applied equally to both types of service, since no real distinction could be drawn between them. Nevertheless, they continue to be treated differently in many bilateral air service agreements and within many countries in their own regulations on domestic air services.

Two types of charter flights have emerged, namely *ad hoc* charters, that is, one-off flights where aircraft are chartered for a specific event such as a sports fixture, a religious festival or a sales promotion, and *series* charters. The latter are charters involving multiple flights which may be on behalf of tour operators, oil companies, the military or others requiring the regular and systematic transfer of people. They normally have a set timetable and are operated as a regular series.

Traditionally, within the Europe–Mediterranean area, which is the largest charter market, the vast majority of passenger charter flights have been inclusive tour charters (ITCs). These are where the whole of an aircraft is chartered by one or more tour operators who combine the round-trip seats with hotel or other accommodation into 'package' holidays. The passenger buys a holiday package from a travel agent or tour operator at a single price and is unaware of the cost of air travel within that total price. Inclusive tour holidays accounted for two-thirds of foreign holidays taken by UK residents visiting Europe or North Africa and travelling by air in 2000. Some charter packages may involve minimal accommodation or may include car hire, boat hire, cruises, camping or other services in addition to or instead of hotel accommodation. Apart from inclusive tour charters there are some affinity group and student charters within Europe, but these other forms of charters have been relatively limited compared with inclusive tour charters, which have dominated the market. Out of the United Kingdom around 95 per cent of passengers on charter flights in 2000 were on such inclusive tour or package charters.

In recent years, however, the European charter market has been undergoing change. First, there has been strong growth of self-catering inclusive tours, where the package does not include a hotel and meals but provides only accommodation in houses or apartments. Currently about one-third or more of the UK inclusive tour market goes on self-catering packages. Self-catering packages are also important in other European markets. Second, over the last fifteen years there has been a growing shift within the charter industry away from dependence on short- or medium-haul markets between northern Europe and the Mediterranean towards long-haul leisure markets previously the preserve of scheduled airlines. There has been above-average growth in charter flights from Europe to Florida, the Caribbean and Indian Ocean destinations such as Sri Lanka and the Maldives. This change resulted in part from growing consumer demand for cheap access to new and more distant destinations and in part from the introduction of smaller long-haul twin-jet aircraft with low operating costs. The use of Boeing 767-ER or A310-300 aircraft made the operation of long-haul charters more viable. Moreover, these aircraft could also be flown to denser Mediterranean resorts in summer months. For the airlines this change has resulted in a better balance of long- and shorter-haul markets. More important, the longer-haul routes tend to peak in the European winter and can be used to generate cash flow in what, for charter carriers, is the low season. Long-haul charters have generally developed on routes where scheduled services cannot meet the high seasonal demand for leisure travel.

The third and potentially most significant change has been the continued growth of seat-only sales on charter flights. This is not entirely new. The ability to buy seats on charter flights without any other 'package' features has been possible in some European markets for many years. However, the 1993 Third Package of liberalisation measures removed all restrictions on intra-EU charter flights. As a result seat-only sales have now become possible in all markets and they are an important feature of charter economics. The trend has been led by German charter airlines. To obtain lower seat kilometres costs they bought larger wide-body aircraft earlier than their British counterparts. They had to focus on seat-only sales to fill up the spare seats on these large aircraft which the tour operators did not always require. So from early days German charter airlines have sold seats direct to the public. Such sales make an important contribution to total revenues. German charter airlines sell around 20 per cent or so of their total capacity to seat-only passengers, though the share is up to 30 per cent in some markets. They do this by offering very low fares, even stand-by or last-minute fares which are particularly cheap. For instance, in October 2000 the German charter airline LTU was selling a stand-by return fare for the two-hour sector Dusseldorf to Palma in Spain for $135. Moreover, it was flying five flights a day on this sector, thus offering the stand-by passenger a high probability of getting a seat. This was below the cheapest return fare in October for a similar sector from London to Palma with one of the British low-cost no-frills carriers such as easyJet. German charter airlines have also redesignated their charter flights out of Germany as 'scheduled' flights. So they appear in timetables and computer reservation systems, which facilitates direct seat-only sales. Among British charter carriers seat-only sales still account for only around 5 per cent of the total traffic. They too have launched a few scheduled flights to tourist destinations or declared their flights to be scheduled so as to increase public awareness of the availability of seat-only tickets on many flights. They have also opened up direct Internet sales for such seats, though most seat-only sales are still channelled through travel agents or tour operators. This trend to more seat-only sales on charter flights is likely to increase as a result of charter airlines' awareness that seat-only passengers can add to profits. One consequence will be increased head-on competition for the independent leisure traveller in those European markets such as London–Palma which are also being targeted by the low-cost no-frills operators such as easyJet.

Inclusive tour charters are distinctive in that most passengers on these services buy a holiday package of some kind which includes the flight. Nevertheless, one can also buy inclusive tours using scheduled services. However, less than 20 per cent of the UK air inclusive tour market flies on scheduled flights; the rest fly on charters. In summary, there are two key features which distinguish inclusive tour charters and other forms of charter services from scheduled flights. The first is that the majority of passengers do not buy a seat direct from the airline, as scheduled passengers can do, since most seats are sold as part of a holiday package. The whole package is bought through an intermediary such as a tour operator, travel agent, student union, and so on. This distinction may be cosmetic rather than real, since in many cases the intermediary selling agent may be owned by the same parent company as the charter airline. Generally only a small proportion of the seats will be available for direct sale to the public. On some flights there may be none at all. The second distinguishing feature is that flights are put on by the charter airlines not in the hope of generating demand from individual travellers but in response to specific advance contracts from tour operators. It is the latter and not the charter airlines themselves who determine the routes and frequencies to be served. This is true even when the charter flights, as previously mentioned, have been redesignated as scheduled.

6.3   The charter industry

Passenger charters are big business. Charter flights handle over 9 per cent of the world's passenger traffic (Table 6.2). But since most of the charter traffic is international rather than domestic, the charter industry's share of

Table 6.2 Significance and distribution of passenger charters, 2000 (%)

Traffic	Share of world's passenger kms		
	International services	Domestic services	Total all services
Scheduled			
Scheduled airlines	87.0	98.5	91.4
Charter			
Scheduled airlines	7.2	1.3	4.9
Charter airlines	5.8	0.2	3.7
Total	100.0	100.0	100.0

Source: Compiled by the author using ICAO data.

international business is even greater. In 2000 charters generated around 13 per cent of the world's international traffic. Surprisingly, over half of this charter traffic appears to have been carried not by the specialist charter airlines but by scheduled airlines operating charter flights. This is partly because scheduled airlines tend to operate primarily in the long-haul charter market and partly because some charter airlines have been redesignated as 'scheduled' carriers to facilitate the selling of seat-only tickets. Because charters, and more specifically inclusive tour charters, have been most developed in Europe their market share here has, of course, been much higher. By the mid-1990s just over 50 per cent of international passenger traffic within the European Union (measured in passenger kilometres) was estimated to be travelling on charters. After 1996 the latter's market share began to slip because of the extremely rapid growth of the new entrant European low-cost no-frills carriers such as Ryanair, easyJet and Go.

The international passenger charter market is dominated by specialist carriers which are either privately owned non-scheduled airlines or separate charter subsidiaries of scheduled airlines (Table 6.3). There are in addition a significant volume of charter flights operated by airlines that are primarily conventional

Table 6.3 Major carriers of non-scheduled passenger traffic, 2000 (million passenger kilometres)

Rank	Independent charter airlines		Charter subsidiaries of scheduled airlines		Charter flights of scheduled airlines
1			Condor (Lufthansa)	24,000	
2	Britannia	21,747			
3			LTU (Swissair)	19,100	
4	Airtours	18,750			
5	Air 2000	17,950			
6	JMC	14,300			
7	Hapag-Lloyd	14,250			
8	Monarch	13,650			
9	Air Transat	12,850			
10	Corsair	11,000			
11			Martinair (KLM)	10,550	
12	Premiair	10,000			
13	Air Berlin	7,800			
14	Aero Lloyd	6,600			
15			Transavia (KLM)	6,150	
16					Finnair 5,100
17			Futura (Aer Lingus)	4,550	
18	Amtran	4,300			
19					Spanair 4,300
20					Garuda 4,250

Sources: *Flight International*, IATA and ICAO.

Notes
Top five share of world international non-scheduled: 35%. Top twenty share of world international non-scheduled: 81%.

scheduled carriers. This latter group is the third segment of the charter industry. Several of the charter carriers are relatively large, with traffic levels exceeding those of many national scheduled airlines. Their size and import-ance can be gauged from the fact that the largest of them, Condor of Germany and Britannia Airways (UK), each generated more passenger kilometres on international services in 2001 than any of the scheduled airlines in South America or Africa, more even than SAS in Europe.

There are many charter airlines based in tourism destination countries, such as Futura in Spain, Eurocypria in Cyprus, or Pegasus and Onur Air in Turkey. However, it is a feature of the European charter industry that the large and powerful charter carriers are virtually all in the tourist-originating states of northern Europe and primarily in Germany and the United Kingdom, by far the largest charter markets. This is evident from Table 6.3. Only three of the top twenty charter carriers in 1999, Spanair and Futura from Spain and Garuda from Indonesia, were from tourist receiving states. It is also indicative that there are only two North American charter airlines, Air Transat and Amtran, in this top group, although there are several smaller North American charter carriers such as Ryan International, World and Champion Air. There is only one Asian airline, Garuda, in the list, and ranked twentieth in size. This is because a combination of regulatory constraints and aggressive pricing by Asia's scheduled airlines have kept charters at bay. In Asia, Africa and South America most charter flights by local carriers are operated by scheduled airlines.

The charter industry is becoming increasingly concentrated. While in 1987 the five largest charter carriers accounted for 24 per cent of the world's total international charter traffic, the figure had risen to 35 per cent in 2000. Moreover, the top twenty airlines now control over two-thirds (81 per cent) of the market (Table 6.3). But as a result of mergers and acquisitions among major tour operators between 1999 and 2001 several of the airlines listed in Table 6.3 now belong to the same parent company. Condor and JMC are now part of the same German-owned group. Britannia, Hapag-Lloyd in Germany and Corsair in France are part of the Preussag group of companies. UK Airtours also owns Premiair in Denmark. If each of these groupings are considered as single airlines, the top five airlines' share of the world's total non-scheduled passenger traffic rises to 52.7 per cent in 2000. Consolidation among charter carriers has gone much further than among scheduled carriers.

Most of the major non-scheduled carriers in Europe are equipped with large and modern fleets of aircraft, often bought new. In 1999 the average age of Condor's fleet was around seven and a half years, while Britannia's aircraft were on average about a year younger. European charter fleets are markedly younger than the fleets of many European or US scheduled airlines. It is only some of the smaller charter airlines that are more dependent on older equipment. But the view that most charter carriers traditionally operate old second-hand aircraft is the opposite of the truth. In Europe, at least, their fleets are young and modern.

6.4   Vertical integration and consolidation

The European charter industry has long been characterised by a strong tendency towards vertical integration between tour operators and charter airlines and in some cases with hotel groups as well. This is in marked contrast to the United States, where anti-trust regulations prevented it. Moreover, this key feature of European charter operations partly explains their much greater success and long-term growth. In the UK, Britannia Airways has always been part of the Thomson Travel Group, which owns Thomson Travel, Britain's largest tour operator, and also has interests in a number of hotels. The Airtours charter airline is owned by the Airtours Group, which even includes cruise ships and the second largest UK travel agency, Going Places. In Germany in 1998 Condor, the largest charter carrier in the world, set up a joint-venture leisure company, C&N Touristic, with Neckerman, one of Germany's largest travel and tour agencies, with which Condor had been co-operating for years.

This strong tendency towards *vertical integration* between holiday companies and charter airlines is a common feature in all the tourism-originating countries of Europe. Such vertical integration means that most charter airlines do 80–100 per cent of their flying for their own in-house tour operator(s). Britannia Airways, for example, did less than 10 per cent of its flying in summer 2001 for tour operators not in the Thomson group, but this rose to over 10 per cent in the winter months. But there are a few charter operators that are not vertically integrated. These include most of the charter airlines based in destination countries as well as the charter operations of scheduled airlines such as those of Garuda and Tunis Air.

The second and more recent characteristic of the European charter industry has been a strong trend towards consolidation, that is, *horizontal integration*. As a result of a spate of mergers and acquisitions the United Kingdom in recent years has seen five large groups emerge that control almost 90 per cent of charter traffic flown by UK airlines (Table 6.4).

An attempt in the summer of 1999 by Airtours to merge with First Choice was turned down by the European Commission. The Commission felt that the combined group would be in a monopolistic position in the UK short-haul leisure market, controlling 37 per cent of this market. The new group would also control 2,900 travel agents, nearly double the number controlled by Britannia (1,000) or Thomas Cook (700), its main competitors. On the airline side the merger would have created an airline group making up around 35 per cent of the UK charter industry (Table 6.4).

If further integration and consolidation at the national level were likely to fall foul of the European Commission the only way the large leisure travel companies could expand was through cross-border acquisitions. There was a spate of these in Europe in 1999 and 2000. The major tour operating companies were hoping through mergers and acquisitions to achieve economies of scale in distribution, in the provision of charter flights and in the buying of hotel beds. Greater control of the various European markets would also enable them to squeeze out over-capacity and thereby push up the charter

Table 6.4 Vertical integration and consolidation in the UK charter industry, 2000

Airline	Share of UK charter passenger km (%)	Linked tour operator or owner	Main travel agent
Britannia	22.1	Thomson	Lunn Poly, Pegasus, Sibbald Travel, etc.
Airtours	20.5	Airtours	Going Places, Travelworld
Air 2000	16.8	First Choice	Travelchoice, Baker's, Dolphin, Hays Travel, Holiday Express, etc.
JMC[a]	15.6	Thomas Cook	Thomas Cook, Orchid Travel
Monarch	14.0	Cosmos	
Total five majors	89.0		
Other UK airlines[b]	11.0		
Total UK charters	100.0		

Notes
a JMC created by merger of Caledonian Airways and Flying Colours in 2000.
b Traffic of smaller charter airlines and on charter services of UK scheduled airlines.

rates. Over-capacity seems to be endemic to the package holiday industry as the large operators fight for market share by offering more capacity.

While most of the larger charter airlines with linked tour operators were British, the drive for consolidation was led by two large German companies, Preussag and C&N Touristic, which is 50 per cent owned by Lufthansa. The reason was simple. These two companies, because of interests outside the travel/tourism sector, were too large to be taken over by the British travel companies.

By early 2001 Preussag, a German conglomerate not previously heavily involved in tourism, had bought control of TUI, Germany's largest travel agent, and of the Thomson Travel Group in Britain. It also had a 34 per cent stake in the French travel company Nouvelles Frontières. Through these three travel companies it also controls three charter airlines, Hapag-Lloyd, Britannia and Corsair. Cross-border consolidation was also being undertaken by C&N Touristic. Towards the end of 2000 C&N acquired Thomas Cook, the United Kingdom's second largest tour operator. In the process it took over Thomas Cook's charter airline, JMC, which had been created earlier the same year when Flying Colours took over Caledonian. The whole C&N group was subsequently rebranded as Thomas Cook. The European leisure travel industry was reflecting the trend towards consolidation and internationalisation in other sectors of industry.

For the charter airlines this trend will inevitably mean more mergers and the concentration of the European charter business into fewer and fewer larger airlines. As pointed out earlier, the five largest airline groups in Europe generate over 50 per cent of the world's passenger charter traffic. This trend has been reinforced by the mixed financial results of charter airlines in recent years.

6.5   Financial performance

The performance of the passenger charter airlines has not been uniformly good. Two sectors of the industry have faced serious problems. The first is the sector based in destination countries, such as Spain or Turkey. Many charter airlines have been set up, often with the participation or help of north European airlines or leisure companies, to try to capture some of this market. Examples include Spanair in Spain, which is 49 per cent owned by SAS, and another Spanish airline, Futura, majority-owned by Aer Lingus. The proliferation of such carriers, which has pushed charter rates down, their relatively small size compared with their northern competitors, and the absence of a sufficiently large winter market from their home base, have undermined the financial viability of many of them. Many such airlines have gone out of business. This aptly describes the situation in Turkey, with failures such as Noble Air and Sunways. Other failures in destination countries during the mid to late 1990s include Centennial Airways in Spain, Venus and Apollo, both Greek airlines, and Air Columbus in Portugal. To overcome the inherent weaknesses mentioned above, some charter airlines in destination countries have launched domestic or international scheduled services to reduce the imbalance in their cash flows between summer and winter. Both Spanair and Air Europa in Spain started off as charter airlines but now carry half or more of their passengers on scheduled services.

The other problem area is that of the smaller charter airlines in the large charter markets such as Germany, France and more especially the United Kingdom. Those without strong vertical integration or links with large tour companies have struggled to survive. As the number of independent tour operators diminishes and the major holiday groups increasingly concentrate their flying in-house on their own charter airlines, the demand for smaller charter airlines is constantly being squeezed. Even in the buoyant years of the mid-1990s several smaller UK charter carriers failed, including Excalibur Airways (1996), All Leisure Airlines (1997), Ambassador Airways (1994) and Leisure International (1999).

The operating margins of the six largest (in terms of revenue) of the UK charter and scheduled airlines for the financial year 1999 are shown in Table 6.5. It is clear that there is a wide range in performance among both groups but the four larger charter airlines had operating margins which were significantly higher than those of the larger scheduled carriers such as British Airways, Virgin or British Midland. Small unaligned charter carriers, as Caledonian Airways was in 1999, without vertical linkages to tour operators, appear to have less certain prospects, with operating margins towards the lower end of the scale. This explains why in 2000 Caledonian was taken over by Flying Colours to create JMC, a charter airline linked with Thomas Cook.

The inherent instability of the charter industry not only in Europe but worldwide can be gauged from the fact that, of the twenty largest charter operators in 1987, identified in the second edition of this book (Doganis,

Table 6.5 Operating margin of larger UK scheduled and charter airlines, financial year 1999

Airlines	Operating margin (%)
Scheduled	
Virgin Airways	4.2
British Regional	4.1
British Midland	1.5
British European	1.4
British Airways	1.3
KLM UK	−4.7
Charter	
Air 2000	11.4
Flying Colours	9.5
Airtours	6.9
Britannia	6.0
Monarch	3.7
Caledonian Airways	−0.5

Source: Compiled by the author using CAA (2000a).

Note
Operating margin is operating profit (loss) before interest as percentage of revenue.

1991), eleven have since collapsed or been merged with other carriers. They do not appear in the 2000 list of the industry's top twenty (Table 6.3 above). Nevertheless, the larger non-scheduled airlines have generally shown themselves more adept than many scheduled airlines at matching supply and demand in a way which both generates profits for the producers and meets consumer needs. A key element in this matching process is the ability of charter airlines to produce at low unit costs and in consequence sell seats at very low prices.

6.6   Cost advantages of charter operations

In order to appreciate how non-scheduled operators can produce such relatively low unit costs one must examine separately each element of the costs of a charter service and compare it with the costs of a comparable scheduled service. To eliminate the effect of differing aircraft types and stage lengths, any cost comparison must assume the use of similar aircraft on the same route. The London–Athens route would be a suitable example, since Boeing 737-400 aircraft have been used by both sectors of the industry on this route.

6.6.1   Direct operating costs

Flight operations are the largest single element of direct costs. Here charter operators may enjoy some limited advantages. Traditionally, flight crew with charter operators have received lower salaries than those in scheduled airlines.

However, the shortage of pilots in recent years has pushed up the salaries of charter pilots in Europe. There is now little difference in most cases in the salary levels of pilots flying the same aircraft whether on charter or on scheduled services. This is so unless the charter airline is based in a destination country such as Turkey, Greece or Cyprus, where pilot salaries are appreciably lower in the charter sector.

Fuel costs should be similar for both charter and scheduled carriers if they are flying the same type of aircraft on the same route, since they are likely to be paying very similar prices for fuel. The larger charter airlines should be able to negotiate just as favourable fuel prices at their home base, because their uplift will be very high, as the scheduled carriers do in their own bases. If, however, charter carriers have only a limited number of charter flights to a particular destination, their fuel uplift at that destination may be rather limited and they may be unable to negotiate as good a price as the scheduled carriers. This may be so at Athens airport. In this case the charters may have a cost disadvantage. Conversely, there will be destination airports where charter flights may be more numerous than scheduled flights and the former may get a better fuel deal. The level of competition among fuel supplies at any airport is, however, likely to have a much greater impact on the cost of fuel than the volume of fuel uplifts by individual carriers.

En-route navigation charges will be identical when charter and scheduled airlines are operating the same aircraft. On the other hand, charter operators may pay lower *airport charges* by using cheaper airports, especially in their home country. Scheduled services between London and Athens fly mostly from Heathrow and one or two from Gatwick. But charter flights may use Gatwick, Stansted or Luton, which are also in the London area. In summer 2000 a charter flight with a Boeing 737-400 from Gatwick in off-peak times would have been charged around £827, including a one-hour parking fee. A similar scheduled flight from Heathrow, also timed to be off-peak, would have had to pay £1,172. Not a large differential but it would mean £3 to £4 more per passenger.

Maintenance costs for both charter and scheduled operations would be broadly similar if using the same aircraft on the same routes. There is less variation in the wages of maintenance staff between carriers than of other airline employees.

Insurance costs are only a very small part of total costs but large well-established operators (whether scheduled or charter) would both tend to benefit from lower rates.

Depreciation costs per hour would also be the same if both charter and scheduled airlines achieved the same utilisation. In practice this is unlikely. First, aircraft used by the scheduled airlines will be used on different routes, many of which are relatively short. The need, for instance, to use the London–Athens aircraft on other much shorter scheduled sectors inevitably reduces the annual utilisation which that aircraft could achieve flying only on longer sectors such as London–Athens or London–Canary Islands, which is what charter aircraft would be doing.

Second, during the peak summer months the charter airlines will be flying their aircraft night and day. Aircraft on scheduled short- to medium-haul routes have a limited fourteen- to sixteen-hour operating day, since scheduled passengers do not like departing much before 0700 hours or arriving after 2200 hours. Scheduled short-haul aircraft frequently spend the night hours on the ground. Not so charter aircraft. Charter passengers seem prepared to put up with considerable inconvenience in order to fly cheaply. The flight time is also only one element in the overall package they are selecting. Leisure packages with night-time departures or arrivals are cheaper than day flights (see Table 6.1). Leisure passengers will accept departures or arrivals at any time of the night, or at least some of them will. As a result, except where constrained by night bans or limits, charter airlines programme their aircraft to fly through the night during the peak months. By doing so they can frequently get three rotations, that is, round trips, of the aircraft on a two- to three-hour sector during a twenty-four-hour day. A scheduled airline would plan for only two rotations. On a longer sector, such as between northern Europe and Turkey, the charter airline will achieve two rotations while the scheduled airline will manage only one or one and a half. Increasingly restrictive noise regulations at certain (mainly German) airports make achieving the maximum number of rotations a matter for careful scheduling but can usually be accomplished by arriving and departing from Mediterranean points in the middle of the night.

Charter services, however, have much more marked seasonal peaks and troughs, so that in the off-peak winter months daily utilisation of aircraft may drop below that of scheduled aircraft. This is more than compensated for by the very high peak utilisation achieved by using the night hours. In addition, some charter airlines are able to lease out aircraft during their own off-peak periods to airlines in other parts of the world that face peak demand at that time. Thus Monarch and Air 2000 in the United Kingdom have often leased some of their aircraft to Canadian carriers which used them for winter charters to the Caribbean. As an alternative, airlines such as Condor or Britannia, operating medium-range, wide-bodied aircraft on charters to the Mediterranean in the summer, can switch them to Caribbean, East African or Indian Ocean routes in the winter months.

The average aircraft utilisation of a selection of European airlines operating the Airbus A320 and the Boeing 757 is shown in Table 6.6. It is clear that the net result of the above factors is heavily in the charter carriers' favour. They achieve between three and six hours' per day more flying than their major scheduled counterparts when using the same aircraft on intra-European operations. As a result, with up to 50 per cent or so higher annual utilisation, the depreciation cost per hour will be reduced by around one-third. Higher aircraft utilisation should also lead to better utilisation of flight and cabin crews.

A consequence of this high utilisation, however, is the poor punctuality of charter services. Charter services across all international routes from the United

Table 6.6 Aircraft utilisation rates, UK scheduled and charter airlines, 2000

Airlines	Average daily utilisation (hours)	
	Boeing 757	Airbus A320
Scheduled:		
British Airways	6.8	6.5
British Midland	–	9.1
Charter:		
Air 2000	11.7	11.9
Airtours	11.9	11.2
Britannia	10.8	–
JMC	–	13.2
Monarch	10.0	11.3

Source: Compiled using CAA (2001) data.

Kingdom are consistently delayed on departure by about twenty to thirty minutes more than scheduled services. It may not be feasible to sustain this intensity of operation in the future as passenger service expectations rise while growing airport congestion leads to extended journey times and possibly penalties for persistently late operation.

In summary, a charter operator flying London–Athens or any other charter sector may obtain some cost advantage by achieving higher daily utilisation of its aircraft so as to reduce its hourly depreciation costs and, possibly, by using cheaper airports. Since airport charges and depreciation of flight equipment together typically account for 12–15 per cent of total scheduled airline costs, savings in this area would have only a limited effect on a charter airline's total operating costs (Table 4.4). Overall a European charter operator is likely to achieve only marginally lower direct operating costs when competing with a scheduled carrier on a particular route and flying the same aircraft.

6.6.2 Indirect operating costs

The differences in direct operating costs between European scheduled carriers and charters have been highlighted above. Such differences are not large. It is in the area of indirect operating costs that the costs of charter and scheduled services begin to diverge markedly.

Charter's *station costs* should be lower. Charter airlines can save money by subcontracting out most of the aircraft, passenger and baggage handling activities at their destination airports. This may be expensive on a per-flight basis but it means that they avoid a heavy year-round commitment. The seasonal nature of their operations means that they have no need for permanent staff or offices or other facilities at most of the out-stations they serve. At their larger destinations they may base one or a small number of their own staff to supervise local ground handling agents. Even where they do need staff dedicated to their operations, they may be in a better position to use seasonal staff. In contrast, most major scheduled airlines with daily or more frequent flights to, say, Athens will employ a station manager in Athens, together with assorted other station and handling staff. They will have offices at the airport and perhaps off the airport as well, with associated rents and other costs. They will have cars and possibly their own ground handling equipment. While it might employ some seasonal staff, a scheduled airline would have high year-round costs in Athens. Even if it out-sources some of its ground handling a scheduled airline will have many more staff at its out-stations. In Europe, as in many parts of the world, scheduled airlines now provide special dedicated lounges at airports for their business or executive club members, or they may pay for access to other airlines' business lounges. This is an additional expense avoided by charter companies. As a result of all these differences, charter airlines are likely to have lower station and ground costs.

Charter airlines will also have lower expenditure on *passenger services*. They will try to have fewer cabin staff than a scheduled airline would have in the same aircraft type, while providing the statutory minimum required for safety. For example, a British charter airline would normally have one cabin crew member per thirty-two passengers on a Boeing 737 aircraft, compared with British Airways, which carries one cabin crew for every twenty-one passengers on the same aircraft. Moreover a higher proportion of the cabin staff will be seasonally employed and will not be a cost burden for the rest of the year. Some charter airlines employ up to half their staff for a six-month peak season only. Furthermore, some charter airlines pay low basic salaries to cabin staff, who are expected to augment their earnings through commission on in-flight sales. Salary differentials are more marked in the case of cabin attendants than in that of pilots. For instance, in 2000 British Airways and British Midland were both spending on average £18,600 and £19,700 per annum respectively on each cabin attendant. Yet the average cost per attendant for Airtours was £16,400, for Britannia £15,300, for Air 2000 it was £13,100, for Monarch £14,700 and for JMC only £11,500 (CAA, 2001). Because there is no shortage in the supply of cabin staff, charters should be able to achieve lower cabin crew costs. Charter airlines also save money by scheduling crew rotations to avoid having to accommodate crew outside their home country, thus eliminating a huge amount of overnight expense. For instance, British Airways night-stops crews and aircraft in Athens to provide early morning departures back to London for its business and connecting traffic. Fewer cabin staff at lower average wages and with lower expenses help charter carriers reduce their overall cabin crew costs.

Another significant saving in passenger service costs comes because it is not necessary for charter airlines to offer a business-class cabin with the more expensive business-class catering, newspapers, magazines, etc., that are a feature of the scheduled airlines' services. Though meals and bar service on charter flights are generally very good, an attempt is made to provide simpler

Table 6.7 Expenditure on passenger services, UK scheduled and charter airlines, financial year 1999–2000

Airline	Expenditure (in £) per:	
	Passenger	000 passenger km
Scheduled:		
KLM UK	7.29	13.82
British Midland	9.64	12.86
British Airways	27.15	8.22
Charter:		
Britannia	11.17	4.20
Monarch	10.82	3.76
Airtours	8.43	2.89
Air 2000	6.92	2.66
JMC	6.09	2.57

Source: Compiled by the author using CAA (2001) data.

Note
Passenger service costs include cabin crew salaries and expenses plus meals and other services provided to passengers and passenger insurance.

in-flight meals to reduce the cost of in-flight catering. Charter airlines will not normally have responsibility for connecting passengers (the principal exception being the German charter operators, who hub at various German airports in order to serve all the major German cities). They thereby escape the hotel, food, transport and other costs associated with such passengers which scheduled airlines have to meet.

The impact of all these various cost savings is reflected in the dramatically lower passenger service costs that UK charter airlines achieve compared with their scheduled rivals (Table 6.7). In terms of passenger service expenditure per passenger carried the charter airlines spend much less than British Airways but not much less than other scheduled airlines. However, spend per head is partly dependent on the length of the flight. A more instructive comparison is passenger service costs per 1,000 passenger-kms, a measure which takes into account the average distances travelled by each airline's passengers. On this basis, charter airlines' passenger service costs are way below those of both the scheduled short-haul carriers and those of British Airways (second column in Table 6.7). British Midland's and KLM UK's costs per 1,000 passenger-kms are so very high not only because they are primarily scheduled but also because they operate very short sectors, in both cases close to 500 km. (For the impact of sector length on costs see Chapter 5.6.) On the other hand, British Airways' average sector distance is just under 2,000 km, which is not much below that of the charter airlines in Table 6.7, whose sectors are between 2,250 km and 2,500 km. Yet British Airways' service costs per 1,000 passenger-kms are two to three times as high.

The greatest savings obtained by charter airlines arise in *ticketing, sales and promotion*. Charter operations do not require large reservation computers or other expensive ticketing facilities, since the whole plane is chartered to one or perhaps a handful of agents or clients who then become responsible for distributing the tickets and allocating the seats. Even if they sell some capacity on a seat-only basis they will do so either through agents, as Monarch does, or directly through the internet. For the package holiday operator, the airline often merely prints tickets and hands over to the tour operator a book for each flight chartered and has no further ticketing or reservation costs. Some airlines require tour operators to print their own tickets and so enjoy an even greater cost advantage. In contrast, it has been estimated that scheduled airlines spend an average of $7 to $13 on the paperwork and administration associated with issuing each conventional airline ticket.

A charter airline has minimal sales costs. Since all or the vast bulk of its capacity is not sold direct to the public, it has no retail sales offices or staff, nor does it pay commission to others for selling its tickets. Yet agents' commission is an important cost for scheduled airlines. In the financial year 1999/2000 commission paid (net of commission received) represented 11.6 per cent of British Airways' operating costs and 7.8 per cent of British Midland's costs. A charter airline sells its services not to passengers but to travel agents, tour organisers or other charterers. There is no commission to be paid. In the United Kingdom, as in Germany or Switzerland, there are a small number of very large tour operators and a somewhat larger but diminishing number of medium-size ones. Most of a European charter airline's capacity is sold to the tour operator(s) in the same travel group. The vast bulk of seats are sold to a handful of large tour operators in each country. The balance is sold to a small number of independent tour operators. Thus a charter airline's annual selling and promotion costs may be no more than the cost of a few meetings and lunches with the key buyers of charter capacity. The charter airline's managing director, with a handful of back-up sales staff to do the detailed costings and negotiations, is probably all that is required. There is little need to sell or promote its services to the travelling public, so a charter airline is unlikely to have a promotion or advertising budget. Alan Snudden, who, during the 1980s, was managing director of Britain's then second largest charter airline, Monarch, claimed that in 1987 it 'achieved a turnover of £111 million based on the selling activities of one sales director, three salesmen and two typists with an advertising budget of £10,000, which I have to say was underspent'.

Commission payments arise only when charter airlines sell capacity to the public on a seat-only basis. Here, too, charter airlines make great efforts to avoid or minimise commission payments. Overall, enormous cost savings accrue to charter airlines from the virtual absence of ticketing, sales and promotion expenditures. This is evident when one compares the marketing costs per passenger, including commission paid, of UK scheduled and charter airlines (Table 6.8). While the larger scheduled airlines spend £7 to £38 for

Table 6.8 Marketing costs, UK scheduled and charter airlines, financial year 1999–2000

Airline	Ticketing, sales (including commission) and promotion costs per passenger (£)
Scheduled:	
British Airways	37.63
Virgin Atlantic	27.51
British Midland	9.65
KLM UK	7.29
Charter:	
Britannia	1.20
JMC	0.06
Monarch	0.04
Air 2000	0.04
Airtours	0.01

Source: Compiled by the author using CAA (2001) data.

each passenger they carry, all the charter airlines except one, Britannia, spend less than £1 per passenger. Several spend only a very few pence.

Charter airlines tend to have very much lower general and administrative costs because they require fewer administrative and accounting staff. Many functions which are crucial to scheduled airlines and absorb significant resources either do not exist within a charter airline at all or, because of the different nature of charter operations, require relatively few staff. A charter airline, for example, does not need a large planning department with forecasting and yield management staff or large numbers of accountants to sort out revenue and sales accounting and inter-airline ticketing debts.

A charter airline can make economies in virtually all areas of indirect costs. Its station and handling costs are lower. Its passenger service costs are half to a third those of scheduled competitors. Sales, ticketing and promotion costs, which for international scheduled airlines average around 15–16 per cent of total costs, are minimal for charter carriers. Administrative costs too are much lower. As a result, charter airlines' indirect costs may be less than half those of scheduled airlines operating on the same routes.

Major savings in indirect costs, together with slightly lower direct costs, suggest that flying similar aircraft a non-scheduled operator may have total round-trip costs between 20 per cent and 30 per cent lower than those of a scheduled operator on the same route. This is clearly insufficient to explain the wide differentials in charter and scheduled passenger fares which exist in the European market and which were illustrated earlier by reference to the London–Athens route in summer 2000 (Table 6.1). However, the initial 20–30 per cent operating cost advantage is magnified by two key elements in the economics of non-scheduled air services: high seating densities and very high load factors.

6.6.3   High seating density

In summer 2000 British Airways was flying many scheduled services in Europe using an Airbus A320 for some flights. Typically this had 149 seats. It is a popular aircraft with charter airlines but they put up to 180 seats in it (Table 5.8 above). By putting around 21 per cent more seats in the aircraft than their scheduled competitors, the charter airlines can reduce their seat-kms costs by about 17 per cent. In practice, seating on British Airways will be less than 149, since several rows of six-abreast seats will be reduced to five-abreast to provide for a business-class cabin. Eight rows of business class would reduce the seating capacity to 141. The scope for higher seating densities and therefore for even lower seat-kms costs is sometimes greater on wide-bodied aircraft. Non-scheduled airlines operating Boeing 767 aircraft would normally expect to have close to 325 seats in a charter configuration. Yet the same aircraft flown on scheduled services by British Airways, including one daily flight to Athens, has only 247–56 seats. In this case the charter configuration increases the seating capacity by nearly 32 per cent and reduces the seat-kms costs by almost a quarter.

Several factors explain the ability of charter operators to push up the seating capacity on their aircraft. With very few exceptions, non-scheduled aircraft are in a single-class layout and at a constant seat pitch (the distance between each row of seats). No space is lost accommodating first- or business-class passengers in separate cabins with greater leg room and low seat densities. If scheduled airlines operate a three-class cabin on medium- and long-haul scheduled flights this further reduces the total seating capacity. Within Europe, benefits achieved by scheduled airlines during the 1980s from eliminating first class and operating a higher-density layout are diminishing as competitive pressures force airlines to upgrade their business class. For instance, Air France, Swiss and British Airways, among others, all now have convertible seating units in their narrow-body aircraft, allowing them to change from six abreast to five abreast in their business cabins.

Whatever the cabin layout, the charter configuration will also have a lower seat pitch, that is, less distance between each row of seats, so that more seat rows can be installed within the length of the cabin. A 29 in. seat pitch would be acceptable in a short-haul charter layout, whereas 31–4 in. would be more normal for economy-class seating on a scheduled flight. On wide-body aircraft an extra seat across the cabin (e.g. ten abreast instead of nine abreast) would be used on the MD-11 for charters. Charter airlines tend to increase the floor area on the main deck of the aircraft available for seating by reducing the number of toilets and galley space and by eliminating other space uses such as coat cupboards, and so on. Galley space can be reduced because in-flight catering tends to be less lavish than on scheduled flights. The absence of first- or business-class passengers helps in this. In wide-bodied aircraft, such as MD-11s, the galleys could be placed on the lower deck with an internal lift providing access. This is possible because aircraft on non-scheduled flights generally carry little if any cargo.

Table 6.9 Passenger load factors on international services, 1999

Scheduled international services, short/medium haul	Seat factor (%)	Non-scheduled services, all routes	Seat factor (%)
	UK airlines		
British Airways	62	Airtours	92
British Midland	62	Flying Colours	92
KLM UK	59	Air 2000	91
		Britannia	90
		Monarch	89
	Other European airlines		
KLM	70	Finnair	88
Cyprus Airways	69	Hapag-Lloyd	84
Spanair	67	Condor	82
Iberia	66	Transavia	81
Lufthansa	64	Spanair	80
SAS	59	LTU	78
Finnair	56	Maersk	78
Olympic	56		
	North American airlines, all routes		
		Canada 3000	85
		World	66
		Amtran	66

Sources: ICAO *Digest of Statistics*, Series T; AEA (2000); CAA (2000a).

6.6.4   High load factors

Not only do non-scheduled airlines put more seats into their aircraft, but they also fill substantially more of them. Whereas scheduled airlines would be pleased to achieve year-round passenger load factors on their international services of 65–70 per cent, especially for short-haul operations within Europe, charter airlines would be aiming for around 85 per cent or more. The stark contrast in the seat factors of the two sectors of the industry is illustrated in Table 6.9. In 2000 none of the scheduled European airlines listed achieved seat factors above 70 per cent (considered very high by scheduled standards) on their short- to medium-haul services. The majority had seat factors in the middle 60s and several were less than 60 per cent. By contrast, the major UK charter operators shown achieved very high seat factors of over 89 per cent while other European charter airlines achieved seat factors a few percentage points lower. The slightly lower seat factors of German charter airlines compared with their UK counterparts may be due, in part, to their greater reliance on seat-only sales. One can conclude that, in general, passenger seat factors are at least 20 per cent higher on non-scheduled than on comparable scheduled services. Finnair is a good example, with a seat factor of only 56 per cent on its short- to medium-haul scheduled flights but achieving a high 88 per cent on its non-scheduled operations, most of which were within Europe. It is noticeable that World and Amtran, the two largest US charter carriers, in contrast to their European or Canadian counterparts, have much lower seat factors. This is a function of the very different nature of their business, with much less reliance on inclusive tour holiday packages.

The achievement of the very high load factors shown in Table 6.9 is due not to the non-scheduled operators themselves but to the efforts of the tour operators and leisure companies, for it is they who have the responsibility for retailing the seats they have bought wholesale. By careful programming and scheduling of flights and other components of the total package such as hotel beds, self-catering apartments, ground transport, and so on, the tour operators can achieve very high seat factors on the aircraft and high occupancy factors for the beds and other facilities they have booked. Vertical integration between tour organisers, who may be hotel owners too, and charter airlines facilitates the process of closely matching and programming the supply of and demand for hotel beds and aircraft seats. Load factors must be kept high to ensure low and competitive prices. Charter airlines which are not vertically integrated with major tour operators, such as Transavia or Maersk, tend to achieve lower seat factors.

Several features of the charter market help in achieving such high load factors. Charter passengers are given limited flexibility in terms of choice of departure days and almost none on the choice of the return days. Particularly with inclusive tours, passengers can stay for only a fixed period at their destination – usually seven or fourteen days on intra-European charters, or perhaps twelve nights on some long-haul charters. Most of the travellers on an outward flight will come back together on the same return flight and on the same day of the week that they flew out on. Aircraft loads are not subject, as in scheduled operations, to the whims of different individual travellers who want to be away for different periods of time and travel on different days of the week. Moreover, once made and paid for, charter bookings are difficult to change and cancel except at a considerable cost to the passenger concerned. Ticket brokers are also used by aircraft charterers to fill up spare capacity on inclusive tour or advanced-booking charters. The ticket brokers try to sell spare seats to other travel agents or at a discount to the public. If things go really badly, a tour operator with a large number of unsold seats on a flight it has chartered may cancel the flight (though it will pay a large penalty to the airline if it does that late in the day) and 'consolidate' its passengers on to someone else's flight where seats may be available. However, this practice is becoming less frequent. Both tour operators and charter airlines benefit from such an arrangement. Loads on individual flights are carefully monitored to ensure high load factors. A finely tuned and highly differentiated price structure for charter-based inclusive tours is used to induce a potential customer to travel on less popular days or times or seasons of the year. Such incentives include lower holiday prices, two weeks for the price of one, free car hire, no charge for a child, and so on.

Higher load factors substantially reduce the passenger-kms costs of charter as against scheduled services. The twin impact of higher seating densities and very much higher seat factors on the unit costs of charters can be illustrated by reference to two British airlines, British Airways and Britannia, both of which have been flying Boeing 767 aircraft on European routes such as London–Athens. Britannia operated this aircraft in a charter configuration with 325 seats. Its average load factor in 1999 on international charter operations was 90 per cent. This would have resulted in a load of 292 passengers. British Airways' scheduled Boeing 767 aircraft on European services had 247 to 256 seats and its average load factor on intra-European operations within Europe was 62 per cent (Table 6.9). This gives an average load of 153 passengers for a capacity of 247 seats. Even if on a particular route the operating costs of the two airlines were the same, and we have seen that they are not, the costs per passenger round trip or per passenger kilometre for Britannia would be about 48 per cent lower than for British Airways, purely because it was carrying 292 passengers instead of 153. On a smaller narrow-body aircraft, where the capacity difference is not so great, the cost reduction would be less. In essence, by spreading the total round-trip operating costs over many more passengers, the non-scheduled operator can significantly reduce the trip cost per passenger. The above example shows that the higher charter seating densities and load factors together have a greater impact on reducing the charter costs per passenger than do the savings in operating costs.

The preceding analysis indicates that non-scheduled operators start with an initial round-trip cost advantage of 20–30 per cent. This arises largely because of their lower indirect operating costs. By putting more seats into their aircraft they magnify it into an even greater cost advantage per seat kilometre. Then, by filling 85–90 per cent of a larger number of seats, the costs per passenger kilometre become even less *vis-à-vis* those of scheduled operators. The net effect may be to convert the round-trip cost advantage of only 20–30 per cent into a cost advantage per passenger carried which may range from 55 to over 65 per cent.

An attempt has been made in Table 6.10 to show the various potential cost savings which a charter airline might expect when competing head-to-head with a conventional scheduled airline. With each cost reduction, the charter airline's costs per passenger cascade down to only 31 per cent of the scheduled cost. In practice the differential between scheduled and charter costs will depend on several factors such as the sector distance, whether night flying is allowed, the seat factors actually achieved by the scheduled or charter carriers, and so on. But Table 6.10 summarises where cost savings are most likely to be achieved by a charter carrier competing head-on with a conventional scheduled airline.

6.7 Planning and financial advantages

Apart from a straightforward operating cost advantage, charter airlines enjoy other planning and financial advantages which are inherent in the workings of the charter market, particularly for inclusive tour charters (ITCs). The peak

Table 6.10 Cascade analysis: charter versus scheduled cost, London–Athens

Cost saving	Charter adjustment to scheduled cost	Cost index
Total scheduled cost per passenger[a]		100
1 Charter cost savings		
Direct operating costs:		
Higher aircraft/crew utilisation	−3	97
Indirect operating costs:		
• More outsourcing at airports	−2	95
• Fewer cheaper cabin attendants	−2	93
• Economies in other passenger services	−2	91
• Minimal ticketing, sales, promotion or commissions	−15	76
• Lower administration costs	−2	74
2 Higher charter seating density[b]	−17	57
3 Higher seat occupancy[c]	−26	31
Derived charter cost as % of scheduled		31
But no compensating revenue from cargo		

Notes
a Assuming 65% year round seat factor.
b 20% more seats on narrow body.
c Assumed 88% on charter.

period for ITC holidays is during the European summer from mid-June to mid-September. The marketing and retailing of those holidays begins the previous summer, with peak sales generally during January to March – though a number of passengers will be booking even earlier, on returning from their previous summer holiday! Because of early sales, the major tour operators have to publish their summer brochures with full details of their various package holidays the previous summer. To do this they must plan and schedule their flights and 'buy' the hotel beds they need some months earlier. This planning phase is carried out twelve to fifteen months in advance. The same pattern of charter contracts finalised a year in advance exists for winter inclusive tour charters to ski resorts or to long-haul destinations such as those in the Caribbean or the Indian Ocean.

The commercial pressure on tour operators and travel agents to plan and sell their holiday packages so far in advance works to the benefit of the non-scheduled operators. By May or early June one year a charter operator would expect to negotiate several contracts for a twenty-four to twenty-five-week summer season starting around the following April or Easter. Each contract may require numerous return flights per week and may involve hundreds or thousands of hours of flying. The routes to be flown, aircraft types, frequencies, days of the week and departure times will all have been specified. If the charterer is not the airline's in-house tour operator or a major travel company, staggered but high cancellation fees may also be agreed. Usually up to about 10 per cent of flights may be cancelled if it is done well in advance and before January or February, when the agreed flying programme is finally firmed up. After that, cancellation fees may have to be paid. So there is a strong incentive not to cancel flights.

Charter operators are in an enviable position. Having negotiated contracts with their various customers they are in a position to know a year in advance the routes and frequencies they will be operating and the aircraft and crews they will need. Moreover, most airlines are protected by contract provisions allowing an upward revision of charges to tour operators in the event of significant fuel price increases or currency fluctuations. They can plan their productive resources so as to ensure that supply precisely matches demand and that it does so as efficiently as possible. Knowing their total revenue in advance, charter airlines can adjust and reorganise their costs to ensure that costs do not exceed revenues. In contrast to this, scheduled airlines normally do not know their revenues until the costs have been incurred and it is then too late to make any significant adjustments.

The charter airline has further safeguards. The negotiated price for the series of charter flights is normally a fixed fee per round trip or per block hour for a minimum number of trips or block hours per season. If this minimum number is exceeded, the trip or hourly fee may decline. Conversely, if too many flights are cancelled the cost per block hour of the remaining flights operated may go up. But the price is based on the airline's input costs at a datum point and will include actual or forecast fuel prices, airport fees and navigation charges and assumed exchange rates for relevant currencies. In the case of UK airlines this would be the sterling to dollar rate. The airline is obliged to advise the charterer of any net change of costs in relation to the datum costs a certain number of days before a flight. If costs have gone up there will be a surcharge to pay. If they have gone down the charterer may be entitled to a rebate. The minimum period of notice is often ninety days, so the charterer has time to pass on any surcharge to those passengers who have not yet bought their holiday package. This system of surcharges on the negotiated charter price in theory insulates charter airlines against any sudden adverse variations in their input costs. In practice, since most charter passengers buy and pay for their flights several months in advance, imposing surcharges on package holiday prices is virtually impossible. So charterers generally prefer to hedge against fuel price escalation and adverse exchange rate fluctuations so as to reduce the need to pass on any increased costs to their customers. This is especially so if their major or only customer is their own in-house tour operator. (For fuel hedging see Chapter 5.3.)

Another key feature of charter operations is that charter fees are paid rapidly. In a few cases involving small tour operators or one-off charters, flights are paid for before they take off. In most cases flights are paid for very soon after they take place. This contrasts with scheduled carriers, who may wait for months after a particular flight to collect all the revenues due from ticket agents, credit card companies and other airlines. Moreover, all payment accrues to the charter airline. There are no commission or credit-card fees, no chasing of delinquent accounts. While charter flights are paid for quickly by the charterer, many charter airline inputs such as fuel may be paid in arrears. This creates large positive cash balances during peak periods which can earn substantial interest payments while on deposit with banks or financial institutions.

The charter operator's cash flow is also helped by the high volume of on-board sales of spirits, cigarettes, perfumes, watches, and so on. On-board sales per passenger in Europe are much higher for charter than for scheduled passengers. This may be due partly to the fact that many charter flights are to or from secondary airports, particularly in destination countries, with poor retail facilities of their own, and partly to the high proportion of regular travellers on scheduled flights, who may be less inclined to spend money on board. On-board sales also receive a lower priority on scheduled flights with more competing demands on the cabin crew's time; on charter flights commission earned on in-flight sales may be a vital addition to the salaries of cabin crews. Their salaries in any case tend to be lower. However, in July 1999 duty-free sales on flights within the European Union were abolished. Since the profit margins on such sales were very high this was a real financial setback for the charter airlines. They have tried to respond by focusing sales on high-value goods such as watches, jewellery, cosmetics. This has been a success but profit margins are lower. Nevertheless there are many charter markets outside the European Union where on-board duty-free sales continue. These include Turkey, Egypt and other North and East African destinations, the Americas, the Indian Ocean and South East Asia. For flights to these destinations, many charter airlines have embarked on aggressive selling of their in-flight goods in advance of passengers' departure through mail order and other direct sales techniques. This enhances sales revenues. Before the abolition of duty-free sales on intra-European flights in July 1999, European charter airlines were generating up to a third of their overall profits from in-flight sales. Now such sales have declined, but contribute up to about 20 per cent of profits.

While in-flight sales are a positive element for non-scheduled operations, the absence of freight revenue clearly reduces the potential revenue from any one flight. Authorisations for passenger charter flights to and from destination countries outside the European Union, even under some 'open skies' bilaterals, normally exclude the right to carry any freight. Even where charter carriers are allowed to carry freight they have no distribution system, so shippers must bring their own shipments to the airport. As a result freight loads are minimal or non-existent. Generally, charter operators cannot top up their passenger revenue with freight revenue as their scheduled competitors can. For the latter freight can add up to 10–15 per cent of the revenue on a passenger flight. The price at which the charter airlines sell their capacity must therefore reflect this difference.

The charter airlines' planning and financial advantages described above are also the cause of their major headache, which is the constant fear of over-capacity in the market and intense price competition. Signed contracts to provide many hours of flying a year or so later can be used to facilitate the raising of loans to purchase aircraft to meet the charter contract. The ease with which finance can be raised once a contract has been signed may well induce new entrants into the market or existing airlines to expand their capacity too quickly. If there is over-capacity charter rates tend to drop and margins are squeezed. The fear that more new charter airlines will be set up reinforces the pressure towards vertical integration between airlines and the leisure companies. As more tour operators become financially linked with particular charter airlines, the scope for independent airlines and new entrants diminishes. Yet new and ever-hopeful charter airlines are regularly being set up, especially in newer destination markets, such as Turkey and North Africa.

The early negotiation of charter contracts and the ability to adjust charter rates in response to changes in input costs provide non-scheduled operators with a level of certainty and financial security that is unique in air transport. They can sell their product in advance, at a price which can be adjusted if their costs go up. They can then go out and procure the resources necessary to provide the capacity they have sold. Scheduled airlines are handicapped because they have to do the exact opposite. They first decide to provide a level of scheduled capacity which they judge necessary to meet the anticipated demand; they then allocate resources to it and subsequently try to sell it. Scheduled operators must plan their output in advance, without knowing for certain how much of it they will sell. As a result, they face much greater problems in trying to match supply and demand than do the charter airlines.

6.8   Charter versus scheduled competition

There can be little doubt that non-scheduled operators enjoy several cost and other advantages when competing with conventional scheduled air services. These advantages are particularly marked in the short-haul leisure markets within the Europe–Mediterranean area. When faced with head-on competition from charters, European scheduled airlines have had difficulty in maintaining their market share. Some, such as Olympic Airways or Air Portugal, have tried to fight back by entering the charter market themselves. This is rarely a financial success, since scheduled airlines can match the prevailing charter rates only at a loss. This is because they have to carry and recoup the high indirect and overhead costs of a scheduled airline. At the same time they lack the flexibility of a specialist charter operator. If their aircraft are being used on both scheduled and charter flights, they may be unable to use charter seating densities. They may also be unable to tender for all sectors of the charter market if aircraft have to be used for scheduled services for much of the day. While some conventional scheduled airlines continue to operate both scheduled and charter services, as Finnair still does, most have reduced their involvement in charters. For instance, British Midland has cut back its once extensive overnight and weekend charters.

The difficulties involved in competing directly in the charter markets have pushed European scheduled carriers in different directions. Some set up separate but subsidiary charter companies with their own dedicated aircraft and crews, employed under different terms and conditions from those of the parent scheduled company. Subsidiaries such as Condor (Lufthansa) are now large and successful charter airlines in their own right. Others have bought into well-established, previously independent charter airlines. For instance, Alitalia bought into Air Europe, KLM purchased a controlling share in the Dutch charter company Transavia and Swissair took a 49.9 per cent stake in LTU in Germany. Such moves give the major carrier the opportunity to use the low-cost subsidiary to supplement its own services, to dominate the wider air transport market (i.e. including charter) in its home country and in the case of Swissair to obtain a foothold in markets otherwise closed to it as a carrier which, at that time, was outside the European Union. On the other hand several scheduled airlines have found the charter markets too competitive and closed down their own charter subsidiaries. Both British Airways and Air France did this in the mid-1990s.

An alternative and long-established response to charter competition has been the growth of so-called 'part-charters' or other charter-competitive fares on scheduled services within Europe. Scheduled carriers can sell off blocks of seats to travel agents or tour operators, who then package the seats into inclusive tour holidays. In many cases there may not be a separate part-charter fare but the airlines may give tour agents a discount on the group inclusive tour or consolidation fare to enable them to put together inclusive tour holiday packages. These are often competitive with charter airline passenger costs. Between 7 per cent and 8 per cent of international passengers on UK scheduled airlines were carried on a part-charter basis in 2000.

The concept of part-charter and inclusive tours on scheduled services is not merely a competitive response to low-cost charters; it offers scheduled carriers other advantages. By mixing normal traffic and charter-like traffic, scheduled carriers can fill up otherwise empty seats and improve load factors. In the process they may also be able to switch to large aircraft sooner and thereby get the benefit of lower seat-kms costs. The marginal cost of these seats may therefore be very low and this has made it more difficult for charter airlines to compete on long-haul routes if there is an established scheduled service offering charter-competitive fares. By mixing traffic in this way it may also be possible to sustain scheduled services on routes with leisure demand where the scheduled traffic would otherwise be insufficient to maintain a commercially viable frequency.

There is, however, an inherent danger in scheduled airlines trying to match charter fares. Scheduled costs are on average much higher than charter costs. If the proportion of part-charter, inclusive tour or other very low-fare passengers is controlled and mixed with an adequate proportion of high-yield passengers, the total revenue on the scheduled service may be pushed up. On the other hand, too many very low-fare passengers are a recipe for financial disaster, since the total scheduled costs cannot be recouped. Yet during the 1980s and 1990s some European scheduled airlines, such as Olympic Airways or Air Portugal, in their desperation to head off charter competition, ended up with too high a proportion of part-charter and low-yield passengers on some of their intra-European holiday routes. As a result they frequently lost money on such routes without effectively stemming charter penetration. These very low charter-competitive fares should be introduced by scheduled airlines only as part of an effective yield management programme.

In Europe the charter airlines' response to part-charters on scheduled services has been to try to introduce seat-only sales on charter flights. Airline deregulation within the European Union since 1993 has made this easy for charter carriers flying on intra-EU markets such as UK–Spain and Germany–Greece. For markets outside the European Union, such as Turkey, providing such service may require a regulatory 'fig leaf' such as providing the passenger with a voucher for derisory accommodation which is not meant to be used.

Part-charters, very low charter-competitive fares on scheduled services and seat-only sales on charter flights are further eroding the remaining distinctions between scheduled and charter services in markets where both are allowed to operate. The two sides of the industry are moving closer together. In Europe this tendency has been reinforced by the redesignation of many charter flights as scheduled services. Nevertheless the two markets remain distinctive. While scheduled services and routes are developed in response to demand from individual passengers and are sold very largely to individual travellers or their businesses, charter flights and destinations are determined by the demands of leisure companies and tour operators. The bulk of charter capacity is sold to the latter for resale as part of holiday or other leisure packages. Only a small proportion of charter seats is sold by the airlines themselves to individual travellers. This distinction in market characteristics in turn means that the economics of the two types of service are also different.

The real question is to what extent the key elements of charter economics, such as low indirect operating costs, higher seating densities and higher passenger load factors, can be adopted by scheduled services in order to reduce their own costs. It is the low-cost no-frills scheduled airlines, led by Southwest Airlines in the United States, that have successfully adopted some of the features of the charter airlines. In Europe low-cost carriers are also targeting certain leisure markets previously dominated by charter carriers. According to a former Deputy Managing Director of Britannia Airways, 'charter airlines are an integral element in the low-cost sector' (Parker-Eaton, 2000). It follows that perhaps the low-cost no-frills carriers may well represent more of a threat to the charter airlines than do the conventional scheduled airlines. While there is some overlap in the markets targeted by charters and European low-cost carriers, their operating and product characteristics are sufficiently different to ensure that they each have a role to play. Though they will undoubtedly compete head-on in some markets, they each offer an alternative and distinct low-cost business model for the airline industry.

7 Airline marketing

The role of passenger demand

Marketing is not just a bolt-on specialism which can be added to existing management structures, but an integrated approach to the whole conduct of profitable business.

(Sir Colin Marshall, Chief Executive, British Airways, 1988)

7.1 The interaction of supply and demand

The discussion so far has concentrated to a great extent on the supply aspects of international air transport and in particular on the costs of providing air services. There is a tendency among airline managers to concentrate on supply considerations at the expense of demand factors. Within many airlines great emphasis is placed on operational safety and efficiency and on reducing the costs of production. A large range of performance indicators are produced to enable the airlines to monitor various aspects of supply: engine shut-down rates per 1,000 hours, punctuality, annual utilisation of aircraft and crews, maintenance man hours per aircraft and unit costs per tonne kilometre are just a few of the indicators used to monitor supply conditions. By contrast, performance indicators on the demand or revenue side are relatively few and often less importance is attached to them. Too many airlines, among them smaller international carriers, assume that if their supply of services is efficient and low-cost that is enough: profitability should follow.

Yet, as emphasised in the opening chapter, airline management is about matching the supply of air services, which management can largely control, with the demand for such services, over which management has much less influence. To be successful in this an airline can be a low-cost operator or a high-cost operator. What determines profitability is the airline's ability to produce unit revenues which are higher than its unit costs. Low unit costs are no guarantee of profit if an airline is unable to generate even the low unit revenues necessary to cover such costs.

In fact, profitability depends on the interplay of three key performance variables: unit cost (usually measured *per available tonne kilometre*, that is, per unit of capacity), unit revenues or yields (measured *per revenue tonne kilometre*, that is, per unit of output sold) and load factor, which indicates how much of the capacity produced has actually been sold. (It is the revenue tonne kilometres expressed as a percentage of available tonne kilometres.) Clearly, if yields are low they can be compensated for by higher load factors. But high or very high load factors, in themselves, do not ensure profitability if yields are too low in relation to costs. Conversely, low load factors may not be critical if yields per unit sold are high (see Chapter 10.1 below).

To achieve a profitable matching of supply and demand airlines need to get the balance between unit costs, unit revenues and load factor right. For this it is crucial for airline managers to have a thorough understanding of the demand they are trying to satisfy. Such an understanding is fundamental to every aspect of airline planning. Aircraft selection, route development, scheduling, product planning and pricing and advertising are just some of the many decision areas which ultimately are dependent on an analysis of demand for the transport of both passengers and freight. As in all industries, supply of and demand for air services are not independent of each other. On the contrary, each affects the other. Aircraft types and speeds, departure and arrival times, frequency of service, the level of air fares, in-flight service, the quality of ground handling and other features of supply will influence demand for an airline's services. Conversely, the demand will itself affect those supply features. The density of passenger demand, its seasonality, the purpose of travel, the distance to be travelled, the nature of the freight demand and other demand aspects should influence the way in which air services are supplied and will impact on costs. (The impact of demand patterns on costs has been discussed briefly in Chapter 5.2 above.) Thus airline planning is a dynamic and iterative process.

An understanding and evaluation of the demand for air transport leads to the provision of services which themselves affect the demand. New adjustments to the supply then take place to meet changes in the demand, and this interactive process continues. The more competitive and unregulated the market the more dynamic the interaction becomes and the greater are the headaches for airline managers. Marketing is concerned with this dynamic and interactive process of matching supply and demand.

7.2 The role of airline marketing

There is a widely held misconception that marketing is about selling what is being produced. It is much more than that. Marketing is involved in deciding what should be produced as well as how it should be sold. As such it is the lynchpin of any industry. It is all-pervasive. It is important to recognise that virtually everyone within the airline can contribute to the marketing process.

The essence of marketing is to identify and satisfy customer needs; to be consumer- or market-oriented rather than production- or supply-oriented. If an airline concentrates on merely selling what is produced before identifying what customers want and are prepared to pay for, it is doomed to failure. A good example is supersonic air services. The Concorde aircraft was produced largely because it was technically feasible, with little reference to whether passengers would ultimately be prepared to pay the excessively high cost of travelling in the aircraft or whether people were prepared to pay the full cost of supersonic air travel to save two or three hours. British Airways' and Air France's Concorde services survived only because they were not expected to cover their full costs, since the capital costs were written off by their respective governments. No more Concorde aircraft were built after the initial batch of sixteen.

The first step in marketing is to identify markets and market segments that can be served profitably. To do this one uses the whole range of market research methods, from desk-based statistical analyses to surveys of current and pro-spective users of air services. The aim is to gain an understanding of the needs of different market segments and also the degree to which such needs are not currently being satisfied. This leads on naturally to the production of traffic forecasts, which should be as detailed and segmented as possible.

The second stage of marketing is to decide, in the light of the preceding market analyses, the air services that should be offered in the market and their product features both in the air and on the ground. This is product planning. Price is the most critical of the product features but, as discussed later in Chapter 9, there are many other aspects of the airline's product that must also be decided on. Product planning is related to three key factors: the market needs which have been identified, the current and expected product features of competing airlines and the costs of different product features. In assessing the costs of proposed products, the supply and demand sides of the industry are brought together, for there is a trade-off between the two. The product planners must balance the costs of desired product features against what customers are prepared to pay for.

The third stage is to plan and organise the selling of the products on the basis of a marketing plan. This involves setting up and operating sales and distribution outlets both airline-owned, such as sales offices or telephone and Internet sites, and indirect outlets involving a range of agents, sub-agents and on-line agencies. In order to attract potential customers, the marketing plan will also include a detailed programme of advertising and promotion activities.

Lastly, marketing is concerned with reviewing and monitoring both the degree to which the airline has been able consistently to meet the service standards and product features planned and customers' responses to them. Such monitoring through weekly sales figures, customer surveys, analyses of com-plaints and other market research techniques should enable airlines to take short-term corrective action, where possible, and also to make longer-term changes in their service and product features.

It is not the aim of this book to analyse airline marketing in detail but rather to assess its role in the process of matching the supply of air services with the demand. Marketing starts with an understanding of demand. This chapter considers certain characteristics of the demand for air travel and examines the various factors which affect the level and growth of demand in any given market. This understanding of demand leads on naturally to an examination of the forecasting techniques most widely used by airlines (Chapter 8). This is followed by a brief assessment of product planning and distribution (Chapter 9), of which a key element is pricing (Chapter 10). The cost implications of marketing strategies have been considered earlier (Chapter 5.2).

7.3 The motivation for air travel

The bulk of air travel is either for business or for leisure. Business travel involves a journey necessitated by one's employment and paid for by the employer. The business traveller and the employer may in some cases be the same person, but even then the traveller will be paying not directly out of his own pocket but out of the firm's. The leisure market contains two distinct categories, holiday travel and travel whose primary purpose is visiting friends or relatives (often referred to as VFR). Each of these can be further subdivided. For instance, holiday travel can be for short- or long-stay holidays. Leisure travellers, unlike those travelling on business, invariably pay their own fares out of their own pockets. A number of important differences between the business and leisure markets stem from the fact that in the former case the passengers are not paying for their own travel whereas in the latter they are. These are discussed later.

There is, finally, a small proportion of air passengers who do not fit into the business, holiday or VFR categories. These include students travelling to or from their place of study, those travelling for medical reasons, and migrants moving to another country. They may be grouped together as a miscellaneous category. In the United States this type of travel is sometimes categorised as 'personal business' (BTS, 1996).

The mix of air passengers by purpose of travel will vary from market to market. The UK-originating air travel market provides an interesting case. In 1999 UK residents took 37.5 million trips abroad by air. Of these only 17.1 per cent were business trips, though their share has been rising slowly in recent years. Two-thirds of the trips (67.4 per cent) were for holidays and a further 13.3 per cent were to visit friends and relatives. As air fares have declined in real terms the share of such VFR travel has tended to rise. Ten years earlier in 1988 only one in ten of air trips by UK residents were for that purpose. Finally, a small share of trips, 2.3 per cent, is for a miscellany of other reasons (ONS, 2000). Thus leisure travel – taking holidays and visits to friends or relatives together – accounts for around 81 per cent of the UK-originating air travel market.

It is significant that in 1999, 15 million trips, representing two-thirds of the 25 million holiday visits, involved inclusive tours, the majority of which would have been on charter flights. Charters thereby absorb a large but in fact declining proportion of the total holiday market. Conversely, business travel is almost entirely confined to scheduled flights. As a result, on many scheduled flights the business proportion of the traffic is much higher than the 17.1 per cent overall business share would suggest.

While only about one in eight UK residents flying abroad do so to visit friends or relatives, in some markets such VFR traffic can be more important. On routes to Canada, to the Caribbean or to South East Asia and Australia as much as one-third of the UK-originating traffic may be visiting friends or relatives.

In contrast to the United Kingdom, a 1995 survey of long-distance (over 100 miles) travel within the United States showed a quite different motivation profile. Of those travelling by commercial air services 49.6 per cent were on business, 24.5 per cent were visiting friends or relatives and only 16.7 per cent were undertaking leisure trips. The balance, 9.2 per cent, were travelling for a variety of other purposes categorised as personal business (BTS, 1996).

In other regions of the world the split between business, holiday, VFR and other trips will vary. As a general rule, the higher the personal disposable income of the population in a country the greater is the proportion of holiday trips in the total international air travel generated by that country (unless, of course, travel or foreign exchange restrictions are imposed on its citizens). Low incomes in most countries of Africa mean that business trips dominate on international air routes within the continent. Conversely, rapidly rising personal incomes in Japan and the newly industrialised countries of East Asia during the 1970s generated a rapid growth of leisure travel, which partly explains the unusually high growth rates enjoyed by airlines in the region during the last decade (Table 1.3). VFR traffic tends to be significant on air routes joining countries between which there have been earlier population movements. Apart from the UK examples previously cited, there are many other air routes with an important VFR component. They include France to Algeria or Morocco, United States to the Philippines and Singapore to southern India.

The variation in passenger mix that airlines have to deal with is illustrated by examining seven markets, three short-haul and four long-haul, served by scheduled air services from London-Heathrow airport in 1999 (Table 7.1). On short-haul scheduled routes out of London, such as those to Brussels, Frankfurt or Paris, business trips, by UK and foreign residents taken together, may generate as much as two-thirds or more of the total traffic. On all services to/from Belgium, 67 per cent (Table 7.1, columns 1 plus 3) were travelling on business, while the figure for Germany was 49 per cent and for French routes 44 per cent. Yet on long-haul flights to the United States the business share dropped to 30 per cent, on those to Singapore or Japan it was 23–4 per cent and to Canada only 21 per cent. Furthermore, the passenger mix by journey purpose will vary by route and for each route by season or even time of the day.

Two other features of airline markets are apparent in Table 7.1. First, that the passenger mix is not the same at each end of the route and can differ substantially. Thus, whereas four out of five UK residents flying from London-Heathrow to Belgium are travelling on business, Belgian and other residents travelling on the route are more or less evenly split between business and leisure passengers. Second, the proportion of the traffic originating from each

Table 7.1 Purpose of travel on air services between London-Heathrow and selected markets, 1999 (%)

London-Heathrow to/from	UK residents		Foreign residents		Total
	Business 1	*Leisure*[a] 2	*Business* 3	*Leisure*[a] 4	5
Short-haul:					
Belgium	41.2	9.7	26.1	23.1	100
Germany	21.4	13.9	27.8	36.9	100
France	20.9	20.4	22.9	35.8	100
Long-haul:					
United States	11.5	25.7	18.9	43.9	100
Japan	7.2	15.9	16.5	60.4	100
Singapore	10.6	48.4	12.3	28.7	100
Canada	6.1	20.3	14.5	59.1	100

Source: Compiled by author using CAA (2000b).

Note
a Leisure here includes VFR and other non-business travel.

end of the route may also differ. For instance, on London–Singapore almost 60 per cent of the passengers are UK residents, but on the London to Japan services only 23 per cent are UK residents. In other words, while there may be some transfer passengers on the Japanese routes who originate outside the United Kingdom or Japan, the majority of the passengers will be based in Japan. Such imbalances in the origin of passengers on each route have important implications for marketing. They explain, for instance, why traditionally Singapore Airlines has been a big spender on advertising in the UK market, whereas Japan Airlines (JAL) has been one of the smallest spenders. JAL believes most of its market originates in Japan.

In any market the mix of passengers between business and leisure or VFR has important implications on marketing and pricing strategies and also on the average yield per passenger. Thus knowing and understanding the passenger mix on each route is crucially important.

The air travel market is smaller than the number of passenger trips recorded, since each individual traveller will normally make more than one flight. The relation between the number of travellers and the passenger trips recorded varies on a route-by-route basis. It is greatly influenced by the proportion of business travellers on the route, since they are the most likely to be frequent users of air services. On many inclusive tour charter routes, the number of travellers is probably close to half the number of passengers recorded on the route, since each traveller will make both an outward and a return trip, while it is unlikely that they will make that round trip more than once a year. In scheduled markets the position is more complex, with a small proportion of frequent travellers generating a high proportion of the total passenger trips recorded. Such frequent travellers will usually be flying on business, but some may also be on leisure trips. In the United States in 1989 frequent flyers who took ten trips or more in the previous year represented only 6 per cent of air travellers but took 41 per cent of all air trips (IATA, 1989).

Travel motivation has an impact on frequency of travel but also on the duration of the trip. While business travellers fly more frequently, they also take trips of shorter duration. Among leisure passengers, those on inclusive tour holidays have the longest trips, since such holidays are normally of fixed duration, often in multiples of a week. As the journey distance increases so does the duration of the trip, whatever its purpose. These two tendencies – longer trip duration for leisure travellers and longer duration for longer-distance trips by all travellers – reinforce each other. A 1999 survey of Heathrow passengers (CAA, 2000a) showed that, while one-third of leisure passengers on international flights out of Heathrow stayed away for over two weeks, a remarkable 21 per cent of business travellers on international routes flew back the same day or the next.

7.4   Socio-economic characteristics of air travellers

Travel motivation and aspects of travel behaviour, such as frequency of travel, the number of people travelling together or the time when bookings are made, are linked with the socio-economic characteristics of the individual traveller. Sex, age, income level, stage in the life cycle, size of family and occupation are some of the many socio-economic variables that impact on travel patterns. The key variables affecting behaviour will clearly be different if one is travelling for business, or leisure, or visiting friends and relatives. They will also differ for the separate market segments within each of these categories. For an airline, the more it knows about its current or potential customers the easier it is to plan and target its services and products to meet the specific needs of each market segment. Surveys both of air passengers and of those not currently using its services as well as more general surveys and market research are used to build up this understanding of what each market place needs. Airlines that fail to use and take account of surveys and market research are frequently the ones who lose their way. While an in-depth analysis of the socio-economic characteristics of different types of air travellers would need to be lengthy and is not appropriate here, it is nevertheless interesting to highlight some of them.

One would expect male passengers to make up the bulk of the business market, but the extent to which males still dominate is perhaps surprising. In the United Kingdom in 1999 about 22 per cent of business air travellers were women (CAA, 2000a), though the figure had been below 10 per cent twenty years earlier. The proportion is somewhat lower on UK domestic air services and lower on international long-haul. This pattern is indicative of the situation elsewhere in Europe too. In the United States the proportion of women among business air travellers is about twice as high at around 41 per cent.

The leisure market manifests a more even split of passengers between the two sexes, though in many European and North American leisure markets women if anything predominate. A 1999 survey of passengers at London's two major airports and at Manchester indicated that slightly over 50 per cent of leisure passengers were women (CAA, 2000a). The proportion of women is even higher among international VFR passengers. In the United States women are dominant in the leisure market, generating well over half the total air trips.

Traditionally, business travellers have been thought to be primarily middle and senior managers and executives and established lawyers, architects, consultants or other professionals. Their seniority inevitably meant that they would be in the middle to upper age groups. However, the business market has been undergoing a fundamental change. The internationalisation of the world's trade and industry and the fall in the real cost of air travel, together with the speed advantage offered, have resulted in recent years in a growth of business travel by more junior staff and skilled workers. Surveys of air passengers at London's airports have found that over one-third of business passengers were supervisory clerical and junior managerial or professional staff or skilled manual workers. Such passengers would tend to be younger and on lower incomes than the more traditional business passenger. As a result the average age of UK business travellers flying from London-Heathrow and Gatwick airports in 1999 was the same, that is, close to forty years, as that of UK leisure passengers flying from those airports (CAA, 2000a). However, since leisure passengers include many children and people beyond retirement age, the age distribution of leisure travellers is wider and more evenly spread than among business passengers. The latter will virtually all be between twenty-five and sixty-five years of age.

The most significant socio-economic variable affecting the demand for leisure travel is personal or household income, since leisure trips are paid for by the passenger, who may also be paying for a spouse and one or more children. As a result, those with higher incomes generate a disproportionately large share of the leisure market. A survey of UK passengers flying out of London-Heathrow and Gatwick airports on international flights in 1999 indicated that the 68 per cent of business trips and 40 per cent of leisure trips were generated by the 13 per cent of the population at the top of the income scale.

The UK experience is mirrored in other countries such as the United States. A small proportion of the population, the high earners, account for a disproportionately large share of international passenger travel and in most cases of domestic travel too. In many Third World countries with low average disposable incomes, international air travel may be limited entirely to the 5–10 per cent of the population with the highest incomes. Elsewhere, international leisure travel may be more widespread but still with a predominance of higher-income earners.

An appreciation of the socio-economic characteristics of passenger demand in each market is helpful to airlines in planning their advertising, promotion and sales activity. It can help them in deciding where to advertise and what features of their services to emphasise in their advertising campaigns. Such knowledge of the market may assist to a certain extent in product planning and in determining tariff policies and possibly even in forecasting.

7.5   Market segmentation

Traditionally airlines have segmented their markets on each route by trip purpose or motivation. Some airlines do this simply by dividing their passengers into business and non-business or leisure passengers. Others, as suggested earlier, make a three or fourfold division into business, holiday, VFR and other. Market segmentation in this way is invaluable, since the separate market segments have varied growth rates and respond differently to internal supply variables such as frequency of flights, departure times and fare changes or to external factors such as exchange rate fluctuations or economic recession. Understanding the size and the characteristics of each market segment on each route is essential for forecasting demand, for many aspects of product planning such as scheduling or in-flight service, and especially for pricing. Airlines without such detailed knowledge of their markets are likely to get into difficulties when trying to match supply and demand.

In recent years there has been a growing awareness among airline managers that this simple approach to market segmentation based on trip purpose has some shortcomings. First, it tends to place too much emphasis on the demographic and socio-economic features of the passengers. Age, sex and social class are perhaps less important than appreciating passenger needs and requirements when travelling by air. Surely, it is more important for an airline to know whether passengers will cancel their reservation at the last moment or whether they are prepared to pay a lower fare for an inconvenient departure than it is to know their sex or age? Unless, of course, age or sex does affect booking behaviour or attitudes to price. Second, air trips may increasingly be multipurpose. A business trip is combined with a holiday, or a wife accompanies a husband on a business trip (or vice versa), while many visits to friends and relatives are considered as holidays. Third, traditional market segmentation oversimplifies the motivational factors involved in travel decisions. All business air travellers cannot be grouped together and assumed to have similar demand characteristics and needs, any more than can all leisure passengers. A senior manager or engineer requiring to go to another country immediately because of an unexpected crisis has different transport requirements and demands from a salesman who plans his regular overseas sales trips months in advance. Equally, the family holidaymaker buying an annual two-week inclusive tour package holiday at a sunshine resort places different demands on the air services from the holidaymaker going independently and making his or her own accommodation arrangements or the couple going for a weekend break from Montreal to New York or from Singapore to Hong Kong.

Most airline planners now believe that market segmentation should be based not on a straightforward fourfold division categorised by journey purpose but

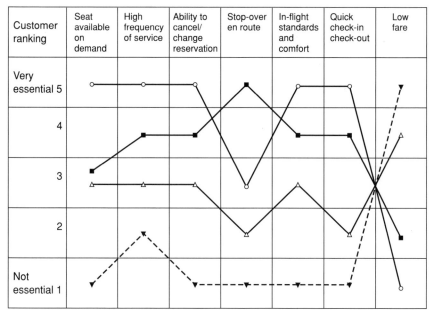

Customer ranking	Seat available on demand	High frequency of service	Ability to cancel/ change reservation	Stop-over en route	In-flight standards and comfort	Quick check-in check-out	Low fare

Key:

▼‑ ‑ ‑▼ Holidaymaker two-week holiday
△——△ Weekend holiday
■——■ Routine business
○——○ Emergency business

Figure 7.1 Market segmentation by trip purpose and passenger needs. Only a sample of possible market segments is shown.

on a more complex division related partly to journey purpose but partly also to passenger needs. Thus the business segment may be further subdivided into routine business and emergency business. The holiday segment of the leisure market could be split into an inclusive tour segment, a multi-destination touring segment and a weekender segment. Other ways of segmenting the market can also be used, depending on each airline's appreciation of what are the key segments of its market. The point about more complex market segmentation is that each segment is likely to have distinct needs and expectations, such as the freedom to change reservations or routeings, the need to make stopovers, the ability to pay particular fare levels, expectations in terms of in-flight service and comfort, and so on. Variations in needs for four of the many possible market segments on a medium-haul route such as London–Athens or Singapore– Hong Kong are shown in Figure 7.1. The contrasting needs of the emergency business traveller with those of the two-week holidaymaker stand out starkly. For the latter a low fare is critical. For the former, high service quality – seat availability, frequent flights, and so on – is crucial and price is relatively unimportant. It can also be seen by comparing weekend and two-week holidaymakers that even in the leisure market there may be distinct segments with their own needs and expectations. It may well be that each of these groups also has different socio-economic characteristics which may help in targeting specific marketing efforts at them. But the key is their needs and expectations. What type and quality of service do they want or need?

The significance of this more sophisticated approach to market segmentation is that it can help airlines in their forecasting, but it can be especially helpful in product planning and pricing. It can help them in planning specific price and product combinations to attract each segment or at least those segments they wish to cater for. It can also be useful in relating fares more closely to the costs imposed by the different segments and also in working out the various conditions attached to different fares to prevent slippage of passengers from high- to low-fare categories.

Another approach is to segment markets not only in terms of motivation and requirements but also in terms of the psychological make-up of passengers. Thus in the late 1980s British Airways categorised its business passengers into 'attention seekers', 'comfort cravers' or 'schedule seekers', each with different demands and flying behaviour. Leisure travellers were 'schedule seekers', 'service seekers' and 'nervous Nellies', though the latter were unlikely to be told this! Some other airlines have also tried to categorise their passengers in a similar fashion. The aim of such market segmentation is to gain a better insight and understanding of passenger needs so as to make the correct marketing decisions. There is a problem, however. The more complex and sophisticated the market segmentation the more complex and costly is the market research which is necessary to establish and monitor the market segments and their needs. Smaller airlines will tend to stick to a more traditional approach.

7.6   The peak problem

Like many transport industries, particularly those dealing with passengers, the airline industry is characterised by marked daily, weekly and seasonal peaks and troughs of demand. The pattern and intensity of the peaks and troughs vary by route and geographical area. Peak flows become a serious problem when they begin to impose cost penalties on the airlines involved. In meeting demand at peak periods an airline may have to provide extra capacity not only in terms of aircraft and flight crews or cabin staff but also in terms of staff, equipment and facilities and other areas such as ground handling, sales or engineering. Such extra capacity will be underutilised during the off-peak periods. The greater the ratio of peak to trough traffic the more difficult it becomes to ensure utilisation of peak capacity in off-peak periods. Such peak capacity then becomes very costly to operate, since it must cover all its fixed and overhead costs during the short period that it is actually in use. Expressed another way, one finds costly equipment and staff required for the peak sitting around virtually unutilised or, at best, underutilised in periods of low demand.

Where the peak traffic season corresponds with the school holiday period in an airline's home country even more extra staff are needed in the peak, since many staff want to take their own holidays during the period and are away from work. It may be possible in some areas to overcome the peak problem by using seasonal staff employed for three to six months. For instance, Olympic Airways in the year 2000 had 7,200 permanent staff based in Greece, but employed an additional 3,190 staff for several months during the summer peak, mainly in ground handling, and a much smaller number as cabin crew. While the number appears very high in proportion to the permanent staff, the increase in annual labour costs was only around 10 per cent since seasonals were paid at much lower rates.

Seasonal peaks in demand for air services to and from each country or on particular routes arise as a result of either institutional or climatic factors. The distribution and length of school holidays, the patterns of annual holidays for factories and offices, religious festivals such as Christmas, the Chinese New Year or the Haj pilgrimage, and the distribution of major cultural and sporting events are the main institutional factors creating seasonal traffic peaks. Climatic factors are important through their effect on holiday patterns or by disrupting surface modes of travel. Where institutional and climatic factors coalesce, seasonal peaks become very marked. In the European area, traditional summer holidays for schoolchildren and employees coincide with climatic conditions in the Mediterranean basin which are ideal for seaside holidays and which are markedly better than those in northern Europe. As a result, during the summer months there is an outpouring of people moving southwards from northern Europe. The effect on airline peaks is dramatic, particularly for the non-scheduled operators who cater for much of this demand. In North America the Christmas holiday season coincides with very cold winter weather in Canada and parts of the United States while Florida and the Caribbean bask in warm sunshine. These conditions create a peak of demand for air services to the Caribbean area in late December and early January.

Daily or weekly peaks are related to the pattern of working hours and days during the week. Business travel creates daily demand peaks usually in the early morning and early evening and weekly peaks on Mondays or possibly Tuesdays and on Fridays. In Muslim countries which have Thursdays and/or Fridays as days of rest the business peaks will be different. On the other hand, leisure traffic is responsible for a peaking of demand at weekends, particularly during the holiday seasons. Inevitably, the split of traffic on any route between business and leisure influences the nature of the daily, weekly and seasonal variations in demand.

The daily and weekly peaks in demand generally pose a less severe handicap than the seasonal peaks, since there is enough flexibility in most airlines' operations to enable them to make sensible use of spare capacity during particular periods of the day or the week. Maintenance and training flights can be programmed for such slack periods, or aircraft can be leased out for charter work. Many international airlines find that, on scheduled routes with a high business component, demand falls off at the weekend and they can reduce their frequencies on Saturdays and Sundays. A few, such as Tunis Air or Finnair, use this spare weekend capacity on charter flights to meet the needs of the leisure market, which prefers weekend travel.

It is the seasonal peaks of demand which create more problems and impose the greatest costs. The monthly variations in demand levels vary considerably between different types of international routes. As a consequence they pose varying problems for the airlines operating each type of route and may require somewhat different responses. The monthly passenger flows in the year 2000 for a selection of routes radiating from London are shown in Figure 7.2. Two are long-haul routes to Singapore and New York and the other three are European short- to medium-haul routes.

As expected, a really problematic route manifesting the most acute peaking problem is that to Palma de Majorca in Spain, a major holiday destination served primarily, but not exclusively, by non-scheduled charter flights. While monthly charter passenger flows are over 100,000 for several summer months, with a peak of 184,000 in August, they collapse to less than 20,000 during the winter months. This is symptomatic of demand pattern on holiday routes, with a clearly defined peak season related to climate. Many routes from northern Europe to the Mediterranean and also from Canada to the Caribbean fall into this pattern. As previously pointed out (Chapter 6.6), charter airlines partly overcome their seasonality problem by flying their aircraft and crews intensively day and night during the peak period, thereby achieving very high annual utilisation of both aircraft and crew. Some may also try to lease their aircraft during their low season to carriers (scheduled or non-scheduled) in other parts of the world who may have a different seasonal pattern of demand.

Scheduled traffic flows to or from holiday destinations, which are again dependent on seasonal variations in climate, also tend to exhibit marked peaks. But these are not as extreme as those where demand is catered for primarily by charter flights. London–Athens is an example (Figure 7.2). Traffic is uniformly high during the Mediterranean summer months from May to September but these levels are nearly twice as high as in the weaker winter months. This contrasts with London–Frankfurt, which also peaks in the summer holiday season but the peak:trough variation is much lower. While on London–Athens the traffic in the peak month in 2000 was double that of the lowest month, on London–Frankfurt the peak was only 50 per cent higher. This is because of the higher business component on the latter route and because leisure traffic on this route is less dependent on the search for good seaside weather!

The two long-haul routes examined also exhibit contrasting patterns. London–Singapore manifests hardly any seasonal variation. Traffic appears to be growing steadily with a mild peak in the European summer and another in December. On the other hand, London–New York appears to have a much more marked summer peak and a lower peak at Easter. Interestingly the peak to trough month ratio for both routes is very similar. It is 1.54:1.00 for the New York route and 1.51:1.00 on London–Singapore. But the absolute traffic levels to

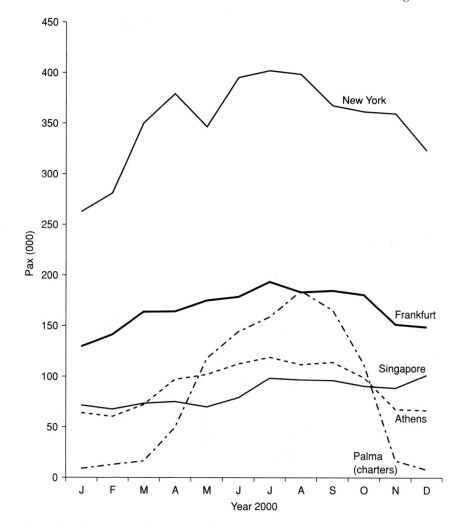

Figure 7.2 The peak problem: monthly traffic on scheduled routes to/from London, 2000–01.
Source: Civil Aviation Authority.

and from New York are so high that having extra capacity for 120,000 to 140,000 passengers for the peak months which is heavily underutilised during January and February places an economic strain on airlines operating this or other similar routes.

A scheduled airline operating on routes with different peak periods can try and shift aircraft and other resources between routes according to the season so as to ensure high utilisation. Figure 7.2 shows that an airline such as British Airways operating a range of services out of London, its home base, would have only limited scope to do this, since on so many London routes peaks and

Table 7.2 Passenger load factor of European airlines, peak summer month, August 2000

Airline	Passenger load factor (%)
KLM	84.4
Aer Lingus	83.9
Air France	83.0
Alitalia	81.3
Lufthansa	81.1
Air Portugal	79.9
AEA[a] average	*79.2*
British Airways	78.0
Austrian Airlines	76.1
Olympic	75.4
Sabena	74.7
Swissair	73.9
SAS	72.5
Finnair	65.6
British Midland	65.6

Source: Compiled by the author using AEA data.

Note
a Association of European Airlines.

troughs of demand fall at the same time of the year. Many other airlines face the same problem. As a result, the capacity provided by most scheduled airlines on international services in the peak season is substantially higher than in the low season. United States airlines seem to face a particularly acute capacity peak, with airlines such as Northwest offering almost twice as many international seat kilometres in their peak month as in their lowest month. Conversely, Asian carriers have the least peaky output profile and this may be an added cost advantage for them.

The high costs of meeting peaks of demand could be offset either wholly or partly by operating at very high load factors during peak periods or by charging higher fares at such periods. The question of peak period pricing is discussed in Chapter 10. Surprisingly, as far as load factors are concerned, only a few of the major European airlines in Table 7.2 achieved passenger load factors in the peak month of August 2000 of over 80 per cent and the highest was only 84.4 per cent. A couple of airlines had peak load factors below 65 per cent, or one seat empty for every two sold. At periods when demand is so high that one would expect scheduled airlines to capitalise by filling every seat, in fact about one out of every five seats on average remained empty. Such relatively low load factors at peak periods aggravate the economic penalties arising from the need to provide sufficient capacity to meet peak demands.

Several factors explain the inability of the scheduled airlines to achieve much higher load factors at peak periods. For airlines with widespread networks, such as some of those in Table 7.2, peak demand may occur at different times in various parts of the network. Then, during the peak month or peak period, there are considerable variations in demand; there are peaks and slumps within the peak. Traffic levels are not the same every month during the peak. Even within the peak months demand will vary by day of the week and also by time of day. To maintain public goodwill, and to facilitate the planning of flight operations, airlines cannot afford to change schedules and frequencies every week or even every month. Timetables are planned and published months in advance and the daily or weekly capacity offered during a timetable period will aim at achieving load factors of over 80 per cent or 90 per cent on certain peak days or times in the certainty that at other times load factors will slump to low levels. On routes where airlines are free to compete in terms of frequencies offered, commercial pressures may push airlines to over-provide capacity at peak periods or on peak days in order to increase their market share.

But as a result they may even fail to achieve the anticipated high load factors. An added problem is that on many routes there is a directional imbalance in the traffic flows. The periods of peak demand in one direction may correspond with an off-peak level of demand in the opposite direction. Directional imbalances in traffic levels exist on many routes and usually arise from institutional differences in the markets at each end of the route, such as the timing of annual holidays. Such directional imbalances are particularly marked on some long-haul routes such as those between North America and Europe or Europe to Australia. Lastly, airlines may be unable to match the capacity they offer closely enough to the demand to ensure very high load factors at peak periods. This is because, in trying to reduce the number of aircraft types in the fleet, the aircraft on some routes may be too large in relation to the demand. Aircraft size and frequencies cannot always be tailored precisely to the demand levels in each market.

Peak problems also exist in the movement of freight by air, but they are frequently less of a problem than peaks on passenger services. With the introduction of the wide-bodied passenger jets which have very considerable freight capacity in their holds, peaks in the flow of air cargo can be met on many routes without the provision of extra peak capacity. A more serious problem in air freighting is the imbalance of flows which arises because freight travels only one way, unlike passengers, who generally make a round trip.

Coping with the seasonal variations in demand is a major headache for some airline managements, since the variations affect so many aspects of airline operations. Pricing policies, operating schedules, maintenance and overhaul checks and advertising campaigns all need to be carefully manipulated in order to minimise the adverse effect of traffic peaks and slumps on aircraft and crew utilisation and on load factors, and through these on unit costs. To mitigate the adverse impact of highly peaked demand, airlines may also lease in aircraft or try to use seasonally employed labour during peak periods. Whatever techniques are used to diminish its impact, the peak remains a problem to a greater or lesser extent for all airlines and is an underlying constraint in many aspects of airline planning and marketing.

Table 7.3 Factors affecting the level and growth of passenger demand

Factors affecting all markets	Factors affecting particular routes
Level of personal disposable income	Level of tourist attraction:
Supply conditions:	Scenic/climatic/historical/religious
Fare levels	attributes
Speed of air travel	Adequacy of tourist infrastructure
Convenience of air travel	Comparative prices
Level of economic activity/trade	Exchange rate fluctuations
Population size and growth rate	Travel restrictions
Social environment:	Historical/cultural links
Length of paid holidays	Earlier population movements
Attitudes to travel	Current labour flows
	Nature of economic activity

7.7   Factors affecting passenger demand

The demand for passenger services arises from the complex interaction of a large number of factors which affect the different market segments differentially. Those factors fall broadly into two groups, which are summarised in Table 7.3: the general economic and supply-related factors that influence demand in all markets and the more particular factors that may influence demand on some routes but may be totally absent on others.

Of the general factors affecting demand, the price of air transport and the level and distribution of personal income in the markets served are perhaps the most important. Much of the growth of air travel during the last forty years can be explained by the falling real price of air transport (as discussed in Chapter 1) and more especially by growth in the world's economies and rising personal incomes. In fact, as Figure 7.3 shows, there appears to be a very strong correlation between the annual rates of growth in the world's gross domestic product (right-hand scale) and the growth rates in air travel, measured in revenue passenger kilometres (left-hand scale). Bearing in mind that the scales on each side are different, Figure 7.3 suggests that, broadly speaking, there is a two-to-one relation between demand for air travel and world GDP. In other words, demand grows or declines twice as fast as any change in GDP.

Accelerated rates of traffic growth in particular markets at particular times have usually been due either to rapid growth in personal incomes or to falling air fares. The more general economic conditions also impact on traffic growth. The world economic climate and the rate of economic growth in particular countries or regions of the world influence demand in a variety of complex ways. They determine the level of industrial and economic activity in each country and more generally the level and nature of international trade. The level of economic activity and trade directly influences the growth of demand for business travel. Indirectly it also influences leisure demand, since it affects the level and growth of personal incomes. Economic factors such as personal incomes or industrial activity have to be understood within a demographic context. The

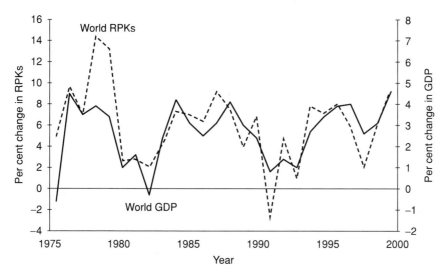

Figure 7.3 Annual changes in world gross domestic product compared with changes in revenue passenger kilometres.

size and the distribution of the populations served by a route impose a major constraint on the level of potential demand. Thus, despite rapidly rising personal incomes in Singapore, the potential demand for Singapore-originating air travel is strictly limited by the small size of the island's population of only 2.6 million. This explains Singapore Airlines' critical need to develop fifth- and sixth-freedom traffic. Conversely, Japan-originating leisure traffic has barely scratched the surface of the potential demand, given Japan's population of about 125 million and its rapid economic growth up to the mid-1990s. While rapid population growth may in theory increase the size of the air market, in practice it may have an adverse effect if it results in lower *per capita* incomes or in a larger population but one with a disproportionate share of young children who are unlikely to be air travellers. Both these phenomena have been evident in Morocco and Algeria, countries with birth rates well above average.

The social environment is also important in all markets, since it determines the number of days of holiday available for travel or leisure and social attitudes to travel. Thus one finds in Japan that workers do not take all the holidays they are entitled to but stay at work. In the same country, though there are many working women with relatively high disposable incomes, it is only in the last fifteen years or so that social attitudes have begun to accept the idea of women holidaymaking on their own, though it is acceptable for men. For both these reasons, and given its high wage levels, Japan represents a huge potential market for air travel which will boom as social attitudes change and people start taking more of their holiday entitlement and as the notion that women can travel on their own becomes more widely accepted. At the other extreme, in much of Western Europe two long holidays away from home, one in the summer and a shorter one in winter, are the social expectation of the middle- and upper-income groups.

Demand and supply do not interact only through the price mechanism. As previously mentioned, various supply conditions other than price affect demand. In the short term, frequency, seat availability, departure and arrival times, number of en-route stops and other supply features influence the level of demand and the distribution of that demand between competing carriers. In the long term, it is the improvements in the overall speed and convenience of air transport that have had the most significant effect on demand. This is particularly true over medium- and long-haul distances where the speed advantage of air increased so dramatically in the 1960s and 1970s that effective surface competition by rail, road or sea has largely disappeared.

In addition to the above general considerations affecting all markets, several other factors, which may be particular to individual routes, also influence demand levels. These are factors which may explain growth on some routes but not on others. Demand for holiday trips is related to the tourist attractiveness of particular destinations. In order to be attractive and have tourist potential, resort areas or towns need two things: they must enjoy certain attractive and preferably unique scenic, climatic, historical or cultural advantages; they must also have the right infrastructure to cater for tourist needs such as sufficient hotel beds of the required standard, adequate ground transport, restaurants, entertainments, shopping facilities, and so on. An attractive tourist location without the necessary infrastructure is not enough to generate a significant volume of demand for holiday travel, as many Third World countries have found. The two must go hand in hand.

Tourist facilities in themselves may not be enough. They must be priced correctly for the market they hope to attract and in relation to competing destinations. Changes in the relative price levels of hotels and other facilities in a tourist resort area may accelerate or retard traffic growth on particular air routes. Changes in the relative cost of holidays in a country may come about as a result of internal economic conditions or even government decisions. But they may also be generated by fluctuations in the exchange rates. Often, switching of tourist demand from one destination to another or a sudden acceleration of outward-bound tourists from a particular country can be related to changes in the relevant exchange rates. During 2000 as the value of the euro, to which several West European currencies were linked, fell sharply in relation to sterling, many European destinations became more attractive to British tourists. Conversely, travel to Britain appeared much more expensive for many in Europe. Exchange rate fluctuations or even political factors may induce governments to impose travel restrictions on their own citizens. These may take the form of a ban on external travel, the imposition of travel taxes on outgoing travellers or restrictions on the amount of foreign exchange which can be taken out for travel purposes. Following the economic crisis which hit several East Asian countries in late 1997, South Korea, the Philippines, Indonesia and Thailand all restricted travel for some time by one or more of these measures. Conversely, when in 1989 Taiwan allowed its citizens to travel to mainland China (via Hong Kong) for the first time there was a sudden boom in air traffic between Taipei and Hong Kong.

Ultimately, of course, leisure travel is also related to taste. Tourist destinations can inexplicably fall into or out of favour. In 1996, when air travel from the United Kingdom to most Mediterranean destinations declined, the number of passengers flying to Turkey shot up by 9 per cent, much of it on charter flights. This surge was attributed largely to a switch of demand from other destinations, notably Spain, Cyprus and Greece, all of whose air traffic from the United Kingdom actually declined in 1996. Very competitive inclusive holiday prices and new hotels may have favoured Turkey, but it was also a question of changing tastes. Yet three years later, in 1999, when air travel from the United Kingdom to these three markets was booming, passenger traffic on UK–Turkey routes collapsed by 17 per cent (CAA, 2000a).

The visiting friends and relatives demand is clearly affected by earlier population movements and migrations, which are very specific to particular routes. The heavy volume of demand on routes between France and Morocco, Algeria or Tunisia is related to the large number of immigrants from those countries living and working in France. There is little VFR traffic on routes between North Africa and the United Kingdom. On the other hand, traffic demand between the United Kingdom and Canada, the West Indies, Pakistan and Australia or from Singapore to southern India or Sri Lanka can be explained only by earlier population movements. The same is true of the demand between the United States and Israel or the United States and Ireland. Many earlier migrations of population were related to the colonial period of history. Colonial ties have also resulted in linguistic and cultural links between particular pairs of countries which generate certain types of leisure travel but also considerable student travel. Large numbers of Singaporean, Malaysian or Hong Kong students go to English-speaking countries such as Australia, the United Kingdom or the United States to study. Students are an important component of demand on the air routes between their home countries and their place of study. The cultural and linguistic ties also generate travel for cultural events, for conferences, and so on. Such ties affect trading patterns and thereby they may also influence business travel. Population migrations for work or settlement are still going on. The United States, Canada and Australia are still attracting and allowing immigrants from certain other countries and these swell the number of air passengers on the respective routes. In other parts of the world since the 1980s relatively dense traffic flows have been generated by movements of migrant labour, such as those from the Philippines, South Korea or Pakistan to Saudi Arabia and other Middle East states.

The demand for business travel is related to several factors, not just the level of trade and commercial interaction between two city pairs. It would seem that the nature of industrial, commercial and other activities in an airport's hinterland is an important determinant of the level of business travel demand. Certain activities appear to generate more business trips than others. At the

London airports, banking and finance generate a disproportionately high level (around 25 per cent) of UK-originating business travel but account for well below 10 per cent of employment (CAA, 2000a). Administrative capitals obviously generate a great deal of government-related travel. Equally there is some evidence that major international ports generate a disproportionate amount of business air travel. Then there are very specific industrial situations which may stimulate, often for a short term, a rapid growth in demand for air services. The exploration and development of a new oilfield or the construction and commissioning of a new industrial complex would be such a case.

The pattern and growth of demand on any route can be understood only by reference to the economic and demographic characteristics of the markets at either end of the route and to the supply features of the air services provided, of which price is the most important. However, when examining traffic growth on an individual route one must also consider any particular or local factors such as those mentioned earlier which may affect demand on that route. These may include the tourist attractiveness of one or both ends of the route, the historical and cultural ties between the two markets served, the impact of exchange rate fluctuations, earlier or current population movements, and so on. These various factors provide an explanation of the growth and current level of demand on a route. Changes in any of them will affect the growth of traffic in the future. None the less, the overall demand for air travel, like that for most goods or services, seems ultimately to be most closely related to its price and to the income levels of its potential consumers. The impact of price and income on demand is therefore worthy of more detailed consideration.

7.8   Income and price elasticities of demand

Historically, leisure travel has shown a marked responsiveness to personal income levels. Early surveys of air passengers, such as those done at the University of Michigan (Lansing and Blood, 1984), established that two things happen as people's personal incomes rise. First, they spend more on all non-essentials. This includes greater expenditure on travel by all modes. Second, air transport, which is the high-cost but more comfortable and convenient mode for longer journeys, becomes more competitive with surface travel and there is a shift of demand from surface modes to air. In other words, higher incomes result in greater expenditure on longer-distance holiday and VFR travel, and at the same time a higher proportion of that expenditure goes on travel by air rather than surface. The relationship between income changes and demand for air travel can be measured by what economists call the income elasticity. This is arrived at quite simply by dividing the percentage change in demand generated by an income change by the percentage change in personal income which brought about that shift in demand:

$$\text{Income elasticity} = \frac{\%\ \text{change in demand}}{\%\ \text{change in income}}$$

Thus, if a 3 per cent increase in personal income results in a 6 per cent growth in demand for air travel, the income elasticity is 6 per cent divided by 3 per cent, which is +2.0. This means that every 1 per cent variation in income will induce a 2 per cent change in demand. Our earlier comparison of annual changes in world GDP and air travel over the twenty-five years 1975–2000 does indeed suggest a GDP elasticity of around +2.0 (Figure 7.3).

In examining traffic development on a route or group of routes over time in order to establish what the impact of income changes has been, a number of problems arise. The first is how to isolate or exclude the impact of other variables, such as fare changes, on demand. This is done by using multiple regression techniques, which in turn pose certain methodological problems discussed in the next chapter. Second, there is the question of how to measure personal income. Ideally, one would like to use a measure of the personal disposable income (after adjustment for inflation) of the population in a market or of the populations served at either end of a route. But disposable income data are not always available and countries tend to calculate them differently. Proxy measures have to be used for disposable income. Gross national product (GNP) or gross domestic product (GDP) are frequently used but they may be converted into *per capita* GDP. The latter is itself problematical in that it assumes a fairly even distribution of income among a country's population, which frequently is not the case. Both the British Airports Authority (BAA) and the UK Civil Aviation Authority (CAA) in their forecasts use an index of consumer expenditure as a readily accessible measure of the income available to consumers in different countries. Third, since air travel for leisure is a relatively new form of expenditure, one can assume a higher rate of growth in the early stages of increasing incomes and then gradual saturation as people on high incomes get to the stage where they cannot easily consume more leisure travel. A study of international leisure trips by air from the United Kingdom found that, whereas income elasticities ranging from 2.2 to 2.5 were obtained for the period 1970–98, they were considerably lower for the more recent period 1984–98 (Graham, 2000). For the short-haul holiday market they had fallen from 2.2 to 1.5, indicating increasing saturation. If income elasticities are changing over time, it may be misleading to base forecasts on elasticities derived from past data. Lastly, there may be difficulties in establishing different income elasticities for the different segments of the leisure market, such as inclusive tours or independent holidays, or for VFR travel.

One would not expect the demand for business travel to be closely related to *per capita* income, since business travellers' expenditure patterns are related not to their own personal incomes but to the needs of their employers. On the other hand, several studies have found that gross domestic product or some other measure of a country's national income or wealth does correlate with the volume of business traffic generated. It is not difficult to accept that business activity and travel will increase as a nation's total wealth grows. Thus it has proved possible to establish income elasticities for business travel but based on changes in national rather than in *per capita* income.

Table 7.4 Predicted income elasticities of demand for international leisure trips to and from London airports

Leisure segment	1989–93	1994–98	1999–2005
Short-haul:			
UK resident	2.0	1.8	1.7
Non-UK resident	1.8	1.8	1.7
North Atlantic:			
UK resident	2.0	2.0	2.0
Non-UK resident	1.6	1.8	1.5
Middle East:			
UK resident	2.0	2.0	2.0
Non-UK resident	2.0	2.0	2.0
Other long-haul:			
UK resident	2.0	2.0	2.0
Non-UK resident	2.2	2.2	2.2

Source: BAA (unpublished).

Most demand studies in recent years have produced results indicating income elasticities for various categories of passengers which are usually between 1.5 and 2.5. As one would expect, these studies indicate lower income elasticities for business as opposed to leisure travel. These are a feature of most studies (e.g. DoT, 1978, 1981; CAA, 1989; Maiden, 1995). They also highlighted that short-haul travel is more income-elastic than long-haul travel. In 1989, using a more disaggregate basis, BAA Plc calculated income elasticities which it could use for forecasting leisure traffic demand through London's airports. The predicted income elasticities for the international leisure segments are shown in Table 7.4. The BAA no longer calculates income elasticities for business demand, since it finds that other independent variables are more significant for business travel than income. Domestic business travel seems to be more affected by the United Kingdom's gross domestic product, while international business travel seems to be linked with changes in the volume of trade between the United Kingdom and major overseas markets (Maiden, 1995). Yet, even when using trade as an income-related variable, one finds that business travel is relatively trade-inelastic. Amsterdam airport has found that the trade elasticity of business travel is between 0.8 and 1.0 (Veldhuis, 1988).

Apart from income, price is the other variable which has, historically, had a major impact on the growth of air travel. The responsiveness of demand to price or fare changes can also be measured in terms of an elasticity coefficient:

$$\text{Price elasticity} = \frac{\% \text{ change in demand}}{\% \text{ change in price/fare}}$$

Unlike income elasticity, price elasticity is always negative, since price and demand must move in opposite directions. If the fare goes up, demand is expected to fall, and vice versa. So there is invariably a negative sign in the equation. If fares go up 3 per cent and demand drops 6 per cent, the price elasticity is $(-6\%) \div (+3\%) = -2.0$.

Most of the problems previously mentioned which have to be faced when estimating income elasticities also arise in price elasticity studies, but there are some additional ones too. In examining traffic and fare data, for a route or several routes, over a period of time, which fare should one choose to indicate price changes? Not only will there be several fares on each route, but the number of fares and their relative levels may have changed over time. Problems multiply when fares vary by season of the year. Some analysts may use the basic economy fare or the most widely used fare or, if it is available, the average yield obtained by the airline. Alternatively, some have overcome the problem by establishing different price elasticities for different fare groups (Straszheim, 1978). It is the real level of the fare in constant value terms that is significant, not the current level. Therefore fares have to be adjusted for price inflation so as to establish the real cost of air travel in relation to the cost of other goods and services. On international routes this means making different adjustments at each end of the route. An additional problem in establishing fare elasticities for scheduled services is posed by the inclusive tour (ITC) passengers, who have no knowledge of the cost of the fare within their total holiday package price. Moreover, fare changes within an ITC package will have a disproportionately small impact on the total holiday price paid by the prospective ITC consumer.

In so far as business travellers do not pay for their own travel, one would expect them to be relatively insensitive to fare changes. This should be reflected in lower price elasticities for business travellers or for high-fare traffic categories which are composed primarily of business travellers. An examination of price elasticities in some studies shows this to be true. Whereas non-business travel tends to have price elasticities greater than -1.0, the price elasticity of business travel is often less than -1.0 and in the case of first-class travel on the North Atlantic it was as low as -0.65 (Straszheim, 1978). This was before the days of separate business-class cabins. Conversely, the most price-sensitive market segments are those at the lower end of the market, that is, the high-discount fare groups and, in Europe, the inclusive tour segment of the market. It is the high elasticity of demand to price changes at the bottom end of the market that explains the very rapid growth of demand for low-cost airlines such as Southwest in the United States and Ryanair and easyJet in Europe.

Economics textbooks deal at length with the concept and the mathematics of elasticity. It is not opportune to discuss the complexities of the concept here. Suffice it to say that, in order to make pricing and other marketing decisions, airline managers need to have a feel for the price elasticity of the various market segments on the route or routes they are dealing with. Without such a feel, they may make major planning and pricing errors. They basically need to know

Table 7.5 Short-haul international daily return service with 200 seats and $100 single fare

Total seats offered per day (200 each way)	400
Business passengers (approx. 50 each way)	100
Leisure passengers (approx. 50 each way)	100
Daily seat factor (200 pax in 400 seats)	50%
Revenue from business market (100 × $100)	$10,000
Revenue from leisure market (100 × $100)	$10,000
Total revenue per day	$20,000

whether their markets are price-elastic or inelastic. If the price elasticity of demand in a particular market is greater than −1.0, that is, if it is −1.1, −1.2 or more, the market is considered to be elastic. This means that a change in the price or fare has a more than proportional impact on demand. If the fare is reduced, demand will grow more than in proportion. Though each passenger will be paying less than before, many more passengers will be travelling, with the result that the total revenue generated will go up. Conversely, a fare increase in an elastic market has such an adverse effect on demand that total revenue will decline despite the fare increase. When the price elasticity is less than −1.0, as in the case of many business markets, demand is inelastic. Fare changes have a proportionally smaller impact on demand levels. In such market conditions, fare increases will generate greater total revenue because demand will not fall off very much. On the other hand, fare reductions will stimulate some traffic growth, but it will be proportionally less than the drop in fare, so total revenue will decline.

The easiest way of appreciating the pricing and revenue implications of different price elasticities is to consider a simple example. Let us assume that on a short-haul international route an airline is flying a daily return service with a 200-seater aircraft. It is the only operator and there is a single fare of $100 one way. The daily traffic and revenue on the route can be summarised as in Table 7.5. Because of an unexpected increase in jet fuel prices, the airline needs to increase revenue on the route by about 4 per cent. In the short term, costs cannot be reduced in other areas, so the marketing manager is required to generate the additional revenue through tariff changes. The instinctive reaction would be to increase fares to cover the increase in costs. However, earlier market research had established that, while business demand is relatively inelastic to fare changes, with an elasticity of −0.8, the leisure market is price-elastic, with an elasticity of −2.0. Using these price elasticities the marketing manager estimates the traffic and revenue impact of a 10 per cent increase in the fare from $100 to $110.

The business price elasticity of −0.8 tells him that, for every 1 per cent increase in the fare, the airline will lose 0.8 per cent of its market. Thus a 10 per cent fare rise results in an 8 per cent loss of business travellers (i.e. change in demand = +10% × −0.8 = −0.8%). So their daily number will decline by 8 per cent, from 100 to ninety-two. Leisure traffic, being more

Table 7.6 Impact of $110 single fare

92 business passengers at $110	$10,120
80 leisure passengers at $110	8,800
172 passengers	Total revenue $18,920
Seat factor: 172 as percentage of 400 seats	43%

Table 7.7 Impact of $90 single fare

108 business passengers at $90	$9,720
120 leisure passengers at $90	$10,800
228 passengers	Total revenue $20,520
Seat factor: 228 as percentage of 400 seats	57%

elastic to price changes, will drop more, by 20 per cent (or −2.0 per cent for each 1 per cent increase in fare), to eighty passengers on average each day. Surprisingly, even a 10 per cent fare increase results in a drop in revenue, not an increase (Table 7.6).

Revenue from business travellers would go up because, though fewer would travel, the drop in traffic is more than compensated for by the higher fare they are all paying. But leisure passengers react in larger numbers to the higher fare, and total revenue from this segment of the market would go down markedly. The net result is that, if the airline followed an instinctive reaction and increased the fare by, say, 10 per cent, it would end up with a significant fall in traffic, and a collapse of the seat factor from 50 per cent to 43 per cent. This in turn would lead to a drop in total revenue. Too often airlines fail to appreciate that increasing fares may reduce rather than increase their total revenue.

What would be the effect of reducing the fare by 10 per cent to $90? Both business and leisure demand would increase – the former by 8 per cent (i.e. −10% × −0.8 = +8%) and the latter by 20 per cent. Using the price elasticities as before, the traffic and revenue implications can be calculated as in Table 7.7. The lower fare would generate twenty-eight more passengers each day and the seat factor would jump to 57 per cent, a creditable improvement from the current 50 per cent. Most of the additional passengers would be leisure passengers, who are more price-elastic, and revenue from this sector of the market would increase. While there would also be more business travellers, business revenue would decline because the 8 per cent increase in passenger numbers would not be sufficient to compensate for the 10 per cent drop in the fare paid. However, total revenue would increase by $520. This might do little more than cover any additional costs such as in-flight catering imposed by the extra twenty-eight passengers. Cutting fares would produce a better revenue result than increasing the fares. It would increase total revenue by 2.6 per cent. But that is still less than the 4 per cent required.

Table 7.8 Impact of two-fare price structure

92 business passengers at $110	$10,120
120 leisure passengers at $90	$10,800
212 passengers	Total revenue $20,920
Seat factor: 212 as percentage of 400 seats	53%

Examination of the above figures suggests that revenue could be maximised by a two-fare price structure. The airline should charge the business travellers more because their demand is relatively inelastic to price. But it should charge the price-elastic leisure market less, knowing that lower fares will generate proportionally more demand and thereby increase total revenue from this market segment (Table 7.8). By introducing separate fares for each market segment, the airline can increase its total revenue by 4.6 per cent and its seat factor by three points to 53 per cent. The net revenue gain might be less because there may be some extra costs involved in carrying twelve more passengers. This solution also presupposes that the airline can create effective tariff 'fences' to prevent slippage of business passengers into the low-fare market. Simply put, the above example illustrates the principle that, in price-elastic markets, low fares may increase total revenue and that conversely, where demand is price-inelastic, higher fares will generate higher total revenue.

It must be emphasised that even on a simple route the best pricing solution is dependent on two variables, the price elasticities of the different market segments and the market mix, that is, the proportion of the total market represented by each segment. In the above example, the pricing policy adopted might be different if business travellers represented 90 per cent of the market or if the price elasticity of leisure demand was −2.4 instead of −2.0.

In order to produce its 1996 medium-term forecasts of European scheduled passenger traffic, the Association of European Airlines estimated the price and income elasticities of demand for air travel between each country in Europe and the rest of Europe (Table 7.9). This was done by calibrating traffic levels, fares and income changes between pairs of countries during the previous twenty years or so. The elasticities obtained show marked differences between countries. They also show that scheduled air travel within Europe is generally not very price-sensitive. This was, perhaps, because the full impact of low-cost carriers was not felt in Europe till after 1996. On the other hand, intra-European travel demand appears relatively sensitive to income changes (measured in terms of GDP), with particularly high income elasticities among some countries with lower *per capita* incomes such as Portugal or Turkey.

The concept of demand elasticity can be taken further to establish the reaction of passenger demand to changes in other variables. For instance, it is possible to calculate the demand elasticities of service elements such as frequency or journey time (e.g. Jorge-Calderon, 1997). Journey-time elasticities would show that business travel is the most responsive to reductions in journey time and VFR demand probably the least responsive. There is also the

Table 7.9 Price and income elasticities of demand for scheduled air travel within Europe

Country	Price elasticity[a]	Income elasticity[b]
High-income countries:		
Scandinavia	−0.27	+2.44
France	−0.66	+1.88
Switzerland	−0.52	+1.80
Germany	−0.62	+2.65
Low-income countries:		
Portugal	−0.12	+3.02
Turkey	−0.56	+3.23
Ireland	−0.81	+1.17
Greece	−0.33	+2.65

Source: AEA (1996).

Notes
a Price is measured in terms of average yield per passenger on intra-European routes.
b Income is the real gross domestic product of each country (i.e. adjusted for inflation).

concept of cross-elasticity. This measures the impact on the demand for air travel of changes in the price of competing goods or services. Changes in fare structure and levels on the North Atlantic have resulted not only in changes in the total demand but also in significant shifts of demand between fare types, between cabin classes and also to some extent between seasons, since fares vary by season. One or two studies have attempted to establish cross-elasticities within the air market (Kanafani *et al.*, 1974).

Different studies even of the same markets seem to produce different income and price elasticities. Airlines may have difficulty in choosing between them. Larger ones may carry out their own studies to establish elasticities on the routes they are most interested in. If they can overcome the data and method-ological problems, they must still face up to the fact that the elasticities are based on historical traffic data, which may be influenced by particular variables other than fare or income which have not been included in their analysis. There is the additional problem that price, income or other elasticities are changing over time. This is inherent and inevitable. Since elasticities are based on proportional changes in demand, such proportions change as the total demand changes. In the simple example used above, once the fares have changed from the $100 starting level to a new fare generating a different level of demand, the price elasticities at that new demand level will have changed too. Though the change may be a relatively small one.

The pragmatic and methodological problems involved in establishing elasti-cities should not induce airlines to abandon the concept. Some understanding of elasticities is so crucial to pricing, marketing and forecasting that they cannot be ignored. Even an approximate appreciation of price and income elasticities for the major market segments will help airlines make more soundly based decisions.

8   Forecasting demand

8.1   The need for forecasts

Forecasting is the most critical area of airline management. An airline forecasts demand in order to plan the supply of services required to meet that demand. Broadly speaking, tactical or operational decisions stem from short-term traffic forecasts covering the next six to eighteen months or so, and are included in the airline's operating plan and budget for the current and the coming financial year. Aircraft scheduling decisions, maintenance planning, advertising and sales campaigns, the opening of new sales offices are among the many decisions which ultimately are dependent on these shorter-term forecasts. There are in addition a range of strategic decisions, many related to an airline's corporate plan and objectives, which stem from long-term forecasts. Decisions on aircraft procurement, the opening up of new routes or markets, the training of additional flight crews, investment in new maintenance facilities and similar strategic decisions all stem from longer-term forecasts of up to five years or more. Almost every tactical or strategic decision taken within an airline stems ultimately from a forecast. At the same time, forecasting is the area in which mistakes are most frequently made and the one about which there is least certainty. There is no absolute truth in forecasting, no optimum method that can guarantee accuracy. Instead, airline forecasters use any one of a range of forecasting techniques, of varying mathematical complexity, each of which has advantages and disadvantages, none of which can ensure consistent accuracy. Yet forecasts have to be made since so many decisions flow from them.

The annual budgets and the longer-term plans on which so many supply decisions hinge start with forecasts of passenger and freight traffic. Forecasting involves different types of forecast, each of which poses different methodological problems. In the first instance, airlines need to forecast traffic growth, assuming a continuation of current operating conditions with no dramatic changes in fares or in other supply factors. They will forecast the global growth of passenger and/or freight traffic on a route, group of routes or geographical region. Such forecasts represent the total demand, from which the airline then has to predict its own share and its own traffic. Essentially they involve an assumption that traffic growth will continue in the future very much as it has done in the past.

Airlines must also be able to forecast the response of demand to a change in the conditions of supply. Such changes may include an increase or reduction in the real level of fares, a change from narrow to wide-bodied aircraft, a market increase in frequencies or a change in departure times. A significant change in supply conditions may be under consideration by the airline itself or change may be imposed by one or more of its competitors. In either case, an airline must be in a position to forecast traffic reaction to such change.

A somewhat different forecasting problem exists when an airline is trying to forecast demand on a new route which is under evaluation. This may frequently be a route on which there have been no direct air services at all previously, or it may be a route on which the airline concerned is a new entrant. In either case the airline has no experience and little or no historical traffic data on which to base its forecasts. This is particularly so if the route has had no previous air services at all. Forecasting in such circumstances is clearly very difficult, with a high risk of error, and may require different forecasting techniques from those normally used.

Lastly, there is the question of segmental forecasting. Passenger traffic on a route is composed of identifiable market segments related partly to purpose of travel and partly to service requirements. Such segments may be further categorised by point of origin. The earlier analysis of demand factors indicated that each market segment is likely to have differing demand elasticities and to be growing at different rates. It should therefore be possible to produce more accurate forecasts by forecasting the growth in each market segment separately and then aggregating them, rather than by forecasting the total traffic from the start. Many airlines already produce forecasts using two market segments, business and leisure, or possibly three based on fare type. Only a small number of airlines have the resources to carry out more extensive segmental forecasting. In the future, however, planning requirements and the need to improve the accuracy of forecasts may push more airlines to consider this disaggregate forecasting. In many airlines there is a dichotomy in forecasting methods. If an airline has a yield management system, its revenue planners may be using very detailed forecasts disaggregated by fare type but with a very short time horizon of a year or so. Yet in the same airline route and fleet planners will be basing their own three-to-five-year forecasts on less detailed models with fewer market segments.

The aim of this chapter is not to suggest the best way of forecasting but to review some of the problems of forecasting and the alternative techniques which are most commonly used in the international airline industry, without going too deeply into the mathematics. As a result, this is not an exhaustive review, since some forecasting tools, little used by airlines, are not examined. The forecasting methods more widely used by airlines, often in combination, fall broadly into three groups of growing complexity: qualitative methods, time-series projections and causal or econometric methods.

8.2   Qualitative methods

8.2.1   Executive judgement

Of the numerous forecasting techniques available to airlines, executive judgement is one of the most widely used, usually to modify and adapt other more mathematical forecasts. Such judgement is based on the insight and assessment of a person, who often may not be a forecaster, but who has special knowledge of the route or market in question. For instance, the country or area managers of an airline are frequently asked to predict traffic growth on their routes. Their knowledge will include an understanding of recent and current traffic growth and of economic and other developments likely to affect future demand. They also have first-hand knowledge of their own market and its peculiarities. They weigh up the factors involved and therefore their judgement and their predictions may be quite soundly based, but the approach is basically crude and unscientific. The more detailed and the more long term the forecast the more likely it is that executive judgement will prove inadequate. On the other hand, executive judgement as a forecasting tool has two distinct advantages. It is quick. Forecasts can be made almost instantaneously and do not require any detailed assessment or working out of data. In addition, the person making the forecast may be aware of extraneous and particular factors which may affect future demand on a route, which the more data-based techniques would not pick up. It is for this reason that many airlines subject their data-based forecasts to assessment and possible modification by certain key managers and executives.

8.2.2   Market research

A wide range of market research techniques can be used by airlines in order to analyse the characteristics of demand for both passengers and freight. These techniques will include attitudinal and behavioural surveys of passengers and, it is hoped, those not travelling by air. They will also involve studies of hotel and tourism facilities, surveys of travel agents and business houses, analyses of trade flows and other business interaction, and so on. Such studies may be commissioned from specialist market research companies or they may be carried out by the airlines themselves. Many larger airlines in any case carry out regular and systematic surveys of their own passengers so as to build up a profile of their needs and characteristics. Others carry out such surveys on an *ad hoc* basis when a specific question needs to be resolved. The aim of all this is to derive empirically an understanding of how demand for air transport varies between different sectors of the population or, in the case of air freight, between different industrial sectors. This knowledge can then be used in combination with forecasts by others of sociological, demographic or economic change to predict future levels of demand.

   In many circumstances such an empirical approach to forecasting may be more appropriate than the more econometric methods. On an air route where the demand for air travel is suppressed by the inadequate number of hotel beds at the destination, a study of hotel and tourism infrastructure projects at that destination may produce a better indication of future travel flows than would an analysis of past traffic trends. Equally the forecasting of air freight demand often lends itself to the use of market research studies, especially on routes where freight flows are relatively thin. On many routes the erratic and irregular growth of air freight makes time-series analyses or other econometric techniques difficult to use. Air freight forecasting models have generally been less successful than models for forecasting passenger demand. On most air routes, the goods freighted by air fall into a limited number of clearly defined commodities. Exports by air from many developing countries are usually confined to one or two commodities, while imports are quite different and cover a wider, though still limited, range of goods. As a result, air freight forecasts may often fruitfully be based on market research analysis of trade developments in a few key commodities.

Market studies are particularly useful as a forecasting tool when past traffic data are inadequate or non-existent, thereby prohibiting the use of time-series and possibly of econometric forecasts too. This happens on many routes from developing countries and is obviously the case on entirely new routes. In these circumstances market research may be the only way of evaluating future demand. Market research also helps airlines to forecast demand reaction to changes in supply conditions and to gain an appreciation of their different market segments if they wish to get involved in segmental forecasting.

8.2.3 Delphi techniques

The Delphi approach requires the building up of a consensus forecast based on the views of individuals who are considered to have sufficient expertise to be able to anticipate future trends. The process is an iterative one, possibly involving several rounds of consultation. In simple terms, a group of experts may be asked to give their forecasts of growth in a region or market. These forecasts are used to build up a composite forecast. This is then communicated to each expert, who may wish to revise his own original forecast in the light of what other experts are predicting. The individual forecast from this second round of consultations can be used to arrive at an agreed or consensus forecast. This is the principle of the Delphi method. In practice the consultative process can be more or less complex, depending on the amount of information exchanged between the experts.

The Delphi technique is more suitable for aggregate forecasts of growth in major markets or regions than for individual route forecasts. As a result it is little used internally by airlines, but it was the basis of the industry-wide forecasts produced annually by the International Air Transport Association (IATA). These are regional forecasts for nearly twenty route areas such as Europe–Middle East or Middle East–Far East. Forecasts by direction are produced for freight traffic too. The forecasts cover the current year and a five-year period ahead and are revised each June, sometimes with interim revisions during the winter. Up to 1986 these IATA forecasts were Delphi forecasts based on a consensus of expert opinion and were arrived at in a series of steps.

The first step involved the development of explicit forecasting assumptions at a meeting of airline forecasters and key experts from outside the airline industry. The purpose of this meeting was to develop the best possible background scenarios and explicit regional assumptions for the changes in the real level of tariffs and in the major economic indicators affecting demand. The assumptions and data bases were communicated to the airlines participating in the forecasting exercise. The airlines were then requested to submit their own forecasts for the industry as a whole and for each route area or market on which they operated. Airlines were free to use whatever forecasting method they preferred in arriving at their own forecasts and could even make alternative key assumptions if they wished to. The results of this first round were distributed to all participating airlines for review before the finalisation meeting. This took place in early June. The experts reviewed the consolidated regional forecasts, made adjustments in the light of more recent developments and might also consider econometric forecasts made by some member airlines.

The IATA forecasts were then finalised and widely distributed throughout the world. These forecasts represented a consensus of expertise within the airline industry. However, this Delphi approach was very time-consuming and since 1986 IATA has reverted to a simpler approach. Preliminary meetings to agree basic assumptions are no longer held. Instead, individual airlines submit their own forecasts for individual routes or markets. A consensus forecast based on a compilation of individual airline forecasts is then prepared by IATA. It is still in essence a Delphi forecast based on a consensus of expert opinion. The IATA annual forecasts are used by smaller airlines as inputs into their own forecasting processes and by larger airlines as a counter-check on their own internal forecasts. Airport authorities, aircraft manufacturers and governments also refer to the IATA forecasts.

8.3   Time-series projections

Time-series or trend projections represent the forecasting technique most widely used by international airlines. Many smaller airlines do little else. Essentially the technique involves a projection into the future of what has happened in the past. It assumes that whatever factors affected air traffic in the past will continue to operate in the same manner in the future. The only independent variable affecting traffic is time, and as time progresses so will traffic.

To establish the relationship between traffic (the dependent variable) and time (the independent variable), it is essential to have accurate and detailed traffic statistics for the route in question. Without such data, trend projections cannot be used. The first step in the forecasting process is to plot the time-series data on a graph so as to show monthly or annual traffic totals against the appropriate month or year. Drawing a freehand curve through the points should indicate

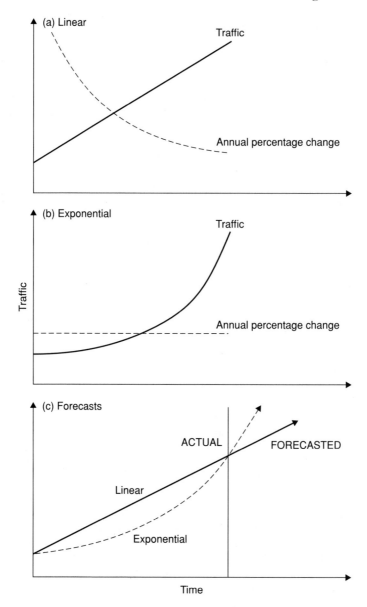

Figure 8.1 Types of traffic growth: (a) linear, $y = a + bt$, (b) exponential, $y = a(1 + b)^t$, (c) forecasts: linear and exponential.

whether the traffic trend on the route is exponential or linear (Figure 8.1). An *exponential* trend is one where traffic seems to grow by a constant percentage with each unit of time. This means that the absolute increase in each time period in passenger numbers or freight tonnes is greater than in the previous period. This is because each successive growth is a constant percentage but of a larger preceding total. The equation of the exponential curve is given by

$$\text{Traffic } (y) = a(1 + b)^t$$

where a is constant and b is the rate of growth and t is time. A linear or straight-line trend is one where the traffic increases by a constant absolute amount with each unit of time. It is expressed in the form

$$\text{Traffic } (y) = a + bt$$

where a and b are constants and t is again time. Because changes for each unit of time are by a constant amount and the total traffic is growing, the percentage growth is gradually declining. There is therefore a fundamental difference between the impact of an exponential as opposed to a linear growth trend on forecasts of traffic growth. Exponential growth means ever greater annual or monthly traffic increments, though the percentage change may be more or less constant. Linear growth would indicate constant increments in terms of numbers but declining percentage changes. Deciding which trend best represents developments of a route will therefore have a major impact on forecasts, especially longer-term ones. There is also the possibility that growth on a route may be linear in its early stages and then become exponential, or vice versa. An added problem is that at times it may be difficult to decide whether an exponential or linear trend fits the data best, yet choosing between them will produce quite different forecasts.

It has been observed that some air routes or markets, after achieving very rapid growth for a number of years, reach a plateau where traffic growth flattens off. It is frequently assumed that this plateau level is reached when the market has matured and is in some sense saturated. If this has happened or is happening on a route, the trend of past traffic data may best be described by growth curves which asymptotically approach an upper limit such as a logistic curve or a Gompertz curve. Both of these are S-shaped and indicate declining absolute and relative growth as markets reach maturity. In practice, international airlines tend not to use logistic or Gompertz trend curves for forecasting. Most time-series forecasting is either exponential or linear. Of these, the former is probably more widely used both because of its simplicity and also because past air traffic trends do often appear to be exponential.

The workings and implications of different time-series techniques can best be appreciated by using them to make forecasts for an actual route. The case study chosen is London to Nice on the French Mediterranean, a short-haul scheduled route with relatively little charter traffic and little indirect traffic transiting via Paris or elsewhere. The case study assumes that one is back in 1984 and wishing to forecast the traffic on the route for 1988, five years hence. For reasons of simplicity the forecasts for individual years prior to 1988 are not discussed.

Table 8.1 Total passenger traffic, London–Nice (both ways), 1972–83

Year	Terminal passengers (000) 1	Annual change (%) 2	Three-year moving average passengers (000) 3	Annual change (%) 4
1972	140.6			
1973	148.5	+5.6	143.8	
1974	142.4	−4.1	151.6	+5.4
1975	163.8	+15.0	158.6	+4.6
1976	169.6	+3.5	166.9	+5.2
1977	167.4	−1.3	174.0	+4.3
1978	185.0	+10.5	187.4	+7.7
1979	209.9	+13.5	206.7	+10.3
1980	225.1	+7.2	225.4	+9.0
1981	241.2	+7.2	245.0	+8.7
1982	268.8	+11.4	259.3	+5.8
1983	268.0	−0.3		

Source: CAA, *UK Airports: Annual Statements of Movements, Passengers and Cargo.*

To make time-series forecasts, a minimum of seven to ten years of past traffic data is required and some forecasters suggest that one should not forecast for a longer period ahead than about half the number of past years for which statistics are available. For the London–Nice route, traffic data for twelve years to 1983 were examined (Table 8.1). These indicated that, though passenger movements almost doubled between 1972 and 1983, growth was at times erratic, with two years, 1974 and 1977, in which traffic actually declined. In practice, many larger airlines would hesitate to forecast so far ahead on the basis of time-series projections alone. Nevertheless, a five-year forecast does enable one to see clearly the impact of different techniques. While the analysis which follows relates to annual traffic volumes and forecasts the annual traffic for 1988, the same forecasting methods could be used with monthly or weekly traffic data. Problems of seasonal traffic fluctuations might arise, but these could be adjusted for.

The London–Nice data underline some of the difficulties faced in forecasting. To start with, examination and plotting of the traffic data do not make it easy to decide whether past growth is linear or exponential. As a result, both exponential and linear forecasts will be made in the analysis which follows. Another major problem facing forecasters using time-series analysis is how far back they should go in examining past traffic data. In the case of London–Nice, ten-year data to 1983 meant 1974 would be the first year. This was known to be a year in which traffic slumped because of the first oil crisis. There was subsequently a very large jump in traffic in 1975. Using a maverick low year as the starting point might produce less accurate forecasts. So forecasters may decide, as has been done here, to go back and extend the time series by two years to 1972. This then raises a different question. Are data and traffic so far in the past a good reflection of what will happen five years in the future? Would it not be logical to take a shorter time series? Is the recent past a better indicator of the future than the more distant past? There is no absolute answer to this enigma. Forecasters must choose the time series which they feel in each case will best allow them to make a realistic forecast. To do this they must ensure that their stream of data embodies the underlying trends and encompasses complete cyclical variations if any exist.

8.3.1   Exponential forecasts

8.3.1.1   Average rate of growth

Many airlines, especially the smaller ones and those that have relatively new routes with only a short stream of data, base their forecasts on the average of the past rates of growth. This approach has the advantage of simplicity. In the London–Nice case, adding up the annual percentage change each year from 1972 to 1983 and dividing by eleven, which is the number of observations, produced an average annual growth of +6.2 per cent. Using the formula

$$y = a(1 + b)^t$$

where a is the actual traffic in 1983, b is the growth rate and t is the number of years forecast, then

$$1988 \text{ traffic} = 268 \times (1.062)^5 = 362.0$$

In this and subsequent equations, traffic volumes are in thousands.

In the London–Nice case the number of observations is relatively small, only twelve, and this is so with many airline forecasts. But it does raise some doubt about whether +6.2 per cent is the true average growth rate. It is possible to estimate mathematically what the possible range of values for the true growth rate may be. The true growth rate at a 95 per cent level of confidence would be 6.2 ± 4.2. If one were to adjust the 1988 forecast accordingly, the range would be very wide. It is for this reason that most airline forecasters would ignore the implications of having a relatively small number of observations.

8.3.1.2   Moving average growth

The use of annual average growth rates should be based, in theory, on data series which are long enough to show what are the random variations and what are shifts in underlying trends. Where the time series is not very long and where there are very marked fluctuations in traffic growth from year to year, as in the case of the London–Nice data (Table 8.1), some forecasters will use moving averages as a way of flattening out wild traffic variations so as to understand the underlying trends. In order to do this, normally three (or more) observations are added together and the average is calculated. It is then given as the actual observation for the middle of the three years (or months if one is using monthly data). For London–Nice the actual traffic for 1972, 1973 and 1974 was added together and divided by three. This produced a three-year moving average of 143,800, which was the traffic attributed to 1973, the middle year (column 3 of Table 8.1). Then 1972 was dropped and the average for 1973, 1974 and 1975 calculated and attributed to 1974, and so on, the final moving average being for 1982. The choice of the number of observations for the moving average is up to the forecaster, whose aim is to eliminate sudden short-term traffic variations without losing sight of longer-term changes. But moving averages cannot be used with small data sets, since one effectively loses data at each end. Examination of the moving average data for London–Nice in Table 8.1 (columns 3 and 4) shows a flattening-out effect. Traffic does not decline in any single year and the growth in the good years is not as high as the unadjusted annual figure would suggest. The highest growth was 10.3 per cent in 1979, following which there seems to have been a downward trend in the underlying growth rate.

The annual average rate of growth can be calculated from the annual changes in the moving average figures (column 4 in Table 8.1). In this case it was 6.8 per cent. Using this to forecast 1988 traffic, then,

$$1988 \text{ traffic} = 259.3 \times (1.068)^6 = 384.8$$

The use of a moving average here seems to have identified a faster underlying growth than was evident previously.

8.3.1.3 *Exponential smoothing*

Some forecasters believe that the recent past is a better pointer to the future than the more distant past. It follows that, in projecting past traffic growth into the future, greater weight should be given to the more recent observations. Mathematically, the technique for doing this is similar to the moving average but adjusted to give a particular weighting to recent as opposed to more distant observations. In a simple form,

$$y + 1 = \alpha y + \alpha(1 - \alpha)y_{-1} + \alpha(1 - \alpha)^2 y_{-2} + \alpha(1 - \alpha)^3 y_{-3} \ldots$$

where α is a smoothing factor ($10 < \alpha < 1$), y is the number of passengers in year y, and $y + 1$ is the first-year forecast.

The greater the value given to α the greater will be the weight given to the more recent observations. The forecaster can decide the value of α. The above formulation is relatively simple but some smoothing techniques can be quite complex. The best known is the Box–Jenkins model. This is a sophisticated and complex model requiring a large number of observations. Though airline forecasters make reference to Box–Jenkins (Nguyen Dai Hai, 1982), few if any actually use it. Simpler formulations are available. One of them is Brown's double exponential smoothing model and another the Holt–Winters model. Both use a smoothing technique to deal with time-series data containing a trend variation. Since the London–Nice traffic data showed a clear trend pattern, the Holt–Winters model was used. The 1988 forecast produced on this basis was 326,200 passengers. This is much lower than the other exponential forecasts because the effect of the smoothing technique is to give much greater weight to the fact that in 1983, the most recent year, traffic declined marginally. While exponential smoothing techniques have been widely used in some other industries, their use is still fairly limited within the airline industry. There is, however, a growing awareness that, by giving greater weight to the more recent observations, forecasters may be in a position to improve the accuracy of time-series projections.

8.3.2   Linear trend projections

8.3.2.1   Simple trend

The underlying assumption is that a straight line best represents the trend of the traffic over time and that traffic increases by a constant amount with each unit of time. The technique involves drawing a straight line through the time series so as to produce a best fit. This is normally done by the least squares method, though other mathematical techniques are also available. The least squares criterion requires that the line fitted to the data should be the one which minimises the sum of the squares of the vertical deviations of the data points from the line. Some of the points are likely to be above the line, and therefore positive, and some below the line, and so negative. These would cancel each other out if one were merely trying to minimise the sum of the deviations. By using the squares of the deviations this problem is avoided.

In fitting a line of the form $y = a + bt$ to the time-series data so as to satisfy the least squares criterion, there remains the problem of how closely the straight line corresponds to those data. The goodness of fit is measured by an index known as the coefficient of correlation (R), or the square of this quantity (R^2), which is strictly speaking the coefficient of determination. In practice the R^2 coefficient is used most frequently. If the fit of the straight line to the data is very poor, the value of R^2 approaches zero. If the fit is very good, the value of R^2 will be close to 1.0. Within the airline industry, experience suggests that accurate predictions using linear trend lines require very high coefficients of determination. They should be above 0.90 and preferably higher.

Fitting a trend line to the London–Nice data produced the following result:

$$y = 111.9 + 12.7t \qquad R^2 = 0.939$$

This indicates that a trend line starting at 111,900 passengers and growing by 12,700 passengers per year (*t*) produces a good fit with the actual traffic in each year, since the coefficient of determination at 0.939 is high. To forecast traffic in 1988 one needs to add 12,700 passengers for each year of the seventeen years from 1972 to 1988 to the starting figure of 111,900:

$$1988 \text{ traffic} = 111.9 + (12.7 \times 17) = 327.8$$

Trend projections are simple and easy to use. But they can be used only if the data exhibit some regularity, without wide fluctuations. Many air routes, however, do exhibit very pronounced traffic variations, with large jumps in traffic followed inexplicably by sudden slumps. In such conditions, fitting trend lines with an adequately high coefficient of determination may prove difficult. One possible solution is to use moving averages.

8.3.2.2 *Moving average trend*

Unusually large variations in the past traffic volumes can be reduced by calculating moving averages and establishing a new time series. This should now contain only the trend component in the traffic and it should be easier to fit a trend line. Using the moving average data for London–Nice (as previously given in column 3 of Table 8.1), the following trend line and forecast were calculated:

$$y = 119.9 + 13.1t \qquad R^2 = 0.961$$

$$1988 \text{ traffic} = 119.9 + (13.1 \times 16) = 329.5$$

On London–Nice, the use of a moving average trend produces a forecast which is very close to the one based on the unadjusted trend. This is because the London–Nice traffic did not exhibit wide fluctuations and therefore using a moving average trend has relatively little impact. It has been done here only for illustrative purposes.

As a result of using alternative time-series techniques, five different forecasts of the London–Nice passenger traffic in 1988 could have been produced. They are summarised in Table 8.2. The difference between the highest and the lowest forecast is around 58,000 passengers a year, equivalent to five round-trip flights a week in an Airbus A320 at about a 65 per cent seat factor. The range is very wide and could play havoc with any airline's strategic fleet planning decisions. Which forecast should the forecasters and planners go for? As a group, the exponential techniques in this particular case produce higher forecasts than the linear trends. This seems to be frequently so in airline forecasts and may be an additional reason why airlines prefer working with exponential rather than linear projections. They prefer to be optimistic in their forecasts.

Table 8.2 Alternative time-series forecasts (made in 1984) of London–Nice traffic for 1988

Forecasting method	No. of passengers forecast
Exponential forecasts:	
Average annual rate of growth	362,000
Moving average	384,800
Exponential smoothing (Holt–Winters)	326,200
Linear trend projections:	
Simple trend	327,800
Moving average trend	329,500
Difference between highest and lowest forecast	58,600

Table 8.3 Actual London–Nice traffic, 1983–88

Year	Terminating passengers (000)	Annual change (%)
1983	268.0	
1984	278.1	+3.8
1985	305.6	+9.9
1986	308.7	+1.0
1987	341.4	+10.6
1988	392.8	+15.0

Source: CAA, *UK Airports: Annual Statements of Movements, Passengers and Cargo.*

What did happen on the London–Nice route by 1988? The year-by-year growth after 1983 seems to have been relatively rapid (Table 8.3). Only in 1986, the year of Chernobyl and a poor year in many markets, did traffic growth slow down. By 1988, 392,800 passengers were travelling on the route. Comparison with the summary of forecasts (Table 8.2) suggests that growth in this market was clearly exponential rather than linear. The linear forecasts were much too low, while two of the exponential forecasts, based on the annual or the three-year moving annual rates of growth, were relatively close to the 1988 outcome. Despite the very high values of R^2 obtained for the linear trends they proved poor predictors of future traffic. This suggests that one should not accept very high values of R^2 uncritically when forecasting.

The exponential smoothing forecast was not very accurate, but this was no doubt due to the fact that 1983 was a year of slight decline. Had one used 1982 as the final year, when traffic grew 11.4 per cent, an exponentially smoothed forecast, which places greater weight on the most recent years, would have produced a much higher forecast. This suggests that exponential smoothing may be too dependent on what has happened most recently and may distort the longer-term trend. Moreover, this technique, though called *exponential* smoothing, is mathematically more akin to linear forecasting. This may explain its low 1988 forecast.

Table 8.4 Alternative time-series forecasts (made in 1995) of London–Nice scheduled traffic for 1999

Forecasting method	No. of passengers forecast
Exponential forecasts:	
Average annual rate of growth	859,700
Moving average	920,700
Exponential smoothing (Holt–Winters)	743,400
Linear trend projections:	
Simple trend	764,200
Moving average trend	745,800
Actual traffic in 1999	980,300

A similar exercise for the London–Nice route carried out ten years later in 1995 to forecast passengers numbers for 1999 produced similar conclusions (Table 8.4). The forecasts were based on annual traffic volumes for the period 1983–94. Once again the exponential forecasts proved to be much closer to the actual out-turn than the linear projections. The exponential forecast, using a moving average, predicted traffic of around 921,000 passengers in 1999 compared with the actual traffic of 980,300. This proved remarkably close, given that in 1996 there was a drastic change in the supply conditions. In that year easyJet, a low-cost carrier, launched services from Luton, one of the London area airports, to Nice, offering very low fares. This had a dramatic impact on demand levels. In 1998, by which time easyJet was well established on the route, passenger numbers grew nearly 30 per cent. All carriers between London and Nice increased their traffic that year. Growth in 1999 was down to 13 per cent. Exponential forecasts appear better able to allow for sudden surges in demand due to changes in market conditions.

The London–Nice case study supports the view of many airlines that traffic growth is more likely to be exponential than linear. But there will be routes where linear trend projections may produce more reliable forecasts. In practice, every airline's forecasting group has developed in the light of its own experience a preference for a particular approach to forecasting involving only one or two of the methods proposed above. Few airlines would bother to calculate more than a couple of time-series forecasts.

Throughout the world the majority of airlines use time-series projections as the starting point of their forecasting exercises. They are simple to use provided that adequate statistical information on past traffic flows is available. They require little else. They are also likely to be reasonably accurate for short-term forecasts. It is relatively easy to forecast tomorrow's traffic if you know today's, or to forecast next week's traffic if you know the average traffic handled in recent weeks. Beyond eighteen months or so the risk of error with time-series forecasts increases as various external factors begin to impact on demand. Time-series projections allow airlines to make individual forecasts for each route. Annual forecasts can be disaggregated into monthly forecasts reflecting seasonal variations without too much difficulty. Alternatively, time-series forecasts can be built up using monthly rather than annual data.

Although they are widely used, time-series forecasting methods do have a fundamental underlying weakness. They are based on the assumption that traffic growth and development are merely functions of time. As time changes, so does demand. Yet our earlier analysis of demand showed that many factors affect the level of demand, such as the level of trade or of personal income, and that these factors are themselves changing over time. Even if they did not do so, there are numerous supply factors, of which the most critical is the tariff level, which are invariably changing and affecting demand in the process. It is clearly an oversimplification to relate demand purely to changes in time. Time can be only a very poor proxy for a host of other critical variables. The longer ahead the time-series projection the less likely it is to be accurate, as there is more time and scope for demand to be influenced by changes in one or more of the many independent variables.

There are two ways in which airline forecasters can try to overcome this underlying weakness. Most airlines start by making time-series projections. They then modify these projections on the basis of market research findings and executive judgement and turn them into forecasts. In this way they can allow for the impact of the expected changes in demand factors and of planned changes in supply which they themselves control. As an alternative, a few airlines, usually larger ones, may try to use econometric or causal forecasting techniques, which relate traffic growth not to time but to a series of assumed causal factors.

8.4   Econometric or causal methods

The underlying principle of all such models is that the demand for passenger transport or for air freight services is related to and affected by one or more economic, social or supply factors. Economic theory suggests that the demand for any product or service depends primarily on its price, on the prices of competing products or services, on the nature of the product and the degree to which it is essential for consumers, on levels of personal income and on consumers' taste. Changes in any one of these variables will affect demand. Econometric models attempt to measure that causal relationship so that by forecasting or even implementing change in any one of the variables one can predict the consequent impact on demand levels.

The starting point in causal modelling must be to identify and select the factors, known as the independent variables, which must be assessed in order to forecast the dependent variable, which is the level of passenger or possibly freight traffic. The second step is to determine the functional relationship between the dependent variables and the independent variables selected. This means specifying the form of the model to be used. Normally for airline fore-casting it will be a *regression* model. Other model forms such as gravity-type models are used in other areas of transport but less frequently in air transport. The third step in the forecasting process involves the calibration of the model and the testing of the mathematical expression for the relationship between the dependent and the independent variables. Should the tests show that the relationship established through the model is significant and statistically robust, one can move on to the final step. This involves forecasting the independent variables or using other people's forecasts in order to derive from them the forecasts of air traffic.

8.4.1 *Regression models*

Most econometric forecasts of air traffic tend to be based on simple or multiple regression models, where traffic is a function of one or more independent variables. The two variables most frequently used are the air fare and some measure of *per capita* income. Thus, for a route such as London to Nice, one might consider a model of the form:

$$T = f(F, \ Y, \ t) \tag{8.1}$$

where T is the annual number of passengers travelling between London and Nice, F is the average fare in real terms, Y is an income measure such as gross domestic product or consumer expenditure per head and t is some underlying time trend. Fare level, income levels or other economic variables have to be adjusted for inflation and expressed in constant value or real terms. The choice of fare is critical. Ideally only change in the lowest fare should be considered, as only this should affect the total market; changes in other fares would affect only the market mix. On many routes it is not as clear-cut as that, since the number of seats for sale at the lowest fare may be strictly limited in number. Many analyses will choose the average yield rather than the lowest fare as the fare variable. Income levels pose the additional problem of identifying those whose income one considers is the variable affecting demand. In the above case, should one use a global figure of UK *per capita* income and another for French income or should one try to establish the income levels in London and those in Nice? If one adjusts the fare level for inflation, one would have to make adjustments to the fare in French francs for Nice-originating traffic and a different adjustment to express the sterling fare in constant terms. This kind of problem would induce many forecasters to develop two separate directional models for the route, based on origin of travel. For London-originating passenger traffic going to Nice the formulation would be

$$T_L = f(F_L, \ Y_{UK}, \ t_L) \tag{8.2}$$

where T_L is the London-originating passenger traffic on London–Nice, F_L is the real sterling air fare from London, Y_{UK} is the *per capita* income in the United Kingdom and t_L is the time trend for London-originating traffic.

In order to convert fares, income or other independent variables into number of passengers, a constant (K) has to be incorporated into the equation

$$T_L = Kf(F_L, Y_{UK}, t_L) \qquad (8.3)$$

Most airline forecasting models assume that the relationship between the independent variables is multiplicative, that is to say, the effects of each of the variables on traffic tend to multiply rather than to add up. The independent variables must represent quite different influences on demand, otherwise the multiplicative relationship may not apply. Expressing the multiplicative relationship between the dependent and the independent variables in logarithmic form turns the relationship between the logarithms into a linear one:

$$\log T_L = K + a \log F_L + b \log Y_{UK} + c \log t_L + u \qquad (8.4)$$

where u is an error term and a, b and c are model parameters, and the higher their value the more impact changes in the corresponding variables will have on the traffic level.

It is not essential for the model to be log-linear, but many empirical studies of demand have found this to be a useful and relevant form.

Many forecasters might decide to go further and relate the percentage change of traffic from one year to the next to the corresponding percentage change in the independent variables, in this case fare and income. The model is then expressed as follows:

$$\Delta \log T_L = K + a\Delta \log F_L + b\Delta \log Y_{UK} + c \log t_L + u \qquad (8.5)$$

where Δ is the logarithm of the percentage change in the variable in question over the previous year. Effectively a and b are now the demand or traffic elasticities. The value of a is, in fact, the fare elasticity of UK-originating traffic on the London to Nice route, and b is the income elasticity of that traffic. It is through regression models of this kind that the price and income elasticities discussed in the preceding chapter are derived.

Having specified the regression model and the independent variables to be initially included, the model is calibrated to past traffic levels and changes in the independent variables. It is usual for time-series data to be used, that is, past data over a period of time. Less frequently a model may be calibrated using cross-sectional data, that is, data at one point in time but covering many routes. Using an iterative process based on the estimation of ordinary least squares, the regression model establishes the value of the constant term (K) and of the coefficients a, b and c.

It is normal for several model formulations to be tested before the independent variables to be used for forecasting are finally selected. While fare and income levels are the most frequently used, many others have also been found to give good results on particular routes or markets. Models for forecasting business travel may well use trade as an index of industrial production instead of income as a variable (CAA, 1989). Models on routes where holiday traffic is dominant may include hotel prices, currency exchange rates or some other variable that is especially relevant to tourism flows. Quality of service variables may also be introduced into the model. The simplest of these is a speed or journey time variable, though a few more complex models have included frequency, load factor or some other service variable (Ippolito, 1981).

Having fitted the data and established the value of the constant (K) and of the coefficients, forecasters need to find out how statistically sound their model is. They can use it as a forecasting tool only if they are convinced of the reliability of the relations the model purports to have established. A number of statistical tests can be used for this purpose. The most straightforward is the coefficient of multiple determination ($\bar{R}^2$), which measures the closeness of fit of the time-series data to the regression model. A very close fit will produce a coefficient approaching 1.0, whereas a low coefficient of, say, 0.5 or less would indicate a poor fit. Using time-series data, one would ideally expect to obtain a coefficient of 0.9 or more if one wanted to use the model for forecasting with some degree of confidence. The $\bar{R}^2$ coefficient may also be used to choose between models with different combinations of independent variables.

While the $\bar{R}^2$ value tells forecasters how well traffic variations fit variations in the independent variable, it does not tell them how traffic is related statistically to each of the independent variables separately. This is done by partial correlation coefficients. These measure how closely traffic is related to any one of the independent variables when all other variables are held constant.

Other tests to establish the validity of the model and the significance of the relationships it purports to measure include Student's *t* test and the *F* statistic. The latter is an alternative to the coefficient of multiple determination and is found by comparing the explained variance of the data with the unexplained variance. It is not the aim of the present book to deal in detail with the conduct and significance of the various statistical tests which can be carried out. These are covered adequately in many statistics textbooks and in one or two specialist air transport texts (Taneja, 1978).

While academic economists have developed quite sophisticated and apparently robust econometric models for forecasting air traffic, airlines tend to use fairly simple models, which often may not be as statistically sound as, in theory, one might wish. One such model was developed in 1977 for forecasting Air Algérie's traffic between Algeria and France. The model took the form

$$\log T = K + a \log \text{GNP} + b \log F + c \log S \tag{8.6}$$

where T is the number of passengers carried by Air Algérie between Algiers and Paris, GNP is a measure of the combined real GNP of France and Algeria weighted in proportion to the share of Algerians in the total traffic, F is the average yield per passenger kilometre on all Algeria–France routes and S is the average speed of all Algeria–France air services.

Effectively the independent variables were income, price and a quality of service variable which was speed. The time series on which the model was based was for the eight years 1968–75. It was rather short, though a similar model for total air traffic between the two countries had a ten-year data base. Using the ordinary least squares method, the coefficient worked out as follows:

$$\log T = 1.0963 + 1.4476 \log \text{GNP} - 1.4135 \log F + 0.2471 \log S$$
$$(0.7890) \quad (8.3352) \qquad\qquad (-2.3490) \qquad\quad (0.6656) \qquad (8.7)$$

where the respective Student t values are given in parentheses below the main equation, $\bar{R}^2 = 0.9732$, the standard error is 0.0381, $F(3.5) = 60.60$ and the value of the Durbin–Watson statistic is 3.24.

The model established a price elasticity of -1.4 on the Algiers–Paris route and an income elasticity of $+1.4$. Since the high t test values validated the significance of the coefficients, the model was used to carry out ten-year forecasts to be used for fleet planning purposes.

Whereas the Air Algérie model was used for specific route forecasts, econometric models are used to forecast traffic development in wider markets. For example, during the early 1990s the UK Civil Aviation Authority divided the traffic at the London airports into eleven discrete market segments based on purpose of travel, place of residence of passengers and type of route. Each market segment had its own causal model and its traffic was forecast separately. For instance, leisure traffic by UK residents on the North Atlantic was a function of UK consumer expenditure, North Atlantic fares and tourist ground costs, which are affected by the sterling–dollar exchange rate (CAA, 1989). The model formulation was:

$$\log \textit{UK-NA LS} = 0.015 + 2.12\Delta \log \textit{CE} - 1.03\Delta \log \textit{TC} - 0.2\Delta \log \textit{AF}$$
$$(8.8)$$

where *UK-NA LS* is leisure passengers between the UK and North America, *CE* is UK consumer expenditure, *TC* is tourist ground costs (as affected by exchange rates, etc.) and *AF* is the air fares. The model suggests that this market is much more elastic to changes in tourist costs, other than transport (elasticity of -1.03), than to changes in the air fare (elasticity of -0.2). A separate model was used to forecast leisure traffic from North America to the United Kingdom. The model formulation was similar, but US gross national product replaced UK consumer expenditure as the income-related variable.

Models can become very detailed and complex, especially if the forecaster splits the market into numerous discrete segments. A good example is provided by BAA, which runs seven airports in Britain, including the three largest London airports. When forecasting traffic for the London area market BAA breaks down its passenger forecasts into fourteen separate route or market areas such as domestic, EU, other European, North Atlantic, Asian and Pacific, and so on. For each of these route areas it produces forecasts for four separate passenger segments, that is, UK residents on business, UK residents on leisure trips and foreign residents travelling on business or leisure. The result is a matrix of fifty-six separate forecasts or cells (four passenger segments for each of fourteen route areas). The BAA forecasting model has been developed and calibrated over time. For each of the fifty-six cells a distinct combination of independent economic variables has been formulated as the basic forecasting equation. Non-economic variables can also be included. For instance, UK leisure trips to other short-haul destinations are forecast as a function of UK consumer expenditure and the cost of air fares and package tour holiday prices. On the other hand, an important variable affecting UK domestic business and leisure air travel is domestic rail competition (Maiden, 1995). In 2001 BAA Plc was using similar econometric models for developing airport forecasts in the United State, Australia and the Middle East.

Another example is the Association of European Airlines (AEA), which developed a series of regression models to forecast air passenger flows between individual countries. After trying alternative formulations using historical data over twenty years, the AEA concluded that airline traffic was best forecast by a multiplicative relationship between the combined gross domestic product of the two countries concerned and the average revenue of the carriers on the route (weighted by the proportion of sales in each country). Both GDP (the proxy for income) and average revenue (the proxy for air fares) are deflated by the private consumption deflators in each country to arrive at real changes in income or fares expressed in constant terms (AEA, 1996).

Very high coefficients of multiple determination are not in themselves a guarantee of causality or even of a close relation between the independent and the dependent variables. A high coefficient of determination may be produced if the error terms produced by the regression equation fall into a pattern. This is called *autocorrelation*, and may occur either when a significant independent variable has been left out or when there is a marked cyclical variation in the dependent variable. One can test for autocorrelation using the Durbin–Watson d statistic. The values of d which will enable one to assess whether autocorrelation is present are related to the number of observations and the number of independent variables. As a general rule, if the Durbin–Watson statistics are below 1.5 or above 2.5 the forecaster will be concerned with the possibility of autocorrelation. The high Durbin–Watson statistic of 3.24 on the Algiers–Paris model (equation 8.7 above) would suggest the existence of negative serial correlation.

Another problem which may exist despite high coefficients of determination is that of *multicollinearity*. This occurs if the independent variables are not statistically independent of each other. For example, air fares and fuel prices may move more or less in unison. Therefore including both as independent variables would result in multicollinearity and would pose difficulties in interpreting the regression coefficients. In particular, they could no longer be strictly considered as elasticities. One can test for multicollinearity by using a matrix showing the correlation between the independent variables. Variables showing a high correlation, say 0.86 or higher, should not really be included in the same model. The possibility of autocorrelation and multicollinearity are two key problems for the airline forecaster using econometric models. There are other more obscure ones, such as heteroscedasticity, which are dealt with in detail in the specialist texts (Taneja, 1978).

Having developed and tested models such as those described above, an airline needs to obtain forecasts of the independent variables used in order to be able to derive from them forecasts of future air traffic. In doing this, particularly for longer-term forecasts, one should not necessarily assume that the elasticities remain constant over time. It is inherent in the way that elasticity is measured that it must change over time as total traffic grows. Because of this, many forecasters build changing elasticities into their predictive processes. Changes in elasticity values can be derived mathematically or they can be assumed. The BAA, for example, in its own forecasts assumes a decline in the income elasticities of most market groups (Maiden, 1995).

It is while forecasting the independent variables that some form of sensitivity test may be introduced into the forecasting process. Airlines may consider what would happen to the economy of a particular country and its *per capita* income if industrial growth did not turn out to be as fast as predicted by the government concerned. Alternatively, they may evaluate the impact of disruption of oil production in the Middle East on the price of fuel and ultimately on economic growth or on the future level of air fares. These sensitivity tests may produce *band* forecasts, suggesting a range of possible traffic outcomes, rather than point forecasts.

For decisions dependent on forecasts over a two-year time span or less, airline managers tend to prefer *point* rather than band forecasts. Decisions have to be taken and giving a range of forecasts is no help to the decision makers. They want precise traffic estimates. They expect the forecasters to have assessed the risks and the sensitivity of the forecasts to external variables and to have made the point forecasts in the light of such assessment. When it comes to strategic decisions stemming from the airline's corporate plan, band forecasts become useful. They should force the airline to maintain flexibility in its long-term planning decisions. An airline must avoid taking decisions which lock it into a size and level of production which it cannot easily vary. This is particularly true of aircraft purchase or other major investments. Band forecasts emphasise the uncertainty inherent in forecasting.

8.4.2   Air freight models

The factors affecting the growth of air freight are complex and often fickle. The tonnage of freight moving on any route is subject to sudden and unexplained variations. There is the added complication that, unlike passengers, who tend to return to their point of origin, freight movements are unidirectional. There is a multitude of commodity freight rates on any route and such rates have also tended to be less stable than passenger fares. Much freight capacity is produced as a by-product of passenger capacity, and as a consequence there is frequently over-provision of freight capacity, with strong downward pressure on freight rates. Tariffs charged often bear little relation to the published tariff, so that even establishing tariff levels is difficult. As a result of all these complexities, it has often been found difficult to relate past freight growth to one or more independent variables, particularly in relation to individual routes, though one of the early studies did develop a model relating freight tonne kilometres to freight rates, an index of US industrial production and a time trend (Sletmo, 1982).

The few causal freight models which have been developed have tended to be used for forecasting global air freight demand or demand in large markets rather than on individual routes. For example, the US aircraft manufacturer McDonnell Douglas has produced directional inter-regional air freight forecasts using simple regression models. For instance, in a North Atlantic westbound model, freight tonne kilometres were found to be positively related to the German mark–US dollar exchange rate and to US real gross domestic product, and negatively related to the real cargo yield (Douglas, 1989). Another manufacturer, Airbus Industrie, derives long-term forecasts of global air freight traffic, measured in freight tonne kilometres, from econometric analyses of 120 directional air freight flow markets. Independent variables driving air freight include economic growth, international trade, air freight yields and industrial production (Airbus, 2000).

The International Civil Aviation Organisation (ICAO) uses econometric models for its long-term forecasts of the world's scheduled air traffic (ICAO, 1997). For instance, using data for the period 1960–91, ICAO developed two separate models, one for passenger traffic and one for air freight. The freight model took the form:

$$\log FTK = -0.41 + 1.58 \log EXP - 0.37 \log FYIELD$$
$$\quad\quad\quad\quad (20.3) \quad\quad\quad\quad (5.1) \quad\quad\quad\quad\quad\quad\quad\quad (8.9)$$

where *FTK* is freight tonne kilometres, *EXP* is world exports in real terms, *FYIELD* is freight revenue per freight tonne kilometre in real terms, and the figures in parentheses are the t statistics and the $R^2 = 0.996$. This clearly suggested that air freight was much more responsive to growth in world trade than to changes in freight tariffs.

Most route-by-route forecasts for freight are based on a combination of executive judgement, market research and, where appropriate, time-series projections. Frequently such forecasts are on a commodity-by-commodity basis, since the number of separate commodities being freighted by air on any route is usually fairly limited. In the late 1970s British Airways also experimented with econometric models for freight flows, but with little success, and subsequently has placed greater emphasis on time-series analysis and on assessing the factors affecting particular commodity flows. The development of causal models of individual commodity flows may ultimately prove more rewarding than attempts to model total freight flows on particular routes.

8.4.3 Gravity models

Time-series analyses or regression models are of little use when trying to forecast traffic on new routes, where there are no historical traffic data, or on routes where traffic records are inadequate or non-existent. Traditionally this problem has been overcome by using a combination of market research and executive judgement. Another possible approach is to use a gravity model. This was the earliest of the causal models developed for traffic forecasting. It has been relatively little used in aviation, even though gravity formulations have played a crucial part in many road traffic forecasting and assignment models.

The gravity model concept has a long history. It was in 1858 that Henry Carey first formulated what has become known as the *gravity concept of human interaction*. He suggested that social phenomena are based on the same fundamental law as physical phenomena and that 'gravitation is here, as everywhere else in the material world, in the direct ratio of the mass and in the inverse one of the distance' (Carey, 1858). One of the first applications to transport was by Lill (1889), studying movements on the Austrian state railways in 1889. Subsequently the concept was taken over by highway engineers, who developed gravity models for forecasting road traffic. The first recorded use for aviation was in 1951, when D'Arcy Harvey, working for the US Civil Aeronautics Administration, developed the gravity concept to evaluate the air traffic flow between two communities (D'Arcy Harvey, 1951).

Translating the concept into aviation terms, one starts with the simple formulation that the air traffic between two points is proportional to the product of their populations and inversely proportional to the distance between them, so that:

$$T_{ij} = K\frac{P_i P_j}{D_{ij}} \tag{8.10}$$

where T_{ij} is the traffic between two towns i and j, K is a constant, P_i and P_j are the populations of the two towns, and D_{ij} is the distance between them.

The top half of the equation, namely the populations, contains the generative variables while the bottom half contains the impedance variables, in this case distance. This is a simple causal model with population size and distance as the independent variables affecting traffic flow. As the concept has been developed, both generative and impedance factors have been modified and the model has become more complex. For instance, the level of air fares has often been considered a better measure of impedance than distance. It has also been thought necessary to modify crude population numbers to take account of purchasing power, nature of economic activity of the population, and so on.

An early study in 1966 involved replacing the population in the interactive formula by the product of the total air traffic of each of the cities concerned (Doganis, 1966). Total airport traffic was thought to provide a good measure of a region's income levels, of the types of economic activity within it and of the effective catchment area of its airport. Using airport traffic obviated the need to incorporate other economic variables into the model. It was also found that raising the distance term to a power other than unity improved the correlation of the model when it was tested against actual traffic levels. This model took the form:

$$T_{ij} = K\frac{A_i A_j}{D_{ij}^p} \qquad (8.11)$$

where T_{ij}, K and D_{ij} are as before, but A_i and A_j are the total passenger traffics of the two airports at either end of the route and P is distance raised to a power of between 1 and $1^1/_2$.

Subsequent studies using gravity models to predict traffic on new or potential routes include one in 1981 by the Economist Intelligence Unit for the European Commission. This used such a model to predict air traffic on intra-regional air services in Europe. A later study, also carried out for the European Commission, involved forecasts of air traffic between airports in the southern regions of the European Community, some of which did not already have direct air links (Westminster, 1989). Various model formulations were calibrated on forty-seven existing air services for 1987. The one which produced the highest correlation of 0.97 took the following form:

$$T_{ij} = K\frac{(A_i A_j)Q^{3/4}}{F^{1/2}} \qquad (8.12)$$

where K is a constant, A_i and A_j are the scheduled passenger traffics at each of the two airports, $Q^{3/4}$ is a service quality variable raised to the power of three-quarters, and $F^{1/2}$ is the normal economy fare raised to the power of half. The quality of service variable (Q) was a measure of equivalent weekly frequencies which makes allowance for intermediate stops and type of aircraft. Whereas a weekly non-stop jet service is given a Q value of 1.0, a one-stop service is valued at 0.5 and a turbo-prop service at 0.7. Services involving two or more en-route stops are ignored.

The value of a gravity model approach is its ability to forecast demand on new routes. Thus, using the model just described, it was possible to forecast the passenger demand between two cities such as Venice and Madrid which did not have air services in 1989 by feeding into the equation the projected forecasts of total air traffic for each of these airports in that year, the current economy air fare and the likely types of air service that could be viably provided. The latter is the quality of service variable and involved some iteration to arrive at the optimum combination of traffic and service level. While using airport traffic as one of the generative factors in a gravity model appears to improve the robustness of the model, it has a major disadvantage in that the model cannot be used where there is no existing airport traffic at one or both ends of the route. In such circumstances one has to revert to using population size perhaps weighted by income levels.

8.4.4 *Assessment of econometric models*

The strength of causal forecasting models is that they are logical. They relate demand to changes in factors which one would expect to have an impact on demand. The models chosen must therefore be logical too, despite the findings of any statistical tests. A model with a high coefficient of determination should not be used if the independent variables are intuitively wrong. The forecaster's direct experience of market conditions and knowledge gained through market research can provide an insight into demand behaviour which may ultimately be more useful than that obtained through statistical analysis and mathematical correlation. The models used must be logically consistent. If they are, it follows that, if one can forecast the independent variables for three or more years, then one should be able to derive longer-term traffic forecasts with a lower risk of error than if one were using time-series projections where demand is related purely to changes in time. Herein lies the strength of causal forecasting but also its weakness. For, by using a causal model in the interests of logical consistency and greater accuracy, airline forecasters transpose their problem. Instead of having to forecast air traffic, they must now use someone else's forecasts of the independent variables and, if these are not available, they must make their own. Many governments, central banks and other institutions do make forecasts of gross domestic product, consumer expenditure, trade and other economic indicators which may be used as independent variables. Such economic forecasts are not always reliable, nor are they necessarily long term. Where more than one institution is forecasting a particular variable, the forecasts do not always agree. If the air fare is one of the independent variables used, then it should in theory be easy for an airline to forecast since it is under airline control. In practice it is difficult for the airlines to predict fare levels more than two or three years hence without getting embroiled in forecasting oil prices or changes in other factors that may affect future fare levels.

Causal techniques pose some further problems too. Like time-series analyses they also depend on the availability of historical data. Clearly, to calibrate regression models in particular one needs not only good air traffic data but also adequate and accurate statistics going back many years of independent variables being used in the model. In most developed countries these should be available. In many Third World countries adequate data are either unavailable or possibly unreliable. Where data are available, the complexity of the modelling work is daunting and time-consuming, especially if an airline wishes to develop separate forecasts for key markets or major routes, each requiring separate models.

It should be borne in mind that econometric forecasting, despite its inherent logic and mathematical complexity, is not a mechanistic exercise. Judgement is involved at all stages, from the model specification to the choice of independent variables, and more especially in the choice between alternative forecasts of those independent variables.

8.5   Choice of forecasting technique

It is clear from the preceding analysis that there is no certainty in forecasting, no forecasting tool that can guarantee the accuracy of its predictions. Even very similar forecasting methods may produce widely diverging forecasts. Whatever the uncertainties, however, airlines cannot avoid making forecasts, because so many other decisions stem from them. Their forecasters must make a choice between the numerous forecasting techniques open to them. Several factors will determine that choice.

The starting point is to determine the prime objective of the forecast. Is it to forecast traffic growth? Is it to predict the reaction of demand to some new development such as a fare increase or frequency change? Or is it to forecast the traffic on a new route? While all techniques enable one to make a forecast of traffic growth under normal conditions, only a few are suitable for forecasting traffic reaction or demand on a new route (Table 8.5). If an airline is planning to open up an entirely new route, it has little choice but to use a qualitative technique or a gravity model.

Having determined the forecasting techniques suitable for the type of forecast being undertaken, speed and data availability become important criteria. A quick forecast means either executive judgement or a straightforward time-series projection. Data availability is crucial for certain of the techniques. Time-series projections need accurate and detailed traffic data over a reasonable period of time. Regression models need all that but also adequate data on the independent variables included in the model. If either traffic data or data on the various socio-economic variables are unavailable and unobtainable, the forecaster is obliged to turn to qualitative methods. Cost may be an important consideration too. Smaller international airlines may not be prepared to meet the high cost of market research, while sophisticated causal forecasting for them would mean using consultants, and consultants do not come cheap. In fact, some smaller airlines are dependent on aircraft manufacturers for their long-term forecasts or use IATA forecasts combined with their own executive judgement for shorter-term planning.

If speed, data availability and cost are not a constraint, then airlines may choose between the forecasting techniques open to them on the basis of their predictive accuracy. This is a difficult judgement to make. The various techniques are listed in Table 8.5 and their accuracy for short-, medium- and long-term forecasts is indicated on a three-point grading of poor, fair and good. However, the gradings are to a certain extent subjective and influenced by one's personal experience and judgement. Different forecasters would use different gradings. Most techniques are fairly accurate for short-term forecasts and some are also reasonable for two-year forecasts. Beyond that time span there is some doubt, but it is likely that qualitative or causal techniques will produce the more accurate forecasts. These techniques are also the most likely to be able to identify and predict turning points in the underlying growth trends. In theory, causal models should produce the better results, but some

Table 8.5 Attributes of airline passenger forecasting techniques

Attribute	Qualitative methods			Time-series projections				Causal models	
	Executive judgement	Market research	Delphi	Annual average growth	Exponential smoothing	Linear trend	Linear trend on moving average	Regression analysis	Gravity model
Accuracy:									
0–6 months	Good	Good	Fair/good	Fair/good	Good	Fair/good	Good	Good	Good
6–24 months	Fair	Good	Fair/good	Poor/fair	Fair/good	Poor/fair	Fair	Fair/good	Fair/good
5 years	Poor	Poor/fair	Fair	Poor	Poor/fair	Poor	Poor/fair	Poor/fair	Poor/fair
Suitability for forecasting:									
Traffic growth	Good	Good	Good	Good	Good	Good	Good	Good	Good
Traffic reaction	Fair	Good	Fair	n.a.	n.a.	n.a.	n.a.	Good	Poor
Traffic new routes	Poor	Fair	Poor	n.a.	n.a.	n.a.	n.a.	Fair	Good
Ability to identify turning points	Poor/fair	Fair/good	Fair/good	Poor	Fair	Poor	Poor/fair	Good	Poor
Ready availability of input data	Good	Poor/fair	Poor	Good	Good	Good	Good	Poor/fair	Fair
Days required to produce forecast	1–2	90+	30–180	1–2	1–2	1–2	1–2	30–90	20–60
Cost	Very low	Very high	Moderate	Low	Low	Low	Low	High	High

Note: n.a. = Not applicable.

aviation experts suggest that there is no compelling evidence that econometric techniques produce more accurate air traffic forecasts than do the simpler and more straightforward approaches.

Within most international airlines a range of forecasting techniques are used. Faced with differing planning requirements, airlines carry out both short-to-medium- and longer-term forecasts. The former tend to be based on time-series projections, frequently modified by executive judgement and by market research findings. The precise time-series technique or techniques used by each airline will depend on its experience and the judgement of its forecasters. Where new routes are being evaluated, the airline's preference may well be to use market research methods to forecast potential demand. For longer-term forecasts beyond a year or two, many smaller airlines continue to use time-series projections, despite doubts about the accuracy of such methods for longer time spans, while some of the larger airlines switch to causal models. Ultimately, so many exogenous and unpredictable factors may affect air transport demand that forecasts beyond three to five years ahead must be thought of as very tentative.

9   Product planning

Our aim is to orient the airline so that it is totally driven by customer needs.
(Steven Ridgeway, Managing Director, Virgin Atlantic, 2001)

9.1   Key product features

As international regulation of air fares, of capacity and of in-flight service has been progressively relaxed or, in many markets, more or less abandoned altogether, the airline industry has become increasingly competitive. Such competition focuses on the products that different airlines offer their customers. As regulations diminish, the opportunities for product differentiation widen and airlines have a much greater range of choices open to them. Product planning is deciding what product features to offer in each market segment in which an airline is hoping to sell its services or 'products'. For each airline, product planning is crucial in two respects. First, it provides the key tool in the process of matching potential demand for air services with the actual supply of services which it offers in the markets it serves. Each airline controls its own supply of services but can influence the demand only through its product planning. Much, therefore, depends on product planning. Second, as previously mentioned, product planning has a direct impact on operating costs (Chapter 6.5 and 6.7 above). It is important as a cost factor because it is an area of costs where airlines have considerable discretion.

In deciding what products to offer in the different markets it has entered, an airline has to bear in mind a number of objectives. It must consider its overall marketing strategy, which will have emerged as a result of its demand analyses and forecasts (Chapter 8 above). It must set out to attract and satisfy customers in the different market segments that it has identified. This means using its understanding of the needs and requirements of these different market segments. Such understanding will have been acquired through a range of market research activities, including passenger and other surveys, the monitoring of its own and its competitors' past performance, and so on. Lastly, an airline will want to maximise its revenues and profits, not always in the short term but certainly in the long run. In brief, the ultimate aim of product

Table 9.1 Key product features affecting travel decisions and choice of airline – but also operating costs

1	Price	Fare levels and conditions
2	Schedule-based	Points served and routeings Frequency Timings Connections Punctuality
3	Comfort-based	Type of aircraft Interior configuration Individual space On-board service Ground/terminal service Airline lounges In-flight entertainment
4	Convenience	Distribution/reservations system Capacity management policy Seat availability
5	Image	Reputation for safety Branding Frequent Flyer programmes/ loyalty schemes Promotion and advertising Market positioning

planning is to attract and hold customers from the market segments that an airline is targeting and to do so profitably.

An airline's potential customers will be influenced by five key product features in making travel decisions and, more important, in choosing between airlines. These are summarised in Table 9.1. An airline must therefore decide how to combine these various product features to meet customer needs in different markets. This is a complex process because customer requirements will vary not only between different market segments on the same route but also between neighbouring routes and geographical areas. For any particular airline product in a given market, different combinations of these five product features can be offered. To a certain extent there may even be a trade-off between them. Greater comfort can be offered, for instance, by reducing the number of seats in an aircraft, but this may necessitate selling at higher fares.

It would seem that the fare level is the most critical product feature for many market segments, especially in many price-sensitive leisure or VFR markets. It may be less important for business markets which are price-inelastic, though even here marked fare differentials between airlines may have an impact. Fares are also the most dynamic product feature in that they can be changed almost daily, at least in deregulated markets. Thus the whole question of pricing and revenue generation merits the more detailed examination provided in Chapter 10. If markets are price-inelastic, or where the fares of different carriers are very similar, because of either regulation or competitive pressures, then product features other than price become relatively more important in determining the market penetration of different airlines.

9.2   Schedule-based features

From a consumer viewpoint, the critical schedule-based features in any market are the number of frequencies operated, their departure and arrival times, the points served and in particular whether flights are direct or involve one or more stops or change of aircraft en route. Conversely, aircraft type is not seen as important, though on some short-haul routes a jet may be preferred to a turbo-prop. Different market segments will have differing schedule requirements. Short-haul business markets generally require at least a morning and an early evening flight in each direction on weekdays so as to allow business trips to be completed in a day. But the ideal is several flights each day. Weekend flights may be less important for business travellers but crucial for short-stay weekend holiday markets. Frequency requirements will also vary depending on the type of market, the length of haul and the level of competition. For instance, offering a once-daily service when a competitor has ten flights a day is unlikely to make much impact on the market.

In the early 1980s the Scandinavian airline SAS asked its passengers what were the most important factors for them in choosing a flight when making their reservations. More than two-thirds of those surveyed said that departure/ arrival times were very important and two-thirds claimed that non-stop direct services were also very important. Other factors were relatively unimportant in travellers' choices. Interestingly, only 3 per cent claimed aircraft type as an important factor in their decision. It was in response to such surveys that SAS effectively grounded its four new A300 Airbuses in 1982 and concentrated on using the smaller DC-9s and later MD-81s and MD-82s with less than half the seats of the Airbuses. The smaller aircraft enabled SAS to offer higher frequencies and to operate direct services on thinner routes for which the Airbuses would have been too large. SAS has continued this strategy to the present day. It is still flying relatively small aircraft on intra-European services. Since smaller aircraft have higher unit operating costs (Chapter 6.5) such a marketing strategy has inevitably pushed SAS into operating with very high unit costs (Table 1.1). However, by concentrating on schedule-based product features, SAS was able to attract business traffic which was prepared to pay the higher fares that such a strategy necessitated. In fact, in 1999 around 32 per cent of SAS's passenger traffic, measured in terms of passenger kilometres, on its intra-European services, was in business class, whereas the average for other European scheduled airlines in the same markets was only 14 per cent.

Most surveys reinforce the importance of schedule-related features. Such features appear to be the core element of the scheduled airline product on short-haul routes and are probably the most important factor for all business travellers. An early survey in 1987 by the International Foundation of Airline Passenger Associations of more than 25,000 passengers, most of whom were likely to be business travellers, shows this clearly. Respondents were asked to identify the three most important features when choosing an airline. Punctuality, convenient schedules and frequency stood out as being by far the most frequently mentioned for shorter sectors of less than two hours, with around half of respondents putting convenient schedules among their list of three. Comfort-based features were much less important on these short sectors. Generally speaking, schedule-based features were more important than comfort for short- or medium-haul flights. However, on the longer sectors, comfort-based features, particularly seating comfort and the quality of in-flight service, increase in relative importance and frequency becomes less important. Low fares were also perceived as being of limited importance, reflecting the business nature of much of the travel undertaken by the respondents.

A survey twelve years later, in 1999, of 3,000 business air travellers from around the world, including the United States, Europe, Singapore and Australia, again reinforced the importance of convenient schedules when it comes to choosing an airline (Table 9.2). Reputation for safety was also highly rated.

Table 9.2 Importance of product features in choice of airline: survey of 3,000 business travellers, 1999

Feature	Rank
Price:	
Cheapest fare	8
Schedule-based:	
Convenience of schedule	1
Punctuality	7
Comfort-based:	
Extra comfort and leg room	4
Efficient check-in	5
Friendly/helpful cabin staff	9
Executive lounges	10
Food and drink	11
Convenience:	
Membership of Frequent Flyer programme	3
Advanced seat selection	6
Image:	
Reputation for safety	2
Award-winning airline	12

Source: OAG (2000).

Since most major international airlines have equally good safety records it is difficult to appreciate how this factor influences choice of airline. Presumably it is a negative reaction to one or two airlines which may have had a recent accident. Membership of a Frequent Flyer programme was the third most important factor. But, again, since business travellers surveyed on average belong to three and a half different airlines' programmes the effect can only be negative. That is, travellers avoid airlines whose Frequent Flyer programme they do not belong to. Among comfort-based features extra on-board comfort and leg room as well as the efficiency of the check-in procedures were highly rated. On the other hand, features that airlines spend much money advertising such as the quality of food and drink, their executive lounges or the awards they have won do not feature highly when business passengers choose an airline. It is also evident that such travellers are not that concerned about obtaining the cheapest fare (OAG, 2000).

Both surveys mentioned earlier highlight the importance of punctuality. Numerous surveys, especially in the United States, have emphasised growing passenger concern with poor on-time performance. It was this which in 1987 induced the then US Transportation Secretary, Elizabeth Dole, to introduce a ruling requiring airlines to submit on-time performance records to operators of computerised reservation systems and travel agents so that they could be seen, if required, by passengers when booking flights. The second leading cause of consumer complaints in the United States was lost or delayed baggage. Here, too, airlines were required to provide comparative statistics on how often they lose, delay or damage baggage. The UK Civil Aviation Authority followed the US lead on punctuality but not on baggage, which is less of a problem in European markets. Since 1989 UK airlines have had to submit punctuality data to the CAA on a route-by-route basis for major domestic and international routes. The Association of European Airlines in Brussels also publishes quarterly data on delays at each of the major European airports.

In the last two decades, a key product development which has affected many scheduled-based features has been the restructuring of many airlines' operations so as to enable passengers to travel between two points without direct services by transferring through a central hub airport. Schedules are planned to minimise the connecting time at the hub. The concept of hubbing is now central to most international airlines' operations. Moreover, one aim of the emerging global alliances is to link major hubs in different continents. The importance and economic impact of hubbing is such that it is examined in greater detail in section 9.6 below.

The main reason why schedule-based features together with the fare are generally the most important product components is that they can be seen and quantified objectively. They are explicit and precise: one can compare one scheduled departure time with another, or the total journey time of a direct as opposed to a one-stop service. By comparison, assessment of comfort, convenience or image-based product features, such as the quality of an airline's in-flight service or of its distribution system, is subjective. Customer perception of these product features will vary for each trip and between different customers on the same trip. They cannot easily be quantified or compared between different airlines.

9.3 Comfort-based product features

The schedule-related features of an air service appear to be more important in most markets than comfort-based features, but they cannot be adjusted rapidly. In many cases they cannot be changed at all, either because an airline already has a network and schedules which meet market needs or because of external constraints such as the bilateral air service agreements or an absence of available runway slots. Yet, as markets have become more competitive, the need for product innovation has intensified. Since schedules, in most cases, can be changed only in the medium term, if at all, airline product development has often concentrated on improving comfort-based features, which can be changed more readily and quickly. Three aspects of the airline product are important in determining passenger perceptions of comfort.

The first is the interior layout and configuration of the aircraft, which affect the width and pitch of each seat and thereby determine the space available for each passenger. Space seems to be the key comfort variable. There is a trade-off between seating density and unit costs in that the more seats that can be put into the aircraft the lower are the operating costs per seat. Thus deciding on seating density has major cost implications (see Table 6.9). A key aspect of comfort relates to the width and pitch of each seat. Pitch is the distance between the back of one seat and the same point on the seat in front, and is a measure of the leg room available. Seat pitch and width and the type of seat provided have a major impact on perceived comfort, especially on long-haul services. But more spacious seats mean fewer seats per aircraft. Thus in 2000 when British Airways announced the introduction of flat-bed sleeper seats for its Club World and a new World Traveller Plus cabin area, for full-fare long-haul economy passengers, with 38 in. instead of the normal economy 31 in. pitch, the number of seats in its Boeing 747 dropped sharply. The standard 747-400 aircraft had 376 seats – fourteen first, sixty-four Club World and 298 in the World Traveller and economy cabin. The new configuration, part of a $860 million investment in the interiors of its whole fleet, would offer only 291 seats – fourteen first, seventy Club World, thirty World Traveller Plus and only 177 in World Traveller. Effectively a quarter of the seats were lost in order to upgrade the product. Other aspects of the interior layout which an airline must decide on, since they affect the nature of the product it is offering, include the number of separate classes of cabin and service, the number of toilets, the types of seats installed, interior design and colour schemes, the size and suitability of overhead lockers, and so on.

The second important area where decisions have to be made is that of in-flight service and catering standards. This covers the nature and quality of food and beverages provided, the number of cabin staff for each class of cabin, the availability and range of newspapers and magazines, in-flight entertainment and communications, give-aways for first- and business-class passengers as well as for children, and so on. A great deal of effort goes into planning airline meals and meeting target catering standards. Again there are cost implications and as a result the composition of meals is planned down to the precise weight in milligrams of a pat of butter or the weight of the sauce going on a meat dish. While airlines place much emphasis in their advertising on the quality of their food and wines, there is little evidence that gastronomic preferences determine choice of airline for a journey. However, catering standards together with the quality and attentiveness of the cabin staff may create a certain image for a particular airline which may be important in marketing terms.

In recent years much effort has gone into improving the quality and range of in-flight entertainment (IFE) facilities in all cabins, but especially for business and first class on long-haul flights. Aircraft seats are now expected to provide interactive multi-channel music and films, as well as sockets for computers, in-flight telephone and facsimile access, and electronic games. Increasingly passengers will be looking to have live television or radio. But all this costs money to install in the seat, and also creates substantial running costs to buy and prepare film and sound programmes which need to be changed monthly. Airline annual investments in in-flight entertainment were less than $400 million in 1990. By 1999 the figure had risen to $2,300 million. Seats also become more costly in order to incorporate all the electronic gadgetry. In 1990 airlines were investing $1,800 per seat to install in-flight entertainment. Ten years later in 2000 the cost was around $10,000 per seat, which means about $3 million to $4 million per long-haul aircraft (*Airline Business*, January 1999). Since the aircraft purchase price may be $150 million to $200 million, in-flight entertainment may account for up to 2 per cent of the total purchase price. Pro-active, innovative airlines, such as Emirates, which was one of the first to introduce seat-back screens and multi-channel films in economy class, gain some initial marketing benefit. But it is a short-term benefit. IFE improvements can be introduced fairly quickly and any competitive advantage is soon lost, but the high costs remain. Currently, most quality airlines have personal IFE systems in first and business class. Therefore it is becoming an expected airline feature by passengers travelling in those cabins. This is why, despite the high spend on in-flight entertainment, most surveys show that it is not an important factor in choosing between airlines.

Third, the services offered to passengers on the ground are a key component of the product. An airline has to consider whether to provide its own check-in and handling staff at out-stations or to use another airline or handling agent. It must decide what is an acceptable average waiting time for check-in for its passengers, since this will determine how many check-in desks and staff it needs for each flight. More desks cost more money. Then the airline must determine the nature of any special ground facilities for first- and business-class passengers, such as special lounges, office services, car parking valets, or the provision of limousine service to collect and deliver passengers from their homes or offices. Surveys suggest that many business travellers are concerned with speed through the terminal rather than comfort as such. This means separate, well-manned check-in desks for business- and first-class passengers. To speed up the check-in process, particularly when baggage is involved, airlines have been experimenting with automated check-in and automated ticket and boarding pass (ATB) as well as off-airport check-in at hotels (SAS) or railway stations (Lufthansa, British Airways). They have also started to introduce arrival lounges for first- or business-class passengers on long-haul flights. The ground environment and quality of service can have an important influence on a passenger's perception of an airline, but they are inevitably also affected by the actions and efficiency of the airport authority. This is why more and more airlines now wish to operate and possibly own the terminals they use. This is fairly common in the United States but rare elsewhere.

A non-measurable and intangible aspect of comfort which underpins all the areas mentioned above is the efficiency, helpfulness and friendliness of staff, both the cabin crew in the air and also the ground staff at check-in, in the airline lounges and at the boarding gates. This appears to be dependent on three factors. First, the quality of the training received by all staff in contact with the public, but also the degree to which they are constantly being retrained. In the late 1980s British Airways transformed itself from an airline with a poor reputation for quality of service to one very highly thought of by ensuring all its staff from the chief executive down went through a programme entitled 'Putting People First'. This was a training programme originally introduced at SAS. Its success at BA was such that other airlines followed suit. The second factor is the success of management in motivating and empowering staff at all levels. Staff need to feel that they 'own' any problems that arise and are empowered to deal with them, rather than pass them on to someone else higher up the management chain. British Airways were successful in this area too, helped, no doubt, by the fact that many staff became shareholders when the airline was privatised in 1987. Giving shares to staff can be an important motivator (Doganis, 2001). But then British Airways blew it. An acrimonious confrontation with cabin crew in 1997 undermined much of the previous success in improving service and motivating staff. Finally, the number of staff employed in each functional area is important. In an aircraft such as a Boeing 747-400 does an airline carry the legal minimum of cabin crew, which is eleven, or something close to it, or does it go for eighteen or nineteen, so as to ensure higher service, though at a higher cost? Similarly, decisions have to be made for the ground staff. The motivation and quality of staff in contact with clients is crucial. Poor staff attitudes can destroy the best-planned product. On the other hand, friendly, warm, welcoming staff, who are obviously trying hard, can overcome short-comings in the product and win customer support.

Product and service planning is a complex task. Product planners must work in two dimensions. They must ensure that their product and service standards match or are better than those of their key competitors. But they must also try to differentiate the products offered in their own aircraft in such a way that passengers in each class feel that they are getting value for money.

It is primarily in the comfort-based aspects of the airline product that distinctions between the products offered to different cabin classes by the same airline become most apparent to passengers. This means that airline product planners have a complex task. They must specify differing comfort-based features for the different market segments they are trying to attract. Not only may product features have to be varied by class of cabin and type of ticket but the same cabin class may require different product features on different routes or geographical areas. Thus business class in Europe does not have the same product specification as business class on services from Europe to Asia.

Because they can be more easily changed and more readily advertised, comfort-based product features are continually being monitored and revised. There is a constant requirement to respond to product changes introduced by competitors and an even greater need for an airline to be the first to introduce innovative changes. Airlines that are innovative can enjoy a competitive advantage until their new product is copied by others. In 1989 Virgin Atlantic made a major breakthrough by introducing its so-called Upper Class on services from London to New York and later to Tokyo and its other long-haul routes. This was an upgraded product but at business-class fares. Seat pitch was 55 in., when all other long-haul carriers were offering only 38–42 in. This, together with a cabin service which was equivalent to other airlines' first class, gave Virgin a major competitive advantage on the long-haul routes it served. It enabled Virgin to expand against head-on competition from British Airways in markets where others, notably British Caledonian, had failed. Virgin offered and still offers its Upper Class but has no first class. During the 1990s several airlines followed suit and abandoned first class on long-haul routes in favour of an enhanced business class. Over this period all airlines gradually improved their business-class product in various ways – more leg room, better seating, interactive in-flight entertainment, improved catering, and so on. But by 2001 Virgin was still offering the most leg room and the widest seats in its business class, especially compared with Air France or Lufthansa (Table 9.3) and continued to gain a competitive advantage as a result.

The next major innovation in long-haul business class was the introduction of seats with 72 in. pitch which convert into fully flat beds. British Airways began introducing these in mid-2000, initially on the North American routes, then, during 2001, on other routes, including those to East Asia. Initially, as no other carrier had flat beds in business class, BA was able to charge a premium during 2000–01 above the prevailing business-class fare on routes where they were available. That is, until its direct competitors also provided flat beds, which would be one to two years later. Virgin was the first to match BA when it began offering flat sleeper seats in its Upper Class (i.e. business class) in mid-2001. This new product was also important in maintaining the BA brand image of providing an innovatory high-class business product.

Another relatively recent product innovation has been the introduction of a premium economy class by some airlines on long-haul routes. Virgin Atlantic was the first to do this in the mid-1990s. The aim is to offer passengers paying

Table 9.3 London–East Asia: business-class seating, early 2001

Airline	Seat pitch (in.)	Width of seat (in.)
European airlines:		
Virgin Atlantic	60	22.0
Lufthansa	48	19.5
British Airways	40	20.0
Swissair	38	18.8
Air France	38	18.5
Asian airlines:		
SIA	52	20.5
Thai	50	21.0
JAL	50	20.5
Cathay	50	20.0
Malaysia	50	19.8

Source: *Which Airline*, 12(1), 2001.

the full economy fare a dedicated cabin with several inches more leg room than the normal economy cabin and better in-flight catering. This development, combined with the spread of flat beds in business class, may eventually lead to more airlines abandoning first class altogether, except on a few dense business routes where there may be sufficient passengers prepared to pay the very high first-class fares. As discussed in Chapter 10 on pricing, first-class services are in any case generally unprofitable unless load factors are high.

Some airlines, among them Virgin Atlantic, Emirates, British Airways and Singapore Airlines, have a reputation as innovators. In Virgin Atlantic's case it arises from a corporate strategy of trying to satisfy passenger needs. Virgin's Managing Director, Steven Ridgeway, explained the strategy as follows: 'Our aim is to orient the airline so that it is totally driven by customer needs. As we all fly the same aircraft it is even more important to be different, and we are always trying to do things on the ground and in the air that have not been done before' (Pilling, 2001). In planning new product or service improvements airlines have to balance three factors – the cost of the innovation, its marketing benefits in terms of revenue generation and the speed with which it can be copied. It is not an easy balance to calculate. The sums involved are substantial. For example, in August 2001 Singapore Airlines announced its SpaceBed concept, a $100 million revamp of its business-class cabin, which would include flat beds. But while the costs of such improvements are easy to quantify, the revenue gains are not.

9.4 Convenience features

Convenience, as a product feature, is concerned both with the availability of seats when requested by customers and also with the ease of customer access to airline reservation and ticketing services and the quality of such services. Frequent Flyer programmes and airline clubs may also play a role both in enhancing convenience and accessibility as well as in improving an airline's image.

Each airline has considerable freedom of action in deciding its capacity management policy. In particular it must decide how much capacity – that is, seats – it should provide in relation to the anticipated demand, especially at peak periods. Does it provide only enough capacity to ensure that it flies at very high load factors throughout the peak period? This in practice means choking off demand or turning passengers away. Or does it provide sufficient capacity to ensure that there are seats available more or less up to the departure date? The latter strategy would probably result in lower overall load factors than the former. At the micro level, seat capacity can also be managed through control of seat sales, using the revenue management system (Chapter 10.6 below). This can ensure both that seats are available, but at a high price, right up to the departure time and also that load factors remain high and revenue per flight is maximised. Another aspect of capacity management is the degree to which over-booking is practised and, more especially, the airline's success in accurately predicting the pattern and number of 'no show' passengers and cancellations. If its predictions are consistently wrong it may end up paying costly denied boarding compensation to its over-booked passengers. Its image inevitably suffers too. From a passenger's point of view, especially if travelling on business or for some kind of emergency, the availability of a seat when required is an important convenience factor that may well differentiate one airline from another.

A key decision area in any airline's marketing is how to distribute and sell its products and, in particular, how far it should use its own shops and sales outlets in addition to independent travel agents, including on-line agents such as Travelocity, e-bookers or Expedia. Since airlines must pay commission on sales through agents, they have a vested interest in trying to sell directly through their own sales offices or over the phone or their own web site. That is, provided the costs of such direct sales outlets are less than the commission they would otherwise have to pay. Traditionally, the major benefit of travel agents was that they were and still are very numerous and widely scattered, giving airlines a much wider distribution network at relatively lower cost than they could achieve themselves. But the development of Internet selling since the late 1990s has undermined and changed the role of high street travel agents.

Part of an airline's product planning is to assess the number, location and nature of its own sales offices as well as other distribution methods, from telephone call centres or Internet sales to automatic self-ticketing machines. Making a flight enquiry or a reservation by telephone or at a sales office and buying a ticket all normally involve personal contact between passengers or their representative and the airline. The ease and quality of that interaction, which may involve several contacts for just one air journey, is an important product feature which can directly affect a passenger's perception of an airline. The layout and spaciousness of the sales office, the speed with which people are seen, the availability of open lines to the telephone reservation system, the helpfulness of counter or telephone staff, are some of the convenience-based features which must be carefully planned and for which service targets must be set. As with other product features, there is a service–cost trade-off. As the service level improves, so the costs go up. An airline must find the right balance to meet market requirements and expectations. British Airways, for instance, has 1,000 telephone sales agents in Britain alone, of whom 300 deal exclusively with travel agents while the rest deal with calls from both the public and agents.

In 1999 ticketing, sales and promotion costs together represented 16.6 per cent of the total operating costs of IATA airlines. It was the functional area generating the highest single cost. Developing on-line sales through their own Web site enables airlines to reduce their distribution costs by up to two-thirds (Doganis, 2001) yet at the same time give an improved level of service. Pat Gaffey, head of e-commerce at British Airways, put it succinctly at the end of 2000: 'We saw the Web as a huge distribution and differentiation opportunity, one that would allow us to perform the magic of cutting costs and increasing customer satisfaction at the same time' (Gallagher, 2001).

Easy on-line access to schedules, routeings and price information as well as reservations, combined with tickets that can be issued electronically, has significantly improved the accessibility and convenience of air travel to both business and leisure passengers. Airlines now compete through the speed, quality and user-friendliness of their web sites. Surprisingly it is the low-cost carriers who have led the field. By early 2001 Southwest Airlines in the United States generated 30 per cent of its total bookings through its own web site, and America West 16 per cent. Of the majors Continental was the highest, with 5–6 per cent. In Europe, low-cost easyJet was selling around 80 per cent of its tickets through its own site and all the rest were through telephone call centres. None were through travel agents or on-line agencies. Nevertheless by mid-2001 only 8 per cent of airlines worldwide were selling more than 10 per cent of their tickets through web-based services and one in four airlines (22 per cent) were not selling on-line at all (SITA, 2001).

The internet itself offers airlines several choices in distribution strategies, as shown in Table 9.4. They can sell purely on their own web site, as easyJet does, or they can combine this with selling through a variety of additional web-based service providers. One option is to sell through sites shared with other airlines or alliance partners. In the United States, Orbitz, in which American, Continental, Delta, Northwest and United invested $145 million but which also has more than thirty additional airlines as 'charter associates', started selling tickets in mid-2001. In the same year a group of nine European airlines launched their own joint web site, Opodo, which was due to be operational by the end of 2001, while Asian carriers were looking to do the same. But there are three additional internet sales outlets. First, large traditional travel agencies such as Thomas Cook or American Express have their own web sites which offer numerous services such as hotels or cruises in addition to travel. The web sites complement their high street sales office and telephone call

Table 9.4 On-line distribution alternatives for airlines

Type	Examples	Additional attributes[a]	Comments
Airline-owned			
1 Own web site	All airlines	Customer relations management Can offer special fares Frequent Flyer Targeted selling	Costly to set up May not cover other airlines Can offer hotels/car hire
2 Multi-airline site	Orbitz Opodo	As above but weaker	Conflicts with own site Lower booking fee than GDS/on-line agencies Does not sell 'distressed' seats Is it anti-competitive?
Not airline-owned			
3 Traditional travel agency	Thomas Cook American Express	Sell all airlines Plus hotels, car hire, cruises, etc.	May not find lowest fare Airlines charged commission Local knowledge/ experience
4 On-line travel agency	Travelocity Expedia e-bookers	Also sell hotels, car hire, etc. May offer special fares	Direct competition to airline sites
5 Auction site	Priceline Hotwire[b]	Sell distressed/unsold seats and hotel at unpublished prices	Good for off-loading unsold capacity Consumers wary

Notes
a Attributes additional to basic schedule and price search and reservation.
b Some airlines have invested in US-based Hotwire.

centres. In addition there are specialist on-line-only agencies, some of which are owned by or linked with the global distribution systems (GDSs). For instance, Travelocity, the largest of these agencies, in 2001 was 85 per cent owned by the Sabre GDS. Finally, there are a number of on-line auction sites such as Priceline or Hotwire, the latter partly owned by six airlines.

Each of these on-line distribution alternatives has its strengths and weaknesses from the airlines' point of view, but also from the consumers' viewpoint. These are summarised in Table 9.4. According to a major survey, most airlines see their own web site as the key to internet sales and are investing heavily in this and in electronic ticketing. A long way behind in importance come the joint airline sites and the GDS-based sites such as Travelocity and Expedia. In fact, airlines are wary of losing control to new on-line players and in particular to the auction sites (SITA, 2001). Yet in the year 2000, when about 4 per cent of ticket sales in the United States were on-line, slightly over half of them were by on-line travel agencies and slightly under half were direct sales through airline web sites. Clearly, by controlling most of its on-line sales through its own web site, an airline can ensure service standards are high and that it does not lose clients to competitors. It can also use the web for interactive marketing.

Despite airlines' efforts to sell direct, and the growing impact of on-line sales, in 1999 74 per cent of US airline ticket sales were still through agents (*Aviation Strategy*, September 2000). The figure would certainly be higher if one excluded Southwest Airlines. Among most European and Asian carriers, too, travel agents and wholesale tour operators were responsible for 70–80 per cent of ticket sales. The role of traditional travel agents is declining as airline-owned web sites and on-line travel agencies get better known and more frequently used. But it is also declining because airlines, during the 1990s, realised that agents, and more especially commission paid to agents, were a controllable cost rather than an externally determined cost.

During the 1980s deregulation and increasing competition meant that airlines had to increase their commission payments to agents to ensure that their tickets were being sold. This was most evident in the US domestic market. In 1978, before deregulation became effective, most of the US domestic trunk carriers were paying out 4–5 per cent of their revenue as commission. By 1993 the average figure was 10.9 per cent. A similar level of commission was being paid by European carriers. In some US markets by 1990 airlines were having to pay 20 per cent or more of the ticket price to agents. This was particularly the case for the smaller airlines and for foreign carriers with only a limited marketing base in the United States such as Thai International or Malaysia Airlines. Outside the United States, attempts by IATA and individual airlines to hold commission rates at low and fixed levels were gradually being eroded in many markets. The higher commission rates arise from the incentives offered by airlines to agents to book passengers on their flights rather than the competitors'. A major incentive is the override commission. This enables an agency to claim a higher commission rate than the normal when it gives an airline a higher share of its ticket sales or surpasses certain agreed sales targets. Through their extra override commission airlines try to tie agents into selling primarily or exclusively their tickets. Since the mid-1990s airlines around the world have made major efforts to cut commission rates on a country-by-country basis. By 2001 in the United States commission had been reduced to 5 per cent of the ticket price, with a cap of $50 for a domestic and $100 for an international round trip. As a result, commission expenses had dropped to between 4 per cent and 6 per cent of revenues for the major carriers, though they were less than 3 per cent for Southwest, in part because around 30 per cent of its sales were through its own Web site. Among European airlines they had also dropped, though they still ranged between 6 per cent and 8 per cent.

There can be no doubt that the role of the travel agent in airline distribution will continue to be crucially important. But it may change in character. Off-line agents will tend to focus increasingly either on leisure travel, where they can more easily offer customers greater choice and various add-ons – hotels, car hire, cruises, specialist holidays – as well as more personal service or on-line travel for large corporate clients. In the latter case they will also provide specialist services such as travel planning, tracking business travellers' expenses or ensuring company travel policies are adhered to. Increasingly, they will charge the corporate client a management fee while buying airline seats net of commission. Despite the fact that they have no direct control over travel agents or their staff, airline marketing managers need to ensure two things: first, that agency staff provide an efficient, speedy and reliable service to any potential customer; second, that, where alternative airline products are available, agents' sales staff give preference to their own particular airline. They have tried to achieve both these objectives through equipping agents with direct links to their own airline's computer reservation system and through paying commission or offering low fares net of commission to buy agent loyalty.

9.5   Airline image

The final group of product features are those associated with the image that an airline wishes to create, both among its own customers and among the public at large. This is done in a variety of ways: through the nature of its advertising and promotions, through the airline's logo, its colour schemes, and the design of its aircraft interiors, sales offices and airport lounges, and through the quality of service provided by its staff in the air and on the ground. Ensuring an excellent safety record is also an important considera-tion. The success of Singapore Airlines' 'Singapore girl' advertising campaigns during the 1980s created the image not only of helpful, smiling, attentive cabin staff but also of an airline that took care of its passengers. This image was an important factor in enabling SIA to maintain unusually high passenger load factors throughout the period and up to the present day. A key element in image building is to ensure that what is promised, before the flight, actually materialises and meets passenger expectations when the flight takes place. This is why marketing and product planning must be all-embracing, covering what is produced and how it is produced as well as how it is sold.

In order to establish an image, an airline needs to first identify its market position and marketing strategy. Southwest Airlines in the United States or Ryanair in Europe position themselves quite differently from, say, United Airlines or Aer Lingus, the Irish carrier. The former are low-cost no-frills airlines which would need to project a different image from the latter. But even within the same sector airlines may adopt a different market position. Among low-cost budget carriers in Europe, Go positions itself at the top end in terms of service quality and price and Ryanair probably at the lower end. Never-theless, Ryanair is highly profitable. Charter airlines, in yet another market niche, need to develop a separate and different image from scheduled carriers.

Airline services have been commoditised. An airline seat from point A to point B on a conventional scheduled airline is perceived by the passenger as being very similar irrespective of which airline actually flies the service. Fares may differ, but otherwise the essential product is very much a commodity. Product planning, as discussed earlier, tries to differentiate an airline's product from that of its competitors. But it can be only partially successful, since so many service elements, such as the quality of in-flight catering or of ground handling, are subjective. This is where the concept of branding comes in. Through product and service improvements, combined with targeted and effective advertising and promotion, airlines attempt to change their product from being a common commodity to being a 'brand'. As a unique brand it becomes more attractive and may even, on certain routes, attract a higher fare than that prevailing in the market. A brand is exemplified not only by service and product standards but also by designs and colours used in the aircraft interior and exterior and on the ground, as well as in more mundane aspects such as crockery, cutlery, ticket covers, and so on.

A first step in this process of branding on international flights was seen in the mid-1980s when airlines began to give their business class distinctive names, even though the product offered in terms of space and comfort was broadly similar. As previously mentioned, Virgin Atlantic called its business class 'Upper Class', and was successful in creating a high-quality brand image, which it still maintains. Many passengers think of it as a first-class product at business-class fares. Later in 1988 British Airways set up brand teams to develop and launch two distinct business-class products, Club Europe and Club World. The aim was to plan and produce two separate products, each of which would have the same distinctive BA product features and quality on whichever route or geographical area they were being offered. These product features would differentiate Club Europe and Club World from other air-lines' business class by creating a distinct image and product. British Airways claimed this policy was highly successful. Passenger numbers in Club World increased by 27 per cent in the first two years after its introduction. On a number of routes, notably on the North Atlantic, where Club World pas-senger load factors regularly exceeded 80 per cent, British Airways was forced to increase capacity in response to demand. In some markets the airline was able to charge a premium over the normal business-class fare for its own dis-tinctive product. Subsequent product improvements, such as the flat-bed seats introduced in 2000, have tried to sustain the Club World brand.

Airlines periodically rebrand themselves if they feel they need a new ident-ity or image, especially if they want to position themselves differently in the market. In the mid-1990s British Airways came to the conclusion, as a result of market research, that in overseas markets it was seen as being too British and not international enough. As part of its rebranding it began to replace the union jack design on its aircraft tails with a variety of non-specific but colourful designs from around the world. The rebranding backfired in part because it was accompanied after 1997 with falling service standards. UK passengers took a dislike to the new colour schemes and the multi-coloured tail fins began to be phased out in 1999. Conversely, in 2001, the consultants advising

Table 9.5 Rating of ten STAR Alliance member airlines by business-class passengers, 2000

Rank out of sixty-six airlines	Airline	Average rating for all service elements out of ten maximum
6	Air New Zealand	7.88
8	Singapore Airlines	7.86
9	Lufthansa	7.79
10	United Airlines	7.72
15	Austrian Airlines	7.70
19	Air Canada	7.61
20	All Nippon	7.61
22	Thai Airways	7.57
31	SAS	7.39
60	Varig	6.46

Source: Inflight Research Services, World Business Class Survey, 2000.

British Midland on its rebranding, prior to launching long-haul services to the United States, concluded that its British heritage was a mark of good quality and service and should be emphasised.

The ever-growing global alliances pose a particular branding and image problem. That is, how to try and create an alliance brand, which can be an effective marketing tool, while not diluting the strength of any existing airline brands. The problem becomes especially acute when there are many airlines within an alliance, since they are then less likely all to have the same high service standards and an equally good image. The STAR Alliance faced exactly this problem in 2001 because it had thirteen or so members with differing service quality. This is evident from Table 9.5, which shows how ten of these airlines were rated by business-class travellers for various aspects of service in 2000. While the best two or three achieved high ranking and quite similar ratings, others were not rated very highly, especially SAS and Varig.

In the mid-1980s airlines began to develop Frequent Flyer programmes (FFPs) both as a way of ensuring passenger loyalty and as a way of improving their image. Under such schemes, passengers are awarded points for each flight with the airline whose programme they have joined. The number of points depends on the length of the flight and the class of travel and sometimes the type or price of the ticket. As the points build up, passengers can redeem them for free flights for themselves or family members, for upgrades to a higher class when they buy a paid ticket or for a variety of other travel or related benefits. However, there are strict conditions as to when and how such redemption is possible. For instance, the award of free seats is normally limited to specific flights likely to have low load factors and only a restricted number per flight can be awarded. This minimises the cost of redemption in terms of lost revenue. The number of points awarded for specific flights or their value when redeemed varies from airline to airline. Thus in 2000 to earn a free return business-class ticket from London to Hong Kong one needed first to undertake six return journeys in business class if flying with Virgin Atlantic, around seven with Cathay Pacific and thirteen with British Airways. This despite the fact that both Cathay and BA were members of the oneWorld alliance! The Frequent Flyer programmes are normally operated as clubs, giving higher grades of membership and more privileges as the number of points earned or journeys made with the parent airline each year climbs above certain thresholds. In theory it is the combination of more points and greater potential rewards, together with the increased privileges associated with higher grades of club membership, that ensures passenger loyalty.

Certainly, as mentioned earlier (Table 9.2), FFP membership appears to be a major factor in airline choice despite the fact that most business travellers normally belong to three or four separate programmes. Frequent Flyer schemes are targeting primarily those flying on business, though many leisure and VFR passengers also fly frequently and belong to FFPs. By 2001 there were over 120 airlines with their own loyalty scheme and another 100 smaller airlines without their own programme but which awarded their passengers points from a partner airline's scheme. The main objective of all loyalty schemes has been to sell more seats. Airlines appreciate that it is much more expensive in marketing terms to attract a new customer than to retain an existing one. Some experts claim it is five times more expensive (Gialloreto, 2001).

The power of Frequent Flyer programmes to ensure passenger loyalty has been slowly eroded as frequent flyers have each become members of more and more schemes or as airline alliances allow such passengers to earn transferable points when flying with an airline to whose scheme they do not belong. As a result airlines are now focusing increasingly on the second objective of such programmes. Loyalty schemes can provide the data base on which airlines can build effective customer relationship management (CRM) while the internet provides the means of communicating with customers. Airlines with long-established FFPs have considerable data on their customers' travel patterns and preferences, family, residence, place of work, and so on. Relatively few have hitherto leveraged these data either to prevent defections or to encourage repeat business. The latter can be done by developing an interactive relationship with FFP members by offering them discounted fares to their favourite destinations, special fares for family members, and so on. By using the internet or telephone to question customers about needs and preferences, by setting up customer panels and through other survey techniques, they can develop customer bonding and loyalty. Most airlines have not yet developed customer relationship management as an effective tool. But it is going to play an increasingly important part in airline marketing.

As competition has intensified image and customer loyalty have become key product features. With the strengthening of airline alliances and global networks during the first decade of the new millennium they will become even more important. Lufthansa, among other airlines, appreciates this. According to its Chief Financial Officer, 'Investing in brand values and customer loyalty has become much more important . . . these two are numbers one and two on the list of quality parameters in the new airline industry' (Kley, 2000).

9.6   The 'hubbing' concept

Following deregulation in the United States, 'hubbing' was developed by all the major companies as a crucial schedule-based product feature. Hub-and-spoke networks in themselves were not new. After all, most airlines outside the United States had always operated radial networks because the international regulations prevented them from doing anything else. What was new was the way in which hubs came to be operated. Hubbing has major implications both for airline economics and for competition policy and thus merits more detailed examination.

The concept of hubbing was first developed in the 1970s by Federal Express for the carriage of overnight express parcels throughout the United States, using its hub at Memphis TN. Effective hubbing requires that flights from different airports, which are at the spokes of a network, arrive at the hub at approximately the same time. The aircraft then wait on the ground simultaneously. This facilitates the interchange of passengers and baggage or, in the case of Federal Express, of express parcels between aircraft in a short period of time before they depart in quick succession back out along the spokes. This process, which involves a wave or 'bank' of arrivals followed shortly afterwards by a wave of departures, is described as a complex. The transfer time between flights in the same complex should be close to the best attainable. A US airline with a major hub will operate several complexes during the day. American Airlines schedules about eight complexes daily at Dallas-Fort Worth. Air France in 2001 had six at Paris Charles de Gaulle, while KLM and Lufthansa operated five complexes each at their respective hubs.

An airline able to develop and operate a hub-and-spoke system with a series of complexes enjoys numerous potential advantages. The increase in city-pair coverage that can be obtained as a result of hubbing is much more dramatic than is often realised. If three point-to-point direct links from cities A to B, C to D and E to F are replaced by six direct services from each of these six airports to a new hub at an intermediate point, the number of city-pair markets that can be served jumps from three to twenty-one. This advantage increases in proportion to the *square* of the number of routes or spokes operated from the hub. Thus, if a hub has n spokes, the number of direct links is n, to which must be added $n(n - 1) \div 2$ connecting links.

The progressively greater impact of adding more links through a hub can be seen in Table 9.6. It is because of this relationship that British Airways was able to claim in 1990 that by taking a 20 per cent stake in Sabena World Airlines, which would serve seventy-five European regional cities through a Brussels hub, more than 2,000 city pairs would be linked (BA, 1990). As the table shows, in fact this was an underestimate! British Airways did not in the end get its stake in Sabena. The ability to reach a large number of destinations

Table 9.6 Impact of hubbing on the number of city pairs serviced

No. of spokes from the hub n	No. of points connected via the hub n(n − 1) ÷ 2	No. of points linked to the hub by direct flights n	Total city pairs served n(n + 1) ÷ 2
2	1	2	3
6	15	6	21
10	45	10	55
50	1,225	50	1,275
75	2,775	75	2,850
100	4,950	100	5,050

from any one origin gives the airline operating the hub system considerable market appeal. Effective hubbing generates substantial volumes of additional traffic, and revenue, but most of it is transferring through the hub airport.

A number of further marketing advantages flow from the increase in city pairs served. By channelling what may be a large number of separate but thin city-pair flows originating at an outlying airport on to a service going into the hub airport, the density of traffic on that particular spoke may be built up. The additional traffic generated by the connections may allow an airline to use larger and more economical aircraft, but also to operate more frequent flights along the spokes. As this will happen on many spokes, the frequencies of possible connecting services via the hub linking two distant spokes, with low traffic between them, increases. Not only does this stimulate traffic but it also inhibits potential competitors from starting a direct service between the two spokes, since they may be unable to compete in terms of frequencies or departure times. The hub operator may also drop its fares on connecting services if it needs to undermine any new competition from direct point-to-point services bypassing a hub. It can do this easily by cross-subsidising the service from other routes where it faces no direct competition. Moreover, where two airports at the periphery of a hub-and-spoke system warrant direct service between them, the hub airline may offer that service to pre-empt a new entrant.

One of the most important benefits to arise from effective hub-and-spoke operations is the extent to which individual airline networks can become self-sufficient in meeting demand, enabling operators to keep passengers on their own services rather than lose them to inter-line connections. This has been illustrated clearly since deregulation in the United States. The proportion of all passengers making an on-line transfer connection with the same carrier rose from 25 per cent in 1977 to over 90 per cent of all transfer passengers. At London Heathrow airport 27 per cent of transfer passengers were British Airways to British Airways in 1984. By 1991 this had grown to 43 per cent and by 2000 it was approaching 60 per cent (Dennis, 2001).

Complexing of flight schedules ensures that the probability of the first outgoing service to any particular destination being by the same airline as the delivering flight is disproportionately high. Interlinable fares, involving transfer from one airline to another, therefore become no longer necessary. Even if a parallel journey from a competitor exists on one leg of a connecting journey, there will now usually be a severe financial penalty for using it. In other words, the hub carrier will offer a lower through fare on its own services than can be obtained by transferring to another carrier at the hub. The passenger also gains in terms of convenience and reliability from single airline service. Frequent Flyer incentive programmes further encourage the use of on-line connections with the same airline rather than interlining on to a different carrier.

Certain pairs of links created by hubbing will generate substantially more traffic than others. Such demand can be stimulated by offering through services. Unlike traditional scheduling methods, whereby aircraft return on the same route from which they originated, they can now proceed on through the hub to the location with which there is most market potential. This is something European airlines rarely do.

The result of all this is to ensure that a major airline at a particular hub in terms of routes and frequencies will become even more dominant in its share of transfer passengers as its operations develop. In the early 1980s, as 'hubbing' began to be implemented in the United States, there were only a couple of the fifteen or so larger airports where a single operator had more than 50 per cent market share in terms of passengers boarding. By the late 1990s half these airports had a dominant carrier with 70 per cent or more of the passenger traffic and at most of the remaining airports the major carriers had a 50–70 per cent share (Table 9.7). The dominance was least marked at major international gateways such as Los Angeles, San Francisco, Miami and the two New York airports. This is inevitable, as many foreign carriers operate into these airports.

The European airlines, despite operating radial networks, were much slower than their US counterparts in developing schedules to provide effective hubbing. By 1990 only some of the smaller carriers such as Swissair at Zurich, Austrian at Vienna, SAS at Copenhagen and KLM at Amsterdam had made progress in implementing a hubbing strategy. Of the larger carriers only Lufthansa had done so. British Airways, Air France, Alitalia and Iberia began to implement such a strategy only during the 1990s. However, the European experience in developing powerful hubs contrasts with that of US airlines in three respects. First, the dominance is not so marked. At only two of the major European airports does the base airline offer more than 65 per cent of the seats available. In 1999 both KLM and Swissair offered 66 per cent of the seats at their respective hubs, while British Airways had only a 39 per cent market share at London Heathrow. This is partly due to the fact that all the European airports are also international gateways. Second, European airlines generally operate only one hub, though some are trying to develop a second hub, as Lufthansa is doing at Munich. Yet, as Table 9.7 illustrates, the US majors tend to operate multi-hub networks with several hubs each. For instance, Northwest operates hubs at Minneapolis-St Paul controlling 80 per cent of the airport's seats in 1999, Detroit with 78 per cent of the seats and Memphis

Table 9.7 Dominant airlines' share of seats at the fifteen largest US airports, 1999

Airport[a]	Airline	Share of seats (%)
Atlanta	Delta	75
Chicago (4)	United	49
	American	35
Los Angeles (2)	United	27
	American	12
Dallas–Fort Worth	American	70
San Francisco (6)	United	52
Denver	United	73
Las Vegas	Southwest	33
Minneapolis–St Paul	Northwest	80
Phoenix	America–West	43
	Southwest	29
Detroit	Northwest	78
Houston	Continental	79
New York Newark (5)	Continental	56
Miami (3)	American	50
New York JFK (1)	American	20
	Delta	15
St Louis	TWA	72

Source: Salomon Smith Barney (SSB) (2000).

Note

a Airports ranked on basis of total passengers handled in 2000. Numbers in brackets indicate ranking in terms of international passengers.

with 76 per cent (Salomon Smith Barney (SSB), 2000). Partly to overcome this shortcoming, European airlines have embarked on alliances with other European carriers in order to develop multi-hub systems (Doganis, 2001). Finally, Europe has no shared hubs where two carriers each have a significant market share at the same airport. This is what American and United do at Chicago O'Hare and to a lesser extent at Los Angeles.

Once airlines have established dominance at a hub through control of a disproportionate share of the flights offered and traffic uplifted, it is very difficult for another airline to set up a rival hub at the same airport, because it is unlikely to get enough runway slots to offer a similar range of destinations. In the United States the hub operator will also control most of the terminal gates. If the new entrant chooses to compete on just a few direct routes from the hub airport, it will face a competitive disadvantage *vis-à-vis* the hub airline in terms of ensuring adequate feed for its own services. Hence the notion of the 'fortress hub'.

Consumers clearly benefit from hub-and-spoke systems in that they can fly to many more points with higher frequencies and, where necessary, shorter connecting times than was the case before hubbing became so finely developed. On the other hand, passengers who as a result of hubbing are deprived of direct services which might otherwise be operated are clearly worse off.

Their journey times may be longer and their fares may be higher if there is no alternative routeing. There may be other disadvantages too. Hubbing is very dependent on excellent punctuality, and delays anywhere can throw whole 'complexes' into disarray, with serious knock-on effects. This is because a delayed flight may be carrying passengers transferring to a dozen or more departing flights, all of which have to be held back. The short transit time between arriving and departing flights can create havoc in trying to handle large volumes of connecting baggage. It is not surprising that passenger awareness of and concern about punctuality and misdirected baggage have increased significantly in the United States as hubbing has spread.

There is also considerable concern about the high fares on routes to fortress hubs as a result of market concentration. The US Department of Justice uses the Herfindahl–Hirschman index (HHI) to assess levels of concentration for anti-trust reviews. The index is calculated by summing the square of individual market shares of all companies operating in a market. For example, if three airlines at an airport have 10 per cent, 30 per cent and 60 per cent of the traffic the index is 4,600 ($10^2 + 30^2 + 60^2 = 100 + 900 + 3,600$). If there is only a single operator it is 10,000 (100×100), suggesting total concentration. The Justice Department considers markets with a Herfindahl–Hirschman index of 1,001–1,800 as moderately concentrated and those above 1,800 as highly concentrated. Of the fifteen US airports listed in Table 9.7 only one, Los Angeles, had an index below 1,800 in 1994! Eight had indices above 4,000, indicating very high concentration (Maldutis and Musante, 1995).

On-line schedule co-ordination can be measured using a connectivity ratio, which shows the degree to which linkages are more than purely random. It allows for varying volumes of flights operated and different minimum connect times at each of the hubs. A ratio of 1.0 suggests connections are no better than would be expected with a random pattern of schedules. A ratio of 2.0 suggests twice as many connections as would be achieved on this random basis. In 1990 among the European majors, Austrian at Vienna, Swissair at Zurich and KLM at Amsterdam stood out as having integrated schedules, with a connectivity ratio around 2.0 (Table 9.8). British Airways, Alitalia and Air France were way behind with connections that were little more than random. By 1995 Air France had shown marked improvement in the use of effective hubbing.

9.7   The economics of hubbing

Hubbing can be an effective schedule-based marketing tool providing wider market spread, generating increased revenues and resulting in market dominance on many routes. But the economics of hubbing are quite complex, since it imposes certain cost penalties on the operating airlines. These are largely of two kinds: those associated with the extra flying required and those arising from the extra passenger handling that is involved compared with direct flights.

Table 9.8 European hub performance, 1989–95

Airport	Hub airline	Connectivity ratio[a]	
		1989	1995
Vienna	Austrian	2.2	
Amsterdam	KLM	1.9	1.8
Zurich	Swissair	1.9	
Frankfurt	Lufthansa	1.6	1.6
Brussels	Sabena	1.6	1.8
Copenhagen	SAS	1.4	
Rome	Alitalia	1.2	1.2
London Heathrow	British Airways	1.1	1.0
London Gatwick	British Airways	1.1	
Madrid	Iberia	1.0	0.9
Paris CDG	Air France	0.9	1.4
Athens	Olympic	0.9	

Source: Dennis (1990, 2001).

Note

a The connectivity ratio is the good connections actually timetabled as a ratio of connections that would be possible if all schedules were purely random.

An example of the extra flying involved can be seen in Sabena's efforts in 2001 to sell London to Rome services via Brussels in the London market. This involved carrying passengers on two sectors London–Brussels, with an aircraft block time of 1.00 h, and Brussels–Rome, with a block time of 1 h 50 m, making a total block time of 2 h 50 m. Yet a direct flight London–Rome requires a block time of only 2 h 10 m. In other words forty minutes of extra block time is required for the passenger hubbing through Brussels. Hub-and-spoke networks, by discouraging direct flying between the spokes, will tend to reduce the average sector distance flown by an airline's aircraft and this will push up the unit costs (Chapter 6.6 above). All direct operating costs will be higher, including airport landing charges, since landings will be more frequent. In a European context, where airport charges are especially high, this may be a severe cost penalty. In order to provide feeder traffic for the first bank of departures from the hub, airlines must night-stop aircraft and crews at the end of the shorter spoke routes and schedule early morning departures to the hub. Such night stops are expensive.

Each passenger making a transfer connection at the hub is involved in two boardings and disembarkations, a transfer of baggage at the hub and the use of two or three departure or arrival lounges. The costs of handling must be high. The airline may also have to pay two airport charges for each passenger. Moreover the complexing of flights at the hub and the need to transfer passengers and baggage in the shortest possible time create tremendous peak pressure on staff and facilities compared with a normal operation where demand is spread through the day. To meet such peaks of demand, extra staff

will be needed and not only additional but also more sophisticated baggage-
and passenger-handling equipment and facilities.

The cost disadvantages of hubbing are particularly severe if one is trying to
operate a short-to-medium-haul hub such as one linking European points.
On gateway hub services connecting short-to-long-haul services the cost penalties are less marked because the increased total in-flight distances as a result
of hubbing are less pronounced.

The economics of hubbing hinge on whether the higher flying- and
passenger-related costs of indirect services via a hub are offset by the ability to
operate larger aircraft with lower unit costs. Larger aircraft should result from
combining several thin flows into a single radial service from the spoke to the
hub. It may also be possible to increase aircraft utilisation because of the higher
frequencies resulting from the denser traffic flows. On the cost side it is a fine
balance. The emergence of small but economical regional jets able to offer
low-cost point-to-point services on thin routes joining the spokes of a radial
network has made the cost economies of hubbing more precarious. A 1999
study compared the costs of connecting two points via a hub using an Airbus
A321 aircraft, offering around 200 seats, with the cost of down-sizing to Boeing
737-300 aircraft, with around 120 seats, on the flights through the hub, while
also offering a direct service between the two outlying points with a Canadair
fifty-seater regional jet. The first spoke was assumed to be 300 km in length.
It was only when the length of the second spoke (sector) reached 900 km or
more that hubbing with larger A321s produced lower unit costs than a direct
link combined with smaller aircraft on services through the hub. The implications are clear: if the spokes of a hubbing operation are relatively short the
unit costs are likely to be higher than offering direct services (Eggert, 1999).

To what extent can increased revenues through improved passenger loads
and/or higher yields per passenger counterbalance the higher costs? Certainly,
airlines have tried to offset the diseconomies of hubbing by increasing their
fares on services through the hub. They can do this in two ways. First by
charging a premium for local traffic going only from the spoke to the hub,
especially if they are the only operator on the spoke. For instance, as a result
of their alliance, SAS and Lufthansa operate as monopolists on the three
major routes from Scandinavia to Lufthansa's Frankfurt hub, namely those
from Oslo, Stockholm and Copenhagen. They can charge high fares for local
traffic on these routes. In the United States a 1998 report by the Department
of Transportation found that 'in the absence of competition, the major carrier
is able to charge direct fares that exceed its fares in non-hub markets of
comparable distance and density by upwards of 40 per cent' (DOT, 1998).

A study of air fares in Europe in January 1997 also found that, where
routes to a hub airport were operated as a monopoly, fares were significantly
higher than if there were two or more airlines on the route. This was
especially so for the lower fare classes (Table 9.9).

Second, by trying to exact high fares when offering hub services between
two points that have no direct links. There may not be many of those.

Table 9.9 Impact of number of airlines on fare levels to/from European hubs, January 1997

Average fare on monopoly routes (euro per km)		Fare level (%)		
		Monopoly routes	Duopoly routes	Three airlines serving
Business	0.44	100	95	90
Economy	0.42	100	93	83
Promotional	0.21	100	83	76

Source: European Commission.

However, if a direct link is offered by another carrier, or if it is possible to travel via another carrier's hub, then competition for this point-to-point traffic will be intense. Fares are likely to drop, particularly if one of the sectors is long-haul. For example, in December 2001 Singapore Airlines was selling a business-class return for London–Singapore in the London market for £2,411. British Airways' price was £3,229 but Lufthansa was offering the same route via its Frankfurt hub for only £1,675. In doing so it was undercutting SIA, its own STAR Alliance partner! This £1,675 revenue had to be split between the two sectors London–Frankfurt and Frankfurt–Singapore, diluting the average yield on both. The economics of hubbing depend largely on having sufficient local traffic from each spoke to the hub, paying a premium price to compensate for the lower yield on hub transfer traffic. This means that a hub which is itself a major traffic generator or attractor has a distinct advantage. It also means that the proportion of transfer traffic on each spoke route should ideally not rise to more than 55–60 per cent.

United States' experience, and more recent experience in Europe and at long-haul hubs such as Singapore, suggest that for an airport to become an effective hub it must possess five attributes: a central geographical position in relation to the markets it is to serve, whether this is purely short to medium haul or intercontinental; ample runway capacity; a single terminal building for the hub airline and, ideally, strong local demand from the hub. Many airports satisfy these criteria. The fifth and most critical requirement is to have a strong hub-based airline prepared to develop effective hubbing by operating banks of arriving flights followed by banks of departures.

During the 1980s and 1990s more and more international airlines, following the US example, restructured their networks and rescheduled their flights so as to operate their base airports as effective hubs. But by 2000 there were some signs that hubbing could be problematical. Increased competition, especially in long-haul markets, as a result of hubbing and the new alliances was pushing yields down at a time when unit costs were being affected by rising fuel prices. Another consequence of competition between hubs was that capacity in many markets was rising too rapidly. Extra seats could be filled only by lowering fares. Unexpectedly in May 1999 British Airways announced a fall of 55 per cent in profits for the financial year 1998–99. Worse was to come. In 1999–2000 it suffered a loss, the first for many years. In developing a turn-round strategy, BA came to the conclusion that its biggest losses were coming from economy-class passengers transferring between short- and long-haul services in London and, to a lesser extent, from short- to short-haul economy transfers. It would reduce its exposure in these two areas. It would above all reduce capacity on long-haul routes by cutting frequencies and, in some routes, reducing aircraft size. It would focus on selling fewer seats but at premium fares. The introduction of fully reclining sleeper seats in long-haul business class in 2001 was part of the strategy. Yet other airlines, notably Air France, between 1999 and 2001 were hell-bent on expanding their short- to long-haul transfer traffic in all classes.

It is also clear that in Europe attempts by some airlines to build both operationally and economically successful hubs have failed. A case in point is Sabena, the Belgian airline. As an ailing state-owned airline it received $1,800 million of government aid in 1991 to fund its restructuring and a further injection of capital in 1995. In the following year, 1996, Swissair bought a 49.6 per cent shareholding. Under Swissair guidance Sabena began to develop Brussels as a European hub. This meant opening routes to new and sometimes quite small European points, increased frequencies and a concomitant expansion of the fleet. Rescheduling produced three complexes of arrivals and departures each day. This strategy was mismanaged. It proved a disaster. After making a small profit in 1998, Sabena went into the red again in 1999 and slumped to a $170 million loss in 2000. It was then announced that the cost of saving the airline would be around $850 million. The hubbing concept had backfired. Sabena had opened too many new routes in Europe. Many had little local traffic and were too dependent on transfer traffic. For instance, on the flights from Dusseldorf or Luxembourg to Brussels, over 85 per cent of passengers were transferring to other flights in Brussels. The higher frequencies required to support three daily complexes meant a substantial increase in the seats available and which needed to be sold. New thin spoke routes, over-capacity, insufficient higher-yield business traffic – within Europe only one in ten Sabena passengers in 1999 were in business class, compared with two in ten for its major competitors and three out of ten at SAS – and competition from other European hubs meant that Sabena's average yields fell to levels that were quite unprofitable. By mid-2001 it was apparent that only by cutting out fifteen to twenty of its European destinations plus most of its long-haul routes, and reducing its hub, could Sabena achieve long-term profitability. But time ran out. The losses could not be stemmed fast enough. In November 2001 Sabena collapsed.

By pushing their hubbing strategy too far, both British Airways and Sabena ended up 'flying off course'. Their example highlights the need to keep hubbing in perspective. The risks of failure are high because of the higher costs of operating a 'complexed' hub. Perhaps more worrying for planners, in airlines that are hub-focused, is the fact that the low-cost airlines which concentrate on point-to-point traffic and avoid transfers appear to produce better financial results. As discussed earlier, in the period 1990–93 the airline industry went through its worst crisis ever (Chapter 1.6). In the United States all the major airlines suffered losses in one or several of those years. With one exception. Throughout that period Southwest, the largest low-cost point-to-point carrier, continued to be highly profitable. At the beginning of 2001, as the airline industry appeared to be entering a new cyclical downturn, history seemed about to repeat itself. While the US majors announced losses or substantially reduced profits for the first half of 2001, Southwest continued producing the same high profits as in 2000. At about the same time most of the European carriers, with one or two exceptions, were also announcing declining profits or losses for 2000 and warning of further deterioration in 2001. Yet Ryanair, the largest European low-cost point-to-point international carrier, was posting 44 per cent higher profits for the year 2000 and planning a major fleet expansion. Even after the slump in passenger demand which followed the terrorist attacks in the United States on 11 September 2001 the low-cost airlines, especially in Europe, were much more successful in restoring their earlier traffic levels.

10 Pricing policies and fare structures

Issues of pricing, fare restrictions and their impacts on passenger choice are just as critical to revenue maximisation as forecasting and optimisation in the yield management systems themselves.

(Peter Belobaba and John Wilson, 1997)

10.1 Objectives of airline pricing policy

Pricing is a crucial element in airline management. It is only one of several product and service features which are planned and combined together in order to generate demand. But it is the key mechanism whereby the demand for air services is matched with the supply. An airline's primary aim must be to sell the capacity it is prepared and able to offer at prices which will generate sufficient demand to ensure an adequate level of profit. A great deal hinges on what each airline considers an adequate profit. For some state-owned airlines it may mean little more than breaking even. For others it may be measured in terms of an adequate rate of return to shareholders or a target rate of return on the value of the assets employed. Some airlines may go further and set out not only to produce a target rate of return on their current assets but also to generate an adequate reserve fund to self-finance, as far as possible, the acquisition of new assets such as aircraft. Singapore Airlines appears in recent years to have followed this latter objective. Thus even the profit objective in airline pricing may have different implications for different airlines. There is also a temporal dimension to the profit objective. While some airlines may be concerned more with current profits, others may place the emphasis on longer-term profitability. They may be prepared to forgo profits in the short term to ensure their longer-term objective.

International airlines will normally have a clear profit objective but it will be only one of a number of corporate objectives. These other objectives may also impinge on pricing policy. Expansion into new routes and new markets figures large in many airlines' corporate objectives. Expansion may be an object-ive in its own right or the ultimate aim may be rapid growth or the attainment of a particular size of operation. Many airlines want to be big! There may be cost advantages from growth but ultimately the purpose of growth seems to be more akin to a revenue-maximising objective. But revenue maximising may not be the same as profit maximising, as Malaysian Airlines found out in the late 1990s. Under new private management it set out on a course of very rapid expansion, only to see its profits evaporate to such an extent that in 2000 control was bought back by the Malaysian government. If the development of new markets or rapid growth are objectives of an airline's pricing policy the pricing strategies it adopts must be coloured by this fact. In the United States during the 1980s, following deregulation, many new entrants, such as Braniff, when moving into international markets with established carriers for the first time, consistently tried to capture market share by offering lower tariffs.

The adverse cost impact of large seasonal or even daily variations in demand may induce airlines to use the pricing mechanism as a way of evening out those fluctuations. This might be done by using high tariffs to restrain or dampen peak demand and lower tariffs to stimulate off-peak traffic. Such a policy may adversely affect the total revenue generated compared with a policy of expanding the supply of services at the peak periods. But revenue maximisation may be less important in the short term than reducing unit costs through a reduction in the peakiness of demand and hence of supply.

Pricing has a further role. It should in theory be a guide to new investment. Where the number of consumers who are prepared to pay the full cost, including a reasonable profit, of the goods or services they consume exceeds the supply, the producers have a clear indication that if they can supply more at the same or a lower price demand will be sufficient to generate further profits. Conversely, if consumers in total do not generate sufficient revenue to cover the full costs of particular services it would be foolhardy to invest in the expansion of such services. If pricing is to be used as a guide to further investment the prices of different services should reflect their cost of production. If not, demand may be artificially high or it may be suppressed. On two or three occasions falling tariffs on the North Atlantic, as in 1999–2000, generated a surge in demand which pushed up load factors to high levels. Some airlines misread the signs and increased the capacity on offer. This happened in summer 2001. While Delta, Continental, British Airways and KLM cut seat capacity and targeted higher-fare passengers, Lufthansa and United were increasing their seats on offer by 11 per cent each (*Airline Business*, June 2001). Yet Lufthansa's average yield on North Atlantic services was well below the average for European carriers; at least, they had been in 1999. On past occasions, adding more seats which could be filled only at very low fares had proved a recipe for financial distress! The low tariffs were feasible only if mixed with a certain proportion of high-fare business and first-class traffic. Putting on extra services to cater exclusively for the low-yield traffic could prove ruinous, since the revenue generated may be insufficient to cover the costs. The pricing mechanism, if used as a guide to further investment, must be used with care.

In short, few international airlines have a single overriding objective in their pricing policy, though the attainment of profitability looms large, especially for privately owned airlines. Most want their pricing policy to achieve a number of internal objectives. But they may also have externally imposed objectives. Some national airlines are required by their governments to stimulate incoming tourism. This may well require a low-fare policy irrespective of its repercussions on the financial fortunes of the airline itself. The attempt to attain different pricing objectives simultaneously may produce conflicts and contradictions in pricing policy. Such conflicts and complexities in pricing are further increased because the same airline may be pursuing different objectives on different parts of its network. It may be trying to maximise profits on some routes, especially those on which there is little or no tariff competition, while on other routes its prime objective may be increasing its market share or its rate of growth. Inevitably within any airline different pricing objectives will prevail at different times and in different parts of their operations.

10.2   Inherent instability of airline tariffs

Profitability, which appears to be an important objective for most airlines, depends on the interplay of three variables, the unit costs, the unit revenues or yields and the load factors achieved. The interplay of these three variables can be illustrated by reference to a specific example. In summer 2001 a West European airline flying a daily Boeing 747-400 from its base airport to New York would have incurred a total one-way operating cost of, say, $80,000. On this basis it is possible to draw a break-even load factor curve (Figure 10.1). This shows the load factor which the airline would have needed to achieve to break even at different average fare levels or yields. At any point along the curve, the average fare shown (on the vertical scale) times the number of passengers carried, or the load factor (horizontal scale), equals $80,000. By plotting on the graph the average fare and the average load achieved on each day's flight in each month or season it is possible to see whether the flight is profitable or not. The plots for three days in the summer season are shown in the diagram. On both Mondays and Saturdays the combination of average fare and passenger load were clearly above the break-even curve. These flights were profitable. The Thursday flight was a problem! Average yields were low and so were loads, averaging close to 40 per cent. What could be done? Two obvious strategies come to mind immediately – push up the loads or increase the fares. At existing fares, which on Thursday were just over $200, the average load factor would need to be pushed up to more than 85 per cent to cross the break-even load factor curve. This seems unrealistic. On the other hand, to break even at the current 40 per cent load factor, the average fare would have to more than double to achieve a profitable operation. But if fares went up so much surely it would be difficult to maintain the same volume of passenger traffic? Clearly the easiest task for Thursday flights would be to try to cross the break-even curve at the nearest point. In other words, try to increase both average yields and average loads. This could be done by targeting high-yield business-class passengers, thereby improving the traffic mix, by focused advertising, and so on. There is a further solution: to try to move the

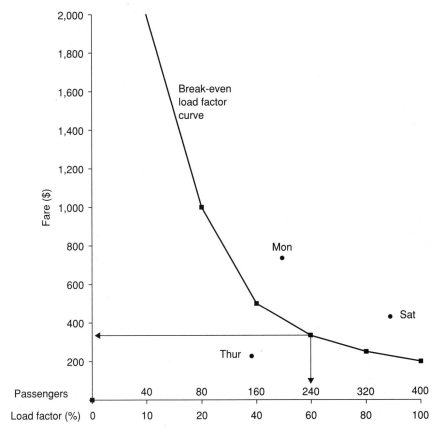

Figure 10.1 Unit cost, yield and load factor trade-off (total operating cost, Europe to New York, one-way = $80,000).

break-even curve downward and to the right by reducing total operating costs, through tighter cost control or, if possible, by operating the Thursday service with a smaller 260–300-seater aircraft with lower trip costs. The airline's planners have three variables to play with in order to achieve profitability.

As in the simple case above, airline managers must juggle with costs, fares and load factors to produce a profitable combination. This is a very dynamic and interactive process, made more difficult by the pricing instability inherent in the airline industry. The industry is characterised by short-run marginal costs which are close to zero. The marginal cost of carrying an extra passenger on a flight which is due to leave with empty seats is no more than the cost of an additional meal, an airport passenger charge, the cost of ground handling and a few pounds of fuel burnt as a result of the extra weight. The problem is that even when operating with high load factors of 70 per cent or more there will be many empty seats. These cannot be stored or sold later. If they are not sold at the moment of production, the seats and the seat kilometres generated are lost for ever. The same considerations apply to unsold freight capacity. An airline committed to operate a published schedule of services for a particular season or a tour operator committed to a series of charter flights finds that its short-run total costs are fixed and cannot be varied. Therefore it makes business sense to try to maximise revenues. Having sold as much capacity as possible at normal tariffs, the airline or tour operator is tempted to sell any remaining empty seats at virtually any price above the very low marginal cost of carrying the additional passengers.

The problem is how to prevent slippage or diversion of traffic prepared to book early and pay the normal tariffs into the lower tariffs. If that happens the total revenue generated may decline. In markets where tariff rules are regulated and enforced, diversion is prevented or minimised by the conditions, the so-called 'fences', which circumscribe the availability of the very low tariffs (see section 10.5 below). In markets where tariffs are not regulated or, if they are regulated, the regulations are not enforced the low marginal cost of carrying an additional passenger (or freight consignment) has a strong downward pressure on all tariffs, including the normal economy-, business- or first-class fares. The inherent instability in such markets is made much worse if there are no controls on the seat capacity offered or if the entry of new carriers is easy. It is in conditions of over-capacity that airlines are most likely to resort to marginal cost pricing. Following the total deregulation of the US domestic system the relationship between costs and tariffs in the early 1980s largely disappeared. Tariffs were determined by competitive factors, and on many routes tariffs approached long-run marginal cost while on others only short-run marginal costs had any relevance to pricing. Since short-run marginal costs were close to zero and long-run marginal costs were below average costs, losses and airline collapses and mergers ensued until a more oligopolistic and less competitive market structure emerged.

In international markets the price instability is aggravated by a number of additional factors. One of these has already been mentioned, and that is the tendency of new airlines entering established markets to try to capture market share by undercutting existing tariffs. For instance, when All Nippon Airways launched its trans-Pacific services in July 1986 it cut the minimum selling price for Tokyo–Los Angeles by $100 from $550 to $450. The most significant factor and the most widespread, even affecting regulated markets, is the availability of sixth-freedom capacity. While the point-to-point, third- and fourth-freedom carriers on a route may be trying to maintain an adequate mix and level of different tariffs, sixth-freedom carriers operating via their own home base may be prepared to charge almost anything to fill empty seats with traffic that they would otherwise not have had. The sixth-freedom operators' tariffs will be particularly low if they want to compensate passengers for a lengthy stopover en route to their destination. The development of hubbing (Chapter 9.6) has aggravated this problem, as it has increased the number of convenient routeings and timings available for many journeys. This, together with so much additional capacity being available, has intensified competition. In most long-haul

Table 10.1 Business-class fares, London–Singapore, September 2001

Airline	Return fare (£)
British Airways	3,229
Malaysia Airlines	2,436
Singapore Airlines	2,411
Qantas	1,936
Lufthansa	1,675
KLM and Swissair	1,666
Gulf	1,561
Finnair	1,540
Royal Brunei	1,236

Note
Fares provided by travel agent/consolidator and exclude airport taxes.

international markets there is a great amount of spare sixth-freedom and sometimes fifth-freedom capacity slushing around and depressing tariffs. On some routes there may be the additional problem of the marginal carrier, that is, the airline for whom the route is marginal to total operations. It may therefore be unconcerned by low fares on the route, particularly if it sees them as a way of attracting traffic on to the rest of its network.

Examples of these and various pressures on price could be found in 2001 on the London to Singapore route. Table 10.1 shows the return business-class fares available through travel agents or, in some cases, direct from the airline. The two third- and fourth-freedom carriers on the route, British Airways (£3,229) and Singapore Airlines (£2,411), had higher fares. British Airways was actually the highest, in part because it was introducing flat beds in business class and partly because it had fewer seats on offer, with two flights per day, compared with SIA's three daily. Most of BA's flights were going on to Australian points, so it had even fewer seats available for local London to Singapore traffic. Qantas has fifth-freedom rights on this sector and offered twelve direct flights weekly. Its fare (£1,936) was substantially lower than SIA's and a great deal lower than BA's, despite the fact that BA owns 25 per cent of Qantas and both belong to the oneWorld alliance. The marginal carrier in this market was Royal Brunei. It has traffic rights on this sector but flies only once a week and is virtually unknown in the United Kingdom. To make any inroads it had to offer very low fares. At £1,236 return for a twelve-hour sector they were clearly the lowest. The various sixth-freedom operators all had low fares around £1,500 to £1,700 return. In the case of the European carriers this was despite the fact that they had to carry passengers on high-cost short sectors from London to their European hubs. In fact Gulf Air went even further. It was offering through on-line agents a first-class return fare to Singapore via Bahrain for £2,592. The exception among sixth-freedom carriers was Malaysia Airlines, which was trying to keep the fares up at a level (£2,436) comparable to that of SIA. This was in an attempt to stem its own mounting losses.

While Table 10.1 shows the apparent price structure, the availability of so many low fares and so much capacity inevitably meant that all carriers but especially the home carriers, BA and SIA, were under tremendous pressure to cut fares, especially on flights when loads were poor. Economy-class fares were even more varied and fluid, with constant price changes in response to market conditions.

On other routes, price instability may be increased by the actions of financially weak or government-supported carriers. Surprisingly it is the weak or loss-making airlines which drop their prices most in competitive markets in order to generate sufficient cash flow to meet their day-to-day payments. During the mid-1990s Garuda Indonesian and Philippine Airlines offered the biggest discounts on services from Europe and the United States to South East Asia. They were losing money and were desperate to improve their cash flow. When the East Asian economic crisis hit them in 1997–98 PAL virtually shut down for a few weeks until a financial rescue package could be put together. Garuda kept flying but withdrew many services. Some state-owned airlines may continue operating on certain routes at yields and load factors which are uneconomic because of government pressure or because they can rely on subsidies to cover their losses. In the process they depress the market for other carriers. Finally, the tendency for airlines to sell seats *en bloc* or on a part-charter basis to tour operators, consolidators or travel agents reduces the airlines' ability to control the tariffs at which those seats will ultimately be sold to the public.

In markets which are effectively oligopolies, where the number of competitors is limited to between three and five or so, and product and service standards are not that different, attempts by any one carrier to gain competitive advantage by dropping prices will invariably be matched by all the others. So they all end up with similar fares but at a lower level and no one is better off in competitive terms. For example, one finds this in many markets between the United Kingdom and points in the United States. In September 2001 the lowest economy return fares from London to Los Angeles and available through agents were £321 with British Airways and £316 with Virgin Atlantic while United and American were *both* offering £294. These were all the carriers with direct non-stop services. Not much to choose between them! Delta and Continental, who required a change of plane en route, were priced slightly lower, at around £290, while Northwest was lower still, at £277, also with a plane change.

This example highlights a new dynamic in airline pricing which has emerged since the early 1990s. The development of computerised reservation systems and later automated revenue management programmes working in real time has given airline revenue controllers, at least those in the largest airlines, instant knowledge of fare changes introduced by their competitors. It has also given them the ability to respond immediately with new or matching fares which can be communicated worldwide in seconds through the Internet and the GDSs. The speed with which new fares can be introduced but also matched in many markets is a new and additional cause of instability in airline fares. The more truly competitive the market, the greater the inherent instability.

The low marginal cost of carrying additional traffic, together with the other factors discussed, which undermine price stability, means that international airlines often have a strong incentive to reduce tariffs often to very low levels. The characteristics of international airline operations are such that even published and agreed tariffs such as those negotiated through IATA are not enforceable unless the airlines themselves decide to enforce them. Even government controls, where they still exist, are ineffective without airline acquiescence, since airlines can find countless ways in which to circumvent regulatory tariff restrictions. Without airline self-control and enforcement of tariffs and tariff conditions the inherent instability of air transport markets may well push tariffs to levels at which no operator can make a profit except for short periods. It is this fear above all else that pushes airlines to try to reach agreement between themselves on tariffs and on enforcement. One way of removing real price competition on routes where there are only two competitors, or where two airlines carry most of the traffic, is for those two airlines to enter into a code-share agreement or even a full alliance, as SAS and Lufthansa have done. As a result there has been little downward pressure on yields on the six major routes between Scandinavia and Germany, all of which are operated by the two airlines as a joint code share, with no other competing carriers.

10.3   Alternative pricing strategies

In developing their pricing strategies international airlines must bear in mind both their pricing objectives and the inherent instability of airline tariffs. Broadly speaking, two alternative strategies are open to them. The first is to relate each tariff to the costs incurred in providing the services used by those paying that tariff. This is 'cost of service' pricing, more frequently referred to as cost-related pricing. The alternative is to base tariffs for different categories of service not on costs but on what consumers are able and willing to pay. This is market pricing or demand-related pricing, though in more traditional textbooks the concept has been called 'charging what the traffic will bear'.

During the 1980s, when in most international markets air fares were still regulated, several regulatory authorities and European governments (CEC, 1981) or the Commission of the European Communities (CEC, 1984) argued most strongly in favour of cost-related pricing. The UK Civil Aviation Authority as long ago as 1977 outlined the fundamental principles to be pursued in developing airline pricing policies (CAA, 1977). It suggested that 'charges . . . should be at the lowest level which will cover the costs of efficient operators, including an adequate return on capital; each charge should be related to costs, and that tariff provisions should be rational, simple and enforceable . . .'.

The arguments in favour of cost-related pricing hinge on the twin issues of equity and economic efficiency. It is considered inequitable that some consumers of air services should be charged more than the cost of providing those services either to generate excess profits or in order to cross-subsidise consumers who are paying less than the full cost of the services they consume. From this point of view, the 50 per cent discount for children under the age of twelve is clearly inequitable. It does not cost less to carry a child than an adult and by charging children only 50 per cent of the fare other adults have to pay more to compensate for the revenue loss. If tariffs are not cost-related then they may well be discriminatory. That means that certain consumers will be discriminated against not on the basis of the costs they impose but on the basis of their age, or their marital status or, for instance, because they want to spend less than six nights at their destination.

There are efficiency implications as well. If prices are above cost for some services, demand for those services will be suppressed even though it would be profitable to supply that demand at prices that were cost-related. Conversely, prices below cost may generate excess demand for particular services and induce airlines to expand such services even though consumers are not meeting their full costs. This would clearly be a misallocation of resources. Unless tariffs are cost-related, inefficient high-cost airlines will continue to operate, protected by high tariffs. Consumers are thereby denied access to lower-cost facilities. In truly competitive markets where there are several existing airlines or potential new entrants, tariffs for different services will tend to the level of the most efficient operator, as happens in the European charter market. In markets where real competition is restricted or where there are barriers to the entry of new carriers, there are no competitive forces to push tariffs to the level of the lowest-cost operator. Tariffs may be agreed bilaterally by the airlines concerned or through the IATA mechanism and will represent a compromise between the pricing strategies of the carriers on the route, each with different cost levels. There may also be a tendency to charge what are effectively monopoly prices for certain inelastic market segments. Market forces cannot ensure that tariffs reflect the costs of the most efficient suppliers. Regulatory authorities and other bodies, such as consumer associations, have argued that it is primarily in regulated markets that cost-related pricing is needed to ensure equity and that tariffs reflect the costs of efficient suppliers. Cost-related pricing is supported both on social grounds in order to reduce discrimination between consumers and on economic grounds in the belief that it creates pressure towards improved airline efficiency and a sounder allocation of productive resources.

On the other hand, several arguments can be put forward against the principle of cost pricing. The first is that there is no satisfactory way for transport industries to allocate costs to particular users because of the incidence of joint costs. This means that a high proportion of fixed costs have to be allocated arbitrarily. Joint costs arise when in producing one service another is inadvertently provided. A daily scheduled flight aimed at a business market produces freight capacity whether or not there is a demand for freight services. Its operation will also inevitably result in vacant seats which may be sold off to meet tourism demand. How is one to allocate the costs of that flight between business passengers who were the prime objective in setting it up and freight or holiday travellers? Any allocation of joint costs must have an element of arbitrariness in it. The same applies to certain fixed direct operating costs and to indirect costs. In practice many but not all the problems of airline cost allocation can be overcome, as indicated later. But some arbitrariness remains and it is argued that many airlines end up calculating what is more akin to an average cost for all users than a separate cost specific to different categories of users.

Another argument against cost-related pricing is that on some routes such a pricing strategy would not generate sufficient revenue to cover costs and would therefore fail to ensure the continued operation of services. On a simple route with one fare and one class of service a cost-related fare may not generate sufficient demand to ensure profitability. On the other hand, if two market segments with different price elasticities can be identified, the airline concerned may generate higher revenue by charging the two market groups two separate fares even though there may be no difference in the cost of transporting them. Without discriminatory but market-related tariffs the services might be abandoned and all consumers would be worse off. Such a case was illustrated earlier (Chapter 7.8) when discussing the concept of price elasticity. Finally, attempting to improve efficiency by setting tariffs at the level of the lowest-cost operator may be meaningless in international air transport. Many international air routes, particularly on short- or medium-haul sectors, are dominated by the third- and fourth-freedom carriers of the two countries at either end of the route. These airlines may have quite different costs for reasons quite unconnected with questions of efficiency. The prevailing wage levels in each country may be different, as may the price of fuel or other factor inputs. Exchange rate movements may also have an adverse impact on one airline's costs. Cost-related pricing would produce a different set of tariffs for each airline, yet the lower tariffs might not necessarily be those of the most efficient carrier in terms of the resources used.

From an airline viewpoint, demand-related pricing strategies make sense. A scheduled airline that is committed to a published timetable of flights and has brought together the productive resources to operate that timetable finds that its short-run total costs are more or less fixed. In those circumstances it needs the freedom to price its services in such a way as to be able to generate sufficient revenue to cover its costs. This may mean charging more than cost to price-inelastic segments of the market and less than cost to elastic market segments. In competitive conditions competition between carriers should ensure that market-related pricing is not abused to produce excessive profit for the airline. Where effective competition does not exist there may well be a danger of excessive profits being made through discriminatory pricing with or without some capacity control. In such situations regulatory or government intervention to monitor costs, tariffs and airline profits may be necessary to prevent this happening, though there must be some doubt as to how effective such intervention can be. Deregulation of tariffs, of capacity controls and of

Table 10.2 Pricing case study: Athens to a Greek island ($)[a]

	Passengers' willingness to pay	Fares paid by passengers willing to travel		
		Average cost pricing		Market pricing (three separate fares: $300, $150 and $90)
		Fare based on cost per seat = $120	Fare based on cost per pax at 60% Seat factor = $210[b]	
	1	2	3	4
1	310	120	210	300
2	310	120	210	300
3	280	120	210	150
4	260	120	210	150
5	230	120	210	150
6	210	120	210	150
7	160	120		150
8	110			90
9	90			90
10	55			
11	55			
12	50			
13	40			
	etc.			
Total revenue		840	1,260	1,530
Surplus-deficit		−360	+60	+330
Seat factor (%)		70	60	90

Notes
a Ten-seater aircraft; total operating cost = $1,200 (one-way).
b Cost per pax $200 plus $10 profit margin.

market access would be the most effective way of minimising the likelihood of excessive profits. Meanwhile, airlines can argue that they should have the freedom to offer a range of services at a range of prices which meets some or all segments of demand in a way which ensures the continued supply of such services whether or not individual prices are cost-related.

A simplified example illustrates the basic differences in approach between cost-based and market-based pricing. The daily demand for air services between Athens and a small but important Greek island is shown in the first column of Table 10.2. This shows how much each potential passenger is prepared to pay to fly to the island. It is a measure of the value or benefit to each passenger of this service. Some wealthy Athenians have holiday homes on the island and would be prepared to pay $300 or more for easy access and to avoid the six-hour boat services. Effectively column 1 is the downward-sloping demand curve and shows how the demand increases as the cost or fare goes down. The total one-way operating cost of this service with a small ten-seater twin is $1,200 for a forty-minute sector. This means that the average cost per seat is $120. If a fare of $120 is charged, there would be seven passengers daily, that is, all those who, on the strength of their willingness to pay (as shown in column 1), value the trip more than $120. The seat factor is good, 70 per cent, but the service would make a loss (column 2) of $360 per trip. Clearly the airline's planners should base the fare not on the cost per seat but on the cost per passenger. If they target a 60 per cent seat factor, the cost per passenger would be $200. The airline could build in a profit margin of $10 per passenger and charge $210. It would then get six passengers, and total revenue would rise to $1,260, yielding a small profit. However, it is clear by comparing columns 3 and 1 that several passengers are paying a lot less than the value to them of the service. What economists call the 'consumer's surplus', which they enjoy, is substantial. Two who are prepared to pay $310 for the flight are getting it for only $210. Market-related pricing aims at ensuring that producers do not lose out in this way. If one introduced a three-tier fare structure, as indicated in the final column (4), where fares were more closely aligned with market demand than with costs, seat factor and revenue could be pushed up markedly. In this case a significant surplus of $330 per flight and a seat factor of 90 per cent would result from the proposed fare structure.

In practice, pricing is not as simple as the example would suggest. But the basic principle applies. Market-related pricing may, in most but not all markets, enable airlines to generate higher revenues. The complexities of implementing such pricing are discussed later. For instance, in the case above, barriers would need to be devised to prevent high-fare passengers using the lower fares. Another complication may be government intervention to try and keep fares low. Up to the year 2001, on routes from Athens to smaller islands, the reality was that the Greek government would not allow the airlines to charge even average-cost fares. Government pressure over the years had resulted in single fares that were below average cost per passenger. As a result most such routes were loss-making.

While in the short term a strategy of market-oriented tariffs makes sense as a way of maximising revenues, it does not in itself guarantee profitability, especially in price-competitive markets. Because of the inherent instability in airline tariffs, discussed above, which is due to very low short-run marginal costs, market-related tariffs may reach such low levels that the total revenue generated is insufficient to cover total costs. This is particularly so if extra capacity is provided to cater for the demand generated by the low tariffs. While revenue maximising may be a short-term pricing objective, in the longer term airlines are likely to adopt a profit-generating or loss-minimising objective.

In order to achieve such objectives through their pricing strategies, airlines must be in a position to do three things. First, they must have a fundamental understanding of the different market segments in each of their markets and of customer needs and requirements, in terms of both product features and price (as discussed earlier in Chapter 7.5). Second, since in many markets airlines will decide on or will be forced to introduce fares which are market-related rather than cost-based, they must introduce effective yield or revenue management in order to ensure that revenue dilution does not occur through slippage of high-fare passengers into lower-fare categories and that they max-imise their revenues. Finally, they must ensure that, broadly speaking, each major market category or traffic group covers, where possible, the costs which it imposes on the airline. This, together with the need to evaluate the feasibility of aircraft investments, of new routes and of different products, pushes airlines to consider carefully the costs of the different services they provide. Whatever pricing strategy they are forced to adopt by the market conditions on each route, the starting point for their pricing procedures should be and normally is an evaluation of the costs of the different services they provide. Even market-related pricing cannot ignore costs. Understanding the relationship between pricing and costs is fundamental to effective airline management. In brief, the key to successful revenue generation is market knowledge, effective revenue management and cost awareness.

10.4   Choice of price and product strategies

The fare charged is only one aspect of the product or service provided by an airline to different classes of passenger. Other product features include fre-quency, timings, seat comfort, the quality and nature of ground and in-flight services, and so on. These have been analysed in Chapter 9, though price is often the most important, particularly for leisure and VFR travel. In planning the supply of services on each route it serves, an airline must also decide on the various price and product mixes which it feels will generate the level of demand it requires. In markets which are less regulated and where there is a high degree of price competition, the pricing options available are much wider but the choice between them is more difficult to make.

The starting point for deciding on a pricing strategy, that is, the structure and level of tariffs and the product features associated with them, must be an assess-ment of demand and of the airline's pricing objectives. Is an airline setting out to meet a particular profit target, to expand rapidly, to capture market share, or does it have some other objective it wishes to achieve? Given the objectives of its pricing policy, an airline must examine the costs of the different products it can put on the market in relation to its assessment of what potential con-sumers want and are prepared to pay for. It must also consider its own posi-tioning within each market. Is it setting out to meet the needs of all market segments or is it trying to attract only certain segments? It could concentrate on only the high-fare and high-product quality end of the market, as Swissair (now Swiss) and SAS have done in recent years. By going for the top end of the market such airlines aim for high-yield traffic and accept that it may mean lower load factors and a smaller market share. In those international markets where there is still some government oversight of tariffs, a pricing strategy must also be acceptable to the airline's own government and to the govern-ment at the other end of the route. The other government's response will be dependent on the interests of its own airline and in particular on the relation-ship of the tariffs proposed to its own airline's costs and objectives.

In more price-competitive markets the pricing strategy may need to be dynamic and changing in response to price or product changes introduced by competing airlines. Airlines have many difficult decisions to make. Should they match a competitor's lower fares when they know the competitor has lower unit costs, or is prepared to face a loss, or may be heavily subsidised by its government? What proportion of its capacity should an airline offer at price-competitive fares? Is there any point in undercutting a competitor's tariff if the latter is going to match those lower tariffs? These and other considerations will affect the pricing strategy and tariff levels that airlines adopt in each of their markets. The ultimate aim must not be forgotten, however: that is, to bring supply and demand together in such a way that the airline achieves its corporate objectives.

10.5   Structure of passenger fares

The structure of publicly available fares on international routes is very complex. Many of the fares are negotiated each year by the Tariff Co-ordination Conferences of IATA. In fact, IATA tariff conferences are a series of regional meetings run throughout the year at which airline representatives from each region or sub-region in turn come together to agree fares within their region or between regions. Other tariffs may be agreed between the third- and fourth-freedom carriers on a route or may be published unilaterally by one or more carriers. Since the mid-1980s the IATA-agreed fares have not really been binding, since airlines, especially the third-, fourth- and fifth-freedom carriers, have flexibility to diverge from these tariffs. In addition, many major airlines, such as Cathay Pacific or SIA, while being trade members of IATA, do not take part in tariff co-ordination and are free to set their own tariffs. Nevertheless, the IATA fares are guideline prices which most international airlines use in some parts of their network while diverging from them elsewhere. But the main value of the IATA fares for all airlines is that they provide the basis for allocating between airlines the revenue from interline passengers who travel on two or more carriers on a single journey (section 10.8 below).

While there is much conformity worldwide in the structure of international air fares, there is an important exception. In Europe, low-cost airlines offering international air services operate entirely outside the IATA framework and have their own individual pricing structures. They represent a different business model, as do the charter airlines. As a result, they are not interested in interline or transfer passengers and therefore have no need to conform to any IATA rules or practices on fares.

The complexity of normal international tariffs is of two kinds. First, there is a multiplicity of fare types. These include first-, business- and economy-class fares as well as preferential fares and a range of promotional fares. Second, there is normally a host of very detailed and complex conditions attached to each one of the individual fares within each fare type. For instance, on most intra-European routes the only fully flexible fare is the normal business-class fare.

But many airlines also offer a lower 'restricted' business fare, which is fully flexible except in one respect: reservations can be changed but only to other flights offered by the airline issuing the ticket. Unlike the normal business fare, one cannot use the 'restricted' ticket to fly with another airline. Conditions attached to the various promotional fares are particularly complicated.

10.5.1   Normal fares: first, business and economy

Partial or total deregulation of airline tariffs on many routes, together with differences in the pricing strategies of major international airlines, has made it increasingly difficult to identify what one might call 'normal' fares. But on most international routes there are three basic fare types corresponding to the separate cabin classes, that is, first, business and economy. On most European routes and a few long-haul routes there may be a first-class fare, agreed through IATA, but no first-class services, since many airlines no longer offer first class on such routes. While normally there will only be a single first-class or business fare, or in some cases a couple of such fares, there are frequently several different fares available for the economy cabin. It is the full economy fare that is considered as the basic 'normal' fare for the economy cabin. But there are in addition numerous promotional economy-class fares which are discussed below.

Point-to-point IATA tariffs have an agreed mileage attached to them. This is normally the great circle distance between the two points. In travelling from one point to the other passengers can deviate from the IATA distance by up to 20 per cent in mileage terms (15 per cent on some longer routes) without any increase in the normal fare. This freedom may not apply to some of the promotional fares. The free 20 per cent add-on to the permitted distance allows passengers to take quite circuitous routes to reach their ultimate destination, often with stopovers en route at no extra cost. This is particularly so on tickets to distant destinations where a 20 per cent deviation on a distance of several thousand kilometres can give passengers considerable scope for roundabout routeings. On a few very long-haul routes there may be several sets of normal fares, depending on the routeing taken. This is done partly to avoid misuse of the 20 per cent add-on. Thus between London and Sydney there is one set of fares for services via the eastern hemisphere or the trans-Siberian route, and higher fares for travel via the Atlantic or the polar routes.

10.5.2   Preferential fares

Preferential fares are those which are available only to passengers who meet certain requirements in terms of age, family kinship or occupation. They are usually expressed as a percentage discount on the normal fares and are generally applicable over large geographical areas. The most widely accepted and used are the 33 per cent or sometimes 50 per cent discount on the economy or more expensive fares for children under twelve years of age and the 90 per cent discount for infants under two but without the right to a seat. Child discounts on promotional fares, if available, may be similar or not so substantial. In particular IATA Traffic Conference areas there may be discounts for students travelling to or from their place of study, there may be spouse discounts for husbands and wives accompanying their partners on business trips or publicly available group discounts. There may also be discounts for military personnel or ships' crews. Seamen's fares, involving a 25 per cent discount on the economy fare, are another common feature. Traditionally the aim of preferential fares has been partly developmental, to encourage demand from particular groups within the community, and partly social, through the choice of groups to be encouraged, that is, families with young children or students. Interestingly, child discounts are not normally available on charter flights.

10.5.3   Promotional fares

Promotional fares, sometimes referred to as discount or deep discount fares, are various low fares, usually with one or more restrictions on their availability, which offer passengers significant savings on the normal economy fares. Such fares are not of general application, as most preferential fares tend to be, but are separately negotiated and agreed for each point-to-point link. Promotional fares have tended to be most widely used on routes where there is charter competition, such as within the Europe–Mediterranean region or on routes where there is considerable leisure traffic, and on routes where there is over-capacity arising from the operation of fifth-freedom or indirect sixth-freedom carriers. They have been least developed on routes where the airlines concerned have wanted to maintain high fares or have believed that demand was likely to be inelastic to fare reductions. The latter is the case on many international routes to and within Africa.

The early development of promotional fares was aimed at stimulating particular market segments, such as off-peak demand or the demand for inclusive tours, while taking advantage of the low marginal cost of scheduled air services once airlines were committed to a published timetable. Off-peak fares, night fares and group (GTX) or individual inclusive tour (ITX) fares were of this kind. Subsequently a wide range of promotional fares has been developed. The economic rationale for some, such as advanced or late purchase fares, was discussed earlier. Fundamentally there can be only one justification for them. They must increase an airline's net revenue and hopefully its profits too. They can do so only by increasing traffic by a greater amount than is needed to overcome not only the revenue loss arising from the lower fares and the possible diversion of higher-fare traffic but also the increased cost due to the greater volume of traffic. On the other hand, higher traffic volumes may allow the use of larger aircraft and thereby lead to lower unit costs.

Promotional fares involve considerable risk. There is the risk that newly generated traffic will not come up to expectations or alternatively that it may be so heavy that it will displace higher-fare traffic. Traditionally tight 'inventory' control, which means control of the number of seats sold at different fares, has been necessary to ensure that this does not happen. The other risk is that too many passengers will be diverted from full fares or other high fares and will travel at the promotional fares, thereby deflating total revenue. To minimise this risk 'fences' or conditions are attached to each promotional fare. A promotional fare tends to have one or more of the following fences built into its conditions.

10.5.4   Duration limits

Most promotional fares have a minimum and maximum stay limit. Within Europe, several categories of promotional fares include a requirement that the passenger must stay at least one Saturday night at his destination and no more than one month or, in some cases, three months. On the North Atlantic many excursion fares require a minimum stay involving a Saturday night as well as a three- or six-month maximum. Inevitably duration limits mean that passengers must buy return tickets. The primary aim of most duration limits is to prevent the use of these fares by normal business travellers who, as previously pointed out (Chapter 7.3), prefer short trips and avoid weekends away from home.

10.5.5   Departure time limits

It is also common to limit the availability of many promotional fares to particular times of the day, or days of the week, or seasons. The aim here is to generate off-peak demand or to try to fill seats that would otherwise be expected to remain empty because of the timing or day of particular flights. Many of the lowest fares in Europe and on routes to North America are available only on weekday flights, Monday to Thursday.

10.5.6   Purchase time restrictions

In order to be able to direct demand more effectively than can be done with departure time limits, restrictions on the timing of purchase have been introduced for many promotional fares. These require either advance reservation and simultaneous full payment a minimum number of days before departure, or late purchase, normally within twenty-four hours before the flight or actually at the time of departure. Advance purchase fares originally required the purchase and payment of tickets at least thirty or forty-five days before departure. The aim was to use them to push traffic into days where projected demand was expected to be low. But competitive pressures in some markets, especially long-haul ones, have resulted in the minimum number of days being reduced to ten or fifteen, or in the requirement being ignored. Effectively the so-called APEX or PEX fares have then become the most widely used economy tariffs on many services, especially on long-haul routes. Advance payment also reduces airline costs by improving cash flow.

10.5.7 Routeing conditions

Most promotional fares can be bought only as round-trip fares. In some cases the return trip must be booked at the time of reservation and neither the outward nor the return booking can subsequently be changed without forfeiting a substantial part of the fare. The aim is to reduce passenger flexibility, thereby making the fares unattractive to business passengers or independent holidaymakers, while at the same time ensuring high load factors by cutting out last-minute changes and no-shows. Higher load factors, by reducing unit costs, justify the lower fares. A number of additional routeing restrictions may also be used as a way of reducing the cost of handling low-fare traffic. These include reduced or no stopovers between the original and ultimate destination; a point-to-point restriction which prevents both stopovers and use of the 15 per cent distance add-on rule; and a 'no open jaw' rule to force passengers to start their return trip from the original destination point. Finally, some very low fares may preclude interlining; that is, they can be used only on the airline which issued the ticket. This prevents any revenue loss by the airline from pro-rating of the ticket with other carriers (see section 10.8 below). In a few cases restrictions aimed at reducing costs may be combined with normal fares. For instance, on the London to Hong Kong route there is a low point-to-point business fare.

10.5.8 Inclusive tour requirements

There is finally a range of promotional fares which are not publicly available but which can be purchased by travel agents or tour operators and used to package into inclusive tours. (For an example see Table 6.1.) Such packaged holidays normally include accommodation but may involve some other element such as car hire or tickets for a cultural or sports event instead of or in addition to the accommodation. On some routes there is a single inclusive tour fare while on others there may be a separate ITC fare for individuals and a lower fare for groups. Inclusive tour fares have been aimed at meeting the needs of the independent holidaymaker. At the same time on some routes they may allow scheduled airlines to compete with charters in the package holiday market. As such they are a defensive response.

Most promotional fares (whose names tend to differ by region) will have conditions attached to them involving several of the above limitations. On certain routes the complexities of the numerous fares available and the conditions attached to them have posed administrative problems for both airline staff and travel agents and have become counterproductive in marketing terms. This is particularly so when passengers become aware of the simplicity of the fares offered by low-cost airlines such as Southwest, Ryanair or easyJet. Airlines are under both internal and external pressure to try to simplify tariffs and the conditions attached to them, some of which are outdated if not absurd. For instance, it is generally impossible to buy a one-way promotional ticket on a conventional airline, as one can on a low-cost carrier. All the low tariffs require passengers to purchase a round trip.

During the 1990s progressive liberalisation and increased competition resulted in the widespread introduction of more and more promotional fares. As a result the proportion of passengers travelling on such fares as opposed to full first, business or economy fares has steadily increased on most major international routes. In Europe between 1985 and 1996 promotional traffic on scheduled services went up from around 59 per cent of the traffic to over 70 per cent while during the same period the average promotional fare dropped from being 57 per cent of the full economy fare to around 46 per cent (AEA, 1997). Another example is that more than three out of every four passengers on the North Atlantic are travelling on promotional fares of various kinds. In other very competitive markets, too, airlines have found themselves selling virtually their entire economy cabin at promotional fares. On London to South East Asia routes promotional fares that were originally introduced as advanced purchase (APEX) fares have become effectively the most widely used economy fare, with hardly anyone paying the full economy tariff. This trend is a major factor explaining the long-term decline in average yields. A higher proportion of passengers are travelling on promotional fares than was the case ten or fifteen years ago and at the same time the discounts many are obtaining are much deeper.

The use of the various 'fences' outlined above in conjunction with some degree of computerised control of seat inventory allowed airlines to implement some degree of *yield management* and *revenue management* even before these terms became widely used. The aim was to ensure a good mix of high-yield and low-yield passengers on any route by preventing slippage of high-fare passengers into lower-fare categories. But the approach was not very sophisticated and was not pro-active enough to respond to changing market conditions on a day-to-day basis. Many smaller international airlines still use such traditional methods to try to maintain adequate passenger yields. The development and application of information technology during the 1980s revolutionised revenue management and made it much more effective. At the same time the liberalisation of tariff controls in many markets and the development of hubbing made it a necessity.

10.6   The role of revenue management

For a long time it was thought that the 'fences' or booking conditions attached to different fares were sufficient safeguard to ensure that yields or revenues were not diluted by high-fare passengers switching to low fares. However, they failed to ensure that revenues on each flight were being maximised. In many cases the opposite happened. The introduction of new low fares as a result of tariff liberalisation created a surge of demand for them. Airlines found themselves putting on extra capacity to meet the demand, but with so much low-yield traffic on each flight they often failed to cover their costs even though load factors increased. This happened in the United States during the 1980s, following deregulation, especially with low-fare airlines such as Braniff or People Express. In the early 1990s Philippine Airlines' fares between Manila and the United States were so low that it was capturing around 70 per cent of the market, operating at very high load factors, and yet was losing money on the route. Its break-even load factor was over 100 per cent because the yields were so low.

Yield management became an essential marketing tool as a result of US deregulation and the complexity of fares and fare types that emerged within a very competitive and rapidly changing market. It involves the management of seat access through an airline's reservations control system in order to maximise total passenger revenue per flight. This is not the same as ensuring the highest load factor or the highest average yield. In fact maximising revenue may in many cases mean that neither of these aims is achieved.

Yield management is based on the simple economic concept of utility, as expressed through the demand curve. There is a maximum price which each consumer is willing to pay for goods or a service. That price is equivalent to the utility or benefit he gets from consuming it. He will happily pay less for it but will not pay more. Different consumers gain varying levels of utility from particular goods or services and therefore each will only buy them if the price is no greater than that utility or benefit. For air services, as for most products, the lower the price the greater the demand. By summing up the demand for a service at different price levels we can draw a demand curve. On a simple diagram showing the air fare on the vertical axis and seats demanded on the horizontal axis one could draw the demand curve for an air service between two cities. This has been done for a hypothetical route in Figure 10.2a. It shows a downward sloping demand curve, indicating the number of seats which would be bought at different fares.

An airline wishing to provide this service with a 100-seater aircraft has estimated a one-way total operating cost of $3,500. It sets a target seat factor of 70 per cent, which means carrying seventy passengers. If pricing were purely cost-based the airline would charge a $50 one-way economy fare. At that fare, the demand curve tells us, the airline would get only fifty passengers, thereby generating an income of only $2,500, which would result in a substantial loss (Figure 10.2a). The load factor achieved would be 50 per cent, not 70 per cent.

The demand curve also tells us that many passengers who paid $50 would have been willing to pay more. They are getting a good deal. The utility or benefit they get from using the service is greater than the price paid. The difference between the $50 fare and the utility they enjoy is called the *consumer surplus* and is measured by the shaded area in Figure 10.2a. One aim of yield management is to maximise revenue by transferring some of the consumer surplus to producers, that is, the airlines. The demand curve also shows us one more important fact – that half the seats are empty if the fare is $50 but that there are people who would be keen to fly at fares below $50.

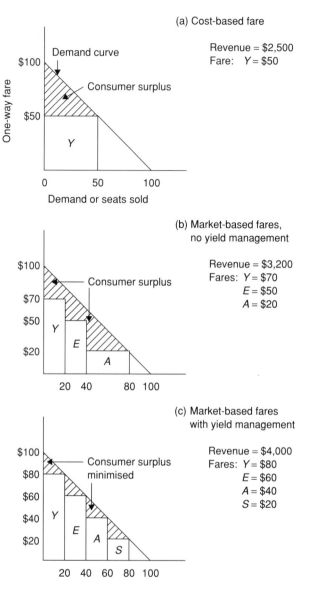

Figure 10.2 Interplay of demand curve and pricing strategies: (a) cost-based fare, (b) market-based fares with no yield management, (c) market-based fares with yield management. Types of fare: *Y* full economy, *E* excursion, *A* APEX, *S* Super-APEX.

The airline, conscious of both the 'consumer surplus' issue and the need to fill empty seats, now decides to introduce a three-part tariff: a full economy fare of $70, an excursion fare of $50 and an advance purchase APEX fare of $20. There are various conditions attached, notably that the APEX fare must be bought in advance. In practice, because of the ability to buy cheap seats in advance, many passengers opt for the APEX fare and sales boom. But in the end too many seats (forty) are sold at this cheap fare, leaving insufficient seats, only sixty, for those passengers prepared to pay more but who generally book later. The outcome is shown in Figure 10.2b. The seat factor has shot up to 80 per cent, but though revenue has also increased to $3,200 it is still not enough to cover costs. Moreover, since many passengers are still paying less than they would be prepared to pay, the airline is still failing to capture for itself an adequate share of the 'consumer surplus'.

In theory, to maximise revenue and capture the consumer surplus, the airline should sell each seat at the maximum that each passenger is prepared to pay, from $100 down to $1 for the hundredth passenger. This is clearly impractical. But to try and maximise revenue more realistically it might introduce four separate fares: a full economy fare of $80, an excursion fare of $60, an APEX fare of $40 and a Super-APEX fare of $20. If it could sell twenty seats at each of these fares its total revenue would be $4,000 per flight, producing a profit of $500 with a seat factor of 80 per cent (Figure 10.2c).

The fundamental problem is how to ensure that twenty seats are sold at each fare, and more especially how to avoid the earlier situation where too many seats were being sold at the lowest $20 fare. This is the function of *yield management*. It is the day-to-day monitoring and control of seat availability in each fare group on each flight to ensure that revenue is maximised. This is done by highly trained staff using the constantly updated information on sales and other key data in the reservation computer. Booking conditions attached to different fares and seat availability are the tools used to channel seats to the passengers paying the higher fares. The tariff conditions or 'fences' should separate the demand for particular fare types into discrete segments which have different booking characteristics. By controlling the seats available for sale one can then direct that demand on to flights where it is needed to maximise revenues.

The need for yield management arises because high-fare passengers tend to book nearer the departure date, while many low-fare passengers do not mind booking early, especially if they are travelling for leisure. The latter must not be allowed to fill seats that could be sold later at a higher price. Yield management is also required because, in practice, all fare types are being sold simultaneously in many locations at the same time, further diluting the effective yield. The risks can be seen if one examines British Airways' London–Frankfurt service. The aircraft have a movable partition between the business and economy cabins so seats can be sold at either fare. But the revenue from this sector for promotional tickets in economy class for flights from Canada or New York to Frankfurt via London may be less than 20 per cent of the revenue that could be obtained by selling the same seat in Frankfurt or London to a business-class passenger. Yet the airline's sales offices in North America are under pressure to generate higher sales revenue. Similarly, even a business-class ticket sold by British Airways in Singapore for Frankfurt via London would generate much less revenue for the London–Frankfurt sector than a ticket sold locally. Thus with tickets for passengers to travel on, for instance, BA's London–Frankfurt flights being sold all over the world as part of multi-sector journeys, the danger of airlines such as BA losing control of the total sales in each fare group is very real.

To overcome this, fares on each route are allocated to different reservation or booking classes. This is crucial, since some routes, such as London–New York, may have up to sixty fare types. Most large airlines will work with ten to twelve booking classes, and could go up to twenty or twenty-five. Each booking class may contain several fare types. Thus for the London–Frankfurt sector a BA through ticket sold in New York or Montreal would be put into a very low booking class. But some airlines can still cope with only three classes. Assuming that flights come on to the reservation system a year before the departure date, twelve-month forecasts of demand for different booking classes are used to allocate the number of seats available to each booking class on each flight. When the number of seats allocated to a particular class are sold out, that booking class is withdrawn from sale, even though seats may be available in other higher-fare classes. If, later on, sales in those other classes fail to come up to forecast the previously closed booking class may be reopened for sale.

The forecasts of sales by class are reviewed periodically in the period starting twelve months before departure, and booking classes may be closed or opened accordingly. But it is during the last month that most of the critical decisions and changes are made by the yield managers or controllers. A large airline may employ up to 100 of them, working in groups controlling particular parts of its network. Using data from the reservation computer on sales by booking class to date and on past booking trends they must make rapid and critical decisions, closing, opening or wait-listing particular booking classes on each individual flight scheduled during the coming month. The aim is always to maximise revenue per flight. If sales are going badly as the departure date approaches it may mean allocating more seats to lower-fare types. Conversely, if demand is high, low-fare booking classes may be closed very early on and before they are sold out. It is a complex and critical task that could not be done without a sophisticated software program backing up the reservations system. While some decisions on opening or closing booking classes can be made automatically by the computer system itself, much depends on the revenue manager. At British Airways the European revenue manager will have around 2,500 European flights at any one time on which decisions are pending as to whether the number of seats allocated to any particular booking class should be changed. The task of the yield controllers working for him is made particularly difficult by a number of factors.

In the first place, accurate forecasting of demand by booking class is the key to success but demand is influenced by many external variables. The closer to the departure date the more accurate forecasting becomes. The yield controller must monitor not only current sales but also external developments which may affect future sales. Second, the same fare type sold in one country may be worth more when sold in another because of fare and currency variations. For instance, as mentioned earlier, seats on British Airways' London to Frankfurt flights are on sale through its offices and agents worldwide at different fares and in different currencies. It becomes particularly difficult trying to control and manage sales in different markets, but it is not impossible. There is a risk, however, of upsetting local sales staff who can sell at the published fares but are stopped from doing so by the yield managers at head office. A third problem area is how to deal with interline passengers on multi-sector routes. The *pro-rating* or allocation of the through fare to the separate sectors flown usually means that an airline may get very low yields from carrying interline passengers, travelling on multi-sector tickets issued by other carriers, on one of its own sectors. Group travel provides an important volume of business but poses yet another problem. Group bookings are made far in advance, when they are easy to accept, but are usually firmed up only three or four weeks before departure, and the take-up rate – that is, the number of passengers compared with the number of seats originally booked – may be very low. Requests for advance deposits may help to alleviate the problem. In addition agents offering groups may be vetted on the basis of their past performance before bookings are accepted. Then there is the problem of no-shows. They may go up to 10–15 per cent for most airlines, but may be higher on some flights. Over-booking can compensate, but one can still end up off-loading passengers or having empty seats. Getting the over-booking right for each flight means more revenue and more satisfied passengers. To do this one must develop models to predict no-show rates and introduce booking conditions which discourage no-shows or even penalise passengers who fail to turn up by cancelling their onward bookings.

Yield management must also tackle the question of cheating. The guilty parties are travel agents or the airlines' own sales staff, who, to meet their sales targets, book passengers in one booking class which is open but actually sell them a fare which is in another class which has been closed. Checks have to be introduced to control this. Finally, in markets where fares are not strictly regulated, yield managers must constantly monitor the fares being offered by competitors. While they must maximise revenue they must also have an eye to market share. Losing market share may mean higher unit costs.

Numerous studies have shown that airlines can increase their revenues by 5–10 per cent when they introduce effective yield management on competitive routes. 'The revenue gains come from forcing consumers to pay fares closer to their willingness to pay' (Belobaba and Wilson, 1997). The impact is greatest if the competitors have not implemented revenue management themselves. Thus revenue management may be crucial in ensuring profitability. The latest development in revenue management, which a few airlines are experimenting with, is to focus revenue maximisation on the end-to-end fare for multi-sector routes rather than on optimising the revenue for individual sectors. Inevitably this requires extremely complicated modelling.

The wider, more complex and more competitive an airline's network becomes the greater is the need to implement effective yield management, which means having up to ten or twelve booking classes. It is an essential concomitant of market-related pricing. While some consumers end up paying more than would otherwise be the case, or travelling in more congested aircraft, consumers as a whole should be better off. By mixing high- and low-fare passengers to generate higher revenues, flights are operated that would otherwise not be viable. A wider range of fare types can be made available while protecting last-minute access to seats for those who must travel at short notice and are prepared to pay for it. Hopefully, the frequency of off-loading over-booked passengers should also be reduced.

10.7   Relating passenger tariffs to costs

The starting point for any price-setting exercise is the costing of a particular route or flight. In allocating costs to routes airlines have to make some arbitrary decisions, particularly with regard to the allocation of certain overhead and fixed costs. Studies of European and other international airlines have indicated that there tends to be considerable uniformity in the allocation methods used, and these have been discussed earlier, in Chapter 4.7. Where there are marked divergences in the allocative process they tend to be in smaller cost items which have a relatively minor impact on the total route costs. There are three major cost categories that need to be identified. The first are the costs which are directly attributable to each route, that is, those costs which were described in Table 4.5 as the *variable direct operating costs*. They are the costs which would be escaped if a particular service or route was not operated at all. They include fuel costs, variable flight and cabin crew costs, landing and en-route charges, ground handling charges paid to others, in-flight catering, and so on. Most of these are easy to identify and cost specifically for each route. The one difficult area is that of direct maintenance. This is allocated either on the basis of block hours flown on each route or a combination of block hours and number of landings.

The second cost category is that of the *fixed or standing direct costs*. These comprise aircraft standing charges, that is, depreciation and insurance, the fixed annual flight and cabin crew costs, and engineering overhead costs. Most airlines tend to convert these costs into a cost per block hour for each aircraft type. They then allocate them to each route on the basis of the block hours generated on that route. The third category of costs that needs to be allocated is that of the *indirect operating costs*. These include the station and ground costs that are not route-specific; passenger service costs on the ground, including passenger insurance; ticketing, sales and promotion costs, and the general and administrative overheads. These tend to be allocated on the basis of some output measure. But if a station at an airport on a route is used only for the services being costed then all the staff and other ground expenses associated with that station should be attributed to that particular service. The same applies to the cost of any sales offices and promotion, advertising or other costs which are specific to that route or service.

All these route- or service-specific costs need to be split between the passengers and the cargo carried on the route. This is the next allocative step for pricing purposes. Certain of the above costs are passenger- or freight-specific, so that they can be allocated directly to these categories of traffic. On the passenger side they include the costs of in-flight services such as meals, free drinks, papers and give-aways as well as the costs of cabin staff or passenger sales and ticketing. On the freight side they include the costs of cargo warehousing and handling, of cargo sales and advertising, and so on. Having separated out the passenger- or cargo-specific costs one is left with the joint costs of a particular route or flight, such as fuel, landing fees or aircraft depreciation. These joint costs have to be split between passengers and freight. This may be done on the basis of the capacity payload or usable volume available for the two types of traffic or on the basis of the tonne kilometres expected to be generated by each, or even on the forecast revenue split. (The allocation of joint costs between passengers and freight is discussed in Chapter 11.6.) On routes primarily intended for the carriage of passengers some airlines may allocate virtually all the costs to the passenger side. This is a grey area in which it is difficult to argue that any solution is optimal. Once a proportion of the joint route costs have been allocated to the passenger side the passenger-specific costs need to be added back to them. Then the next step is to calculate the cost per category or class of passenger.

To understand the process whereby one arrives at a cost per passenger it is easiest to examine an example. One might consider the case of a wide-bodied Boeing 777-300 on a long-haul flight with three cabins, each with a different seating configuration and seat pitch producing 18 first, 49 business and 265 economy seats. This was Singapore Airlines' configuration for the 777-300 aircraft in 2001. If the aircraft was operated with full economy seating only, it would be possible to arrive at a cost per seat. If the total allocated route cost per economy seat is then assumed to be 100, it is possible to establish what the cost of providing the first- and business-class seats should be after allowing for the extra space they require, both because such seats have a longer seat pitch and because there are fewer seats abreast across the aircraft. Such an analysis (using seat pitch and seating layout similar to SIA's and those of other airlines) indicates that, purely on the basis of their space needs, the ratio of costs and therefore of fares in the three classes should be 366:208:100 (line 5 of Table 10.3). An IATA analysis of costs based on space required in different classes in 1999 came broadly to the same conclusion with ratios of 271:187:100, though they vary between airlines, aircraft types and routes (IATA, 2000). Also, most of the airlines in the IATA study did not at that time have fully reclining first-class seats with 78 in. pitch or more, as SIA did. This explains why IATA's first-class differential is not as high as that suggested here.

In our example an adjustment might also be made for the greater proportion of space allocated to toilets and galleys, though it has not been done here.

Table 10.3 Unit costs of different classes on long-haul Boeing 777-300

Variable	First (F)	Business (J)	Economy (Y)
1 Cost per seat if all economy			100
2 Seat pitch (in.)	78	52	32
3 *Seat cost index allowing for seat pitch*	*244*	*162*	*100*
4 Number of seats abreast	6	7	9
5 *Seat cost index allowing for pitch plus seats abreast*	*366*	*208*	*100*
6 Planning load factor (%)	50	65	80
7 *Cost per passenger adjusted for load factor*	*732*	*320*	*125*
8 Passenger-specific costs	40	25	10
9 Cost per passenger including passenger-specific costs	772	345	135
10 *Cost per passenger if Y = 100*	*571*	*255*	*100*

What if the planned load factors of the three classes were different too? Airlines often plan to achieve average year-round load factors of no more than 50 per cent on first- and 65 per cent on business-class traffic so as not to turn away any high-yielding demand. On the other hand, they will use promotional pricing and their revenue management systems to try and ensure that year-round load factors are close to 80 per cent in the economy cabin. Differences in planned load factor can be used to convert the cost index per seat into an index of cost per passenger (lines 6 and 7 of Table 10.3).

Lastly, the passenger-specific costs need to be added in to the costing exercise. These include the cost per passenger of the different in-flight services such as meals, drinks, in-flight entertainment, and newspapers or magazines and of any exclusive ground facilities. The higher ratio of cabin staff to passengers in first and business should also be adjusted for. All this is reflected in the assumed passenger-specific costs (line 8, Table 10.3).

Adding these passenger-specific costs to the passenger cost indices in Table 10.3 produces a final index of relative costs per passenger between the first, business and economy cabins of 571:255:100. The significance of these indices is that having earlier calculated the total passenger-related costs per flight of operating a Boeing 777-300 on the route in question the relative tariffs which need to be charged for each fare class can be derived. If purely cost-based, the business fare should be two and a half times the normal economy fare and the first-class fare almost six times as high. In so far as passengers in economy and, for that matter, in business or first may be travelling at different market-related fares, this proposed relationship should apply to the average yield per passenger or passenger kilometre in each class rather than the fare. To what extent do actual long-haul fares and yields for each cabin class reflect a 5.7:2.5:1.0 cost relationship between first, business and economy?

The London–Hong Kong route can be used as a case study to assess the relation between fares and the assumed costs per passenger as analysed above.

Table 10.4 London–Hong Kong fares, summer 2001

Fare type and (booking class)	BA return fare (£)	As % of economy excursion fare
First (F)	7,598	609
First – restricted point-to-point (F)	6,031	484
Business class (J)	4,591	368
Restricted business class (D)	3,734	300
Economy (Y)	4,573	367
Excursion (B)	*1,246*	*100*
World Traveller Plus (T)	1,374	110
World Traveller (T):		
Low	867	70
Shoulder	960	77
Peak	1,067	86
PEX (H):		
Low	634	51
Shoulder	727	58
Peak	835	67
APEX (V):		
Low	467	37
Shoulder	560	45
Peak	667	54

Source: British Airways, *Fares Fortnightly – September 2001*, and BA telephone call centre.

Note
Except first and full business/economy fares, all others have varied restrictions. Another five booking classes in economy not shown above.

An examination of fares on this route in summer 2001 shows that the full economy fare is very similar to the business fare (Table 10.4). But very few passengers travel at this fare because there are so many cheaper economy fares available, though with different restrictions and 'fences'. A better indicator of what one might call a 'normal' economy fare is the excursion fare, which is also one of the least restrictive. If one expresses all the other fares as a percentage of the excursion fare (as shown in the final column of Table 10.4) the ratio of first and business fares to economy fares becomes 6.0:3.7:1.0. This is close to the cost relationship between the three cabins identified earlier, except that the business fare is higher than the cost ratio indicated. The London–Hong Kong example suggests that, while airlines use market-related pricing, they still try to maintain some relation to costs, particularly in terms of the costs per passenger in each of the three cabins.

Another feature of the London–Hong Kong fare structure is the multiplicity of fares and booking classes available. Not all published fares are shown in Table 10.4. There were over sixty fares on offer from British Airways, with very similar fares from Cathay Pacific and Virgin. Many fares were seasonal

Table 10.5 Europe to/from North East Asia: passenger results by class of service, 1999

Measure	Cabin class		
	First	Intermediate	Economy
1 Passenger yield per RPK (US cents)	26.7	17.8	4.9
2 Yield index (Economy = 100)	545	363	100
3 Break-even load factor (%)	55	43	85
4 Load factor achieved (%)	29	54	81

Source: Compiled by the author using IATA (2000).

or restricted in some other way. These restrictions, together with the variations in fares for different times of the year, had two purposes: to meet the needs of and attract different market segments, but also to maximise revenue per flight.

This was done through a yield management system with at least twelve booking classes for paid tickets and probably at least another four booking classes for redemption tickets awarded for Frequent Flyer points.

All the promotional fares were actually well below the excursion fare. In fact the lowest fare available, the low-season APEX fare, was only 37 per cent of the former. The large number of promotional fares suggests that the average yield in the economy cabin could be well below the excursion fare. If this is the case, the imbalance in average yields generated by passengers in British Airways' three cabins would have been even greater than 6.0:3.7:1.0 as suggested by the earlier analysis of fares. In fact, in 1999 this was the case. British Airways' average yields on all its services from Europe to North East Asia, including the London–Hong Kong route, were 4.75c per passenger kilometre for economy passengers, 22.52c for business passengers and 33.67c for those in the first-class cabin. In essence, the first-class yield was seven times as high as the economy yield and the business yield around four and a half times. On the basis of our earlier cost analysis this would suggest that yields in business class appear to be relatively high in relation to the cost of providing for a business passenger. Does this mean that business is the most profitable market sector on long-haul services?

From an economic analysis by IATA based on returns from twelve airlines for their services between Europe and North East Asia, including Hong Kong, in 1999, one can draw some interesting conclusions. First, the relationship of average passenger yields by cabin class for first, business and economy is 5.5:3.6:1.0 (Table 10.5). This is very close to the ratios based on the fares analysis for London–Hong Kong. Average first and business yields are not as high as those of British Airways. Second and more important is the fact that only business class is profitable. The business load factor, 54 per cent (line 4), is well above the break-even load factor of 43 per cent. For economy the actual load factor is close to but below the break-even, indicating losses. But of greater concern is the fact that the first-class load factor, 29 per cent, is only just over half that required to break even, 55 per cent. In other words, on services between Europe and North East Asia, first class is very unprofitable.

Table 10.6 Passenger yields and load factors by class for selected route groups in 1999

Category	North Atlantic	North and mid-Pacific	Within Europe	Within Far East	North America–South America
First class:					
Yield (cents per RPK)	37.4	20.4		23.9	8.5
Actual seat factor (%)	**41**	32		24	54
Break-even seat factor (%)	36	48		108	117
Intermediate class:					
Yield (cents per RPK)	19.2	12.9	41.3	18.7	7.3
Actual seat factor (%)	**55**	**45**	**40**	49	67
Break-even seat factor (%)	37	41	33	57	93
Low class:					
Yield (cents per RPK)	4.1	4.6	14.4	8.6	7.7
Actual seat factor (%)	81	68	69	**74**	**61**
Break-even seat factor (%)	94	78	80	62	55

Source: Compiled by the author using IATA (2000).

Note
Where actual seat factor is above break-even it is shown in bold type. RPK = revenue passenger kilometre.

   This pattern of profitable business-class services, marginal economy class and totally unprofitable first class appears to be the pattern in many international air markets. This was so even in 1999, one of the better years for most international airlines. The average passenger yields, the break-even load factors and the actual load factors recorded by IATA reporting airlines in that year are shown for a sample of five market areas in Table 10.6. Only if the actual load factor is above the break-even factor are the services profitable. Conversely, if the actual is below the break-even, losses are being sustained. In the five route areas examined first class was unprofitable everywhere except the North Atlantic. In fact on routes between North and South America and those within the Far East the load factor required to break even on first-class services was over 100 per cent, clearly an impossibility. In contrast to first class, business was profitable in the three largest market areas and especially profitable on the North Atlantic. But in these same three markets where business class was profitable, load factors in the economy cabin were way below break-even. Conversely, on North to South American routes and those within the Far East, economy services appear profitable while first and business are not. On the North Atlantic, the world's largest international market, first and business appear to be highly profitable, while economy class loses money. This is why airlines were so badly hit when, as a result of the US economic downturn in 2000–01, the outbreak of foot and mouth disease in the United Kingdom in 2001 and also the terrorist attacks in New York and Washington in September

Table 10.7 Passenger yields on scheduled services, 1999 (US cents per passenger tonne kilometre performed)

Rank	North American		European		Asian	
1			SAS	172.4		
2			Lufthansa[a]	109.9		
3					JAL	101.8
4			Air France	100.2		
5			Iberia	96.8		
6			British Airways	95.0		
7	Air Canada	91.6				
8	American	90.1				
9	Delta	86.6				
10	United	84.5				
11	Continental	82.6				
12	Northwest	79.5				
13			KLM	64.7		
14					Cathay	62.2
15					Korean	61.8
16					SIA	56.3
17					Thai Airways	56.0
18					Malaysia	49.3

Source: ICAO *Digest of Statistics*, Series F, *Financial*.

Note
a Figures for 1998.

2001, first- and business-class travel across the Atlantic declined sharply. The low yields and very high break-even load factors in economy class on the North Atlantic and within Europe also explain British Airways' decision in 2000 to focus increasingly on the higher-yield business sector.

10.8   Determinants of airline passenger yields

While pricing is an important element in an airline's marketing strategy, from a revenue point of view the level and structure of passenger fares are less important than the yield that an airline actually obtains. Yield is the average revenue per passenger, per passenger kilometre or passenger tonne kilometre performed. These all measure the average revenue per unit of output sold.

The range of passenger yields achieved by different airlines, some of them based in the same geographical area, is surprisingly wide even though many factors such as average sector distance, strength of home currency, and so on, will affect the yields. The diversity is evident from Table 10.7, which shows yields per passenger tonne kilometre for major North American, European and Asian airlines. European carriers generally have the highest passenger yields – some are exceptionally high – while the lowest yields are achieved by Asian carriers other than JAL. Yet, as has been emphasised previously, by combining low passenger yields with low costs and relatively high load factors one can achieve profitability, though of course overall performance depends on the combined passenger and freight yields. The outstanding example is Singapore's SIA, whose passenger yield is exceptionally low, close to half that of some European airlines. But SIA's passenger load factor in 1999 was 77 per cent, three to five percentage points higher than most of the other carriers in Table 10.7. This, together with SIA's very low costs, ensured high profits. The North American carriers, in terms of passenger yields, are lower than the Europeans but generate yields well above those of the Asian carriers.

The passenger yields indicated in Table 10.7 are global figures for each airline's total operations, including its domestic services. Direct comparisons may, therefore, be somewhat misleading. Yet even when operating on the same or neighbouring routes airlines end up achieving markedly different yields, as evidenced by European carriers in 1999 on their intra-European services (Table 10.8). British Midland, SAS and Austrian Airlines earn more than twice as much per passenger kilometre as does Air Portugal or Olympic. Why do yields vary so widely between carriers? The discussion so far has tacitly assumed that an airline can determine its revenue levels and its yields through the pricing strategies it adopts and in particular by the structure and level of passenger tariffs. In practice this is only partly so, since the relation between fares and yields achieved is much more complex and is influenced in varying degrees by a number of factors, of which the fare structure itself is only the starting point.

A key factor affecting passenger yields is the geographical areas in which an airline is operating. For a number of reasons, such as past government controls on fares or, more recently, the impact of increased competition, fare levels vary significantly between different parts of the world. Historically, fares per kilometre have always been high for flights within Europe, whereas in most Asian markets fares on short- to medium-haul routes have been much lower. This is evident from Table 10.6 above. But, even within Europe, fare levels on routes within northern Europe have tended to be well above those in southern Europe, reflecting the higher standard and cost of living in the former. This partly explains why Iberia, Air Portugal and Olympic find themselves at the bottom of Table 10.8 with the lowest yields among European carriers. The routes that an airline operates also impact on fares and yield levels. For instance, because of the long-term appreciation of the Japanese yen and the high cost of living in Japan, as well as the traditionally high costs of Japanese airlines, fares per kilometre out of Japan have been extremely high. This explains Japan Airlines' very high passenger yields, almost double those of other East Asian airlines (Table 10.7). Any foreign airlines flying to Japan will also benefit from these high fares.

Our earlier analysis of operating costs showed that unit costs decline as sector distance increases (Chapter 5.6). It is not surprising, therefore, to find that unit fares per kilometre also decline with distance. In fact fare analyses by ICAO over the years show a close correlation between increasing route distance and falling unit fares or yields in most major markets (ICAO, 1988).

Table 10.8 Average passenger yield of European carriers on their intra-European services, 1999

Airline	Average yield (cents per passenger km)	Average sector distance (km)
British Midland	23.09	586
SAS	22.32	730
Austrian Airlines	21.68	947
Aer Lingus	20.08	546
Air France	19.74	895
Lufthansa	19.61	814
Swissair	18.81	748
Sabena	16.94	733
Alitalia	16.62	902
European airlines average	*16.54*	*886*
British Airways	16.37	989
Malev	13.23	1,012
Iberia	12.92	1,158
Air Portugal	10.73	1,348
Olympic	10.03	1,301

Source: Compiled by the author using Association of European Airlines data.

Note
Yields here are per passenger kilometre but in Table 10.7 per passenger tonne kilometre.

This relationship can be seen in Table 10.6 above. The average yields for the two really long-haul markets, the transatlantic and trans-Pacific routes, are less than half those of intra-European services, which are on primarily short-haul, that is, less than three-hour, sectors. Since fares per kilometre taper downward with distance, the yields an airline obtains are much influenced by the sector lengths it operates. This is clearly apparent when looking at the intra-European operations of Europe's major airlines (Table 10.8). The three airlines with the lowest yields in 1999 also had by far the longest average sector distances within Europe. Olympic's average European sector was 1,301 km, Air Portugal's was 1,348 km and Iberia's 1,158 km, whereas the weighted average for all the European carriers was 886 km.

Conversely, three of the four airlines with the highest yields, namely British Midland, SAS and Aer Lingus, also had the shortest sectors.

The yield per passenger kilometre on any route depends less on the level of individual fares than on the traffic mix. There are two aspects to this. First, is the overall mix between high-yielding first- and business-class passengers and the much lower-yielding passengers in the economy cabin. Some airlines, as part of their marketing strategy, target the business market and plan their products and in-flight services to try and attract high-fare passengers. The improved services may cost more to provide but can be compensated for by the higher fares that passengers may be prepared to pay. In Europe, while all carriers try to attract business passengers, both SAS and Aer Lingus have made a special effort to capture this market segment. As a a result, 33 per cent of SAS's European traffic in 1999 was in business class, as was 28 per cent of Aer Lingus's. Yet the average for all European carriers was only 14 per cent. This is another reason why these two carriers achieved such high yields in 1999 (Table 10.8). Given Olympic's very low yields, it is not surprising to find that business passengers accounted for only 3 per cent of Olympic's European traffic. Thus Olympic is doubly disadvantaged in terms of yields. It operates long sectors and has failed to attract sufficient business traffic.

The second aspect of traffic mix relates to the availability and level of discount and promotional fares. This will particularly impact on yields in the economy cabin. In international markets low promotional fares are more widespread and most used where there is the greatest competition. In Europe, this is usually in the leisure routes between northern Europe and Mediterranean leisure destinations. The competition here comes from charter airlines. Scheduled carriers such as Olympic, Iberia or Air Portugal tend to offer a range of charter-competitive fares to ensure that they do not lose all the leisure passengers to the charter carriers. The result is that their economy yields are sharply depressed. One sees the same phenomenon on other routes such as those between Europe and Florida or between Canada and the Caribbean where charters pose a major competitive threat to scheduled carriers.

Exchange rates and currency fluctuations also impact on yields. If an airline's home currency is devalued and sales in its home market represent a significant share of its revenues, its average yield when converted to say US dollars will be adversely affected. One reason why the yields of Thai International and Malaysian airlines were so low in 1999 (Table 10.7) is that both their currencies had been substantially devalued during the East Asian economic crisis of 1997–98. For large international carriers exchange rate fluctuations in any one of their major markets can push up or depress their average yields. The greater volatility of exchange rates since the 1980s has increased the risks of revenue dilution from sudden movements in exchange rates.

Another major source of revenue dilution arises from the pro-rating of revenue from interlining passengers. An interline or on-line passenger travelling with a single ticket on two or more sectors is charged the end-to-end fare, not the sum of the separate fares on each sector. Because of the taper of fares with distance the end-to-end fare to be charged is normally less than the sum of the separate fares. Pro-rating is the method used to share the revenue earned between the different sectors flown. The basic principle used is to share the revenue in proportion to the distance of each sector. But shorter distances are given greater weight to allow for the higher costs of operating short sectors. These weighted distances are published each year by IATA and may change as the relative costs of different sectors change. The method of pro-rating on the basis of weighted distance is illustrated in Table 10.9. For a business-class ticket used to fly London to Athens via Hamburg the revenue dilution is considerable. The airline carrying the passenger on the London to Hamburg leg receives 55 per cent less than the full business fare for that

Table 10.9 Pro-rating of London–Athens full business ticket (£950) used to fly London–Hamburg–Athens, summer 2001

Fare	Return business fare	Distance (miles)	Pro-rate calculation based on weighted distance factors (£)[a]	Revenue dilution of pro-rate fare (%)
Fare paid				
London–Athens	950			
Pro-rating				
London–Hamburg	668	450	$950 \times \dfrac{1,086}{3,421} = 301.60$	−55
Hamburg–Athens	798	1,270	$950 \times \dfrac{2,335}{3,421} = 648.40$	−19
Total		1,720[b]	950.00	

Notes

a Weighted distance factors (found in IATA's *2001 ProRate Factor Manual*) are London–Hamburg 1,086 and Hamburg–Athens 2,335. Adding them together gives 3,421.

b London–Athens direct is 1,494 miles but permitted mileage is 1,791 or 20 per cent higher. Therefore routeing via Hamburg permitted.

sector. On the Hamburg to Athens leg the revenue shortfall is only 19 per cent. The same basic method is used to pro-rate cheaper fares as well if such fares allow interlining. Pro-rate calculations based on distance have become increasingly complex in some markets, especially where airlines on the same routes offer different fares. In those markets where IATA-agreed fares are not those actually used by the airlines, the value of such IATA fares is that they provide the framework and basis permitting worldwide interlining. This is of great benefit to passengers.

Pro-rate dilution is greatest when passengers take advantage of the 20 per cent additional mileage rule to travel on a circuitous routeing between their origin and their destination, particularly if travelling long-haul. The end-to-end fare has then to be split over several sectors. Pro-rate dilution will also increase if a domestic sector is included in the ticket and the domestic airline insists on receiving the full fare or a high proportion of it, leaving even less revenue to be shared between the international sectors. Pro-rated interline traffic used to represent as much as a third or more of an airline's total traffic and was particularly prevalent on routes serving geographical gateway airports such as Heathrow, Amsterdam, New York or Singapore which were major interlining centres. However, one consequence of the development of effective hubbing (see Chapter 9.6) has been that interlining, the transfer of passengers from one airline to another at a hub, has tended to decline as airlines have focused on transferring passengers to their own flights at their hubs. But whether the passenger switches to another airline at a transfer airport or switches to another aircraft of the same carrier the revenue dilution as a result of pro-rating the fare still remains.

The final source of revenue dilution is that arising from long-haul passengers even where there is no interlining involved. This is because of the taper of unit fares with distance. An airline carrying its own passenger on a 6,000 km flight with two stops en route will earn less than if it had carried three separate shorter-haul passengers each of whom flew only on one of the three sectors on the route. Thus SIA or Cathay, each of whose passengers travel more than 4,000 km on average, have a distinct revenue disadvantage, while the shortness of many European sectors is one explanation as to why European airline yields are so high (Table 10.7).

The yields which an airline achieves on each of its routes will depend partly on the level of the normal fares, on the availability and level of promotional fares and on the degree of further discounting through consolidators or special offers. Within that framework of fares it is the traffic mix which ultimately determines the total revenue earned and thereby the unit yield. That is why effective yield management is so important. But revenue will be diluted by the pro-rating of interline tickets and possibly by exchange rate fluctuations. The proportion of interline traffic is therefore a further important determinant of the yield. The final yield will bear little relation to any single published fare. This further complicates the issue of airline pricing. In deciding on its pricing strategy, and in working out the tariffs for different market segments, airlines must balance and juggle with all these factors which transform the various fares into an average yield. It is the yield in conjunction with the achieved load factor and the unit costs which will determine whether an airline's revenue and financial targets can be met.

11 The economics of air freight

Our customers expect globally functioning logistics and distribution networks.
(Dr Klaus Zumwinkel, CEO, Deutsche Post,
WorldNet, October 2001)

11.1 Freight traffic trends

Many of the concepts and principles of airline economics discussed so far apply equally to the cargo side of the industry. At the same time there are particular issues and difficulties which arise in the carriage of air freight which require separate analysis and treatment. The importance of freight is too often under-estimated, yet just over one-third of the output of the international airline industry, measured in tonne kilometres, is generated by freight rather than passengers and for some airlines it is considerably more (Table 1.5). Though the revenue contribution of freight is much less, at only one-eighth of total revenue, it makes a significant contribution to the profitability of many air services. While there are a number of airlines that carry only freight, air cargo is an integral part of most passenger airlines' operations.

Since the 1960s the annual rate of growth of international air freight has been outpacing passenger growth at times by two or three percentage points. In the 1980s the growth of international air freight was around 7.2 per cent per annum. During the 1990s the annual growth rate improved to 7.7 per cent. Though air freight has generally continued to grow faster than passenger traffic the gap between the growth rates of the two sides of the industry has recently been much smaller. However, growth rates for air freight swing wildly and are much more volatile than those for passengers. Thus, while international freight tonne kilometres grew 16.2 per cent in 1997, there was a drop of 0.8 per cent in 1998, followed by a 6.5 per cent jump in 1999 (ICAO, 2000). Volatility plays havoc with the industry's economic performance.

Until the mid-1970s European and North American airlines were dominant in the carriage of international air freight, attracting between them close to three-quarters of the freight traffic (Table 11.1). Since then their dominant position has been eroded by the exceptionally rapid penetration into the freight markets by East Asian and Pacific region airlines. Based in export-oriented

Table 11.1 Regional distribution of scheduled international air freight

Region of airline registration	Regional share of international freight tonne-kms (%)	
	1972	*1999*
Europe	44.8	32.8
Asia and Pacific	12.3	37.3
North America	29.0	19.8
Latin America/Caribbean	5.8	3.8
Middle East	5.0	4.3
Africa	3.1	2.1
World	100	100

Sources: ICAO (1990, 2000).

and rapidly growing economies, the latter airlines have over the last twenty years or so expanded their international freight traffic particularly rapidly. Airlines such as Korean Air, Cathay Pacific and SIA have grown their freight business at annual rates well above the world average and significantly higher than those being achieved by European or North American airlines. As a result there has been a fundamental restructuring of the international air freight industry, with the centre of gravity shifting towards East Asia and the Pacific. As a group the Asian and Pacific carriers overtook North American airlines in the carriage of international freight by the end of the 1970s and they caught up with their European counterparts in the early 1990s. Today the Asian Pacific airlines dominate the international air freight markets, carrying over 37 per cent of the world's scheduled international freight (Table 11.1). In the year 2000 four of the Asian carriers, Korean Airlines, SIA, Japan Airlines and Cathay Pacific, ranked among the world's ten largest international freight carriers, with Korean and SIA ranked the second and third largest overall (Table 11.3 below).

Just over four-fifths (83 per cent) of the world's air freight is international and less than one-fifth domestic. But much of the domestic freight, in fact most of it, is transported within North America (Table 11.2, column 1). A noticeable characteristic of international air freight is the degree to which it is dominated by three major route groups, namely the Europe to Asia routes (24.2 per cent of international freight tonne kilometres in 2000), the North and mid-Atlantic (22.4 per cent) and the north and mid-Pacific routes (20.6 per cent) (IATA, 2001a,b). These three route groups together generate around two-thirds of the total freight tonne kilometres performed on international air services. Interestingly, the very largest freight carriers such as Lufthansa, Air France, Federal Express or British Airways, as well as the Asian carriers previously mentioned, are all heavily engaged in at least two of these three route groups. This seems to be a prerequisite if an airline aims to be really big in international air freight.

Table 11.2 Major scheduled freight markets, 2000

Route area	Share of freight tonne-kms (%)	
	World total	International
Europe–Asia	20.2	24.2
North and mid-Atlantic	18.7	22.4
Trans-Pacific	17.2	20.6
Intra-Asia (International)	6.3	7.5
Europe–Africa	3.3	3.9
Europe–South America	2.7	3.2
Other	15.1	18.1
Total international	83.5	100.0
North America domestic	13.0	
Asia domestic	2.2	
Other domestic	1.3	
World total	100.0	

Source: Compiled by author using IATA (2001a).

While in the early days air freight was considered essentially as a way of filling spare capacity on passenger aircraft, its very high rate growth in the 1960s induced many airlines to introduce scheduled all-cargo services. These could be introduced only where freight traffic was already dense enough to support them but they had a strong stimulatory effect on demand. Narrow-body aircraft in a passenger configuration had relatively little capacity available for freight and were in any case unsuitable for large or awkward consignments. All-cargo aircraft, even narrow-body ones, facilitated the carriage of large unit loads and consignments and accelerated the introduction of specialised handling and sorting equipment which speeded up the movement of freight. Improved handling and the flexibility to send freight independently of passenger aircraft, which, among other things, permitted the use of night hours, allowed airlines flying all-cargo aircraft to reduce freight transit times while offering considerably more capacity. As a result, scheduled all-cargo operations generated new traffic and captured a growing proportion of it. On most major routes the proportion of international freight carried by IATA airlines on scheduled freighter aircraft grew rapidly and peaked at around 43 per cent in the mid-1970s.

After 1973 the market penetration of all-cargo services began to decline. They were hit by two major developments. First, the huge jump in aviation fuel prices in 1974 and again in 1978–79 impacted much more severely on all-freighter than on passenger services. This was because fuel costs represent a much higher proportion of total operating costs for freighter than for passenger aircraft, since the latter incur many additional costs such as those of cabin crew, in-flight catering, and so on. With fuel prices going up fivefold between 1973 and 1980, freighter operating costs jumped sharply and many such services were no longer viable. Second, the gradual introduction and spread, during the 1970s and 1980s, of wide-bodied aircraft, such as the Boeing 747, on long-haul routes, and the Airbus A310 and Boeing 767 on medium-haul services, produced a huge jump in belly-hold cargo capacity compared with that of the narrow-bodied aircraft they were replacing. Moreover the new aircraft carried large containers and other unit load devices (ULDs) which facilitated the loading and handling of cargo. Airlines discontinued their narrow-bodied and fuel-costly freighters and began switching cargo to the bellies of their new wide-bodied passenger aircraft.

The relative decline of all-cargo scheduled services was reversed in the mid-1990s as a result of the rapid growth in demand for air freight, especially from the export-oriented economies of East Asia. On several trunk routes, belly-hold capacity on passenger aircraft could no longer cope with the demand. In these and other markets airlines began to increase scheduled and charter freighter services. By the year 2000 around 44 per cent of cargo on IATA international scheduled services was being carried by IATA- member airlines on all-cargo flights. This level of penetration had last been achieved in the mid-1970s.

Within Europe, however, most distances are so short that the economics of all-cargo services have never recovered from the two oil shocks of the 1970s. Today most intra-regional air freight in Europe is trucked by road. It is cheaper and faster to do it that way, especially as distances are relatively short and most major centres are within an overnight road journey of each other. Even long-haul freight may be trucked by road for the first part of its journey. British Airways, like other major European cargo operators, operates a European freight network. Trucks (generally leased in) collect freight from all over Europe, including Scandinavia and Spain, and deliver it to BA's cargo centre at Heathrow. In this way British Airways can compete with SAS in Scandinavia for freight destined for the United States or Mexico. But SAS also competes for long-haul freight in the UK market by trucking it by road to Copenhagen. Most of Europe's major cargo carriers are heavily involved in trucking. Europe's motorways are criss-crossed nightly by heavy lorries, some with flight numbers, carrying 'air' freight!

International air freight services are regulated by the same bilateral air service agreements as passenger services and broadly speaking in the same way. That is to say, traffic rights and capacity for freight and more especially for freighter services on any international air route will be constrained by the relevant bilateral agreement. Cargo tariffs are agreed through the IATA machinery and in theory approved by governments. In practice, in many key international markets, such as those between Europe and the United States, *de facto* liberalisation of air freight preceded the *de jure* loosening of regulations which occurred as a result of the open skies agreements signed by the United States during the 1990s (see Chapter 3.4–5). This was partly in response to market pressures and partly because the supply of air freight services became so varied, when the integrators expanded, and the pricing so complex and unstable that economic regulation by governments became difficult if not impossible. The capacity or frequencies offered by freighter services are still controlled in some major markets, for instance between the United States and Japan. But control of cargo tariffs is largely non-existent or ineffectual. The IATA Tariff Co-ordination Conferences still agree cargo tariffs on over 200,000 separate routes. But these tariffs bear little relevance to what is actually charged in the market place (section 11.7 below). Their prime purpose is to facilitate the interlining of cargo from one airline to another and as an aid to freight forwarders.

11.2 The key players

Historically, the looser regulation of air freight services compared with that of passenger services has led to the emergence of a fairly heterogeneous industry with several different key players. Clearly the most significant group is that made up of the conventional scheduled airlines which transport both passengers and cargo. These are the so-called *combination carriers* who offer three kinds of cargo service. They carry cargo in the freight holds of their scheduled passenger flights and some also operate scheduled all-cargo flights. A smaller number operate so-called combi aircraft. These are normally wide-bodied aircraft where part of the main upper deck as well as the belly-hold capacity is used for the carriage of freight. Combi aircraft tend to be used on routes where the demand for air freight is substantial while that for passengers is relatively thin. The combination carriers are the prime focus of the present chapter.

In addition to the combination carriers there are a few *all-cargo carriers*, who tend to operate both scheduled services and *ad hoc* charters. There used to be many more, some with well-established names such as the US cargo carrier Flying Tiger. But many collapsed following the fuel crises of the 1970s or were taken over by the integrators. The only independent, all-cargo operators of any size still operating are Cargolux, based in Luxembourg, which in 2001 was partly owned by Swissair, and the Japanese company Nippon Cargo Airlines, in which All Nippon Airways has a minority 21 per cent stake. Both of these fly primarily scheduled networks but also offer aircraft for *ad hoc* charters or for leasing. There are in addition a variety of smaller scheduled and charter all-cargo carriers such as Emery Worldwide, Evergreen or Polar Air Cargo in the United States. Some are niche carriers, operating within a particular region. One example is Channel Express in the United Kingdom.

The distinction between combination carriers and all-cargo airlines will become increasingly blurred if other airlines follow the example of Lufthansa and Singapore Airlines. Both have split off their cargo divisions as separate companies with their own accounts, but also with their own staff, pilots and fleets of freighter aircraft. In addition to operating scheduled freighter services, these cargo companies buy and pay for belly-hold capacity on passenger aircraft from the parent airline. They are a new breed of all-cargo airline.

The third group of key players are the so-called *integrators*. This is the fastest-growing and most dynamic sector of the industry. Unlike combination and all-cargo airlines which traditionally provided an airport-to-airport service with only limited collection and delivery, the integrators provide a door-to-door service. This requires the provision of road trucking for collection and delivery

Table 11.3 The world's largest international freight carriers, 2000 (million international scheduled freight tonne kilometres)

Rank	Combination carriers		All-cargo airlines		Integrated carriers	
1	Lufthansa	7,096				
2	Korean	6,357				
3	SIA	6,020				
4	Air France	4,968				
5	British Airways	4,555				
6					Federal Express	4,456
7	JAL	4,321				
8	Cathay Pacific	4,108				
9	KLM	3,964				
10			Cargolux	3,523		
11	United	2,777				
12	Northwest	2,409				
13			Nippon Cargo	2,186		
14					UPS	2,174
15	American	2,166				
16	Swissair	1,930				
17	Malaysia	1,812				
18	Alitalia	1,734				
19	Thai Airways	1,678				
20	Qantas	1,531				

Source: IATA (2001b).

Note
If domestic freight is included, Federal Express becomes by far the largest carrier.

of freight. They were also first in offering guaranteed delivery times and a pricing structure to match. Their success during the last twenty years has been such that integrators are now among the world's largest cargo carriers. In global terms, two in particular, Federal Express and United Parcel Service (UPS), are very large. There are, in addition, two medium-sized integrators, DHL and TNT, and a number of smaller regional companies.

The relevant role in the carriage of international air freight of the three key groups discussed so far can be gauged from Table 11.3. This shows the international traffic in 2000 of the world's twenty largest cargo carriers. The industry appears to be dominated by the combination carriers. Only two all-cargo operators and two integrators appear in the top twenty. The table is somewhat misleading because domestic air freight services and, in particular, the huge US domestic market are not included. Within this market, the large integrators have totally eclipsed the combination carriers. As a result, in terms of total freight, that is, scheduled plus domestic, Federal Express is by far the largest cargo carrier in the world and UPS is the fourth largest. This is why the impact of the integrators needs further examination (see section 11.4 below).

A fourth group of players consists of the postal authorities, especially those in Europe. Traditionally letters and small packets have been the domain of government post offices. Domestically and for short international services they have in the past used their own road vehicles, the railways and in some countries their own small aircraft or aircraft chartered in to operate regular overnight services. For longer international distances they handed their mail to scheduled combination carriers, usually their own country's flag carrier. Post offices continue to play a role in air freight, particularly for small parcels. Thus Royal Mail in the United Kingdom operates a fleet of over thirty small aircraft on domestic and short-haul international services. However, the laxity of international regulation of air freight, mentioned earlier, allowed the integrators to divert a growing share of the documents and small parcels business away from the national post offices. In the second half of the 1990s the post offices began to hit back. One of the first was the Canada Post Corporation when it acquired Purolator Courier Systems. In Europe, the German Deutsche Post bought a 25 per cent shareholding in DHL, in which two combination carriers, Lufthansa and Japan Airlines, also held 25 per cent each, though the Japanese airline sold its share in 2000. In September 2000 Deutsche Post AG bought a majority stake in DHL and in March 2001 assumed full control of DHL International, based in Brussels. Meanwhile, in 1996 the Dutch postal service had purchased TNT. Effectively two of the four main integrators are today controlled by national postal authorities.

Recent years have seen the emergence of a relatively new player in the international air cargo market, the *contract freighter operator*. This is the airline which operates all-cargo aircraft but primarily on behalf of other airlines, on a wet-lease contract basis. The best-known and most significant example is Atlas Air in the United States, which started flying in 1993. At the start of 2001 Atlas had a single type fleet of nearly forty Boeing 747s. These are wet-leased on an ACMI basis to combination carriers, such as British Airways, Emirates, Lan Chile and Korean Air, or less frequently to scheduled all-cargo operators, to meet their freighter requirements. Normally, these are three- to five-year contracts with a guaranteed minimum number of block hours per month. A fixed hourly charge covers aircraft, flight crew, maintenance and insurance (ACMI) costs. All other costs are met by the lessee. The ACMI charge is in US dollars and insulates Atlas from currency fluctuations. Moreover the lessor is not exposed to traffic fluctuations or drops in cargo yield, since the hourly ACMI charge is totally independent of traffic or revenue levels. Yet for the airlines ACMI contracts are attractive. They provide great flexibility in adding or reducing cargo capacity, and the low-cost structure of a specialist such as Atlas means that this capacity can be provided at rates 30 per cent or more below the airlines' own costs of providing such capacity (Shifrin, 2001). Several all-cargo operators may also lease out their aircraft on an ACMI basis, but often for shorter periods. For Atlas Air it represents 97 per cent of their business. In 2001 Atlas acquired Polar Air, which was facing difficulties because of the downturn that year in the freight market. But the intention was that Polar Air would continue as a separate company and as a traditional all-cargo carrier.

Atlas Air, in terms of international freight tonne kilometres generated, is certainly among the top five or so airlines in the world. But none of this traffic is carried in its own name. It is all on behalf of other airlines. More significant is the fact that the ACMI cargo operations appear to be the most profitable sector of the air freight industry. Atlas Air appears to be relatively free of exposure to risk. As a result its net profit margin after tax and interest in the five years to 1999 averaged over 9 per cent of revenues. Few airlines could match that. However, during the downturn in the freight market in late 2000 and 2001 Atlas was not immune. It had difficulty leasing out all its aircraft and seven of its thirty-seven Boeing 747s were grounded by August 2001. This was bound to impact on profit margins. An interesting question is whether the Atlas business model could also be applied to the passenger side of the airline business.

The final group of key players in air freight are the *freight forwarders and consolidators*. Their role parallels that of the travel agent and tour operator on the passengers side. They provide the link between the airline operator and the ultimate customer who is the shipper. Their role in this respect is discussed in a later section. But some of the larger forwarders are crossing the line and setting up their own scheduled air services. The pioneer in this trend of vertical integration was Panalpina, a large European forwarder. From the late 1980s it started wet leasing or chartering aircraft from Cargolux and others to operate scheduled services on routes of its choice, particularly on routes short of freight capacity. Some of these were entirely for its own needs, other flights were on a shared risk basis with the cargo airline or other forwarders. By the mid-1990s some other large forwarders were beginning to operate their own flights too. In 1999 Danzas, another large European forwarder, began a transatlantic operation from Hahn (Frankfurt) to Charlotte in North Carolina. In the United States, Eagle Global Logistics (EGL), a large forwarder, built up a network of freighter services in the United States, Mexico and Puerto Rico and in 2000 launched a trans-Pacific service to Taipei in Taiwan. While other US forwarders, such as Emery Worldwide or BAX Global, developed domestic air services they were initially hesitant to set up international operations. This is now changing. The attraction to freight forwarders of operating their own flights is that they can then offer a complete door-to-door service on key routes within a single company. This has two advantages: they can generate higher yields, but it is also a way of fighting back against the integrators who are trying to cut the forwarders out of the logistic chain.

11.3 The demand for air freight services

Since air freight is much more heterogeneous than are passengers there are several ways of categorising it. One may, for instance, consider the commodities being sent, or one can classify freight by the weight of individual consignments or by the speed of delivery required. As with passenger traffic, it is valuable to try to segment the freight market in terms of the motivation of the shipper rather than in terms of the product, since this has implications for the type of air freight services which need to be provided and for their pricing.

The most obvious role for air transport is the carriage of emergency freight. This includes urgently required medicines such as vaccines and spare parts for machinery or for equipment of various kinds which may be immobilised until the arrival of the replacement parts. Increasingly during the last two decades such emergency freight has involved documents of various kinds, such as business contracts or other legal papers, medical records, financial papers, articles and reports, as well as films, photographic negatives, artwork and computer tapes or disks. Many such shipments were best handled by the express parcels operators or by the companies providing courier-accompanied services. They provided the basis for the growth of the integrated air carriers discussed below. While the electronic (facsimile) transmission of documents began to undermine the traditional courier services during the 1990s, the further globalisation of trade and commerce has ensured the continued rapid growth of express cargo for the carriage of documents and small parcels.

Air is also used in emergency when surface communications become congested or are disrupted by natural or other causes or when the national postal services are slow or inadequate. In all such circumstances speed is of the essence and cost of shipment is relatively unimportant. Demand to meet emergencies is irregular, intermittent and unpredictable in volume and in the size of individual consignments. It is therefore difficult for airlines to plan for. The need of shippers for high frequencies and good last-minute space availability means that, if adequately catered for, emergency freight demand results in low freight load factors and high unit costs. On the other hand, since the demand is relatively insensitive to price, higher tariffs can be charged.

Goods with an ultra-high value in relation to their weight are also normally carried by air primarily because of the much higher security offered. Speed is important not in its own right but because it reduces the time during which the goods are at risk. Gold, jewellery, diamonds, valuable metals and rare furs or works of art fall into this category. Security is of overriding importance, while the cost of air freighting, given the value of the goods being sent, is unimportant.

Both emergency and high-value freight require a high quality of service. Shippers of such consignments normally want to reserve space on specific flights with a guarantee of on-time arrival. They demand preferential handling and clearance through customs and up-to-date information on the progress of their shipments. From this point of view, too, such freight is more costly to handle.

The majority of air freight shipments involve what is called routine freight, where the shipper's decision to use air transport is based on an assessment of available transport options and is not a response to a sudden and unexpected problem; nor is it imposed by security considerations. There are many categories of routine air freight. A simple and widely used division is into perishable and non-perishable freight. In the case of perishables, the market for the commodities being shipped is dependent on air transport. The commercial life of the products – fish, out-of-season vegetables, newspapers, newsfilm, high-fashion textiles, to name but a few – is short and the gap between producer and consumer must be bridged before that commercial life expires. Only freighting by air can do that. The freighting costs are quite high in relation to the price of the product, but they can be justified if the final consumers are prepared to pay a premium because no local substitutes are available. In the case of foodstuffs, the premium consumers are willing to pay for unusual or out-of-season produce is limited. As a result, the demand for air freight is fairly price-sensitive. For all foodstuffs being shipped by air there is a tariff level at which the demand virtually dries up because the final market price of the products is no longer attractive to consumers. Since the initial price of many foodstuffs is quite low, that critical tariff level may itself be quite low.

Airline pricing strategy then becomes crucial. To develop new flows of perishable freight, airlines may need to offer specific cargo tariffs well below prevailing levels on the routes in question. The bulk of perishable freight movements are highly seasonal, with very marked and often short-lived demand peaks followed by long periods when demand dries up completely. This happens with the movement of early grapes from Cyprus to the United Kingdom, where the period during which air freighting is viable, despite its high costs, may last only two to four weeks. After that, later grapes transported cheaply by road from Italy or France become available. More expensive air-freighted grapes from Cyprus can no longer compete in the shops. The seasonality of much routine perishable freight means that high year-round load factors are difficult to maintain. On the other hand, the demand patterns are known in advance and airlines can try to stimulate demand from other products during the off-peak periods.

Routine non-perishable freight is sent by air because the higher transport costs are more than offset by savings in other elements of distribution costs. Any one of a variety of costs may be reduced as a result of delivery by air. Documentation and insurance costs will normally be lower, but the biggest direct cost savings are to be found in packaging, ground collection, delivery and handling. These are all transport-related costs. There may also be savings in other areas from reduced stock holdings and therefore lower warehousing costs and from the lower capital tied up in goods in transit. Relatively high interest rates in some countries in recent years have made shippers and manufacturers very conscious of the high cost of maintaining large inventories. It pushed them to re-examine their logistics chain with the aim of reducing their stock holding to a minimum. This has led to the concept of 'just in time' (JIT). Air freighting is particularly suitable for JIT logistics chains because of its speed and its dependability. These indirect benefits of air freighting tend to be more marked on long-haul routes where a consignment which may take twenty to sixty days or more by sea and land may reach its destination by air in an elapsed time of two days or less. Taken together, the total distribution costs by air, including the costs of warehousing stock or of inventory in transit, should be lower than or close to those of competing modes for air to be competitive.

Routine non-perishable freight consists largely of fragile high-value goods such as delicate optical and electrical goods, clothing and machinery of various kinds, as well as semi-manufactured goods needed in various production processes such as micro-chips. These benefit not only from the higher speed but also from the increased security provided by air transport in terms of reduced damage and loss. This, together with the high value of such commodities, sometimes means air may be preferred even when its total distribution costs are not the lowest. For instance, some shippers or manufacturers may use air freight as a way of breaking into and testing new and distant markets without the need to set up expensive local warehousing and distribution systems. If they are successful, they may then switch to lower-cost surface modes.

Consignments of routine non-perishable freight tend to be regular, known in advance and often of relatively constant size. Although speed is important, small delays of a day or two in collection or delivery can be coped with by the shippers. Non-perishable freight is less price-sensitive than perishable freight because of its higher value, but it is nevertheless responsive to the total distribution costs of air transport, especially in relation to the costs of competing surface modes.

Most goods being sent by air have a high value-to-weight ratio. Since cargo rates are generally based on weight, the higher the value of an item in relation to its weight, the smaller will be the transport cost as a proportion of its final market price. Therefore the greater will be the ability of the goods to absorb the higher air transport tariffs. This tendency for high-value goods to switch to air transport is reinforced if they are also fragile and liable to damage or loss if subject to excessive handling, or if the surface journey times are very long, involving the tying up of considerable capital in transit. Consumer demand in many industrialised countries is switching more and more towards goods with high value-to-weight ratios such as cameras, video machines, home computers, calculators, expensive shoes, and so on. It is goods such as these that lend themselves to carriage by air, so the future prospects for air freight must be good. What is more important from the airline's point of view is that the countries manufacturing such goods will become the largest generators of air freight demand. This is one reason why the growth of freight traffic among South East Asian airlines has in recent years far outstripped that of other regions and why JAL, Korean, Cathay Pacific and Singapore Airlines are now among the top ten airlines in terms of international freight tonne kilometres (Table 11.3 above).

While freight can be categorised and split into market segments in terms of shippers' motivation, it remains very heterogeneous, with a wide range of different manufactured and semi-manufactured goods, raw materials and agricultural products that may have little in common. The commodity mix will vary from route to route, but some broad generalisations can be made. Worldwide, about one-third of total international air freight is composed of manufactured goods (groups 6 and 8 in the Standard International Trade Classification). These include office equipment, computers, electronic goods and components. Another one-third is machinery and transport equipment (SITC group 7), including motor vehicle parts and equipment, construction machinery, industrial machinery, communications equipment, and so on. The remaining third or so is made up of a variety of commodities, among which fresh foodstuffs and other agricultural produce, medical and pharmaceutical goods and chemicals are all relatively important. The heterogeneity of goods going by air poses numerous marketing problems for airlines, particularly when trying to identify and develop new markets.

Another aspect of this heterogeneity is that freight comes in all shapes, sizes, densities and weights. There is no standard unit or size for a freight consignment or any standard unit of space. Freight density is crucial to the economics of air freight. Cargo payload on an aircraft is limited by weight, but also by volumetric capacity. Since tariffs are based on weight, an airline can maximise freight revenue on a flight by carrying dense, heavy freight that fully utilises its weight payload. Low–density shipments may fill the cargo space with a low total weight and a lower total revenue. Surcharges are frequently applied to shipments having a density below a certain level. An airline must try to achieve an average density in its freight carrying which makes maximum use of both the volumetric capacity and the weight payload of its aircraft. Because of the variety of goods being carried, the risk is that volumetric capacity is used up before the payload capacity in terms of weight.

The difficulty of handling large numbers of relatively small individual consignments of different size, shape, weight and density created considerable pressure towards unitisation of air freight, both as a way of speeding up its handling and in order to reduce handling costs. As a result, most air freight now moves in a variety of unit load devices (ULDs), which fall into four major groups. There are various built-up or half-pallets which may be rigid or flexible. Some are no more than a rigid base with netting to cover the goods being sent. Second, there are IATA-approved lightweight fibreboard or plywood containers or boxes which fit on to full-size or half-pallets. The third group are rigid containers, which come in a number of standard sizes designed to fit into the holds of wide-bodied aircraft. These rigid airline containers now account for the larger proportion of total air freight, since much of that freight is being moved on wide-bodied passenger aircraft or freighters. Last, there are ISO intermodal-type containers which can be used only on wide-bodied freighters such as the Boeing 747F. These various unit load devices may be used and filled by the shippers or the forwarders and presented for carriage to the airline. On many routes the lower costs of handling such devices may be passed on to them through low tariffs related to particular types. The fact that much of the freight comes forward in unit load devices, each perhaps packed with a variety of different goods, perhaps originating from different shippers, is an added complexity in the marketing of air freight services.

A key characteristic of the demand for air freight is that it is unidirectional. While passengers generally fly round trips, or at least return to their origin, freight clearly does not. As a result, considerable imbalances in freight flows can arise. While freight flows on some major international freight routes such as Amsterdam to New York are more or less balanced in each direction, on most routes there is a marked imbalance. On major freight routes it is common to find that the traffic in the densest direction is twice or almost twice as great as in the reverse direction, as is the case on the Hong Kong to Tokyo or the Bangkok to Hong Kong routes. On secondary but still important freight routes the imbalances may be even more marked, with the outward flows sometimes as much as three or four times greater than the return flows, as happens on the Hong Kong to New York route.

On many routes the tonnage imbalance is aggravated by cargo-pricing policies that try to stimulate demand in the low-density direction by offering lower tariffs. The result may well be an even more marked revenue imbalance as the low tonnages in one direction end up paying the lower cargo rates. Where freight is being carried largely on passenger aircraft, weight and revenue imbalances are easier to absorb, though sometimes airlines may find themselves with inadequate belly-hold capacity in one direction. But large imbalances are particularly detrimental to the operation of all-cargo services, since they result in low overall load factors with no possibility of compensating revenue from passenger sales on relatively empty return sectors. The absence of assured return loads creates marketing and pricing problems which are unique to the cargo side of the industry.

11.4   The challenge of the integrated carriers

The biggest change in the air freight industry in the last twenty years or so has been the growth of the express parcels sector, spearheaded by Federal Express (FedEx) in the United States. Launched in 1971, this company realised that the traditional airlines were ignoring two key needs of a large segment of the potential freight market. The need was for high-speed carriage and rapid handling of small parcels, many of an emergency or crucial nature such as legal documents. The second requirement was for door-to-door service with no other intermediary. With these two product features in mind, Federal Express set up a parcels 'hub' in Memphis TN, and in effect introduced hubbing long before the passenger airlines appreciated its benefits (Chapter 10.6). Complexes of aircraft arriving in Memphis from all over the United States within an hour or so of each other in the middle of the night were able to swap their parcels and return within a couple of hours. Operating in this way, Federal Express could guarantee overnight delivery anywhere in the United States and could ensure it by running its own collection and delivery vans in the cities it served. The freight product was redefined. Instead of weight and price being the key product features, convenience, speed and reliability became the critical aspects of the product. Services were segmented and priced on the basis of speed of delivery. Already by 1990 Federal Express was offering different services, including 'Overnight Letter', 'Priority One' (delivery within the United States by 10.30 the next business day) and 'Standard Air', which offered delivery no later than the second working day. Freight forwarders and other middlemen were cut out, since bookings and all contacts were made directly with Federal Express.

The door-to-door express parcels business in the United States boomed, its growth rate outstripping that of the more traditional air freight sectors. The FedEx model was adopted by others. During the 1980s courier and parcel companies which had previously used scheduled airlines for their courier services and express deliveries, as well as road vehicles, followed the FedEx example and set up their own airline operations. A number of such integrated carriers emerged, including Emery Worldwide, Airborne Express, DHL Airways, United Parcel Services (UPS) in the United States and DHL International and TNT, which were stronger in Europe. Unlike Federal Express, they did not limit their business to parcels but accepted larger consignments as well. In time, Federal Express began to do so, too. Integrators use their own aircraft but also buy space from the scheduled passenger and freight airlines as appropriate. The essence of such integrated carriers is that they offer a total service, including pick-up and delivery, transport, customs clearance, paperwork processing, computer tracking of individual consignments and invoicing. A single system can handle all kinds of cargo worldwide and guarantee delivery within specified time periods.

In 1999 the four integrators between them operated 172 aircraft throughout Europe each night. Of these eighty-one were operated by the integrators themselves, while the remaining ninety-one were chartered from other airlines. In the following year FedEx and UPS between them were using for their worldwide operations nearly 600 owned or leased jets, of which 264 were wide-bodied (IATA, 2001b). This is a measure of the significance of the integrated carriers.

Having captured the major part of the US domestic market by the late 1980s, the integrated carriers turned to developing their international operations. In 1985 Federal Express established a European hub initially at Brussels airport, though it is now based in Paris. In June that year it began its first transatlantic service and launched its first route across the Pacific to Tokyo three years later. DHL also opened its European hub in Brussels in 1985, while UPS had earlier based its operations at Cologne–Bonn airport in Germany. This expansion abroad by US companies was accompanied by the rapid purchase of courier and road-based freight companies in many parts of the world. TNT, originally an Australian company, likewise bought up small express parcel and distribution companies as well as small airlines as a way of expanding its European network most rapidly. Initially things did not go smoothly. The US integrators faced some problems in Europe. The labour environment was different and more unionised. Frontiers created smaller markets and regulatory issues. In certain countries hostility from freight forwarders and combination carriers sometimes created further difficulties. FedEx and others had to pull back from some markets. In fact FedEx eventually focused more on trans-atlantic and long-haul services and left the intra-European market to DHL, UPS and TNT. It was not till the late 1990s that European operations had settled down and began to show real profitability.

The success of the integrated carriers in the United States can be gauged by the fact that in 1977 they had close to 4 per cent of the US domestic air cargo market. But by offering speed, on-time delivery, reliability and responsiveness the integrators have increased their share of the US market to over 60 per cent. It is estimated that integrators have a much smaller share of the *international* air cargo market – only about 6 per cent (Doganis *et al.*, 1999). On the other hand, their very high market penetration within the United States shows the degree to which they could represent a real threat to the traditional combination carriers.

A major issue facing the traditional passenger-oriented combination airlines during the first decade of the century is whether they can meet the challenge of the integrated carriers or whether they are doomed to lose much of their freight traffic. To survive the challenge they must capitalise on their major assets, which are high-frequency passenger flights to a wide variety of destinations, and combine them with a high-speed door-to-door integrated service. Lufthansa set out to be a world leader in air cargo. As part of its long-term strategy, in May 1990, together with JAL, Lufthansa joined a Japanese trading company, Nissho Iwai, in buying a share in DHL's two holding companies. This was a significant alliance, linking two of the world's top three freight airlines with a major integrated door-to-door operator, giving the airlines direct access to the fast-growing express freight market. As mentioned earlier, Deutsche Post bought control of DHL in September 2000, but Lufthansa remains a shareholder. As a result DHL enjoys a good working relationship with Lufthansa Cargo. In fact all integrators not only use their own aircraft but also send shipments on scheduled passenger flights and may buy space on all-cargo flights, often using block space agreements. Closer co-operation between integrators and combination carriers, especially when the latter are grouped into global alliances, may be a partial answer to the challenge posed by the former.

Hitherto, the freight forwarders have taken the view that the challenge to them from the expansion of the integrators was limited to the small parcels end of the market, which in any case was costly for the forwarders to handle. However, in recent years the integrators have started to go for heavier consignments, a market which the forwarders previously thought was their own. They felt that the weight and diversity of many such shipments did not lend themselves to the logistics-oriented approach of the integrators. But since 2000 the two larger integrators have both moved to acquire freight forwarders and road haulage companies as a way of accessing this market. For instance, UPS acquired Fritz Companies and FedEx bought American Freightways in the United States. Freight forwarders may increasingly be challenged in all sectors of their business.

11.5   The role of freight forwarders

The process of moving freight is considerably more complex than that of moving passengers. It involves packaging, more extensive and complex documentation, arranging insurance, collection from the shipper, customs clearance at origin and destination, and final delivery. The complexity involved has encouraged the growth of specialist freight forwarders who carry out some or all of these tasks on behalf of the shipper and provide an interface between shipper and airline. Such firms may be relatively small IATA-approved or non-IATA agents which feed their consignments directly to the airlines or to large freight consolidators. The latter will be handling freight directly for their own customers but may also be collecting and consolidating consignments from smaller agents. There is considerable fragmentation within the industry, with shippers, forwarders, consolidators and airlines all involved to varying degrees with different consignments. Such fragmentation has made the marketing and product planning of freight particularly difficult for the airlines. Any one of the chain of activities necessary to move freight by air may go wrong and undermine the total service being offered, yet the airline may have no control over the activity. The airline is also frequently torn between marketing and selling its service direct to the shipper or concentrating its selling efforts on the forwarders.

Larger forwarders and consolidators have expanded vertically to develop new markets and sources of freight, since they deal directly with the shippers, and to provide more and more services, such as ground collection and delivery, which were previously often undertaken by the airlines themselves. Large forwarders may publish their own flight schedules and tariffs. In many markets, such as UK–North America, a handful of large consolidators may come to control over half the freight being shipped. This gives them considerable market power. By consolidating numerous small shipments into large consignments they can obtain substantial bulk discounts. In other words, they buy in bulk and sell retail. On certain routes they can go even further. If the tonnage they send is high, they can play off the airlines against each other and obtain very low contract rates, particularly on routes where there is over-capacity. In this process airline freight yields are pushed down, but the ultimate shipper may not be given the full benefit of the lower rates the consolidators have squeezed out of the airlines.

On markets where there has been over-capacity, airlines have tried to stimulate total demand or to increase their market share by offering special discounted rates to large forwarders or consolidators. Large numbers of small agents have been unable to generate sufficient freight to take advantage of these special low rates. They have also been wary of consigning via large consolidators for fear of losing their customers to them. Economic pressure from smaller agents eventually led to the establishment of a new specialist, the *freight wholesaler*. They are now an important phenomenon. They buy space in bulk at rates comparable to those of the large consolidator and resell to

Table 11.4 Impact of consolidators and wholesalers on airline revenues: 500 kg
low-density consignment, London–Nairobi, 2001

	£ per kg
Tariff structure:	
Normal general cargo rate	5.32
Quantity general cargo rate for 100 kg plus	4.43
Lowest specific commodity rate (car parts)	2.50
Contract rates	0.90–1.60
Selling rates:	
Airline's contract rate to consolidator	0.90
Consolidator resale rate to forwarder	1.00
Forwarder's rate to shipper	1.20–1.50
Revenue earned:	
Shipper pays forwarder for 700 kg at, say, £1.50/kg	£1,050
Forwarder 'splits' volumetric weight with consolidator, pays 600 kg at £1.00/kg	£600
Consolidator mixes with dense cargo to lose volumetric weight penalty, pays airline 500 kg at £0.90/kg	£450
Airline revenue (£450) as percentage of shipper's payment (£1,050)	43

Note
Volumetric weight for charging: 700 kg.

smaller agents. Unlike consolidators, they do not compete directly for the
shippers' business and therefore pose no threat to their customers, the smaller
forwarders. They are simply brokers of freight capacity.

The growing concentration of freight demand in the hands of a small number
of consolidators and wholesalers created two key difficulties for the airlines
that supply freight services. First, it cut them off from the ultimate customers,
with the result that they were possibly less aware of and less responsive to
customer needs and new opportunities. Some airlines tried to overcome this
by acquiring or establishing their own freight-forwarding subsidiaries. Second,
and potentially more damaging, was the downward pressure on cargo yields
which, as mentioned earlier, resulted from the activities of consolidators or
wholesalers.

The general impact of consolidators on airline yields can be gauged from
the example of a 500 kg consignment on the London to Nairobi route
illustrated in Table 11.4. The ready availability of low contract rates on this
route in 2001, well below the lowest specific commodity rates, encouraged
consolidators and wholesalers to buy space from the airlines at these very low
rates. They then sold the space to smaller freight forwarders at a higher rate,
who in turn sold it on to shippers at an even higher rate. But the shipper was
pleased to be paying less than the published tariffs. The result was that the
airlines were often receiving less than half the monies paid by the shippers for

the transport of their goods; the balance was going to the middlemen. The dilution of freight revenue in this way clearly undermines the profitability of air freight. The growing power of these middlemen, and in particular their ability to force cargo tariffs down when and where there is spare capacity, is a continuing problem for international airlines.

World trade in non-bulk products is dominated by a few hundred companies in key sectors such as high-tech equipment, motor car manufacturing, electronic goods or pharmaceuticals. During the 1990s many of these companies began consolidating into larger enterprises with manufacturing bases in many countries and with worldwide sales. The traditional nationally based freight forwarder alone cannot meet their needs. Such large global shippers require worldwide reach and total logistic support. This may include warehousing, inventory control, packaging and despatch, multimodal collection and delivery, as well as the more traditional functions of the freight forwarder. Hitherto logistics was supplied by what were originally ground-based trucking firms such as Ryder in the United States or Exel and Danzas in Europe. In response to the changing needs of these large shippers, logistic and freight forwarding providers are merging and consolidating into larger companies to provide the global reach and total multimodal logistic support that these large shippers now require. For instance, early in 2000 the Ocean Group, parent company of MSAS, a major worldwide forwarder, merged with Exel, the largest logistics company in Britain. During a short period between 1998 and 2001 Deutsche Post bought the European logistics branch of Nedlloyd, a Dutch shipping company, the Swiss-based forwarder and trucking company Danzas and the American forwarder AEI. It also became majority shareholder in DHL. As a result of such mergers and acquisitions companies such as MSAS, Kühne & Nagel, Danzas and Panalpina are becoming truly global players.

For the airlines, these *global logistics suppliers*, as they are now called, represent really large customers, but also a threat, since they have the market power to squeeze substantial tariff discounts out of them. This will exacerbate the downward pressure on cargo yields. One response may be to tie them into joint ventures. This is what Swissair's cargo subsidiary SAirLogistics did in 1999 when it entered into a joint venture with Panalpina, though this broke up two years later, in 2001. While vertical integration and consolidation are taking place at one end of the market there are still about 4,500 IATA-accredited freight forwarding agents around the world and several thousand more who are not accredited. In particular markets or countries some of these smaller agents continue to be important.

The market power of the larger forwarding agents and global logistics suppliers can be seen in Table 11.5. This shows the share of cargo sales of the largest eight agents in each of three major international air freight markets, those of Hong Kong, Germany and Singapore, in 2000. In each of these markets the top eight agents control between one-third and half of the market. It is noticeable that certain global logistics suppliers are key players in two or three of these countries. This pattern is repeated in most of the key cargo markets.

Table 11.5 Role of major freight forwarders in key markets (Hong Kong, Germany and Singapore): IATA cargo sales, 2000

Hong Kong	%	Germany	%	Singapore	%
MSAS (Exel)	6.8	Schenker	11.5	MSAS (Exel)	12.4
Danzas	4.5	Kühne & Nagel	11.0	Danzas	10.4
Nippon Express	4.4	Panalpina	6.8	KWE-Kintetsa	7.6
Hellman	3.4	Danzas	6.8	BAX Global	6.5
Panalpina	3.4	MSAS (Exel)	5.1	Eagle Global	5.2
Expeditors	3.3	Dachser	3.0	Geologistics	5.0
Emery	2.9	Geologistics	2.3	Nippon Express	4.6
Star	2.5	ABX	2.3	Emery	3.4
Top eight	31.2	Top eight	48.8	Top eight	55.1
Others	68.8	Others	51.2	Others	44.9
Total	100.0	Total	100.0	Total	100.0

Source: Compiled by the author using IATA (2001b).

Note
Sales are those made through the IATA Clearing System (CASS).

11.6   The economics of supply

In assessing the economics of carrying air freight and, in particular, the degree to which it is a profitable business, a major dilemma is how combination carriers should allocate costs between passengers and cargo. The problem arises because so many costs are joint costs and are not specific to the carriage of either passengers or freight. For instance, while cabin crew costs are specific to passengers and are needed only if an aircraft is carrying passengers, the costs of the flight crew are joint costs. The pilots are needed to fly the passengers, but, in the process, capacity is also generated for the carriage of freight. Another joint cost is airport landing fees, which are calculated on the basis of an aircraft's maximum take-off weight (MTOW) and are independent of what is actually being transported. The issue of cost allocation arises primarily when freight is carried in passenger aircraft, or in combi aircraft. The latter are aircraft whose main passenger deck is not used solely for passengers but where part is separated off as a main deck cargo compartment.

11.6.1   Belly-hold capacity

Slightly over half of international air freight travels in the belly holds of the passenger aircraft. Traditionally combination carriers have regarded it as a by-product arising from the supply of passenger services. Provided freight revenues covered those costs, such as ground handling, cargo sales and marketing, or extra fuel burn, which could be directly attributed to the carriage of freight, any revenue in excess of such costs made a contribution to offsetting the costs of passenger services. The significance of this contribution can be gauged from the fact that in 2001 British Airways estimated that close to 60 per cent of its freight revenues on passenger flights went to cover freight-related costs, while the balance of 40 per cent could be used to cover the other costs which would be incurred whether or not freight was carried on the aircraft. Inevitably, on this basis, belly-hold freight appears to British Airways and others to make a valuable contribution to airline profitability.

The by-product approach to costing, however, leaves open the question of whether freight should bear its share of other costs. Should the major costs of operating a flight be considered as joint costs which need to be split and allocated in some way to both passengers and freight? This argument is strengthened by the fact that the lower freight decks of wide-bodied aircraft have possible alternative uses as galleys or lounges. Freight must at least cover the opportunity cost of foregoing these alternative uses. One could also argue that the shape, size and capacity of wide-bodied aircraft have been influenced by the requirement to carry cargo in the belly hold and that therefore cargo must share all the aircraft-related and direct costs. However, the allocation of joint costs inevitably involves some arbitrariness. The International Air Transport Association's Cost Committee recommends that the profitability of air cargo on passenger and combi aircraft can be truly assessed only after all operating costs have been fully allocated between cargo and passengers. This should be done on the following basis:

1   *Direct operating costs* should be apportioned on the basis of the usable volume of the aircraft allocated to each. These direct costs include the costs of fuel, of flight crews, aircraft maintenance, weight landing fees and aircraft standing charges, that is, depreciation or lease rentals as well as airframe insurance (see Chapter 4.3). While IATA recommends that these should be allocated on the basis of volumetric capacity as between passengers and freight, one could use other allocative criteria. For instance, direct operating costs could be allocated in proportion to the revenue generated by the two traffics. In practice, allocation is most widely based on volume.

2   *Cargo-specific or passenger-specific costs* should be separately identified and allocated as appropriate. They include most, but not all, of the indirect operating costs. On the cargo side, specific costs include those associated with cargo sales and marketing, the collection and delivery of consignments, ground handling and warehousing, airport cargo charges and cargo insurance, as well as the administrative costs of the cargo department. On the passenger side one would need to include the costs of ticketing, sales and reservations, of cabin crews, ground handling and ground staff, passenger-related station expenses, passenger insurance, the costs of in-flight catering, airport passenger fees, and so on.

3   *Administration and other indirect overhead costs* should be split between passengers and cargo in proportion to the sum of all the other costs (i.e. 1 + 2 above).

If joint costs are allocated in this way, the carriage of belly-hold freight becomes marginal or unprofitable. In most markets belly-hold freight fails to cover its fully allocated costs. Nevertheless, the carriage of such freight on some individual routes, such as Europe to/from East Asia, may still be highly profitable. An increasing number of airlines, Air France among them, do their cargo costing in this way. But many, particularly smaller carriers, still prefer to think of belly-hold cargo as a profitable by-product making a significant contribution to overall revenue, rather than as a marginal or loss-making joint product.

From both the suppliers' and the consumers' points of view, belly-hold freight offers numerous advantages. It is certainly low-cost if costed on a by-product basis. The higher frequency of passenger services is attractive to shippers, particularly for emergency-type freight, and they are prepared to pay a premium for the better service. This, together with the fact that passenger aircraft tend to carry a higher proportion of small consignments which do not get bulk or quantity discounts, means that average freight yields from belly-hold freight on most routes are generally higher than average yields on freighters.

11.6.2   Combi aircraft

There are routes where the enormous payload of wide-bodied aircraft in all-cargo configuration is too large for the freight demand, while belly-hold capacity may be insufficient or unable to cope with bulky consignments. In such circumstances the wide-bodied combi aircraft, on which both passengers and freight are carried on the main deck, may prove a commercially attractive proposition. By adjusting the main deck space allocated to passengers or freight in response to the demand mix and seasonal variations on each route, total revenue can be maximised. For instance, at times of peak passenger demand the whole cabin may be used for passengers.

In a combi operation the allocation of joint costs to the freight side is essential. Freight revenue must be seen to cover its share of capacity costs, since without freight on the main deck the passenger service would use a smaller aircraft or a lower frequency and reduce its total costs. This means that freight pricing must move towards a full cost-recovery basis rather than be based on the by-product pricing strategy that might be adopted for belly-hold freight. Market conditions will determine whether it can be done. The method of allocation varies between airlines, but a small number of airlines – KLM and Air France among them – have done the exercise and have convinced themselves of the commercial advantages of combi aircraft. During the 1990s Air France, one of the largest freight operators, was carrying as much as 35 per cent of its total freight traffic in combi aircraft. Another 55 per cent went in freighters and only 10 per cent went on passenger aircraft. However, the current trend is for combi aircraft to play a diminishing role in the carriage of air freight.

For combi aircraft the allocation of joint costs on the basis of volumetric capacity is relatively simple. On a Boeing 747-300 with space on the main passenger deck for six pallets or containers and with seating reduced from 410 to 360, the volumetric breakdown would be as follows:

Passenger capacity: 360 at 36.1 ft³/passenger = 12,996 ft³, or 65.4%

Cargo capacity: six pallets plus belly-hold = <u>6,867 ft³ or 34.6%</u>

Total = 19,863 ft³ = 100.0%

So cargo would need to cover 34.6 per cent of the joint direct operating costs, plus its own specific costs and a share of the small administrative and indirect overheads.

A few airlines, Lufthansa, SAS and SIA among them, have separated out their cargo operations as stand-alone businesses. Once this has been done the question of joint costs on passenger or combi aircraft has to be resolved head-on. Lufthansa Cargo or SIA Cargo, which was launched as SIA's largest subsidiary in July 2001, operate their own freighters with their own flight crew and do all the cargo selling and handling within their own facilities and cargo warehouses. Costing all this is not a problem. But they also need to buy space on their parent companies' passenger flights. This now has to be done on a fully costed basis. In SIA's case, SIA Cargo buys belly-hold space at a price which reflects joint costs allocated on the basis of the volumetric capacity dedicated to cargo. This space has to be paid for by SIA Cargo. With cargo costs made explicit and real, it will be easier to assess the true profitability of carrying cargo on passenger flights.

11.6.3 All-cargo aircraft

The major economic advantage of the freighter is that it increases its payload by half or more compared with the same aircraft in a passenger configuration. By stripping out unnecessary passenger-related facilities, thereby saving weight, a Boeing 747 freighter may carry a cargo payload of 100–110 t; the same aircraft with a main passenger deck and belly-hold freight has a typical payload of around 60–67 t. In theory, the greater payload should reduce the direct operating costs per tonne kilometre of freighters by up to one-third or more. In practice, the cost differential between fully allocated costs on freighters and cargo on passenger aircraft appears to be less. According to IATA, in 1998 cargo on freighters cost 14 per cent less per available tonne kilometre than cargo carried on IATA-member airlines' passenger or combi aircraft (Table 11.6). In 1999 the differential had narrowed to 6 per cent as direct operating costs on passenger aircraft were reduced.

The full costs of carrying freight on all-cargo aircraft can readily be identified so that, in theory, tariff strategies could be adopted to ensure that revenues exceeded costs. In practice, over-capacity and competition have meant

Table 11.6 Cost and yield comparison for cargo on passenger/combi services and on freighters, 1998–99

Cost and yield	1998	1999
Total cost[a] (cents per available ATK):		
Passenger/combi aircraft	18.8	17.3
All cargo aircraft	16.2	16.3
All cargo costs as % pax/combi	86	94
Yield (cents per revenue tonne-kms):		
Passenger/combi aircraft	25.5	22.7
All cargo aircraft	22.7	21.7
All cargo yield as % pax/combi	89	96

Source: Compiled using IATA (2000).

Note
a Total cost is operating cost plus interest.

that tariffs are market-based rather than cost-based. Moreover, yields on all-cargo freight, much of it travelling at bulk discount or contract rates, have been appreciably lower than those from freight on passenger aircraft. As a general rule, airlines have found that yields from all-cargo services are around 5–10 per cent or so lower than the yields achieved from the carriage of freight on passenger aircraft (Table 11.6), though it varies significantly between different markets. As a result, where airlines have managed to sustain high load factors on freighter services, such services have proved profitable.

The factors which appear to be necessary to ensure the continued viability of long-haul freight services are a high level of demand, preferably from both ends of a route, an insufficient volume of cargo space on passenger aircraft and some limit on the provision of all-cargo services. In many long-haul markets limitation is being achieved by the third- and fourth-freedom carriers operating freighter services jointly rather than in competition. This is done by SIA and British Airways between London and Singapore and by SIA and Lufthansa on their Singapore–Germany services. Such joint operations avoid over-provision of freighter capacity, which tends to undermine cargo rates. The North Atlantic is one of the least profitable of the long-haul routes, largely because there is too much capacity available. Conversely, the more limited freighter services between Europe and East Asia and the high demand levels from East Asia to Europe have ensured reasonable profits for many all-cargo operations in this market. The high value of the Japanese yen has also contributed.

The danger of over-capacity is present in all markets and in consequence many airlines are loath to operate freighter aircraft, preferring to concentrate on carrying belly-hold cargo. Yet there is clearly a role for the freighter. Many carriers will continue to operate freighters as a necessary adjunct to their overall freight operations. They need them to provide a better overall service for their customers by using them to transport the 10 per cent or so of freight that is too large or dangerous for belly holds as well as the larger consolidations. All-cargo schedules can also be geared to the needs of shippers. On some routes, where the demand for passengers is thin, belly-hold capacity may in any case be insufficient to meet cargo needs. This may also be so on routes where payload or range restrictions reduce the effective cargo capacity on passenger flights. The introduction of very long non-stop passenger flights with Boeing 747-400 or other aircraft has resulted in the loss of belly-hold cargo capacity on routes where the extra fuel required for non-stop sectors necessitates cutbacks in the freight payload that can be uplifted. When in the mid-1990s airlines began replacing Boeing 747s with smaller twin-engine aircraft, such as the Boeing 767, on long-haul routes there was again a reduction in belly-hold cargo capacity, creating a need in some markets for more freighters.

11.7   The pricing of air freight

11.7.1   Structure of cargo tariffs

The structure of cargo tariffs is very complex. This is because there exists a wide range of publicly available tariffs in parallel with a host of confidential tariffs agreed between airlines and their larger individual customers. As with passenger fares, the published international cargo tariffs have traditionally been agreed by the airlines through IATA and subsequently approved by governments, though the latter is a formality. With the spread of liberalisation, and with over-capacity in many markets, IATA cargo tariffs have tended to become less significant worldwide. Nevertheless they are negotiated by IATA's Tariff Co-ordination Conferences every two years. These IATA tariffs provide the basis for the interlining of freight between carriers, though there is not much of this, and also act as the basic rates which the public or an individual shipper sees. In many instances shippers may be charged the IATA rate by the freight forwarder, who will actually be paying the airline a much lower negotiated rate.

The European Commission's Directorate General of Competition has long felt that fixing cargo tariffs through IATA was anti-competitive. As a result of a 2001 agreement between the Commission and IATA the latter agreed to discontinue the joint setting of rates for the air transport of freight within the European Economic Area (EEA) as from February 2002. Tariffs between EEA states and third countries continued to be negotiated through IATA. These publicly available cargo rates are composed of several different categories.

The majority of international city pairs involving major and secondary cities have an IATA *general cargo rate*. Like all air freight rates it is expressed as a rate per kilogram and there may be a minimum charge per consignment. An examination of general cargo rates around the world shows that the rate per kilometre tapers with route distance. But the taper, which in theory is cost-related, is neither regular nor always evident. In addition there are significant variations in the general cargo rate for each direction on the same route. Thus the general rates from African points south of the Sahara to Europe have traditionally been as low as two-thirds or less of the rates for cargo originating in Europe. Similar north–south imbalances in rate levels have also existed on air routes between North and South America. For instance, in 2000 the general cargo rate from Buenos Aires to Los Angeles was 40 per cent lower than the return rate from Los Angeles. Such rate variations have clearly been aimed at reducing the imbalances in freight flows and more particularly at generating more northbound traffic. IATA tariffs are expressed in the local currency of the originating point. If this happens to be devalued the rate imbalance in each direction will clearly worsen.

On most routes, tariffs are available which will be lower than the normal general cargo rate. First, there may be *quantity general cargo rates* where the rate per kilogram decreases as the size of the consignment increases beyond certain agreed weight break points. While most routes may have only one or two quantity rates, 45 kg and 100 kg are common break points, routes to and from the United States tend to have many more break points with successively lower rates as consignment weight increases.

While the quantity general cargo rates encourage consolidation into large consignments they fail to stimulate the air freighting of particular goods or commodities. This is done by *specific commodity rates*, which are individual low rates for specific and clearly defined commodities. Some routes may have only one or two commodity rates while others may have forty or more. Such rates will reflect and encourage the types of goods most likely to be sent by air on each route and in a particular direction. Many commodity rates also include quantity discounts with lower rates as consignment size increases. The level of the commodity rates varies widely but on occasions they may be as low as 40 per cent or less of the general cargo rate.

The third type of discount rates consists of those related to particular unit load devices, known as *ULD rates*. Such rates are not available in all markets. There is a fixed minimum charge per unit load device which declines proportionally as the size of the pallet or container increases. The minimum charge is for a given weight for each type of unit load device, known as the *pivot weight*. If the contents of the unit load device weigh more than the pivot weight there is a charge per kilogram for each kilogram above that weight. The ULD rates are normally lower than the quantity general rates or most of the specific commodity rates. Their aim is to encourage shippers and forwarders to pack as much into the unit load devices as possible. Moreover, by mixing shipments of different weight and density in a container, one can reduce the average cargo rate paid to the airline. The aim of unit load device rates is also to encourage shippers to use containers or other unit load devices which, from an airline's viewpoint, are easier and cheaper to handle than disparate consignments.

A somewhat different category of cargo tariffs are the so-called *class rates*, which involve a reduction (for unaccompanied baggage or newspapers) or a surcharge (for gold or human remains, for example) on the general commodity rate. They have been applied to certain commodities whose carriage calls for special treatment. Only a very small proportion of freight travels at these class rates.

For major cargo carriers such as British Airways as little as 5 per cent or less of their freight is carried at the published IATA rates. This share will be higher for smaller airlines such as Olympic or Philippine which traditionally have not attached much importance to air freight. Most of the freight is carried at tariffs which are negotiated directly with freight forwarders and are not publicly available. Many airlines will have a special *account-holder tariff* or something similar for their customers. These are tariffs with a similar structure to the IATA tariffs, that is, with quantity break points and ULD rates. They are lower than the published IATA rates but generally higher than the prevailing market rates. They are made available to freight forwarders who generate sufficient business to be regular account holders. Each airline will offer its own rates to these regular account holders. Though not public, such account-holder tariffs are known to agents and available to most freight forwarders.

The lowest rates, often reflecting the prevailing market rates on any route, are the *contract rates* negotiated directly between individual airlines and customers prepared to guarantee a minimum tonnage of freight over a given period. A large cargo airline may find that the fifteen to twenty largest global freight for-warders, such as Danzas or MSAS, with offices around the world, generate two-thirds or more of its business. These, together with very large forwarders in individual countries, can negotiate individual contract rates. The growing market power of freight forwarders and the competitive pressure on airlines to sell excess capacity has created a situation on the North Atlantic, on the North Pacific and some other routes where very low contract rates dominate the market and where freight pricing bears little relevance to published IATA tariffs. Contract rates may fall to 20 per cent or less of the general cargo rate. In addition, to attract and keep business from freight forwarders with offices in many countries, airlines will often offer incentives in the form of rebates payable at the end of each year if the total business generated exceeds certain agreed levels.

Finally, in order to fill anticipated spare capacity in certain markets and at particular times, airlines may offer *spot prices*. These are the cheapest rates and are available to all comers, usually within the last two weeks before the departure dates.

In recent years, as a response to the challenge posed by the integrators with their door-to-door logistic chains and guaranteed delivery times, a few airlines have launched time-definite cargo products and *time-definite rates*. The aim is to increase yields and margins both by offering collection and delivery and by guaranteeing delivery within specified elapsed times. Whereas traditional cargo products focus on flight schedules and flight departure times, in marketing time-definite (td) services the focus is on the total elapsed journey time, from collection to delivery. That is all that concerns the forwarder or the shipper. In Europe time-definite pricing was pioneered by Lufthansa Cargo. In April 1998 it launched three time-definite products: 'td.Flash', which guaranteed delivery within twenty-four hours, 'td.X', with delivery within forty-eight hours, and 'td.Pro' for delivery within seventy-two to ninety-six hours. The tariffs were obviously higher for the faster services. Within a year of the launch Lufthansa claimed that around 20 per cent of its standard cargo was travelling on time-definite rates and that the average yield from time-definite freight was 30 per cent higher than from other cargo (Kraus, 1999). A few other conventional airlines, such as SAS and Singapore Airlines, have also introduced similar time-definite services and tariffs. Collection and delivery are normally contracted out to specialist trucking firms.

11.7.2 Pricing strategies

The preceding review of the structure of cargo tariffs suggests that they bear only a tenuous relation to cargo costs. Different commodities on the same route may be charged at widely different rates with no marked differences apparent in the costs of handling and freighting them. General cargo rates vary markedly between sectors of similar length being operated with similar aircraft. Rates on the same route differ in each direction. The taper of rates per kilometre with distance is neither consistent nor closely related to costs. While IATA and some airlines have tried to dress up the cargo tariffs as being somehow cost-related, there can be little doubt that the underlying philosophy, especially for commodity rates, is ultimately 'charging what the traffic will bear', that is, market-oriented pricing. Such a pricing strategy was encouraged by the by-product view of air cargo. As a by-product of passenger services the carriage of freight appeared to impose low additional costs and any revenue in excess of these low costs made a contribution to the overall profitability of the services.

It could be argued that market pricing is discriminatory, since it entails charging some shipments more than the costs they impose and others less. This is undoubtedly the case, but it is difficult to see how market pricing could be avoided, given the nature of the air freight market. It has two distinctive characteristics which bedevil any attempt to establish cost-related tariffs. First, the existence of freight consolidators and wholesalers not only cuts the airlines off from their true customers and distorts the pricing mechanism but also gives such large freight agents considerable market power. Second, the carriage of freight is inherently more competitive even in regulated markets than is the carriage of passengers. This is because most freight, except emergency freight, is indifferent to the routeing it is offered from its origin to its destination. A shipper is unconcerned whether his shipment goes from New York to Lisbon on a direct flight or via Amsterdam or Frankfurt or Copenhagen, even with a six-hour transshipment at one of those airports, provided it gets to Lisbon within the expected time. Few passengers would put up with circuitous and lengthy journeys. Thus in most cases there are numerous routeings (and airlines) that freight can use to get to its destination. This ensures a degree of inter-airline competition which may be absent for passengers on the same routes. If one superimposes on these market characteristics the availability on most air services of surplus belly-hold capacity, any attempts to establish cost-related cargo tariffs will inevitably be futile. Airlines have little choice but to pursue a strategy of setting rates aimed at maximising revenue. In prevailing market conditions on most major routes this means charging what the traffic will bear.

In an environment of market-oriented pricing, where consolidators and wholesalers have had a major influence on freight tariffs, and where combination carriers are losing market share to the integrators, it seems inevitable that tariffs will increasingly move towards a three-tier pricing structure related to the speed of delivery. The level of charges within such a structure will of course reflect market conditions in each market or route. They will be highest where the demand for freight capacity exceeds the demand.

11.7.3 Freight yields

The prevailing cargo tariff levels in the major markets served by an airline and that airline's traffic mix are clearly the major determinants of an individual airline's freight yields, that is, the average revenue actually received per tonne kilometre carried. Other factors also impact on yields. Particularly important is the degree to which the general cargo rates have been eroded by the introduction of low specific commodity rates and ultimately by contract or other deep discount rates. This will be determined by market conditions, notably the availability of spare capacity and the degree of inter-airline competition. Consignment mix in terms of the size of various shipments is important in determining the rates paid to the airline. The length of haul of those consignments also impacts on yields, since cargo rates per kilometre tend to decline with distance. Similar factors will also affect the freight yields achieved in various parts of an airline's network.

The wide range of freight yields obtained in different geographical areas by member airlines of IATA in 1999 is illustrated in Table 11.7. It shows that, on passenger and combi aircraft, the lowest yields in 1999 were being achieved where there was most over-capacity, most notably on the North Atlantic. While the yield on North Atlantic freighters appears comparable to that on other long-haul markets, one would expect it to be markedly higher, given that many individual routes across the Atlantic are significantly shorter than, say, trans-Pacific routes. Once again, over-capacity and competition appear to be the cause. Conversely, on the very long trans-Pacific routes average yields appear to be high on both passenger aircraft and freighters. It is also evident that on the relatively short European routes, where much air freight goes by road, yields are exceptionally high. This suggests that much of the international air freight within Europe is composed of relatively small and high-rated consignments, often of an emergency nature. Yields are also high on routes within Asia, partly because of the shorter distances, but partly, too, because capacity is more limited.

Table 11.7 Freight cargo yields in selected markets, 1999 (US cents per revenue tonne kilometre)

Market	Pax or combi	Freighters
Long-haul:		
North and mid-Pacific	23.0	22.6
Europe/Middle East to Far East	22.0	20.5
South Atlantic	21.2	20.2
Europe/Middle East to South East Asia	17.7	16.2
North Atlantic	14.5	22.9
Short/medium haul:		
Within Europe	51.2	36.7
Within Far East	41.9	38.5

Source: Compiled by the author using IATA 2000.

Table 11.8 Freight yields of European airlines on the North Atlantic, 1999

Airline	Cents per freight tonne-kms
Aer Lingus	33.87
Air Portugal	24.02
Austrian	23.25
Malev	21.83
SAS	20.85
Turkish Airlines	20.01
Iberia	18.08
Air France	16.27
Alitalia	15.54
Average European airlines	*14.00*
British Airways	12.75
Lufthansa	12.49
Swissair	9.36

Source: Compiled by the author from Association of European Airlines data.

The average freight yields individual airlines achieve will depend on several factors, but three are crucial. First, the degree to which they operate all-cargo aircraft, since yields on them tend to be lower. Second, the markets they are operating in and the degree of competition, but also the sector lengths over which they are flying cargo, since shorter sectors tend to produce higher yields because tariffs per kilometre are higher. Finally, the mix of cargo carried, particularly the balance between smaller, higher-yielding shipments and large bulkier consignments normally travelling on the lowest contract rates. If an airline has high time-definite rates for cargo requiring rapid delivery this too will have an impact on its average cargo yields.

It is variations in these key factors that explain why freight yields on the same route may vary so much between airlines (Table 11.8). It is noticeable that in 1999 the highest freight yields on the North Atlantic among European carriers were being obtained by airlines on the geographical periphery of Europe facing less direct competition from the big cargo operators, from high-frequency passenger flights or from all-cargo services. These included Aer Lingus, Air Portugal and SAS. Conversely yields were very low for the major cargo carriers operating in the largest and most competitive markets, who were fighting for market share by using their road trucking services to feed their hubs and who had enormous amounts of capacity to fill. This was either because of the very high frequency of their passenger flights across the Atlantic or because they were operating freighters or because of both. The four biggest cargo operators, British Airways, Lufthansa, Air France and Swissair, who together generate around two-thirds of North Atlantic cargo carried by European airlines, all had very low cargo yields. It is unlikely that their transatlantic operations, if fully costed, were profitable at such low yields. Competition appears to have pushed them too low.

As a general rule, yields per freight tonne kilometre are less than half the revenues generated from passengers when converted into a yield per passenger tonne kilometre. In 1999 the average yield per passenger tonne kilometre on the international scheduled services of IATA-member airlines was 82.1c. The average freight yield was 21.8c per tonne kilometre, equivalent to 27 per cent of the passenger yield (IATA, 2000). Ten years earlier it had been 34 per cent. The imbalance in yields is worsening, since over time freight yields have fallen faster than passenger yields. The relatively low freight yields explain why freight represents close to one-third (29 per cent) of airline production worldwide but generates only one-eighth of airline revenues (Table 1.4). Inevitably the airlines very heavily involved in air freighting, such as Lufthansa or Air France, will have overall yields (for passenger and freight traffic combined) which are lower than those of passenger-dominated airlines.

11.8 Marginal profitability

For combination carriers as a whole the overall profitability of air freight appears questionable. This is especially so if one allocates joint costs on passenger and combi aircraft to freight on the basis of volumetric capacity, as suggested by IATA. If this is done, the performance of air freight during the 1990s is fairly dismal. Between 1990 and 1993 cargo, like other sectors of aviation, was adversely affected by the cyclical downturn in the world's key economies. Though there were exceptions, the carriage of freight, whether in passenger or combi aircraft or on freighters, was generally unprofitable. According to the IATA Cost Committee, average yields were well below unit costs for both types of air cargo (Figure 11.1). In other words the operating ratio was below 100 per cent. As the world's economies began to improve after 1993, the carriage of cargo on freighters became profitable again. But the profit margin, as expressed by the operating ratio, was very low, generally 1–3 per cent (Figure 11.1). Only in 1995 did it exceed 5 per cent. However,

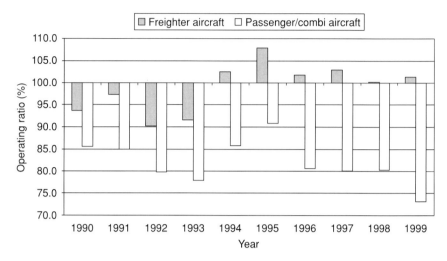

Figure 11.1 Operating ratio for freight on passenger or combi aircraft and on freighters. The operating ratio is profit or loss as a percentage of revenue.
Source: Compiled by Cranfield College of Aeronautics from IATA (2000).

freight on passenger and combi aircraft, if bearing its fully allocated costs as recommended by IATA, was unable to generate profits. On the contrary, even in the good years of the late 1990s the yields from belly-hold or combi freight was 15 per cent or more below cost.

Freight is no different from passengers. Its profitability depends on the interplay and balance of the same three variables, namely unit costs, unit revenue or yield and the load factor achieved. One of the reasons why freight on passenger/combi aircraft appears to be so unprofitable is that its load factors are too low. An analysis of air cargo results in 1999 for IATA airlines shows this clearly. In that year the operating ratio for cargo on passenger and combi aircraft was on 73.2 per cent. In other words, revenues were almost 27 per cent below costs. On the other hand, cargo on freighters was marginally profitable, with an operating ratio of 101.4 per cent. Yet, as was evident earlier (Table 11.6 above), unit costs and average yields for freight on passenger/ combi aircraft were only marginally higher than those for freight on all–cargo aircraft. As a result, the break-even load factors for the two types of freight were very similar, at around 74 per cent. But what undermines the profitability of freight on passenger/combi aircraft is the appallingly low load factors being achieved. In 1999 it was only 54 per cent, that is, twenty percentage points below the break-even load required.

Such low load factors for freight on passenger aircraft are inevitable. Passenger aircraft generate some cargo capacity on all the routes they operate, irrespective of the level of demand for freight on each route. Most airlines operate many passenger routes where demand for freight is minimal, yet the freight capacity is substantial either because flight frequencies are high or because wide-bodied aircraft are being used. Since such excess or unwanted freight capacity is included when calculating the overall load factor (and total allocated costs) for freight on passenger/combi aircraft it inevitably deflates the load factors to unprofitable levels. Put simply, an airline's cargo manager must try to balance unit costs, yield and load factor, yet has no effective control over capacity so as to push up the load factors. An impossible task, since much of his cargo capacity is generated by the demands of the passenger side of the business.

Nevertheless, there are clearly many individual routes, with strong demand for air freight in both directions, where cargo load factors on passenger and combi aircraft are sufficiently high to cover fully allocated costs. Such routes include many sectors between Europe and the Far East and certain trans-Pacific routes.

Overall, the profitability of freight is also linked with the costing approach adopted. IATA recommends the full allocation of joint costs between passengers and freight in proportion to the volumetric capacity used by each. It is on this basis that in general freight on passenger/combi aircraft appears to be so unprofitable for many airlines. But many airlines, including British Airways, consider belly-hold freight as a *by-product* of passenger services rather than as a *joint product*. They assess freight in terms of its contribution to total revenue on their passenger services, after deducting from the freight revenue all costs specific to the cargo side. On this basis, belly-hold freight appears to make a valuable contribution to the overall profitability of many routes. Cargo managers tend to prefer this approach.

Scheduled freighter services, whether operated by combination carriers or by integrators, are more likely to be profitable, in large part because it becomes easier to match the capacity provided with the demand in particular markets. Load factors can be pushed up, since they can be influenced directly by an airline's cargo managers and salesmen. Apart from competition from other carriers, the major difficulty they may face in achieving adequate load factors arises from the imbalance in freight flows in each direction on the same route. Very high loads in one direction may be offset by negligible flows in the return direction. Where loads are good in both directions and the supply of freighters by all carriers is not too great it should be possible to achieve good load factors and good yields. Market conditions have a major impact on the profitability of all-cargo services. While such operations in general appear to be marginally profitable, results vary considerably both between major markets or routes and between airlines operating freighter services.

It is noticeable that, historically, the profit margins of integrated freight carriers such as UPS or FedEx have been much higher than the margins achieved by the traditional combination carriers or the all-cargo airlines such as Cargolux. Thus in the year 2000 both these integrators generated much higher operating profits in proportion to the freight they carried than either Lufthansa, the largest freight operator among combination carriers, or Cargolux, the largest all-cargo operator (Table 11.9). This discrepancy in results arises because, by offering a door-to-door service, the integrators provide much more added value

Table 11.9 Profitability of different types of freight carriers, 2000

Type of carrier	Freight tonne-kms (million)ᵃ	Operating profit ($ million)
Integrators:		
UPS	6,336	4,512
FedEx	11,389	999
Combination carrier:		
Lufthansa Cargo	7,666	200
All-cargo airline:		
Cargolux	3,813	36

Source: Compiled by the author using *Air Transport World*, July 2001.

Note
a Includes domestic (unlike Table 11.3 above).

and can charge substantially more for their services, especially those offering guaranteed and fast delivery. This is why the cargo subsidiaries of airlines such as Lufthansa and Singapore Airlines are focusing increasingly on the provision of door-to-door and time-definite services.

11.9   Future prospects

Air freight is very sensitive to the prevailing economic climate. Past experience suggests that the demand for air freight has an income or GDP elasticity of 2 or slightly more. That is to say, a 1 per cent growth in the world's gross domestic product in one year produces a 2.0–2.5 per cent growth in air trade. A decline in GDP would produce a corresponding drop in demand for air freight. Consequently, even before the terrorist attacks in the United States in September 2001 and the subsequent war in Afghanistan, the air freight market was suffering as major economies began slowing down. Whereas 2000 had been a good year, with overall freight traffic up by 7–8 per cent and yields rising marginally, a serious downturn was apparent by mid-2001. This was due not only to the deteriorating economic climate but more especially to the decline in high-technology sectors which followed the collapse of Internet-related and high-tech shares in March 2000. Trade in high-tech products, including computers and telecommunications equipment, which accounts for a quarter or more of air freight, had dropped dramatically by mid-2001. This hit outbound freight volumes from East Asia to Europe and North America, traditionally two of the strongest freight flows. During 2001 the worsening economic climate began to affect other key types of air freight such as car parts and high-value clothing. By the end of 2001 the economic downturn in the United States and Japan had turned into a recession, inevitably affecting other key economies in Europe and East Asia. If the pattern of the early 1990s was to repeat itself it was unlikely that the air freight business would recover before 2003 or 2004.

On the other hand, the long-term prospects of air freight appear to be good. This is precisely because of its dependence on the world's economic climate. All long-term economic forecasts predict that world GDP will grow on average 2.0–2.5 per cent each year during the decade 2001–10 despite any short-term downturns such as those in 2001–02. This means that air freight should grow during the decade at a long-term rate of 5–6 per cent per annum. In brief, the air freight industry is faced with short-term uncertainty but long-term promise.

There are several challenges to be faced. The traditional view that combination airlines are involved in supplying two joint products, the carriage of passengers and the carriage of freight, which are inextricably entwined, will progressively be replaced by the belief that they are two quite distinct products. These two products manifest demand patterns which differ both geographically, in terms of routes, and temporally in terms of seasons and timings. They require airlines to offer different service and product features which are marketed and sold through separate and different distribution channels. They are two quite separate businesses, and as both are developed further the differences between them will become more pronounced and apparent. Certain sectors of the airline industry have known this for a long time. In Europe and elsewhere, the charter airlines have focused almost exclusively on carrying passengers. Though they inevitably generate cargo capacity on their passenger charter flights, with few exceptions they have not entered the freight business. For the low-cost no-frills airlines carrying freight is also anathema, since it would screw up their economics, which are dependent on fast turn-rounds and minimal ground handling. On the other side of the business, the integrated carriers have also seen the advantages of product specialisation – in their case on freight only.

As a result of both economic and operational pressures to separate the two businesses there is likely to be growing polarisation among combination carriers in their approach to freight. At one end there will be airlines such as Ethiopian Airlines, Air Portugal or the Polish airline LOT, which will basically see themselves as primarily passenger carriers. Such airlines will not view freight as a key part of their business, in which they are prepared to invest substantial resources or effort. They will carry some belly-hold freight but will treat it as a by-product, one hopefully making a contribution to the passenger side, not as a separate business in its own right. Less than 20 per cent of their revenue tonne kilometres will be generated by freight as opposed to passengers, and freight will produce less than 10 per cent of total revenues. Moreover in the course of time both these percentages will be depressed further. Inevitably these airlines' share of the freight traffic on the routes they operate will also decline.

At the other end of the spectrum will be a few airlines who see freight as a major and potentially profitable business activity with its own needs and requirements – but an activity sufficiently different from the passenger side of their business to merit separate treatment. These airlines will increasingly follow the example of Lufthansa, SAS, SIA and others and establish their cargo operations as separate and independent subsidiary companies. The latter will operate their own freighter aircraft with their own flight crew and will undertake all their own marketing, selling, ground handling, warehousing, administration, and so on. They will buy and pay for belly-hold capacity as required from their parent passenger airline. Some may be floated on the stock exchange, with the parent airline retaining some shares, or they may be sold off entirely.

Lufthansa started this trend in 1995 when it split off Lufthansa Cargo into a separate company with its own management and accounts. Subsequently, Swissair set up SAirLogistics and in 2001 SAS created SAS Cargo. A year later, in July 2001, Singapore Airlines' cargo division became a separate company, SIA Cargo, operating its own nine Boeing 747 freighters and responsible for marketing the entire belly-hold space in SIA's passenger aircraft fleet. A few other airlines, including Northwest in the United States and Iberia, adopted similar strategies. One major advantage of such a move is that it facilitates the whole process of costing air freight, especially that carried on passenger aircraft, since these cargo businesses will have to negotiate a price with passenger airlines for any belly-hold capacity they use.

These large, cargo-oriented airlines or airline subsidiaries will be able to concentrate their business exclusively on freight. More important, they will refocus their activities away from the traditional view that air freight is about transporting goods from A to B. Success in the future will depend on understanding that it is much more than that. Air freight is about providing a delivery service and about supply chain management. This is why the integrators have been so successful and why large freight forwarders and even postal authorities have been making incursions into activities and markets previously the preserve of the airlines.

If refocused in this way, will the air freight airlines be able to meet the long-term threat of the integrated carriers? In order to do so they will need to face up to two other operational challenges.

The first will be to undertake the substantial investment required to improve their IT systems and to reorient these systems to providing a time-definite integrator type of service. This means high-speed tracing and tracking of shipments, high-technology warehousing, automatic and customer-focused reporting systems and the provision, in-house or through ground handling agents, of time-guaranteed collection and delivery. If the traditional airlines are to succeed in the freight sector, they must appreciate that there has been a logistics revolution. They must invest heavily in distribution networks, in electronic data interchange (EDI) and in other facilities which are needed to meet shippers' requirements. Their aim should be not just to transport freight by air but to add value to the shippers' products. In doing this they may be able to charge more for their services and thereby counteract any downward pressure on rates. Only the larger airlines astride major freight flows are likely to have the resources to invest sufficiently to remain big players in air freight.

The second challenge which must be met is how to provide a global delivery service. Big users of air freight such as IBM, Nokia, Ford or General Motors manufacture or source their products in many countries, and sell worldwide. They and most of the other big shippers need global scope and coverage from their providers of air delivery services. For the traditional airlines this means creating cargo alliances, to provide a global network. Two major cargo alliances were launched in 2000 and others are bound to follow. In May 2000 an alliance, NewGlobalCargo, linking the cargo businesses of Lufthansa, SAS and Singapore Airlines, was announced. It was renamed WOW in September 2001 when a new harmonised express service was launched. In September 2000 the Sky Team global alliance (Air France, Delta, Korean and Aeromexico, later joined by Alitalia) announced the creation of a cargo alliance focusing on joint selling of their cargo services in the United States and eventually of harmonised products. Added together, the cargo traffic of each of these alliances exceeds that of FedEx or UPS, even when the latter's domestic freight is included. However, to succeed in the long run such cargo alliances still have a number of problems to overcome. They must launch a common portfolio of products with common brand names in all markets; they must integrate their IT systems so they can communicate with each other; they must also develop standard handling processes and harmonised service standards and they need to integrate their sales teams and marketing efforts. Such integration will take time. Only if it succeeds will airlines be able to stand up to the challenge and long-term threat of the integrators.

Appendix
Freedoms of the air

Negotiated in bilateral air services agreements

First freedom   The right to fly over another country without landing.

Second freedom   The right to make a landing for technical reasons (e.g. refuelling) in another country without picking up/setting down revenue traffic.

Third freedom   The right to carry revenue traffic from your own country (A) to the country (B) of your treaty partner.

Fourth freedom   The right to carry traffic from country B back to your own country A.

Fifth freedom   The right of an airline from country A to carry revenue traffic between country B and other countries such as C or D on services starting or ending in its home country A. (This freedom cannot be used unless countries C or D also agree.)

Supplementary rights

Sixth freedom   The use by an airline of country A of two sets of third- and fourth-freedom rights to carry traffic between two other countries but using its base at A as a transit point.

Seventh freedom   The right of an airline to carry revenue traffic between points in two countries on services which lie entirely outside its own home country.

Eighth freedom or *cabotage* rights   The right of an airline to pick up and set down passengers or freight between two domestic points in another country on a service originating in its own home country.

Sixth-freedom rights are rarely dealt with explicitly in air service agreements but may be referred to implicitly in memoranda of understanding attached to the agreement. In the application of many bilaterals there is also *de facto* acceptance of such rights.

Seventh-and eighth-freedom rights are granted only in very rare cases. But in the 1991 US–UK bilateral the United States granted UK airlines seventh-freedom rights from several European states to the United States. They have never been used.

Glossary of common air transport terms

Aircraft kilometres are the distances flown by aircraft. An aircraft's total flying is obtained by multiplying the number of flights performed on each flight stage by the stage distance.

Aircraft productivity is calculated by multiplying an aircraft's average block speed by its maximum payload in tonnes to arrive at the tonne kilometres per hour. Or one multiplies block speed by seat capacity to produce seat kilometres per hour.

Aircraft utilisation is the average number of block hours that each aircraft flies. This is generally measured on a daily or annual basis.

Available seat kilometres (ASKs) are obtained by multiplying the number of seats available for sale on each flight by the stage distance flown.

Available tonne kilometres (ATKs) are obtained by multiplying the number of tonnes of capacity available for carriage of passengers and cargo on each sector of a flight by the stage distance.

Average aircraft capacity is obtained by dividing an airline's total available tonne kilometres (ATKs) by aircraft kilometres flown.

Average stage length is obtained by dividing an airline's total aircraft kilometres flown in a year by the number of aircraft departures; it is the weighted average of stage/sector lengths flown by an airline.

Block time (hours) is the time for each flight stage or sector, measured from when the aircraft leaves the airport gate or stand (chocks off) to when it arrives on the gate or stand at the destination airport (chocks on). It can also be calculated from the moment an aircraft moves under its own power until it comes to rest at its destination.

Break-even load factor (per cent) is the load factor required at a given average fare or yield to generate total revenue which equals operating costs. Can be calculated for a flight or a series of flights.

Cabin crew refers to stewards and stewardesses.

Code sharing is when two or more airlines each use their own flight codes or share a common code on flights operated by one of them.

Combination carrier is an airline that transports both passengers and cargo, usually on the same aircraft.

Flight or cockpit crew refers to the pilot, co-pilot and flight engineer (if any).

Freight tonne kilometres (FTKs) are obtained by multiplying the tonnes of freight uplifted by the sector distances over which they have been flown. They are a measure of an airline's cargo traffic.

Freight yields are obtained by dividing total revenue from scheduled freight by the freight tonne kilometres (FTKs) produced (often expressed in US cents per FTK).

Grandfather rights are the convention by which airlines retain the right to use particular take-off and landing slot times at an airport because they have done so previously, and continuously.

Interlining is the acceptance by one airline of travel documents issued by another airline for carriage on the services of the first airline. An interline passenger is one using a through fare for a journey involving two or more separate airlines.

Online passenger is one who transfers from one flight to another but on the same airline.

Operating costs per ATK are a measure obtained by dividing total operating costs by total ATKs. Operating costs exclude interest payments, taxes and extraordinary items. They can also be measured per RTK.

Operating ratio (per cent) is the operating revenue expressed as a percentage of operating costs. Sometimes referred to as the Revex ratio.

Passenger kilometres, or revenue passenger kilometres (RPKs), are obtained by multiplying the number of fare-paying passengers on each flight stage by flight stage distance. They are a measure of an airline's passenger traffic.

Passenger load factor (per cent) is passenger kilometres (RPKs) expressed as a percentage of available seat kilometres (ASKs). (On a single sector, this is simplified to the number of passengers carried as a percentage of seats available for sale.)

Revenue tonne kilometres (RTKs) measure the output actually sold. They are obtained by multiplying the total number of tonnes of passengers and cargo carried on each flight stage by flight stage distance. (Revenue passenger kilometres are normally converted to revenue tonne kilometres on a standard basis of 90 kg average weight, including free and excess baggage, although this has been increased by some airlines, e.g. British Airways have increased the average weight from 90 kg to 95 kg as a result of a CAA directive. So, RPKs divided by 11.111 equals RTKs.)

Seat factor, or passenger load factor, on a single sector is obtained by expressing the passengers carried as a percentage of the seats available for sale; on a network of routes it is obtained by expressing the total passenger kilometres (RPKs) as a percentage of the total seat kilometres available (ASKs).

Seat pitch is the standard way of measuring seat density on an aircraft. It is the distance between the back of one seat and the same point on the back of the seat in front.

Scheduled passenger yield is the average revenue per passenger kilometre and is obtained by dividing the total passenger revenue by the total passenger kilometres. This can be done by flight route or for the network.

Slot at an airport is the right to operate one take-off or landing at that airport within a fixed time period.

Stage or sector distance should be the air route or flying distance between two airports. In practice many airlines use the great-circle distance, which is shorter.

Transfer passenger is one who changes planes en route at an intermediate airport.

Transit passenger is one who continues on the same aircraft after an intermediate stop on a multi-sector flight.

Weight load factor measures the proportion of available capacity actually sold. It is the revenue tonne kilometres performed expressed as percentage of available tonne kilometres (also called the overall load factor).

Wide-bodied aircraft are civil aircraft which have two passenger aisles (e.g. the Boeing 767); narrow-bodied aircraft, such as the Airbus A320, have only one aisle.

Yield is the average revenue collected per passenger kilometre or tonne kilometre of freight carried. Passenger yield is calculated by dividing the total passenger revenue on a flight by the passenger kilometres generated by that flight. It is a measure of the weighted average fare paid.

Bibliography

AEA (1996) *Medium-term Forecast of European Scheduled Passenger Traffic, 1996–2000*, Brussels: Association of European Airlines.
— (1997) *Yearbook 1997*, Brussels: Association of European Airlines.
— (2000) Statistical Appendices to *Yearbook 2000*, Brussels: Association of European Airlines.
Airbus (2000) *Global Market Forecast, 2000–19*, Blagnac: Airbus Industrie.
Airline Monitor (1999) 'Commercial aircraft monitor', *Airline Monitor*, August, pp. 1–50, Ponte Vedra Beach FL: ESG Aviation Services.
ATA (1990) *Air Travel Survey 1989*, Washington DC: Air Transport Association of America.
BA (1990) *British Airways Investor*, No. 3, summer, London: British Airways.
BAA (1978) *Long-term Airport Traffic Forecasting*, London: British Airports Authority.
Belobaba, P. and Wilson, J. (1997) 'Impact of yield management in competitive airline markets', *Journal of Air Transport Management*, 3 (1), pp. 3–10.
Bruggisser, Philippe (1997) 'Controlling Costs', Third International Airline Conference, UBS, London, February.
BTS (1996) *American Travel Survey, 1995*, Washington DC: Bureau of Transportation Statistics, US Department of Transportation.
CAA (1977) *European Air Fares: A Discussion Document*, CAP 409, London: Civil Aviation Authority.
— (1989) *Traffic Distribution Policy for the London Area and Strategic Options for the Long Term*, CAP 548, London: Civil Aviation Authority.
— (2000a) *UK Airports: Annual Statements of Movements, Passengers and Cargo, 1999*, CAP 705, London: Civil Aviation Authority.
— (2000b) *The Air Navigation Order, 2000*, London: Civil Aviation Authority.
— (2000c) *1999 UK Airport Survey Report: Gatwick–Heathrow–Manchester*, Ref. C–99, London: Civil Aviation Authority.
— (2001) *UK Airlines: Annual Operating, Traffic and Financial Statistics*, CAP 713, London: Civil Aviation Authority.
CAB (1975) *Report of the Special Staff on Regulatory Reform*, Washington DC: Civil Aeronautics Board.
Carey, H. (1858) *Principles of Social Science*, I, Philadelphia, pp. 41–3.
CEC (1981) *Scheduled Passenger Air Fares in the EEC*, COM (81) 398 Final, Brussels: Commission of the European Communities.
— (1983) *Council Directive concerning the Authorisation of Scheduled Inter-regional Air Services between Member States*, Brussels: Commission of the European Communities.

— (1984) *Progress towards the Development of a Community Air Transport Policy*, Civil Aviation Memorandum No. 2, COM (84) 72 Final, Brussels: Commission of the European Communities.

— (1987a) *Council Directive of 14 December 1987 on Fares for Scheduled Air Services between Member States*, 87/601/EEC, *Council Decision of 14 December 1987* on the sharing of passenger capacity on scheduled air services between member states, 87/602/EEC, Brussels: Commission of the European Communities.

— (1987b) *Council Regulations (EEC) No. 3975/87 and No. 3976/87 of 14 December 1987* on the application of rules of competition in the air transport sector, Brussels: Commission of the European Communities.

— (1988) *Commission Regulation (EEC) No. 2671/88 of July 1955*, *Official Journal*, 24 August, Brussels: Commission of the European Communities.

— (1992a) *Commission Regulation (EEC) No. 2407/92* on the licensing of air carriers, *Official Journal*, 24 August, Brussels: Commission of the European Communities.

— (1992b) *Commission Regulation (EEC) No. 2408/92* on access for Community air carriers to intra-Community air routes, *Official Journal*, 24 August, Brussels: Commission of the European Communities.

— (1992c) *Commission Regulation (EEC) No. 2409/92* on fares and rates for air services, *Official Journal*, 24 August, Brussels: Commission of the European Communities.

CICAT (1969) *British Air Transport in the Seventies: Report of the Committee of Inquiry into Civil Air Transport*, Cmnd 4018, London: HMSO.

Clark, Paul (2001) *Buying the Big Jets: Fleet Planning for Airlines*, Aldershot: Ashgate.

D'Arcy, Harvey (1951) 'Airline passenger traffic pattern within the United States', *Journal of Air Law and Commerce*.

Dempsey, Paul S. (1999) 'Predation in the Air: Competition and Antitrust Law in Commercial Aviation', First International Air Law and Insurance Forum, IIR, London, December.

Dennis, Nigel (1990) 'Hubbing as a Marketing Tool', Air Transport Executive seminar, University of Westminster, London, November.

— (2001) 'The Impact of Airline Industry Changes on Airports', Airport Economics and Finance symposium, College of Aeronautics, Cranfield University, March.

Doganis, R. (1966) 'Traffic forecasting and the gravity model', *Flight International*, 29 September.

— (1991) *Flying off Course*, second edition, London: Routledge.

— (1992) *The Airport Business*, London: Routledge.

— (2001) *The Airline Business in the 21st Century*, London: Routledge.

Doganis, R., Aviation & Travel Consultancy and York Consulting Group (1999) *The Import and Impact of the Express Industry in Europe*, Brussels: Association of European Express Carriers and European Express Organisation.

DoT (1978) *United Kingdom Air Traffic Forecasting: Research and Revised Forecasts*, London: Department of Trade.

— (1981) *Report of the Air Traffic Forecasting Working Party, 1981*, London: Department of Trade.

— (1998) *Request for Comments on Docket OST-98-3717*, Washington DC: US Department of Transportation, 6 April.

DOT (1990) *Secretary's Task Force on Competition in the US Domestic Airline Industry*, Washington DC: US Department of Transportation.

Douglas (1989) *World Economic and Traffic Outlook, 1989–2010*, Long Beach CA: Douglas Aircraft Company.

Eggert, Anselm (1999) 'Calculating the Economic Advantages of Hubbing', Hub Connection Strategy conference, IIR, London, October.

Gallagher, Brendan (2001) 'BA confidently rides the web wave', *Air Transport World* Airline E-commerce supplement, summer.

Gialloreto, Louis (2001) 'CRM: the search for airline customer retention', *Aviation Strategy*, February, pp. 17–19.

Graham, Anne (2000) 'Demand for leisure air travel and limits to growth', *Journal of Air Transport Management*, 6 (2), pp. 109–18.

Hanlon, P. (1966) *Global Airlines: Competition in a Transnational Industry*, Oxford: Butterworth Heinemann.

HMG (1956) *Multilateral Agreement on Commercial Rights of Non-scheduled Air Services in Europe*, Cmnd 1099, London: HMSO.

IATA (1974) *Agreeing Fares and Rates: a Survey of the Methods and Procedures used by the Member Airlines of IATA*, Geneva: International Air Transport Association.

— (1989) *World Air Transport Statistics*, No. 33, Geneva: International Air Transport Association.

— (1996) *Distribution Costs Study*, Hounslow: International Air Transport Association.

— (2000) *Airline Economic Results and Prospects*, IATA Airline Economic Task Force, Montreal: International Air Transport Association.

— (2001a) *World Air Transport Statistics*, forty-fifth edition, Geneva: International Air Transport Association.

— (2001b) *Cargo Agents Worldwide: Annual Sales Report, 2000*, Montreal: International Air Transport Association.

ICAO (1980) *Convention on International Civil Aviation*, sixth edition, Doc. 7300/6, Montreal: International Civil Aviation Organisation.

— (1988) *Survey of International Air Transport Fares and Rates, September 1987*, Circular 208-AT/82, Montreal: International Civil Aviation Organisation.

— (1990) *The Economic Situation of Air Transport: Review and Outlook, 1978–2000*, Circular 222-AT/90, Montreal: International Civil Aviation Organisation.

— (1997) *Outlook for Air Transport to the Year 2005*, Circular 270, Montreal: International Civil Aviation Organisation.

— (1999a) *Safety Oversight Manual*, Doc. 9734-AN/959, Montreal: International Civil Aviation Organisation.

— (1999b) *Digest of Statistics*, Series F, No. 52, *Financial Data, 1998*, Montreal: International Civil Aviation Organisation.

— (2000) *Digest of Statistics*, Series F, No. 485, *Financial Data, 1999*, Montreal: International Civil Aviation Organisation.

Ippolito, R. A. (1981) 'Estimating airline demand with quality of service variables', *Journal of Transport Economics and Policy*, 15 (1), pp. 7–15.

Jorge-Calderon, J. D. (1997) 'A demand model for scheduled airline services on international European routes', *Journal of Air Transport Management*, 3 (1), pp. 23–34.

Kanafani, A., Sadoulet, E. and Sullivan, E. C. (1974) *Demand Analysis for North Atlantic Air Travel*, Berkeley CA: Institute of Transportation and Traffic Engineering, University of California.

Kellner, Larry (2000) 'Building a Global Airline Brand', *2000 Transport Conference*, London: UBS Warburg.

Kley, Karl-Ludwig (2000) 'Will Quality differentiate in a Changing Industry?' *2000 Transport Conference*, London: UBS Warburg.

Kraus, M. (1999) 'Time-definitive Services: the Shift of Paradigm for Cargo Airlines', Tenth World Express and Mail conference, Brussels, May.

Lansing, John B. and Blood, Dwight M. (1984) *The Changing Travel Market*, Ann Arbor MI: Survey Research Center, University of Michigan.

Lill, B. (1889) 'Die Grundgesetze des Personenverkehrs', *Zeitschrift für Eisenbahnen und Dampfschiffsfahrt der Österreichischhungarischen Monarchie*, 35–6.

Lobbenberg, A. (2001) 'Strategic Alliances', Air Transport Executive seminar, Cranfield College of Aeronautics, November.

Maiden, S. (1995) *Heathrow Terminal 5: Proof of Evidence Forecasting*, London: British Airports Authority.

Maldutis, J. and Musante, R. M. (1995) *Airline Competition at the Fifty Largest US Airports: Update*, New York: Salomon Bros.

Morrell, Peter (2002) *Airline Finance*, second edition, Aldershot: Ashgate.

Nguyen Dai Hai (1982) 'The Box and Jenkins approach: a recent short-term forecasting technique applied to air transport', *ITA Bulletin*, September, Paris: Institut du transport aérien.

OAG (2000) *Business Travel Lifestyle Survey, 1999*, Dunstable: OAG Worldwide.

ONS (2000) *Travel Trends: a Report on the 1999 International Passenger Survey*, London: HMSO for the Office of National Statistics.

Parker-Eaton, R. (2000) 'The Challenge to Charter', Accelerating Performance Growth in the Low-cost Segment conference, ENG, Amsterdam, November.

Pearson, Roy (1977) 'Establishing a Methodology for Measuring Airline Efficiency', Ph.D. thesis, London: University of Westminster.

Pena, F. (1995) *Statement of the Secretary of Transportation: International Air Transportation Policy*, Washington DC: US Department of Transportation.

Pilling, Mark (2001) 'Flights of fancy', *Airline Business*, January, pp. 44–7.

Presidential Documents (1978) *Weekly Compilation of Presidential Documents*, 14 (34), 2 August, Washington DC.

Reid, Samuel R. and Mohrfield, James W. (1973) 'Airline size, profitability, mergers and regulation', *Journal of Air Law and Commerce*, 39.

Richmond, S. B. (1971) *Regulation and Competition in Air Transport*, New York: Columbia University Press.

Shifrin, C. (2001) 'Atlas: the making of a cargo heavyweight', *Airline Business*, January.

SIA (2000) *Seamless Connections: Annual Report, 1999–2000*, Singapore: Singapore International Airlines.

SITA (2001) *IT Trends Survey*, Sutton: SITA and *Airline Business*.

Sletmo, G. K. (1982) *Demand for Air Cargo: an Econometric Approach*, Bergen: Institute of Shipping Research, Norwegian School of Economics and Business Administration.

Spinetta, J-C. (2000) 'The New Economics', Air Transport: Global Economics require Global Regulatory Perspectives round table, IATA–AEA, Brussels, November, unpublished.

SSB (2000) *Airline Alliances*, London: Salomon Smith Barney.

Straszheim, M. R. (1978) *The International Airline Industry*, Washington DC: Brookings Institution.

Tae Hoon Oum and Chunyan Yu (1995) 'A productivity comparison of the world's major airlines', *Journal of Air Transport Management*, 2 (3–4), pp. 181–95.

Taneja, N. K. (1978) *Airline Traffic Forecasting*, Lexington MA: Lexington Books.

Veldhuis, X. (1988) 'Forecasting Process at Amsterdam Airport Schiphol', Worldwide Forecasting, 1988–92 conference, IATA, Geneva, September.

Westminster University (1989) *Air Transport and the Southern Regions of the Community IV, Route Forecasts*, London: Transport Studies Group, University of Westminster.

Zumwinkel, K. (2001) 'Challenges for the Future of the Transportation Industry', Sixth annual Transportation Conference, UBS Warburg, London, October.

Index

Note: numbers in **bold** refer to figures (diagrams) and numbers in *italics* refer to tables.